POWER
IN
ORGANIZATIONS

POWER
IN
ORGANIZATIONS

Jeffrey Pfeffer

GRADUATE SCHOOL OF BUSINESS
Stanford University

Cover Design by
Kathy Lammerding

Pitman
Boston · London · Melbourne · Toronto

PITMAN PUBLISHING INC.
1020 Plain Street, Marshfield, Massachusetts

Pitman Books Limited
39 Parker Street, London WC2B5PB

Associated Companies
Pitman Publishing Pty Ltd., Melbourne
Pitman Publishing New Zealand Ltd., Wellington
Copp Clark Pitman, Toronto

Library of Congress Cataloging in Publication Data

Pfeffer, Jeffrey.
  Power in Organizations.

Bibliography: p.
  Includes Index
  I. Power 1. (Social Sciences) II. Organizational
Behavior. III. Decision-Making. IV. Title.
HM131.M417   303.3'3   80–29883

ISBN 0–273–01638–5
ISBN 0–273–01639–3 (pbk)

Manufactured in the U.S.A.

ISBN   0–273–01639–3   Paper
ISBN   0–273–01638–5   Cloth

10 9 8 7 6 5 4 3 2

CONTENTS

CONTENTS

PREFACE

In the last few years there has been increasing interest in a political perspective on organizational behavior. This interest has culminated in several books appearing at about the same time which treat aspects of power and politics in organizations. This growing concern with power and political activity encompasses analyses which use both social psychological as well as sociological perspectives, and incorporates topics as diverse as bargaining and influence strategies and the political aspects of organization development. The expanding effort devoted to understanding power in organizations is at once welcome and long overdue. Organizations are systems in which influence processes play an important part. As part of any study of influence, the topic of power and the political activities through which power is acquired and exercised is important.

Although power is an important topic in the analysis of organizations, it has been difficult in the past to find good teaching materials to use in presenting the subject. It was my own frustration with having to piece together selected articles, some book-length case studies, and examples from diverse sources that caused me to write this book. I have been engaged in the empirical study of power phenomena for several years; I wanted to consolidate my thinking on the subject, and to incorporate into one source many of the ideas and materials that were available for explaining power and the political analysis of organizations.

The perspective adopted in this book is basically sociological. Power is seen as deriving from the division of labor that occurs as task specialization is implemented in organizations. When the overall tasks of the organization are divided into smaller parts, it is inevitable that some tasks will come to be more important than others. Those persons and those units that have the responsibility for performing the more critical tasks in the organization have a natural advantage in developing and exercising power in the organization. Although individual skills and strategies can certainly affect the amount of power and the effectiveness with which it is used, power is first and foremost a structural phenomenon, and should be understood as such.

Two other introductory comments are in order. The literature on power is not particularly large, and the empirical study of power and politics is unfortunately a rare event. For this reason, the book has several aims. One aim is to synthesize what is known about power in organizations, and to develop a reasonably consistent theoretical perspective that can guide analysis and understanding of power phenomena. A second purpose is to point out where there are significant gaps in empirical research. Throughout the book, hypotheses are proposed which have no empirical evidence to support them. Another purpose, then, is to stimulate further research and additional analysis of the phenomena described.

It is also important to recognize that power and organizational politics are topics that make people uncomfortable. Power is a word with an ideological tinge. Politics is barely ethical if one uses it to get something accomplished; it is often seen as quite unethical when someone else uses it against us or in a situation in which we are involved. A third aim of this book, consequently, is to explore both the bases for this unease as well as to demonstrate that power processes are both ubiquitous and beneficial rather than harmful to organizations and to the people who work in those organizations. Power, influence, and political activity all exist. Pretending they do not exist will not make them disappear. For those who will spend their lives working in, buying from, and being served by organizations—and that includes all of us—a knowledge of power is important. The analytical perspective developed in this book can make one a fairly effective forecaster of what organizations are going to do, and can also enhance one's ability to intervene and get things accomplished. Power and politics are inevitable and important parts of administrative activity and should be analyzed and viewed as such. At the same time, because of the ideology associated with political as opposed to rational decision processes, power is a topic that may make the reader uneasy. Some discomfort is preferable to ignorance, however.

The book begins by considering why power has been neglected in the organizations literature. The study of the politics of management literature is a good place to begin to sharpen skills in understanding the use of language and the role of ideology in politics. Management is itself a political activity, and the argument is made that much of the existing literature on organizations serves some power legitimation and maintenance functions. Alternative views of decision making are considered in the first chapter. Although this book will emphasize the political model of organizational choice, other perspectives, and how one might go about distinguishing among them, need to be appreciated. All organizations are not equally political, and it is important for those operating in organizations to be able to figure out the system in which they are working.

In the second chapter, the issue of how to define and assess the power of various political actors in organizations is addressed. In addition to understanding the game, it is helpful to be able to identify the players and their relative strengths. The assessment and measurement of power is also important for those who do research on the topic.

Power is not used all the time or in all circumstances. In Chapter 3, the conditions under which power and political activity are likely to be employed in decision making are considered. The conditions fostering the use of power can, of course, be used to determine how to make decision making less political. The consideration of this question provides some indication of the costs of moving toward a more rational model of operation, as well as some strategies by which this can be accomplished. In addition, understanding the conditions in which power is employed can help predict difficulties in the implementation of normative choice procedures, as well as indicate the circumstances in which such procedures are more or less appropriate. This topic is also addressed in Chapter 3.

Having considered what power is, how to measure it, and when it is used, Chapter 4 explores the question of the origins of power, or the determinants of the power of organizational actors. In understanding where power comes from, one begins to understand what kinds of strategies can be employed to increase power in an organization. Chapters 5 and 6 treat the subject of how power is used in organizational choice—the strategies of organizational politics. Chapter 5 considers coalitions, cooptation, the use of committees, and the legitimation of power through the use of objective criteria and outside expertise. In Chapter 6, the subject of political language is considered in detail. The role of management in using political language to justify and legitimate decisions is important. Indeed, it might be said that one of the major tasks of managers is to make organizational participants want and feel comfortable doing what they have to do.

Chapter 7 considers some examples of power in use, and presents a review of evidence for the importance of power in understanding various aspects of organizations. The politics of careers, of resource allocations, of structures, and of executive succession are all considered.

Power, once acquired, is maintained. Chapter 8 treats the topic of institutionalization. Change is not frequent or easily accomplished. In this chapter, some of the factors that cause the persistence of existing influence distributions are described. An understanding of institutionalization is important for predicting the circumstances in which change is likely to occur, as well as understanding the relative importance of organizational adaptation; this is contrasted with selection processes as sources of change in populations of organizations.

Finally, we conclude by discussing the implications of power and a political perspective on organizations for some rather crucial topics: organizational performance, the selection, training, and skills required by managers, design of organizations, and the likely future of organizations in terms of how politicized they will be. In no case are the implications straightforward. But the importance of power in organizations requires that some attempt be made to explore its implications for the management, design, and performance of organizations.

In order to satisfy publishers, books have to be completed. They are set into type, bound, and distributed. They look finished. I consider these ideas to be very much work in progress. We need to know a lot more about power and political activity in organizations. It is my hope that this book can serve as a stimulus toward that exploration. It is certainly not the final word on understanding power in organizations.

ACKNOWLEDGMENTS

Three types of resources are required in order to complete a project of this sort: intellectual support and stimulation—ideas, time and money (the two are related), and resources required to put the project together, including all the various mechanical details which are involved. I have been helped immeasurably in all three areas.

When I arrived at Illinois in 1971 and met Jerry Salancik, I began an association that has left me considerably better off in a number of ways. Much of the empirical work on power described in this book was done with Jerry. I learned about much of the literature cited in this book through and from him. Our collaboration has been a rich source of ideas and insights. The time I have spent interacting with him has been among the most productive time I have spent. I have learned a great deal from him about organizations and organizational analysis; his insights pervade this book. I am tremendously grateful for his friendship and collaboration.

Many of the insights about the nuts and bolts of organizational political strategies were developed from two of my colleagues at Berkeley, Ray Miles and John Freeman. Ray is one of the most effective administrators I have ever met. Watching him in action was and is truly an educational experience. His understanding of organizations and how to get things done in them is remarkable. I learned a lot, but I suspect not as much as I should have or could have. John Freeman and I spent many a lunch at Kips or the Sinopalace discussing politics and power at Berkeley and I learned a great deal from our discussions. It gave me an opportunity to try out ideas, hear some other insights, and get a better perspective on organizational power and political strategies. Both John and Ray were important in helping me to develop my thoughts.

In addition to theoretical concepts, I also needed examples—sites in which I could observe the various processes in action. For this I am tremendously grateful to many of my current and former students. They have unselfishly provided me with all kinds of data about their organizations, as well as their feedback as I began to develop the perspective represented in this book. Several of them spent a lot of time with me, talking about issues covered in this material, and I am especially grateful for their time and support. Special thanks are in order for Phil Nowak, Larry Fogli, Katherine Strehl, Linnea Bohn, Ellie Chaffee, Richard Harrison, Doug Wholey, and my Business 377 class at Stanford; each in his or her own way contributed in an important respect to this project.

It goes without saying, of course, that I must take full responsibility for the sins of commission and ommission which I have made in the pages that follow. The various reviewers of this project, including Mike Tushman and several anonymous readers, as well as those resources named above, have tried to provide me with their advice and insight. Sometimes, however, I probably failed to see the light.

For the last four years my wife, Susan, has attended law school in the evening while working during the day. These activities have provided the time and helped contribute other resources which have made this project possible. I would probably have been better off with more of her company and fewer manuscript pages, but I am proud of her accomplishments and her drive.

I have been able for the most part, to avoid the time demands and the temptations of consulting and other such activities primarily because of the sound advice and excellent work done by Bill and Anita Lapham and the Lapham Company. As realtors, advisors, property managers, consultants, friends, partners, construction supervisors, and next door neighbors, the Laphams have contributed more to the completion of my work than they can probably appreciate. I am thankful for their friendship and help.

Last, but far from least, the tasks of getting this book together have been accomplished or made less onerous by my secretary, Kathy Lammerding. If progress was slow, she was always willing to ask, "Why haven't you given me anything to type recently?" When impossible deadlines were imposed, not only was she nice about it but completed everything on time. Her sense of humor, pleasantness, and competence made all the tasks associated with putting this book together more enjoyable.

CHAPTER 1

UNDERSTANDING THE ROLE OF POWER IN DECISION MAKING

More than 40 years ago Harold Lasswell (1936) defined politics as the study of who gets what, when, and how. Certainly, who gets what, when, and how, are issues of fundamental importance in understanding formal organizations. Nevertheless, organizational politics and organizational power are both topics which are made conspicuous by their absence in management and organization theory literature (Allen, et al., 1979). Why?

It is certainly not because the terms power and politics are concepts used infrequently in everyday conversation. Both are often used to explain events in the world around us. Richard Nixon's behavior while in the presidency has been ascribed to a need for power. Budget allocations among various Federal programs are described as being the result of politics. Success in obtaining a promotion may be attributed to an individual's ability to play office politics. The fact that certain business functions (such as finance) or occupational specialties (such as law) are frequently important in organizations is taken to reflect the power of those functions or occupations. There are few events that are not ascribed to the effects of power and politics. As Dahl (1957: 201) noted, "The concept of power is as ancient and ubiquitous as any that social theory can boast."

Power and politics are not neglected because they lack relevance in explaining what occurs in organizations. The theme of this book is that these are fundamental concepts for understanding behavior in organiza-

1

tions. In Chapter 7, the effects of power in use will be documented in some detail. For the moment, we can briefly summarize this literature by noting that there is evidence that power affects outcomes ranging from the allocation of budgets to organizational subunits (Pfeffer and Salancik, 1974; Pfeffer, Salancik, and Leblebici, 1976; Salancik and Pfeffer, 1974), to succession to executive and administrative positions (Zald, 1965; Pfeffer and Salancik, 1978: Ch. 9) to the design and redesign of formal organizational structures (Pfeffer, 1978a).

Power has been neglected for several reasons. First, the concept of power is itself problematic in much of the social science literature. In the second place, while power is something, it is not everything. There are other competing perspectives for understanding organizational decision making. These perspectives are frequently persuasive, if for no other reason than that they conform more closely to socially held values of rationality and effectiveness. And third, the concept of power is troublesome to the socialization of managers and the practice of management because of its implications and connotations.

Therefore, we begin at the beginning, with a discussion of these issues as they affect the study and analysis of power and politics in organizations. It is important to understand what power is and what it isn't; what alternative perspectives exist on organizational choice processes; and the place of power in the organization theory literature. With that as background, it will be possible then to proceed to the analysis of organizations using a political perspective.

The Concept of Power

The very pervasiveness of the concept of power, referred to in the earlier quote from Robert Dahl, is itself a cause for concern about the utility of the concept in assisting us to understand behavior in organizations. Bierstedt (1950: 730) noted that the more things a term could be applied to the less precise was its meaning. Dahl (1957: 201) wrote, ". . . a Thing to which people attach many labels with subtly or grossly different meanings in many different cultures and times is probably not a Thing at all but many Things." March (1966) has suggested that in being used to explain almost everything, the concept of power can become almost a tautology, used to explain that which cannot be explained by other ideas, and incapable of being disproved as an explanation for actions and outcomes.

Most definitions of power include an element indicating that power is the capability of one social actor to overcome resistance in achieving a desired objective or result. For instance, Dahl (1957: 202–203) defined

2

power as a relation among social actors in which one social actor, A, can get another social actor B, to do something that B would not otherwise have done. Power becomes defined as force, and more specifically, force sufficient to change the probability of B's behavior from what it would have been in the absence of the application of the force. Emerson's (1962: 32) definition is quite similar: "The power of actor A over actor B is the amount of resistance on the part of B which can be potentially overcome by A." Bierstedt (1950: 738) also wrote of power as having incidence only in cases of social opposition. Power may be tricky to define, but it is not that difficult to recognize: "the ability of those who possess power to bring about the outcomes they desire" (Salancik and Pfeffer, 1977b: 3).

It is generally agreed that power characterizes relationships among social actors. A given social actor, by which we mean an individual, subunit, or organization, has more power with respect to some social actors and less power with respect to others. Thus, power is context or relationship specific. A person is not "powerful" or "powerless" in general, but only with respect to other social actors in a specific social relationship. To say, for example, that the legal department in a specific firm is powerful, implies power with respect to other departments within that firm during a specific period of time. That same legal department may not be at all powerful with respect to its interactions with the firm's outside counsel, various federal and state regulatory agencies, and so forth. And, the power of the department can and probably will change over time.

Although power is relationship or context specific, it is not necessarily specifically related to a limited set of decision issues. Whether or not power is generalizable across decision issues is an empirical question, not a matter of definition. Indeed, one of the interesting aspects in the study of power in organizations is the determination of under what circumstances power is general across decisions, and in what cases the power of a particular social actor is more issue-specific.

Most studies of power in organizations have focused on hierarchical power, the power of supervisors over subordinates, or bosses over employees. The vertical, hierarchical dimension of power is important in understanding social life, but it is not the only dimension of power. As Perrow (1970: 59) wrote, "It is my impression that for all the discussion and research regarding power in organizations, the preoccupation with interpersonal power has led us to neglect one of the most obvious aspects of this subject: in complex organizations, tasks are divided up between a few major departments or subunits, and all of these subunits are not likely to be equally powerful." Implicit in this statement is the recognition that power is, first of all, a structural phenomenon, created by the division of labor and departmentation that characterize the specific organization or set of organizations being investigated. It is this more structural approach to power that constitutes the focus of this book, although at times we will consider what individual characteristics affect the exercise of structurally determined power.

It should be evident why power is somewhat tricky to measure and operationalize. In order to assess power, one must be able to estimate a) what would have happened in the absence of the exercise of power; b) the intentions of the actor attempting to exercise power; and c) the effect of actions taken by that actor on the probability that what was desired would in fact be likely to occur. Because the ability to diagnose power distributions is critical to understanding and acting effectively in organizations, we will consider the diagnosis of power in some detail in the next chapter. For now, it should be recognized that the definition and assessment of power are both controversial and problematic.

THE CONCEPT OF AUTHORITY

It is important to distinguish between power and authority. In any social setting, there are certain beliefs and practices that come to be accepted within that setting. The acceptance of these practices and values, which can include the distribution of influence within the social setting, binds together those within the setting, through their common perspective. Activities which are accepted and expected within a context are then said to be legitimate within that context. The distribution of power within a social setting can also become legitimated over time, so that those within the setting expect and value a certain pattern of influence. When power is so legitimated, it is denoted as authority. Weber (1947) emphasized the critical role of legitimacy in the exercise of power. By transforming power into authority, the exercise of influence is transformed in a subtle but important way. In social situations, the exercise of power typically has costs. Enforcing one's way over others requires the expenditure of resources, the making of commitments, and a level of effort which can be undertaken only when the issues at hand are relatively important. On the other hand, the exercise of authority, power which has become legitimated, is expected and desired in the social context. Thus, the exercise of authority, far from diminishing through use, may actually serve to enhance the amount of authority subsequently possessed.

Dornbusch and Scott (1975), in their book on evaluation in organizations, made a similar point with respect to the evaluation process. They noted that in formal organizations, some people have the right to set

4

criteria, to sample output, and to apply the criteria to the output that is sampled. Persons with such authority or evaluation rights are expected to engage in these authorized activities, and, instead of being punished for doing so, are punished when they fail to do so.

The transformation of power into authority is an important process, for it speaks to the issue of the institutionalization of social control. As such, we will return to this issue when political strategies are considered and when we take up the topic of institutionalized power. For the moment, it is sufficient to note that within formal organizations, norms and expectations develop that make the exercise of influence expected and accepted. Thus, social control of one's behavior by others becomes an expected part of organizational life. Rather than seeing the exercise of influence within organizations as a contest of strength or force, power, once it is transformed through legitimation into authority, is not resisted. At that point, it no longer depends on the resources or determinants that may have produced the power in the first place.

The transformation of power into authority can be seen most clearly in the relationship between supervisors and subordinates in work organizations. As Mechanic (1962) noted, lower level organizational members have, in reality, a great amount of power. If they refused to accept and accede to the instructions provided by higher level managers, those managers would have difficulty carrying out sanctions and operating the organization. Furthermore, the lower level participants have power that comes from specialized knowledge about the work process and access to information that higher level managers may not have. Thus, Mechanic (1962) argued, what is interesting is not that subordinates accept the instructions of managers because of the greater power possessed by the managers. Rather, it is interesting that in spite of the considerable degree of power possessed by lower level employees, these employees seldom attempt to exercise their power or to resist the instructions of their managers.

The point that is being made is important. Although it is true that the manager may have the power to fire employees, to control the amount of money they get paid, and to affect their promotion opportunities in the future, in most organizations such powers are severely limited and, in any event, are seldom exercised. Employees do not consciously compare their power (to withhold labor services, to quit, to withhold information, to do the work poorly) with the power that the manager has (to use and withhold rewards and sanctions), and then decide whether or not to comply depending on the relative power balance. Rather, most of the time in most work settings the authority of the manager to direct the

5

work activities is so legitimated and taken for granted, that issues of relative power and sanctions seldom become consciously considered. Subordinates obey not because the supervisor has the power to compel them to; rather, they follow reasonable instructions related to the control of their work behavior because they expect that such directions will be given and followed. In this way, power becomes transformed into authority, and control can be exercised almost regardless of the balance of power possessed by the interacting groups.

When social understanding and social consensus develops to accept, ratify, and even prefer the distribution of power, then the power becomes legitimated and becomes authority. Authority is maintained not only by the resources or sanctions that produced the power, but also by the social pressures and social norms that sanction the power distribution and which define it as normal and acceptable. Such social acceptance and social approval adds stability to the situation and makes the exercise of power easier and more effective. Legitimation, of course, occurs in a specific social context, and what is legitimate in one setting may be illegitimate in another. The degree and kind of supervisor-subordinate control exercised in U.S. organizations, for instance, may be perceived as illegitimate in the organizations of countries where there is more worker self-management and industrial democracy. Legitimation of power is thus ultimately problematic and far from inevitable. The examination of the conditions under which power and social control become legitimated and transformed into authority is an important undertaking in trying to understand the governance and control of organizations.

Definition of Organizational Politics

The task of defining the term organizational politics is as difficult as that of defining power. The problem is to distinguish between political activity and organizational or administrative activity in general. As in the case of power, if politics refers to all forms of administrative or managerial action, then the term becomes meaningless because it includes every behavior.

From Lasswell's (1936) definition of politics as who gets what, when, and how, and from Wildavsky's (1979) descriptions of the politics of the budgetary process, the inference is that politics involves how differing preferences are resolved in conflicts over the allocation of scarce resources. Thus, politics involves activities which attempt to influence decisions over critical issues that are not readily resolved through the introduction of new data and in which there are differing points of view. For our purposes, organizational politics will be defined as:

Organizational politics involves those activities taken within organizations to acquire, develop, and use power and other resources to obtain one's preferred outcomes in a situation in which there is uncertainty or dissensus about choices.

If power is a force, a store of potential influence through which events can be affected, politics involves those activities or behaviors through which power is developed and used in organizational settings. Power is a property of the system at rest; politics is the study of power in action. An individual, subunit, or department may have power within an organizational context at some period of time; politics involves the exercise of power to get something accomplished, as well as those activities which are undertaken to expand the power already possessed or the scope over which it can be exercised. This definition is similar to that provided by Allen, et al. (1979: 77): "Organizational politics involve intentional acts of influence to enhance or protect the self-interest of individuals or groups."

From the definition of power, it is clear that political activity is activity which is undertaken to overcome some resistance or opposition. Without opposition or contest within the organization, there is neither the need nor the expectation that one would observe political activity. And, because political activity is focused around the acquisition and use of power, it can be distinguished from activity involved in making decisions which uses rational or bureaucratic procedures. In both rational and bureaucratic models of choice, there is no place for and no presumed effect of political activity. Decisions are made to best achieve the organization's goals, either by relying on the best information and options that have been uncovered, or by using rules and procedures which have evolved in the organization. Political activity, by contrast, implies the conscious effort to muster and use force to overcome opposition in a choice situation.

It is useful to contrast the definition adopted here with another one found in the literature. Mayes and Allen (1977: 675) defined organizational politics as:

Organizational politics is the management of influence to obtain ends not sanctioned by the organization or to obtain sanctioned ends through non-sanctioned influence means.

This definition has two problems. First, what is or what is not sanctioned within an organization, in terms of both means and ends, are the results

7

of power and political activity within the organization. To say that an activity is not sanctioned is to say that those undertaking the activity do not have the power in the organization to have their definition of the world generally accepted. Under the definition proposed by Mayes and Allen (1977), the powerful would not engage in political activity (since what they do is likely to be organizationally sanctioned) and the powerless would almost inevitably engage in political activity. The second problem with this definition is that it gives the concept of organizational politics a sense of sinfulness. This may be nice for the sales of books with such a term in the title, but it diverts attention from the inevitability of power and politics in organizations as well as from the functional outcomes that often emerge from political activity.

To assess the consequences of political activity on an *a priori* basis as implied by Mayes and Allen, is to presume that the system knows in advance what is best for it. Influence means that are not sanctioned, which are used to accomplish nonsanctioned ends, are categorized by Mayes and Allen (1977: 675) as being organizationally dysfunctional political behavior. Such a categorization is less likely to be readily accepted when applied to a larger political context, such as the protests against the war in Vietnam. These protests sometimes used non-sanctioned means to accomplish an end which was clearly not sanctioned by the authorities. The definition put forward by Mayes and Allen is important because it is a reflection of the schizophrenia with which concepts such as power and politics have been treated in the literature. Power and politics are fine for understanding and diagnosing events on a national or governmental level; at the level of formal organizations, however, power and politics are considered to be either pejorative terms or illegitimate as analytical concepts for use in understanding bureaucratic or rational systems of decision making.

It is clearly important to be able to distinguish between political activity and administrative action in general, and to distinguish between outcomes produced by social power and outcomes that occur by chance, because of precedent, or because of the application of rational decision procedures. At the same time, analysis should not be unnecessarily diverted by the interminable definitional and theoretical controversies that fill the literature surrounding these concepts. In a study of eighty-seven managerial personnel, Allen, et al. (1979: 77–78) reported:

Respondents were asked to describe organizational political tactics and personal characteristics of effective political actors.

. . . No definition of organizational politics was given to the respondents, nor did any of them ask what was meant by the term.

Similarly, in an interview study of twenty-nine department heads at the University of Illinois, during which each respondent was asked to rate the power of his and the other departments on the campus, only one department head found it necessary to ask for clarification of what was meant by the term power. It seems fair to state that power and politics are terms that have some shared meanings in the world of organizational actors. We shall see when we consider the assessment of power in organizations that such shared meanings guide and are anchored in consensually shared judgments concerning the distribution of power in organizational settings.

The Place of Power
in Organization Theory Literature

If power and politics are terms which are used frequently in everyday conversation, understood at least at an intuitive level by practicing managers and administrators, and, as we shall demonstrate later, can help account for careers, budgets, structure, the relative size of personnel components, and their persistence over time, why then is power neglected in the literature of organization theory? One reason has already been suggested—the issues associated with the definition and measurement of these concepts. A second issue, that of competing perspectives for analyzing organizational choice processes, will be considered later in the chapter. For the moment, consider the place of power in the literature of organization theory and the role served by such literature.

Examination of the major textbooks now current in the field will indicate that the subject of power is either not mentioned at all in the subject index or, if it is, it receives short shrift in terms of the number of pages devoted to it. When the subject of power is found in the index, it is frequently associated with a discussion of the individual bases of power (e.g., French and Raven, 1968) or the need for power. Size, technology, and environment all receive much more time and attention, even in those books with a presumably more sociological perspective. And, in specialized books dealing with topics such as organization design or organization development, power typically receives no mention at all, even though it is a particularly critical variable for some of these more specialized concerns.

It is, of course, possible that this book and its treatment of organizations seriously overstates the importance of power and politics as phenomena of concern and as explanations for behavior in organizations. This argument however, not only flies in the face of a small but growing body of empirical research, but also the popular explanations for organizational phenomena which are found in sources such as *Fortune, Business Week* or the *Wall Street Journal.* If power is unimportant, it is not only this author that has been fooled; I have plenty of company in the business press.

A more likely explanation for the neglect of power in the management and organizational behavior literature is found by considering the role of management writing in the management process, and the position of a topic such as power as implied by the various functions served by management writing. The argument to be developed is relatively straightforward: management writing serves a variety of functions; in virtually all of these functions there is a strong component of ideology and values; topics such as power and politics are basically incompatible with the values and ideology being developed; therefore, it is reasonable, if not theoretically useful, to ignore topics which detract from the functions being served by the writing, and this includes tending to ignore or to downplay the topics of power and politics.

To ask what functions are served by management writing, we can begin by asking who reads management books. The answer is that there are three important categories of persons who read management books, though the books they read are not necessarily the same: students in undergraduate and graduate programs in management and administration who read the books to acquire knowledge about the profession and practice of management; practicing managers and administrators in public and private sector organizations; and the general public, including those not involved with or in private business organizations. Consider next, what books or writings are needed in each case.

In the case of students, there is little doubt that one of the important functions of business education is socialization. This statement reflects both the more general importance of socialization in the educational process, and the specific prominence of socialization with respect to certain occupations and professions. It is not in just the fields of medicine and law that socialization plays an important part of the educational process. Although less frequently empirically examined, there are important considerations of socialization in the education of young, aspiring managers (e.g. Schein, 1968). Socialization involves the inculcation of norms and values that are central to the profession and that are, not incidentally, useful to the organizations in which the professionals are going to work. There is no norm so central to the existing practice

10

and ideology of management as the norm of rationality. The political purposes served by this norm will be developed in more detail in Chapters 5 and 6, but will be briefly summarized here. Rationality and rational choice models focus attention on the development of technologies to more effectively achieve a goal or set of goals, such as profit or efficiency. Concern is directed toward the development of alternatives, the development of sophisticated techniques for evaluating the alternatives, their possible consequences, and the assembling of information that facilitates the evaluation of performance along these specified dimensions. What is less salient and less central in this process of rational choice is the origin of these objectives or criteria and who benefits and who loses by having decisions made to optimize these particular decision criteria as opposed to others.

It is, we are suggesting, not by accident that in choosing among alternatives given certain specified preferences (March, 1978) the role of preferences has been neglected in theories of choice, relative to the role of technologies. It is around preferences, and the values and beliefs implicit in these preferences, that conflicts of interest emerge. And such conflicts may cause a diversion of effort from goal attainment which is not favored by those whose goals are being served well by the present arrangement. The point is that, by even raising the issue of preferences or criteria as problematic, the institutionalized nature of goals such as profits or efficiency is challenged and is threatened by the mere fact of the challenge. It is in this sense that all normative theories of organization, whether within the domains of economics, organizational design, organizational development, or whatever, are inevitably political; it is also the case that most or perhaps all of the the descriptive theories are equally political. These theories are political in the sense that each takes for granted certain assumptions about the world and how it operates, thereby causing the indoctrination of these assumptions. The result is the unconscious, or at best semiconscious, acceptance of the implicit values by a widely varying set of participants. Some actors may benefit from the application of these values and some may lose. This same point has been nicely developed by Walter Nord (1974) in his critique of modern human resource management theory. It is equally and inevitably applicable to all organization theory.

In the socialization of professional managers, there are some components which are distinctly different from the socialization of other professionals. First, in contrast to doctors, lawyers and to a lesser extent accountants, the professional manager will not practice in a relatively small organization with the legal structure of a partnership. Rather, he or she will work in a much larger organization which is legally structured as a corporation. The manager, then, can be expected to operate in a setting substantially more bureaucratized and in which there is a lesser likelihood of attaining such a great amount of ownership or control. Thus, the socialization must focus not so strongly on developing values that will serve the professional in solo or small group practice, but rather that will facilitate the manager's integration into large, formalized bureaucracies. Clearly, the acceptance of legitimate authority as implemented through a hierarchical structure is more important in the socialization of managers. Such authority will be more readily accepted to the extent that it *is perceived* to be legitimate. Given the social values stressing universalism and rationality, any organizational authority system and decision making apparatus that operates according to these values will appear to be more legitimate and will encourage compliance on the part of the managers.

To socialize students into a view of business that emphasizes power and politics would not only make the compliance to organizational authority and the acceptance of decision outcomes and procedures problematic, but also it might cause recruitment problems into the profession. It is certainly much more noble to think of oneself as developing skills toward the more efficient allocation and use of resources—implicitly for the greater good of society as a whole—than to think of oneself as engaged with other organizational participants in a political struggle over values, preferences and definitions of technology. Technical rationality, as a component of the managerial task, provides legitimation and meaning for one's career, fulfilling a function similar to healing the sick for doctors, or serving the nation's system of laws and justice for attorneys.

For the second group of practicing managers, as well as for the student, the ideology of rationality and efficiency provides an explanation for career progress, or lack thereof, that is much more likely to lead to the acceptance of one's position rather than to an attempt at making a radical change. The theoretical foundations of economics, including human capital and labor market theories, emphasize the universalistic nature of the wage determination process. It is scarcely an exaggeration to note that the inclusion of socioeconomic background in multiple regressions explaining wages or change in wages is what distinguishes a sociological from an economic approach to the issues of stratification and inequality. The theory that efficiency considerations, bureaucratic rationality, or both, drive out power and politics, reassures those in or entering into the corporate world, that their success in rising through the ranks will be more a function of their marginal product than of their

12

ability to diagnose power distributions and play politics. Inequality in outcomes becomes justified by the presumed decision making processes which produce such outcomes; this process is deemed legitimate and accepted because of its association with valued social ideals. This acceptance of one's place and rewards in the organization clearly can discourage the unionization of the workforce, and can help to provide continuing motivation and purposefulness to work when career blockages or other career problems occur.

In this way, the ideology of efficiency and rationality provides comforting explanations for practicing managers who find the progress of their careers blocked or less than what they might like, or feel a general sense of malaise about their work and their future. The invisible hands of marginal productivity and human capital have put them where they deserve to be. If power is to be considered at all, it is in terms of individually-oriented political strategies (e.g. Korda, 1975), which provide the managers with the illusion that, with a few handy hints, they can improve their lot in the organization. Explanations which focus on structural variables, as most of the explanations for power and politics developed here do, are less popular, as they provide no easy palliatives and imply a need for much more fundamental change in terms of affecting decision outcomes.

For the third set of readers of the management literature, the general public, the emphasis on rationality and efficiency and the de-emphasis on power and politics, assures them that the vast power and wealth controlled by organizations is, indeed, being effectively and legitimately employed. In this sense, organization theory and economic theory frequently find themselves fulfilling similar roles in explaining the status quo in terms which both justify and legitimate it. The theory of perfect competition or markets argues that when market processes are allowed to operate unimpeded by the intervention of politicians or monopolists, the best allocation results are obtained. Even those writers who have noted the existence of transaction costs and resulting problems (e.g. Williamson, 1975) have argued from a premise assuming efficiency interests on the part of the various economic actors involved.

In a similar fashion, the literature of organizational behavior has been dominated by a parallel form of functionalism. The strategic contingencies theories of organizational design (Lawrence and Lorsch, 1967; Galbraith, 1973; Woodward, 1965; Pennings, 1975) argued that there existed some optimal organizational design, given the organization's technology, size or environmental uncertainty. The assumption was implicit in much of this work that if such contingencies could be uncovered, the implementation of the rational structures would be straightforward. The search for empirical regularities between context and structure presumes some functional imperative for organizations, as a collectivity, to be roughly in correspondence with the requirements of their technologies or environments. Discussion of the size of the administrative component (Pondy, 1969; Blau and Schoenherr, 1971), the degree of centralization and formalization present in organizations (Burns and Stalker, 1961; Thompson, 1967), and the degree of differentiation (Lawrence and Lorsch, 1967; Thompson, 1967). all proceeded from a premise of functional rationality, though only Thompson took pains to make this assumption explicit.

The ideology of functional rationality—decision making oriented toward the improvement of efficiency or performance—provides a legitimation of formal organizations, for the general public as well as for those working within specific organizations. Bureaucracies are, as Perrow (1972) argued, tremendous stores of resources and energy, both human and financial. Bureaucracies also represent concentrations of energy on a scale seldom seen in the history of the world. The legitimation and justification of these concentrations of power are clearly facilitated by theories arguing that efficiency, productivity, and effectiveness are the dominant dynamics underlying the operation of organizations.

To maintain that organizations are less than totally interested in efficiency, effectiveness or market performance is to suggest that it is legitimate to raise questions concerning the appropriateness of the concentration of power and energy they represent and makes it possible to introduce political concerns into the issues of corporate governance. The introduction of these concerns makes the present control arrangements less certain and permanent and would be resisted by all of those who benefit from the status quo.

The argument, then, is that the very literature of management and organizational behavior (as well, we might add, of much of economics, though that is a topic worthy of separate development) is itself political (Edelman, 1964), and causes support to be generated and opposition to be reduced as various conceptions of organizations are created and maintained in part through their very repetition. In this literature, efficiency-enhancing or profit-increasing behavior are not being taken as hypotheses about motivation and causes for action, but rather as accepted facts. Then, a theory is developed which is both consistent with these assumptions and finds excuses for why so much variation in actual decisions and behaviors is missed. Another way of seeing the very strong ideological basis and bias in organization theory is to contrast explanations of organizations developed in the U.S. with those found in the writings of European organizational scholars (e.g., Karpik, 1978; Crozier, 1964). The European treatment of organizations and of knowledge about organizations takes a much more context-specific, historical view. Organizations are much more clearly related to the broader social issues of power and politics in the society and it is assumed that conceptions of organizations themselves are products of a social construction of reality which also constitutes an ingredient of politics played out on a macrosocial level.

Two other sources are also consistent with our position concerning the ideological foundation and political use of organization theory and writings on management. Nehrbass (1979) recently reviewed several streams of research, including the quality of working life studies and the research dealing with participatory decision making, and noted that, in spite of limited empirical research results, certain normatively-valued conceptions remained not only prominent in the literature, but, in fact, the dominant point of view and accepted as established truth. The persistent misinterpretation of the data from the Hawthorne studies (Carey, 1967) is another instance of the willingness of researchers to let values rather than data structure their conclusions. We would add to Nehrbass' list the issue of the premises for decisions made within organizations. Efficiency, effectiveness and profit are normatively valued and legitimate, while conceptions of organizations as political systems are much less consistent with dominant ideology and values. Thus, research demonstrating the non-rationality of decision procedures in organizations or in individuals has been met with relative neglect. The theories of organizations found explicitly or implicitly stated in the principal textbooks and in scholarly research presume bureaucratically rational functional imperatives for management and organizations.

Baritz (1960) has undertaken one of the more systematic examinations of the relationship between research and knowledge on the one hand, and society on the other, in his study of the employment of social scientists in industry, the incorporation of social science, particularly industrial psychology, into management thought, and the consequences of this relationship in the development of critical social theory. Although Baritz focused primarily on the use of the employment relationship to control the direction and development of social science inquiry, it is clear that there are many other forms of influence. These include the part time relationships afforded by consulting opportunities, business firm contributions to universities, business funding of research, and the employment of graduates trained in the various social science skills and ideologies.

Baritz presented details concerning the perceived increase of the importance of social science by business executives which developed during the twentieth century. He noted:

> *American management came to believe in the importance of understanding human behavior because it became convinced that this was one sure way of improving its main weapon in the struggle for power, the profit margin (1960: 191–192).*

This awareness on the part of management was encouraged by the claims made by social scientists concerning their utility in the solving of industrial problems.

Baritz argued that the cooperation between industry and social scientists, which was eagerly embraced by both parties, hindered the development of social science knowledge and its effective use in society more generally.

> *As part of the bureaucratization of virtually every aspect of American life, most industrial social scientists labored in industry as technicians, not as scientists . . . they were hemmed in by the very organization charts which they had helped to contrive. And the usual industrial social scientist, because he accepted the norms of the elite dominant in his society, was prevented from functioning critically, was compelled by his own ideology and the power of America's managers to supply the techniques helpful to managerial goals. In what should have been a healthful tension between mind and society, the industrial social scientist in serving the industrial elite had to abandon the wider obligations of the intellectual who is a servant of his own mind (Baritz, 1960: 194).*

Research and recommendations were colored by and tailored to the wishes of those who either directly employed the social scientists or who indirectly employed them through the support of research and programs within universities. The response on the part of social scientists was, Baritz argued, to ignore this aspect of their work. As in the case of organization theory generally, issues of preferences, values and politics were submerged and therefore ignored. "From the pioneers in industrial psychology to the sophisticated human-relations experts of the 1950's, almost all industrial social scientists have either backed away from the political and ethical implications of their work or have faced these considerations from the point of view of management" (Baritz, 1960: 199).

Clearly, this was true for Mayo, one of the founders of the human relations movement, a researcher involved in the Hawthorne experiments, and an individual who has had a lasting impact on the direction taken by organizational research in the U.S. "Mayo throughout his inquiring and productive life ignored labor, power and politics" (Baritz, 1960: 200).

Baritz argued that because of the influence of the management elite on social science, the problems investigated tended to be both trivial and regarded from a point of view which either vindicated the status quo or accepted as starting premises certain goals, objectives and values established by industry. This point has been echoed by Pugh (1966). Baritz's critique focused primarily on industrial psychology. It could be updated to include the research in organizations conducted since his study, and expanded to include other social sciences, including economics. What is important is not that science has come under these same influences in the same way that one might expect in considering power-dependence relationships. Rather, the critical thing is the extent to which, under the guise of objectivity and data, the ideological bases and premises of much of the study of organizations remain systematically submerged and ignored.

A study of the sociology of organizational science, although an interesting endeavor, is well beyond the scope of this book. Nevertheless, some casual observations about the political and ideological role of organizational behavior literature are in order. Consider a sampling of books randomly selected from the card catalogue of a major U.S. business school library with the terms power or politics in the title. Most of the books are by authors who are either European, political scientists, or sociologists. Few, if any, are in or from U.S. business schools. One could, in general, make the statement that the assumptions and topics covered by organization research are explainable by the political and social context in which researchers are working. This observation has already been made about social psychologists by Cartwright who noted:

> It is true, or course, that the substantive content of the knowledge attained in any field of science is ultimately determined by the intrinsic nature of the phenomena under investigation, since empirical research is essentially a process of discovery with an internal logic of its own. But it is equally true that the knowledge attained is the product of a social system and, as such, is basically influenced by the properties of that system and by its cultural, social and political environment (1979: 82).

17

A study of the politics of knowledge in the organizational behavior area, which traces changes in research issues, conclusions, and expressed values and ideologies, and relates these to changes in funding patterns, consultancy, social values and political trends in the society in general, and to cultural differences, would be productive in terms of developing data and explanations for the phenomena discussed in this section.

Models of organizations which emphasize power and politics have their own political problems. It is important for those analyzing organizations to be able to figure out the kind of analytical framework that can be most usefully employed to diagnose the particular organization of interest. Kaplan's (1964) parable of the hammer is relevant. Because one has a hammer, one tends to use it on everything and for every task. Similarly, there is a tendency to take a noncontingent approach to the analysis of organizations, and to see them all as rational, bureaucratic, or political. Just as it is difficult to play football with baseball equipment, it is difficult to diagnose or effectively operate in an organization unless its dominant paradigm or mode of operation is understood. Furthermore, in order to evaluate the validity of a political approach to organizational analysis, there must be some alternatives with which to compare the model. For both of these reasons—to place the political model in a broader context of competing perspectives on organizational decision making and to raise issues relevant to diagnosing the form of system one is dealing with—we will describe the major contending models of organizational decision making.

Rational Choice Models

The model of rational choice is prominent in the social choice literature. It is not only prescribed as being the best way to make choices in organizations, but frequently claims to be descriptive of actual choice processes as well. The rational model presumes that events are "purposive choices of consistent actors" (Allison, 1971: 11). It is important to recognize, therefore, that the rational model presumes and assumes that "behavior reflects purpose or intention" (Allison, 1971: 13). Behavior is not accidental, random, or rationalized after the fact; rather, purpose is presumed to pre-exist and behavior is guided by that purpose. With respect to understanding organizations or other social collectivities, the rational model further presumes that there is a unified purpose or set of preferences characterizing the entity taking the action. As Allison (1971: 28–29) has noted:

> *What rationality adds to the concept of purpose is* consistency:
> *consistency among goals and objectives relative to a particular*
> *action; consistency in the application of principles in order to*
> *select the optimal alternative (emphasis in original).*

The rational choice model presumes that there are goals and objectives that characterize organizations. As Friedland (1974) has noted, rationality cannot be defined apart from the existence of a set of goals. Thus, all rational choice models start with the assumption of a goal or consistent goal set. In the case of subjective expected utility maximization models (Edwards, 1954), the goals are called utilities for various outcomes, associated with the pleasure or pain producing properties of the outcomes. In the language of economics and management science, the goals are called the objectives or objective function to be maximized. Occasionally, goals are called preferences, referring to the states of the world the social actor prefers. Rational choice models require that these goals be consistent (March, 1976: 70).

Given a consistent set of goals, the next element in theories of rational choice is a set of decision making alternatives to be chosen. Alternatives are presumed to be differentiable one from the other, so that each is uniquely identified. Such alternatives are produced by a search process. Until Simon (1957) introduced the concept of satisficing, it was generally assumed that search was costless and that large numbers of alternatives would be considered. Simon's contribution was to introduce the concept of bounded rationality, which held that persons had both limited capacities to process information and limited resources to devote to search activities. Thus a search for alternatives would be conducted only until a satisfactory alternative was uncovered. The concept of satisfaction was defined in terms of the social actor's level of aspiration (March and Simon, 1958).

Be they many or few, once a set of alternatives are uncovered, the next step in the rational decision making process involves the assessment of the likely outcomes or consequences of the various possible courses of action. If there is risk or uncertainty involved, then estimates of the probability of the occurrence of various consequences would be used in making statements about the values of the consequences of different choices. At this stage in the decision process, it is assumed that consequences can be fully and completely anticipated, albeit with some degree of uncertainty. In other words, everything that can possibly occur as a result of the decision is presumably specified, though which of the various possibilities will actually occur may be subject to chance.

Then, a rational choice involves selecting that course of action or that alternative which maximizes the social actor's likelihood of attaining the highest value for achievement of the preferences or goals in the objective function. In rational choice, decisions are related systematically to objectives (March, 1976: 70); that decision is made which shows the most promise of enabling the social actor to maximize the attainment of objectives. "Rationality refers to consistent, value-maximizing choice within specified constraints" (Allison, 1971: 30).

It is clear that in analyzing choice processes in organizations or other social collectivities, the assumption of consistency and unity in the goals, information and decision processes is problematic. However, one of the advantages of the rational model is that it permits prediction of behavior with complete certainty and specificity if one knows (or assumes one knows) the goals of the other organization. Allison (1971: 13), in reviewing foreign policy analysis, has argued that this advantage is one important reason that "most contemporary analysts . . . proceed *predominantly* . . . in terms of this framework when trying to explain international events." The rational choice model facilitates the prediction of what the other social actor will do, assuming various goals; turning the model around, various goals can be inferred (though scarcely unambiguously) from the behavior of the other actor. It is inevitably the case that "an imaginative analyst can construct an account of value-maximizing choice for any action or set of actions performed" (Allison, 1971: 35).

Thus, to preserve the diagnostic and analytic properties of the rational model, goal consistency and congruity are assumed. In economic theory, the goal of the firm is assumed to be profit maximization. In the theory of finance, the goal is assumed to be the maximization of shareholder wealth. In theories of public bureaucracies, the goals are presumed to be those that are part of the agency's mission and which enable it to fulfill its assigned role in society. As Stava (1976: 209) has noted in discussing choice in larger political bodies, "legal-bureaucratic theories mostly argue that resources are allocated . . . according to some universalistic rules applied in a neutral way and in accord with the prima facie needs of the society." For society, one could as easily substitute the word organization. Stava continued by noting that decisions were presumed to be both formally neutral and rational. "They are neutral in the sense that the necessary value premises for the decisions are given or treated as given. . . . The decisions should also be (formally) rational. This means that they are intended to realize goals" (Stava, 1976: 209).

DIAGNOSING THE USE
OF RATIONAL DECISION MAKING

How can one tell if the organization one is investigating is, in fact, best described in terms of the rational model? One can certainly not tell by investigating the decision outcomes. Any such outcomes can be consistent with rational choice, if the appropriate goals or preferences are assumed. Rational choice describes a *process* of selecting the best alternative course of action. It seems reasonable, then, to diagnose the presence or absence of rationality in decision making by considering the process by which choices are made.

Chaffee (1980), in reviewing the literature on decision making, has developed a set of seven criteria for defining the requirements of rational choice processes in terms of the collection and use of information:

1) Information is received prior to the decision being made;

2) Information is problem-centered and goal-directed;

3) Information documents the existence of and the need to solve the problem or reach the goal;

4) Information includes consideration of more than one alternative for reaching the goal or solving the problem;

5) Information has logical internal consistency in terms of posited cause-effect relationships;

6) Information is oriented toward maximization, in that it demonstrates the value of the various alternatives considered in reaching the goal;

7) Information identifies the value premises on which it is based.

One final condition could be added, which is that the choice is made to accept that alternative which, on the basis of the information provided, seems to provide the best likelihood of achieving the goals or solving the problem.

It is, of course, the case that given a belief and social norms favoring rationality, such a process might be followed to legitimate a decision made, for instance, on political grounds. Thus, it is reasonable to argue that the fulfillment of a process similar to that outlined above is a necessary but not sufficient condition to provide conclusive evidence for the operation of a rational decision making process.

The process concerns outlined above can be usefully coupled with another type of consideration to provide a better way of assessing

21

whether or not the organization in question is operating according to the rational model. In particular, political models of organizations imply that decisions are made on the basis of the preferences of actors within the organization, without regard to the welfare of the whole organization (e.g., Stagner, 1969). Nagel (1975: 29) has defined power as "an actual or potential causal relation between the preferences of an 'actor' regarding an outcome and the outcome itself." By contrast, rational choice involves the selection of the goal-maximizing alternative regardless of which particular interests within the organization favor that alternative. This suggests that rational organizations can be distinguished from more political organizations by investigating the extent to which the choices made consistently reflect the preferences of certain groups within the organizations, or whether such choices are relatively uncorrelated with the prior preferences and positions of the same groups. The rational model presumes that information and value-maximization dictate choice; the political model presumes that parochial interests and preferences control choice. Then, choice should be relatively uncorrelated with the preferences of the same groups and highly correlated with information and the selection of the best alternative.

Bureaucratic Models of Decision Making

The rational model of choice implies the need for some substantial information processing requirements in organizational decision making. These may be unrealistic or unattainable in some cases, and organizations may operate using standard operating procedures and rules rather than engaging in rational decision making on a continuous basis. The bureaucratic model of organizations substitutes procedural rationality for substantive rationality (Simon, 1979); rather than having choices made to maximize values, choices are made according to rules and processes which have been adaptive and effective in the past.

The best explication of what is meant by bureaucratically-rational decision processes can be found in March and Simon (1958) and Cyert and March (1963). In this framework, goals are viewed as systems of constraints (Simon, 1964) which decisions must satisfy. Because of bounded rationality, search is limited and stops as soon as a satisfactory alternative is found. Uncertainty tends to be avoided in that, rather than making comprehensive assessments of risk and probabilities, decisions are made with relatively short time horizons. Conflict among different alternatives or points of view is never fully resolved, and priorities and objectives are attended to sequentially, first, for instance, worrying about profit, then about market share, then personnel problems, and so forth.

Throughout this process, organizations learn and adapt, and their learning and knowledge takes the form of rules of action or standard operating procedures, repertoires of behavior which are activated in certain situations and which provide a program, a set of behaviors for organizational participants, that serve as a guide to action and choice.

Seen from this perspective, decisions are viewed "less as deliberate choices and more as *outputs* of large organizations functioning according to standard patterns of behavior" (Allison, 1971: 67). It is presumed that "most of the behavior is determined by previously established procedures" (Allison, 1971: 79). The model of organizations as bureaucratically rational presumes less conscious foresight and less clearly defined preferences and information. Both rely on habitual ways of doing things and the results of past actions, and constrain how the organization proceeds to operate in the future. Decisions are not made as much as they evolve from the policies, procedures, and rules which constitute the organization and its memory.

Perhaps one of the best examples to consider in understanding the difference between the rational choice model and the bureaucratic model is to examine the effect of precedence on budgeting decisions. The literature on governmental budgeting, for instance (Wildavsky, 1979; Davis, Dempster, and Wildavsky, 1966; Wildavsky and Hammond, 1965), indicates that the best predictor of this year's budget is last year's budget. Analysis of governmental budgeting indicates that precedence, coupled with some very simple rules for handling increased requests, can account for most of the variation in resource allocations. That this process is not perceived as completely rational is evidenced by the fact that great time and attention has been spent on developing alternative resource allocation schemes, such as Planning-Programming-Budgeting Systems (PPBS) and zero-based budgeting. The advocates of these systems argue that what was allocated last year may have little to do with rational, value maximizing goal attainment, and it is necessary to more systematically relate decisions to preferences and new information.

Of course, most of these new decision making processes have had tremendous problems in their implementation. Precedence and other similar simple rules may not be optimal, but they are at least computationally easy and require less heroic assumptions about information processing capacities. Furthermore, one could argue that except in circumstances of sudden and dramatic change in the contingencies confronting the organization, incremental change as might occur through incremental budgeting is sufficient to maintain effective operations through the process of making small adjustments to the organization's operations. Thus, bureaucratic rationality, it is argued, can perhaps effectively substitute for substantive rationality.

DISTINGUISHING
BUREAUCRATIC ORGANIZATIONS

It is relatively simple to distinguish between organizations which operate under the bureaucratic model and those which operate under the rational model. Bureaucratic organizations will typically have much less extensive information search and analysis activities, and rely more heavily on rules, precedent, and standard operating procedures. Less time and resources will be spent on decision making, and fewer alternatives will be considered before actions are taken. Indeed, it is the difference in the amount of analysis, search, and focused attention on goal attainment, that constitutes the difference between the bureaucratic and rational models.

Distinguishing between the bureaucratic and political models of organization may be somewhat more difficult. After all, if the distribution of power is stable in the organization, which is a reasonable assumption, particularly over relatively short time periods, and if power and politics determine organizational decisions, then organizational choices will be relatively stable over time. But, this stability is also characteristic of the use of precedent in decision making, which is one of the hallmarks of bureaucratic organizations. One way of distinguishing, then, would involve looking at the correlates of the incremental changes in decisions and allocations made within the organization. While both models might be consistent with the use of precedent for the bulk of the decisions, there are some implicit differences in how incremental resources will be allocated. In bureaucratic organizations, changes in resource allocation patterns should either follow a proportional basis, be based on some standard measure of operations and performance, or reflect an attempt to shift the resources to better achieve the goals and values of the organization. By contrast, political models of organizations would suggest that power would best predict changes and shifts in decisions and allocations.

Research which attempts to explore the use of rules and standard operating procedures in organizations has typically involved the use of computer programs which simulate the operation of such rules (e.g., Cyert and March, 1963; Crecine, 1967; Gerwin, 1969). Unfortunately, the validation of such models is complex because there may be many ways in which an observed outcome can be produced. This means that just because the application of a set of decision rules produces results that mirror what occurs in an organization, it is not necessarily true that these rules are actually guiding the organization's decision making.

24

Decision Process Models

Although they exist within much the same tradition as the bureaucratic model of organizations, decision process models differ in that they presume even less rationality and more randomness in organizational functioning. As power models depart from bureaucratic rationality by removing the assumption of consistent, overall organizational objectives and shared beliefs about technology, decision process models depart even further by removing the presumption of predefined, known preferences held by the various social actors. Decision process models posit that there are no overall organizational goals being maximized through choice, and no powerful actors with defined preferences who possess resources through which they seek to obtain those preferences. Stava (1976: 209) described decision process models as follows:

> *In* decision process theories *it is presumed that policy is the outcome of a choice made by one or several decision-makers. Which choice is made is determined by the situation in which the decision-maker finds himself. This situation is, in turn, largely caused by the processes preceding the choice. It is impossible, then, to predict policies without knowing the details of the preceding processes.*

March (1966: 180) argued that in such decision process models, although one might posit that the various actors have preferences and varying amounts of power, the concept of power does not add much to the prediction of behavior and choice in such systems.

More recently, March (1978) and others (e.g., Weick, 1969) have questioned whether or not the concept of preferences makes sense at any level of analysis, individual or organizational. One of the arguments raised is that instead of preferences guiding choice, choice may determine preferences. In other words, one only knows what one likes after it has been experienced; or, as Weick has argued, one only knows what one has done after he or she has done it, since the meaning of action is retrospective and follows the action rather than preceeds it. In this framework, goals are seen as the products of sense making activities which are carried on after the action has occurred to explain that action or rationalize it. The action itself is presumed to be the result of habit, custom, or the influence of other social actors in the environment.

One example of a decision process model of social choice is the garbage can model (Cohen, March, and Olsen, 1972). The basic idea of the model is that decision points are opportunities into which various problems and solutions are dumped by organizational participants. "In a garbage can situation, a decision is an outcome of an interpretation of several relatively independent 'streams' within an organization" (Cohen, March, and Olsen, 1976: 26). The streams consist of problems, solutions (which are somebody's product), participants, and choice opportunities. The decision process models developed by March and his colleagues emphasize the problematic nature of participation by various social actors in choices. They note that systems are frequently so overloaded with problems, solutions, and decision opportunities that any given social actor will attend to only certain decisions.

Cohen, March, and Olsen (1972) developed a simulation of the garbage can decision process. One of the important conclusions emerging from that simulation is:

> . . . that although the processes within the garbage can are understandable and in some ways predictable, events are not dominated by intention. The processes and the outcomes are likely to appear to have no close relation with the explicit intention of actors. In situations in which load is heavy and the structure is relatively unsegmented, intention is lost in context dependent flow of problems, solutions, people, and choice opportunities (Cohen, March, and Olsen, 1976: 37).

March (1966) had earlier begun to explore the role of chance in organizational choice situations, and the garbage can simulation represents the formal incorporation of chance and randomness in a theory of choice.

The garbage can model emerged largely from a study of universities and university presidents (Cohen and March, 1974). Universities were characterized as organized anarchies, and garbage can decision process models were believed to be particularly appropriate in such contexts, although the assertion is also made that elements of these models are found in most organizations. Weiner (1976) has summarized some of the main features and assumptions of the organized anarchy model of organizations. First, "the existing theory of organized anarchies does not require that decisions be reached or problems solved by a specified time . . . the theory holds that such requirements are neither generated within the organization nor imposed by the organization's environment" (Weiner, 1976: 226). The garbage can model then, presumes and assumes no deadlines. Decisions are worked on until they are made. The theory also suggests that "the stream of problems entering or leaving an organization" is a "flow that is independent of the other streams of choices, solutions and energy. . . . The theory holds further that problems move autonomously among choice opportunities in search for a choice process in which the problem can be resolved" (Weiner, 1976: 243). Decision making is viewed as an activity which absorbs the energy of those available, works on problems, and comes up with solutions which are determined in large measure by a random stream of events.

DISTINGUISHING ORGANIZED ANARCHIES

The key concept used in diagnosing whether or not the organization is an organized anarchy which can best be understood by using decision process organizational models is that of intention. Not only are there presumed to be no overarching organizational goals, but presumably intention is problematic even at the level of subunits and groups within the organization. Action occurs, but it is not primarily motivated by conscious choice and planning. Although not made explicit, there should be relatively little consistency or consensus over behavior in an organized anarchy. Events should unfold in ways predictable only by considering the process, and not through consideration of value maximization, precedent, power or force.

If that seems like a difficult requirement to fulfill, those who advocate the decision process model of organizations argue that much of the consistency and intentionality observed in organizations is imputed by those doing the observing rather than being a characteristic of the organization being observed. Much as in Allison's (1971) treatment of foreign policy analysis, goals are imputed to organizations by observers rather than being actual properties of the organizations themselves. Similarly, rules and power may also be imputed rather than actually be properties of the system under study.

Although decision process models provide a language for describing the randomness that is sometimes observed, they do not provide a great amount of predictive power. Their theme is that such prediction is largely impossible, except for the use of complex programs of decision routines. Their de-emphasis of intention makes them unpopular with those who view the world in a more proactive, strategic fashion.

Political Models of Organizations

One criticism that has been leveled against rational choice models is that they fail to take into account the diversity of interests and goals within organizations. March (1962) described business firms as political coalitions. The coalitional view of organizations was developed by Cyert and March (1963) in their description of organizational decision making. In bureaucratic theories of organizations, the presumption is that through control devices such as rewards based on job performance or seniority, rules that ensure fair and standardized treatment for all, and careers within the organization, the operation of self-interest can be virtually eliminated as an influence on organizational decision making. Economic or incentive theories of organizations argue that through the payment of a wage, particularly when compensation is made contingent on performance, individuals hired into the organization come to accept the organization's goals. Political models of organizations assume that these control devices, as well as others such as socialization, are not wholly effective in producing a coherent and unified set of goals or definitions of technology. Rather, as Baldridge (1971: 25) has argued, political models view organizations as pluralistic and divided into various interests, subunits, and subcultures. Conflict is viewed as normal or at least customary in political organizations. Action does not presuppose some overarching intention. Rather, action results "from games among players who perceive quite different faces of an issue and who differ markedly in the actions they prefer" (Allison, 1971: 175). Because action results from bargaining and compromise, the resulting decision seldom perfectly reflects the preferences of any group or subunit within the organization.

Political models of choice further presume that when preferences conflict, the power of the various social actors determines the outcome of the decision process. Power models hypothesize that those interests, subunits, or individuals within the organization who possess the greatest power, will receive the greatest rewards from the interplay of organizational politics. In such models, power "is an intervening variable between an initial condition, defined largely in terms of the individual components of the system, and a terminal state, defined largely in terms of the system as a whole" (March, 1966: 168–169). Power is used to overcome the resistance of others and obtain one's way in the organization.

To understand organizational choices using a political model, it is necessary to understand who participates in decision making, what determines each player's stand on the issues, what determines each actor's relative power, and how the decision process arrives at a decision; in other words, how the various preferences become combined (majority rule; unanimity; ⅔ vote; etc.) (Allison, 1971: 164). A change in any one of these aspects—relative power, the rules of decision making, or preferences—can lead to a change in the predicted organizational decision.

DISTINGUISHING POLITICAL
MODELS OF ORGANIZATIONS

March (1966) has argued that it is often difficult to distinguish chance models from power or force models in terms of the predictions that each would make. He argued that evidence for force models would include: whether or not power is stable over time, whether or not power is stable over subject matter, whether or not power is correlated with other attributes, and whether or not power could be experimentally manipulated. These are important criteria to keep in mind when thinking about the evidence for a political model of organizations to be presented in this book.

It is clear that a political or power model of choice need not assume that all issues are equally important and, therefore, equally worthy of effort. In Chapter 3, the conditions under which power is used will be explored. Incorporating ideas of activation in force or power models makes their testing even more difficult.

Power models can be distinguished from rational models if it can be demonstrated that either no overarching organizational goal exists or even if such a goal does exist, decisions are made which are inconsistent with maximizing the attainment of the goal. Power can be distinguished from chance or organized anarchy models by demonstrating that actors in organizations have preferences and intentions which are consistent across decision issues and which they attempt to have implemented. Further evidence for political models would come from finding that measures of power in social systems, rather than goals, precedent, or chance, bring about decision outcomes. Indeed, the ability to measure and operationalize power is critical both for diagnosing political systems and for testing political models of organizations.

Summary

One of the points of Allison's (1971) analysis of the Cuban missile crisis is that it is not necessary to choose between analytical frameworks. Each may be partly true in a particular situation, and one can obtain a better understanding of the organization by trying to use all of the models rather than by choosing among them. This point is different than saying that some organizations are characterized more by the political model and others by the rational model. Allison's argument is that insight can be gained from the application of all the frameworks in the same situation. This statement is true, but only within limits. At some point, the various perspectives will begin to make different predictions about what will occur, and will generate different recommendations concerning the strategy and tactics to be followed. At that point, the participant will need to decide where to place his or her bets.

As we have already discussed, discovering which perspective best describes a particular organization is not easy, and the world will do little to make it easier. Some of the perspectives are more accepted and acceptable than others. This means that language will be used to make it seem that the organization is operating according to the more accepted paradigms. It also means that there will be various informational and other types of social influence imposed on the observer to make him construct a particular view of the organization.

In Table 1-1, the four decision models described in this chapter are briefly summarized along eight relevant dimensions. The ability to perfectly distinguish between the models, using a single dimension in a particular situation, is likely to be limited. However, by considering the dimensions in combination and by using comparative frames of reference, it becomes feasible to assess the extent to which the organization in question is operating according to one or the other of the models.

It is evident from the title of this book what my view is concerning the relative applicability of the four models of organizational decision making. Circumstances of bureaucratically rational decision making occur only in certain conditions on an infrequent basis. As Thompson and Tuden (1959) have argued, consensus on both goals and technology, or the connections between actions and consequences, are necessary in order for computational forms of decision making to be employed. Where there is disagreement over goals, compromise is used; when there is disagreement over technology, judgment is employed; and when there is disagreement about both, Thompson and Tuden characterize the decision situation as one requiring inspiration. In the case of judgment, compromise, and inspiration, it is the relative power of the various social actors that provides both the sufficient and necessary way of resolving the decision.

Furthermore, if intention is not always a guiding force in the taking of action and if preferences are not always clear or consistent, then there are at least some participants in organizations who know what they want and have the social power to get it. The randomness implied by the decision process model of organizations is inconsistent with the observation that in organizational decision making, some actors seem to usually get the garbage, while others manage to get the can.

Standard operating procedures, rules, and behavior repertoires clearly exist and are important in organizations. Much organizational

TABLE 1-1
Overview of Four Organizational Decision Making Models

Model

Dimension	Rational	Bureaucratic	Decision Process/ Organized Anarchy	Political Power
Goals, preferences	Consistent within and across social actors	Reasonably consistent	Unclear, ambiguous, may be constructed ex post to rationalize action	Consistent within social actors; inconsistent, pluralistic within the organization
Power and control	Centralized	Less centralized with greater reliance on rules	Very decentralized, anarchic	Shifting coalitions and interest groups
Decision Process	Orderly, substantively rational	Procedural rationality embodied in programs and standard operating procedures	Ad hoc	Disorderly, characterized by push and pull of interests
Rules and Norms	Norm of optimization	Precedent, tradition	Segmented and episodic participation in decisions	Free play of market forces; conflict is legitimate and expected
Information and Computational Requirements	Extensive and systematic	Reduced by the use of rules and procedures	Haphazard collection and use of information	Information used and withheld strategically
Beliefs about action-consequence relationships	Known at least to a probability distribution	Consensually shared acceptance of routines	Unclear, ambiguous technology	Disagreements about technology
Decisions	Follow from value-maximizing choice	Follow from programs and routines	Not linked to intention; result of intersection of persons, solutions, problems	Result of bargaining and interplay among interests
Ideology	Efficiency and effectiveness	Stability, fairness, predictability	Playfulness, loose coupling, randomness	Struggle, conflict, winners and losers

decision making involves issues that are neither important nor contested, and in such cases, standard operating procedures are sufficient to get the decisions made in an inexpensive fashion. However, it is necessary to be aware that these various rules, norms, and procedures have in themselves implications for the distribution of power and authority in organizations and for how contested decisions should be resolved. The rules and processes themselves become important focal points for the exercise of power. They are not always neutral and not always substantively rational. Sometimes they are part and parcel of the political contest that occurs within organizations.

One of the reasons why power and politics characterize so many organizations is because of what some of my students have dubbed the Law of Political Entropy: given the opportunity, an organization will tend to seek and maintain a political character. The argument is that once politics are introduced into a situation, it is very difficult to restore rationality. Once consensus is lost, once disagreements about preferences, technology, and management philosophy emerge, it is very hard to restore the kind of shared perspective and solidarity which is necessary to operate under the rational model. If rationality is indeed this fragile, and if the Law of Political Entropy is correct, then over time one would expect to see more and more organizations characterized by the political model.

The purpose of this first chapter has been to introduce and define the concepts of power and politics, review some alternative perspectives on organizational decision making, and to consider the ideological function of much management theory and research. It is necessary to be able to diagnose what the game is that is being played and the general normative climate within which the game goes on. Research and writing on organizations is itself political, if not in intent then in outcome. This makes the acquisition of good information and the diagnosis of organizations all the more difficult, but then again, all the more interesting.

Having introduced the game and the central concepts, it is next necessary to understand how to figure out who the players are and what their relative positions should be. This is the topic of the next chapter. Having considered the diagnosis of power distributions in organizations, we will then consider the conditions under which power is more or less important in determining decisions in Chapter 3. Knowing the players, how to assess them, and the conditions under which the game is likely to be political, we next turn our attention to understanding the sources or determinants of power in organizations (Chapter 4), the strategies used in the exercise of power (Chapters 5 and 6), and then in Chapter

7 we will review some evidence of the effects of power in use. That provides an opportunity to bring together, with some more comprehensive examples, ideas developed in the preceding chapters. Finally, we will consider how power and control become institutionalized (Chapter 8), and then conclude by considering some implications and applications of the political analysis of organizations.

CHAPTER 2

ASSESSING POWER IN ORGANIZATIONS

As Pettigrew (1973: 240) has so aptly noted:

> *An accurate perception of the power distribution in the social arena in which he lives is . . . a necessary prerequisite for the man seeking powerful support for his demands.*

The assessment of power in organizations is important for several reasons. In the first place, the exercise and use of power is facilitated by an accurate diagnosis of the political situation confronted by the social actor. Strategies ranging from coalition formation to cooptation require an accurate diagnosis of the political landscape. Second, the measurement and assessment of power is important for those who would do research on the topic. If we are to assess whether or not power is correlated with other attributes, is stable over time, and across decision issues (March, 1966), then power will have to be measured. Third, as Pondy (1977) has suggested, one way of understanding what power is, is to consider how the concept can be examined and used. Thus, the assessment of power will help in the understanding of the concept.

Two tasks are required in assessing organizational political systems. In the first place, the principal organizational actors need to be identified on a meaningful basis. Then, the power of these various actors needs to be assessed. Both issues are covered in the discussion of the assessment of power in organizations which follows.

35

Identifying Political Actors

The first problem confronted by an analyst of organizational politics is to identify the relevant units for analysis. Organizations are, after all, comprised of people, who are grouped into subunits, which may be grouped into departments, divisions, etc. Furthermore, organizations are stratified by level of hierarchy as well as by horizontal grouping. The various people can be distinguished in terms of their race, sex, educational background, type of work, number of years with the company, and so forth. Are cohort groups, which are identified by the time they entered the organization, more important than departmental affiliation? As an illustration of this problem, the following different sets of groupings were among those used by my class for an assignment on diagnosing power within a school of business:

1) quantitative versus non-quantitative subjects

2) administration, faculty, and students

3) subject fields (finance, economics, accounting, management science, organizational behavior, marketing)

4) men and women

5) administration, tenured faculty, untenured faculty, doctoral students, MBA students, undergraduate students

Which are the most useful?

The solution to the problem is not simply a matter of judgment or intuition. What the analyst wants to do is to identify groupings which are as inclusive as possible and which are internally homogeneous with respect to preferences and beliefs on the issues being investigated. In a sense, it is a problem of clustering, in which the criterion is to cluster social actors together to maximize their homogeneity in opinions, preferences, and values which are relevant to the political issue being investigated, or which are the most salient and important in the organization at the time. If one had data on the preferences and opinions of all the various actors within the organization, such clustering would be readily accomplished by using available computational algorithms. However, in most cases it will require judgment to assess whether or not the appropriate units of analysis have been identified. In each instance, the questions to be asked are: is there relative homogeneity in the goals, preferences, and beliefs about technology within the categories of social actors identified; and are there differences among the preferences and beliefs of the

36

social actors so identified? This does not mean that every grouping is necessarily different from every other grouping; indeed, the building of coalitions requires finding areas of common interest. Rather, it is a judgmental decision which involves discerning whether or not there are differences between social actors on enough important issues to justify considering them as analytically separate. And, it is important to recognize that the identification of meaningful political units will change over time and be dependent on the particular set of issues at hand.

In identifying relevant political units, it is wise to start with the labels used in and provided by the organization. As Dearborn and Simon (1958) have noted, departmental identification, for instance, provides a frame of reference and exposure to information that may color one's perception of the world. The demarcations formally and persistently recognized within the organization come to create expectations for behavior which are self-fulfilling. Furthermore, the physical proximity which accompanies such identification, as well as the increased social interaction within such groups, contributes to the development of a common frame of reference which tends to reinforce their validity as distinct political units.

At the same time, it is important to recognize that in organizations, just as in the larger society, people have multiple memberships and interests that are cross-cut in a variety of different ways. A faculty member may be at once: untenured; a specialist in management science; interested in theory and research; opposed to consulting; have a preference to de-emphasize teaching, particularly as a criterion for promotion; and be one of eight persons who entered the organization at the same time. In a business firm, a person may be identified by: his or her disciplinary background (engineering, business, law, etc.); level of education; type of college attended (elite, Ivy League or state university); family social background; functional or departmental background (finance, marketing, consumer products, etc.); length of time in the organization; or age, and this is hardly an exhaustive list. Each one of these ways of characterizing an individual may be relevant in determining meaningful political groupings in the organization.

A HEURISTIC DEVICE

In assessing organizational political systems, the analyst faces the same problems confronted by one who seeks to understand organizational interdependence (Pfeffer and Salancik, 1978), and the problems become greater with the *more* localized knowledge possessed. The problems have to do with taking for granted what the relevant political units are, and thinking one understands when one doesn't what the important dimensions are that form the basis for political cleavage within the organization.

Thus, what analysts of organizational political systems require is some simple way of disciplining the analytical process to avoid overlooking important elements and to avoid reaching premature conclusions concerning the political landscape. One simple, easy to use device is to construct a matrix along the following lines:

Possible Political Actors

	A	B	C	D	....
1					
2					
3					
4					
.					
.					
.					

Relevant Issues or Topics, framed in terms of proposed actions or policies

For each issue or decision, ask yourself, is there likely to be homogeneity on this issue with respect to those persons or subunits grouped under each of the categories? If the answer is no, you have identified categories that fail to match the relevant political cleavages on the issues in question, and another way of identifying political units needs to be tried. If the answer is generally yes within each of the categories and across most or all of the issues, then you have a heuristically useful representation of the political scene. If two of the categories are perfectly correlated, in that their positions on all of the listed issues are likely to be identical, then they can be safely combined into one. The matrix, by the way, does not need to be filled in with great detail; a plus (+), zero (0), or minus (−) representing favor, neutral, and oppose on each of the proposed actions or policies will probably suffice for this part of the analysis.

Of course, by looking at similarities (correlations) among preferences across political actors, potential coalitions of interest can be identified. The more similar the structure of preferences is over a set of decision issues, the more easily the two actors can identify mutual interests and coordinate action. The framework can, of course, be further refined to consider the relative importance of the various issues or actions to the actors, and to consider the relative potency of the actors themselves.

When weighted by the potency of the various political actors, the matrix facilitates the prediction of what particular actions will be, in fact, adopted within the organization. Actions opposed by a majority of the potent actors will probably not be implemented. And, as we shall see in later chapters, the matrix also provides some insights into how to go about obtaining sufficient support in order to get a particular decision adopted.

AN EXAMPLE: CHANGE AT NEW YORK UNIVERSITY

We can use Baldridge's (1971: Chapter 4) discussion of the change in educational orientation at New York University to illustrate the use of the kind of analysis we have been describing. The change was from one of virtually open enrollment and unlimited educational opportunity to one in which there were higher admissions standards, fewer part-time students, and a stronger emphasis on research and graduate education.

> *For many years NYU had a consistent interpretation of its role in New York's higher education. From its founding the university offered educational advantages to all types of people, including underprivileged minority groups. . . . this was to be "a different kind of institution" from the upper-class colleges that dominated American education in the early nineteenth century. As part of this philosophy NYU accepted students of relatively low academic ability . . . (Baldridge, 1971: 39).*

The expansion of public education in the state through a system of state university campuses and junior colleges, as well as the move of City University to a policy of more open enrollment, severely affected NYU's competitive position. NYU was charging among the highest fees in the nation while attempting to compete with state and city universities which charged almost nothing. In the early 1960s, actual NYU enrollments began to fall far below projections (Baldridge, 1971: 41). Spurred on by a planning grant from the Ford Foundation, NYU's educational role came under intense scrutiny by various committees and by the administration. The selection of a new president, James M. Hester, in 1962 facilitated the process of change and self-examination. As a result of this study and planning, the following changes were proposed in a plan submitted to the Ford Foundation for support:

*First, NYU would significantly upgrade undergraduate ad-
missions policies, thus moving itself out of direct competition
with the public institutions for the bulk of the medium-ability
students. . . . This had a drastic effect on several schools in the
university. Second, most of the key decision-makers thought
that the multischool system of undergraduate education would
have to be abandoned so that duplication of efforts could be
avoided. . . . Third, an "urban university" theme was adopted
as a new institutional character . . . carefully articulated
around service to the New York community, research in urban
problems and preparation of urban specialists. . . . Fourth, the
upgrading of quality involved an attempt to get more full-time
students instead of the part-time group that NYU had long
attracted. . . . Fifth, NYU would concentrate an increasing
proportion of its energies toward graduate and advanced professional training. . . . Finally, the faculty recruitment would
concentrate on obtaining more full-time, advanced-degree
people (Baldridge, 1971: 44–45).*

The changes were fundamental and profound in the university, and
unleashed a large amount of political activity and conflict. In Table 2-1,
the various political actors and their positions on the various changes,
as inferred from the discussion provided in Baldridge (1971: Chapter 4),
are displayed. There are several lessons to be learned from this analysis.

In the first place, it is wrong to assume that disciplinary boundaries
demarcate political struggles either within universities or within other
types of organizations. In the case of New York University, the School
of Commerce and the Graduate School of Business were on opposite
sides in several of the issues. The Graduate School of Business was a
separate unit for graduate and advanced professional degrees, while the
School of Commerce was responsible for the undergraduate program
which included a large part-time, evening school component.

*GSB wanted to establish itself as a major research center and
a nationally reputable business education unit. Its professors
were much more oriented to scholarly research . . . and feared
that the undergraduate School of Commerce was severely
damaging the reputation of business studies at NYU. . . . the
Commerce professors rightly believed they might be out of
their jobs if all the changes were instituted. They feared reduced enrollments, a loss of the night-school program, de-*

TABLE 2-1
Political Interests and Their Positions on
Proposed Changes at New York University

Interests

Proposed Changes	University College	Grad. Sch. of Business	Commerce	Engineering	Education	Washington Square College
Upgrade Admissions Standards	+	+	−	+	0	+
Urban Theme	0	0	0	0	0	+
Abandon Duplication in Undergraduate Education	+	0	−	0	−	+
More Full-Time Students	+	+	−	0	−	0/−
More Emphasis on Graduate Education	0	+	−	0	−	+

+ = support
0 = neutral
− = oppose

41

creases in the size of the faculty, and a general lowering of their influence in the university (Baldridge, 1971: 53).

It turns out their fears were justified. "From a high of nearly 300 in the late 1950's the faculty dropped to 61 in 1967–1968 . . . the full-time student enrollment decreased from a high of 2800 to a low of 1000" (Baldridge, 1971: 55). The point is that it is important to consider carefully the extent to which changes are consistently viewed within a political unit. In this case, there is clear justification for treating the Graduate School of Business and the School of Commerce as separate political actors.

Second, the analysis helps to highlight why an attempt at coordinating the various undergraduate programs, although unsuccessful in the past, was now feasible. The basis for the recommendation for consolidation arose from the following conditions:

> *. . . NYU had undergraduate programs in Washington Square College, University College, the School of Engineering, the School of Commerce, and the School of Education. Many of these programs were almost exact duplications, and courses often had the same titles. High administrative overhead, inefficient use of faculty, and the ineffective utilization of space were only a few of the problems that this duplication caused. . . . segregation of the courses into schools meant that often students were isolated and lacked the intellectual stimulation that comes from diversity in the classroom (Baldridge, 1971: 56).*

A previous attempt to consolidate all the undergraduate units, including the professional schools, which was undertaken in the mid-1950s, was unsuccessful. The attempt had provoked serious opposition:

> *The faculties of the various schools felt that their distinctive programs would be undercut and that individual members of the faculty would be hurt by the loss of a favorite course or even a job. The deans were opposed to any decrease in programs for their college, and the department chairmen saw their areas upset by a complete reworking of the course structure. The professional schools feared the loss of their undergraduates, whereas the liberal arts schools feared an influx of professional students who might not be oriented toward liberal arts or who*

42

might not measure up to their academic standards (Baldridge,
1971: 56).

By the mid-1960s, the hand of the administration was considerably strengthened by the growing fiscal crisis which confronted the university. At this time, the administration cleverly bought off some opposition by designing the Coordinated Liberal Studies Program to involve only the first two years of study for Washington Square College, Education, and Commerce. University College, the School of Engineering, and, of course, the Graduate School of Business were no longer interested in opposing the idea. Furthermore, the Coordinated Liberal studies program "meant that Washington Square College would be greatly expanded by the courses that were drawing on Commerce and Education students" (Baldridge, 1971: 57). This plus the increased emphasis on graduate and professional education, located primarily at the Washington Square campus, were sufficient to ensure the support of that important unit.

Looking at the table indicates that the only substantial opposition to the proposals was likely to come from Commerce and Education, with Engineering being largely neutral. Commerce was full of part-time faculty, and thus could not muster effective opposition. Education was already beginning to lose power because of the growing oversupply of teachers. Moreover, in a contest with interests representing arts, sciences, and graduate education, any of the professional schools were at a disadvantage. Thus, the analysis indicates the fundamental viability of the reform package. It also indicates how the various parts of the package gave important items to the political interests whose support was needed.

It should be clear that what this analytical process provides is a structure for exercising judgment about the political structure of an organization and a set of issues. It scarcely takes the place of such judgment, and is not something that can be applied in a mechanical fashion. At the same time, it provides a disciplined way of beginning to think about the identification of the relevant political units, their positions, and the consequences for understanding organizational politics.

Measuring the Power of Social Actors

Having identified the relevant political actors, or in Freeman's (1978) terms, the units of analysis, it is then necessary to develop estimates of their relative power. This measurement of power is important for predicting what will occur, as well as for developing measures of power that can be used in more complete conceptual schemes for analyzing the determinants and outcomes of power. As with the analysis of political units, the problem is subtle but not intractable.

DISTINGUISHING POWER FROM FORESIGHT

If you hold this book above a table, say "fall, book," and then release the book from your hand, the book will fall back onto the table. Does this mean you have power over the book? Of course it does not. Gravity was responsible for the book's falling, not your persuasiveness, resources, or expertise. Because fundamental to virtually all definitions of power is the idea that some resistance or opposition is overcome, or some action is changed from what it would have been without the intervention of the powerful actor, the assessment of power requires the ability to know what would have happened without the intrusion of the power holder. In the case of our book example, this is an easy task. Gravity is a long-established and well-known physical law of nature. The problem is that in many social situations, understanding of social behavior is much less precise or developed. Such situations pose problems for assessing power.

Consider, for example, the problem of assessing power in some kind of legislative body, such as a senate or representative assembly. A simple but naive approach might be to define power as the proportion of the time a given individual is on the winning side of contested issues. Surely, someone who is on the winning side 80% of the time is more powerful than one who is on the winning side only 20% of the time. Such measurement of power neglects the question, of course, of whether or not the various issues were of equal importance to both persons. Sometimes one does not use power because the issue is not important enough. This point will be developed in more detail in the next chapter. But more fundamentally, it may be true that neither of the two individuals is himself very powerful, in the sense of being able to influence the behavior of others. The first person may be much more adept at forecasting which side is going to win and then lining up accordingly. Similar problems of assessment occur in other contexts also. If a given organizational actor consistently supports the job candidate who is eventually hired, it may mean that the individual is powerful in affecting the choice, or it may be that the individual is a shrewd analyst of others' preferences and is able to forecast how the decision is going to turn out.

Dahl (1957: 212) called this the problem of the chameleon, of which the satellite is a special case. The satellite is a given individual who always follows the lead of someone who is actually powerful in the organization. Since satellites will always come down on the same side as the person with power, it would be impossible to distinguish them in terms of their power by merely counting up the number of times each was on the winning side.

Since power is, in part, an attributed property that can be created merely through such an attribution process, the ability to forecast what is going to occur is an important skill. The exercise of such forecasting skill can provide the social actor with the appearance of power and influence because of his or her consistent identification with the winning side of issues. Nevertheless, as Dahl (1957) argued in discussing the power of individual senators, it is important to be able to distinguish between the ability to influence a situation and the ability to forecast what would have occurred in any event.

Discrimination among chameleons, satellites, and the powerful requires observation of the various social actors prior to the decision making event, as well as a knowledge of their preferences before the political activity began. If one knows the initial preferences, the attempts at influence undertaken, and then the final decision, power can be more reliably diagnosed. Clearly, multiple events make it more feasible to infer power, as March (1966) argued in developing the principle of consistency. On any decision occasion, there is some probability that a given social actor will wind up on the winning side by chance. Such a probability of chance occurrence is reduced as the number of decision contexts increases. The probability is reduced even further when the contest among the various positions is reasonably close. It is clear that merely counting up the number of apparent wins versus the number of apparent losses is not an adequate way of assessing power.

Two examples illustrate the pitfalls involved in diagnosing power in organizations. Each year the Budget and Personnel Committee at the University of California at Berkeley triumphantly reports, in a message to the faculty, the large number of personnel cases for both promotion and merit raises within rank it has considered, and how few times its recommendations have been overturned by the administration. These data are supposed to let the faculty know that faculty power is secure (at least as administered through the budget committee) and that the faculty are, by inference, much more in control with respect to these critical personnel decisions than the administration. The reporting of these data omits two very important facts. First, the budget committee, which acts, in the final analysis, in only an advisory way to the administration, submits a preliminary report, particularly on controversial cases. It is not unknown for the administration to ask for reconsideration of the

45

specific personnel case, nor is it unknown for the committee, in reexamining the case, to discover new facts and new information that lead to a change in its position. The budget committee's statistics, of course, deal only with the administration's overturning final recommendations. How often the budget committee acts as a chameleon or satellite is not reported.

But the problem of inference may be even more severe than was at first supposed. For the budget committee may not only change its tentative decision in the light of feedback from the administration, but the initial decisions may be taken in the context of what the committee expects the administration to want. Friedrich (1937) coined the term "rule by anticipated reactions" to describe this situation. Dahl (1957) has argued that there must be some time lag between the actions of an actor who is said to have power and the responses of those over whom he has such power. "A can hardly be said to have power over a unless A's power attempts precede a's responses" (Dahl, 1957: 204). But clearly, this is not the case. The less powerful social actor may and, in fact, probably will take into account the likely response of the more powerful in framing action in the first place. Thus, an attempt to assess power must try to account for the extent to which initial expressions of preference already reflect the power of others in the organization.

Second, most personnel cases are probably relatively clear-cut in any event. Of the total number considered, only a small proportion actually involve any substantial differences of opinion among the various parties concerning what should be done. The budget committee's power can be assessed only by those cases in which there is some disagreement with the administration over whose views are to prevail. By including those cases in which there is consensus, the amount of apparent committee power is overstated.

This point can be nicely illustrated by considering a situation in which admissions or hiring decisions are to be made by three social actors, which might be individuals or organizational subunits. In Table 2-2, some hypothetical data are presented concerning these decisions. For ease of exposition, assume that the final decision is analyzed from the point of view of A's original decisions. Of 100 candidates or applicants, A initially accepted fifty and rejected fifty. B, with more severe standards, rejected all fifty of those that A had also rejected, but also rejected ten of those that A wanted to accept. C, with somewhat more lenient standards, accepted all fifty of those A had wanted to accept, and also wanted to accept ten that A had wanted to reject. In the final decision, all fifty of A's acceptances were accepted, and eight of A's rejections, which were C's acceptances, were also accepted.

Consider the assessment of the relative power of the three parties. A made 100 decisions and got his way 92% of the time. B made 100 decisions also, and got his way 82% of the time. C made the same 100 decisions, and got his way 98% of the time. C is clearly the most powerful, but A is close behind and B still appears to have some significant amount of power in the system. However, a different picture emerges if only the contested decisions are examined. Of A's fifty acceptances, there were ten contested, the ones that B wanted to reject. Of these ten, A and C got ten decisions and B got zero. Of A's and B's fifty rejections, there were ten that C wanted to accept, of which eight were finally accepted. A and B each won two contests, and C won eight. Now we can consider, using the twenty contested decisions, who won, to assess power in this social system. Of the twenty contested decisions, A got his way twelve times, for 60%, B only two times, for 10%, and C eighteen times, for 90%. The power distribution suddenly doesn't look nearly as equal. By considering only those decisions in which there were disagreements, we discovered that B was almost never able to get his way, and C almost always won. A was more powerful than B, but substantially less powerful than C.

This procedure would estimate the relative power only if the decisions were made independently and reflected the actors' true preferences. If A had been merely trying to follow what he thought C would do, the estimate of relative power would be even more distorted. This simplified example should make the point that in assessing power, one must be careful to consider only those instances in which preferences conflict, for they are the only cases in which relative power can be observed.

TABLE 2-2
Hypothetical Selection Decision Data

Actor A	Actor B	Actor C	Final Decision
Accept 50	Accept 40	Accept 50	Accept 50
	Reject 10	Reject 0	Reject 0
Reject 50	Accept 0	Accept 10	Accept 8
	Reject 50	Reject 40	Reject 42

ASSESSING POWER BY ITS DETERMINANTS

One method for assessing power described by Gamson (1968) and others involves developing an understanding of what causes power in the social system under study. This method then evaluates the various social actors by determining how much of each of these causes of power they possess. Thus, instead of trying to measure power directly, power is assessed by considering how much of each of the determinants of power the various individuals, subunits, or groups possesses.

In order to employ this methodology for diagnosing power distributions, it is essential that one understand the determinants of power in the social system under study, the topic of Chapter 4. It is also necessary to be able to assess how much of each determinant or source of power each of the various social actors in the situation possesses. And finally, since power typically is multiply-determined and there are customarily several sources of power, it is necessary to be able to predict which of the sources is likely to be more important in the situation under investigation.

Of the three steps in the process, the assessment of how much of a given source of power a given social actor possesses may be the most problematic. Consider, for instance, power which is derived from specialized knowledge or expertise. Although one may be able to see that this special knowledge is particularly critical in the social system, it is difficult to determine how much of that particular knowledge or competence various participants possess. Knowledge is not something readily observed, like height, weight, or hair color. If various interests within the organization perceive that some specific competency is an important source of power, they will try to make others believe that they are uniquely expert or knowledgeable in the particular area. If marketing expertise is the critical function, then all actors will behave as if they are competent marketers. If fund raising is a particularly critical skill, then each will attempt to demonstrate contacts and abilities in the fund-raising activity. There is a great likelihood of the occurrence of selective self-presentation to enhance status within the organization. Discerning the amount of various power sources actually possessed by various organizational participants requires some skill.

Another issue involved in evaluating power distributions by assessing the distribution of the determinants of power is that some social actors, who might be potentially powerful, may not recognize the determinants or the fact that they possess them. In this sense, the power is not recognized, and hence will not be used. Even if power positions are recognized, organizational actors may choose not to employ their power. However, in this latter case, the power is potentially there for use. In the case in which power is not recognized, however, it does not even exist as a potential to be employed if favorable conditions occurred.

ASSESSING POWER BY ITS CONSEQUENCES

The distribution of power can also be assessed by examining its consequences as these become manifest in decisions made within the organization. Presumably, power is used to affect choices made within social systems. Then, one way of assessing the distribution of power is to see which social actors benefit, and to what extent in contested decisions within organizations. There are many examples of the consequences of power: budget distributions among subunits, the allocation of positions, the making of strategy and policy choices which are favored by and are favorable to various actors, and so forth.

In order to diagnose the distribution of power by looking at the presumed consequences of the use of such power, several things are necessary. First, it must be possible to recognize those situations in which resources or decisions are likely to be determined on the basis of power in the organization. Second, it must be possible to assess which social actors have gained or lost in the decisions that are made on such critical and contested issues. Thus, one must be able to diagnose both those circumstances in which power has an effect, and who has won or lost in these political contests.

In the next chapter we shall consider in more detail some theories about the conditions under which power is employed in decision making. For the moment, it is important to note that it is often more difficult than one might expect to discern the winners and the losers in the various decisions in which power was used. It is not in the interests of many people within the organization to publicize the winners and losers in contests of power. For the social actors who have fared relatively poorly in the decisions, the announcement of these decisions merely reaffirms their position of relative weakness, and helps to solidify that weakness. Furthermore, to lose a decision is to lose face, and unless the publication of such a loss can be used to mobilize further support, there is little to be gained by making public the extent of the loss. For the winners, there are also some disadvantages in discerning how much was gained in the decision. The winning social actors may be confronted with additional demands if others in the organization are able to see the extent of their benefits. In addition, it is considered unseemly to boast over one's victories. Indeed, the victories, if widely promulgated, may set in motion

49

coalitions against the winners, which will make the winning of future decisions more difficult. Power, as we shall learn in Chapter 5, is often exercised most effectively when it is exercised unobtrusively. This implies that those who have fared relatively well in organizational decisions are not likely to make this fact too widely known.

There is another reason why the outcome of organizational politics may not be too readily visible. As Parsons and Smelser (1956) noted, rationality is more than a description of a decision making process, it is a valued social ideal. March (1976: 69) refers to the theory of rational choice using words such as faith and scripture. Rational decision making is an ideal which, even if not empirically descriptive, is to be kept for both external and internal system maintenance at all costs. Thus, it is in the interests of all who share the belief in the myth of rational choice that decisions appear to be made rationally rather than to be based on power and politics. If this requires making the outcomes of such decisions less visible so that the distribution of rewards are less readily discerned, such activity will be taken. In the absence of hard indicators representing decision outcomes, the belief in rational choice processes will be more easily maintained and the norm of rationality preserved as a socially shared myth.

Thus, winners and losers are often difficult to discern. Winners appear not to have won very much; losers act as if they did better than they had hoped, and quite well all things considered. One can see this posturing in political bodies in which there is a certain grace on both sides after the final vote. Discerning power by observing its consequences, therefore, requires access to decision outcomes that may be problematic except in the case of some public organizations. It requires getting the specific results of policy actions. It is in the interests of few parties to make such information too readily available.

ASSESSING POWER BY ITS SYMBOLS

Ironically, although social actors may attempt to hide the extent to which power has affected decision outcomes, there is often much less reluctance to make the distribution of power within organizations visible through the use of symbols of power. Such symbols include things such as titles, special parking places, special eating facilities, restrooms, automobiles, airplanes, office size, placement, and furnishings, and other perquisites of position and power. Such symbols are particularly likely to be employed to distinguish among vertical levels of power within organizations. Managers at different levels may have different size offices. At one large organization in California, the kind of furnishings in the office, as well as whether or not the floor is carpeted, is determined by hierarchical level. One can go into an office in this corporation and determine quickly by visible inspection what is the relative position of the occupant in the status hierarchy.

Such distinctions may also differentiate among individuals and subunits who are ostensibly on the same hierarchical level. In Barrows Hall on the Berkeley campus, one side of the building has a view of San Francisco and the Golden Gate Bridge. Offices on that side of the building are typically occupied by persons such as the dean, associate dean, and ex-deans of the School of Business Administration, very senior full professors, and on other floors occupied by other departments, the leading social and behavioral scientists from those departments. The offices in a major San Francisco law firm were allocated according to the view and position of the office. This led, on occasion, to the placing of people who had worked together in different parts of the building, because placement was done on the basis of seniority, status, and the desirability of the individual office rather than by the relationship of the office to other law firm members. In a major California utility, the shift in power from engineering to law was visible as lawyers began to get offices on the higher floors of the building, and engineers offices on the lower floors. The Transamerica pyramid is perhaps the clearest physical manifestation of the organizational hierarchy, but the general tendency for both higher ranking executives and higher ranking functions to have higher level offices is quite pervasive.

In Figure 2.1, we have shown a partial map of the campus at Berkeley. One can quickly note that the physical sciences, which have tended to be the more powerful departments at Berkeley, are relatively higher up the hillside. The few exceptions to this general rule can be explained by recognizing that there are also laboratory buildings even higher up on the hill; those departments with some power which are relegated to apparently less favorable locations are actually those that have a large proportion of their faculty in offices located up the hill in these other buildings. An interesting study would involve the assessment of the extent to which departmental power in various organizations is correlated with locational favorability, either in terms of view, office space per departmental member, or centrality in the organization's informal communication network as manifested by physical centrality in organizational space.

Whisler and his colleagues (Whisler, Meyer, Baum, and Sorensen, 1967) have developed a measure of organizational centrality which focuses on the dispersion of salaries within organizations. Another useful

51

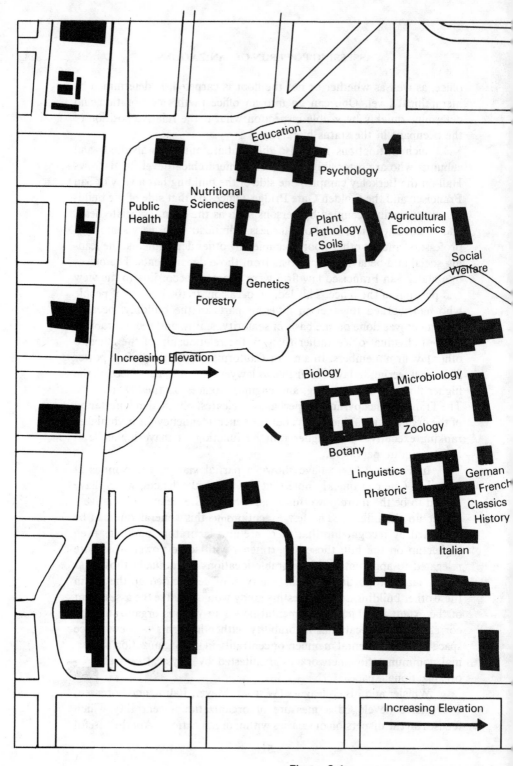

Figure 2-1
Berkeley Campus

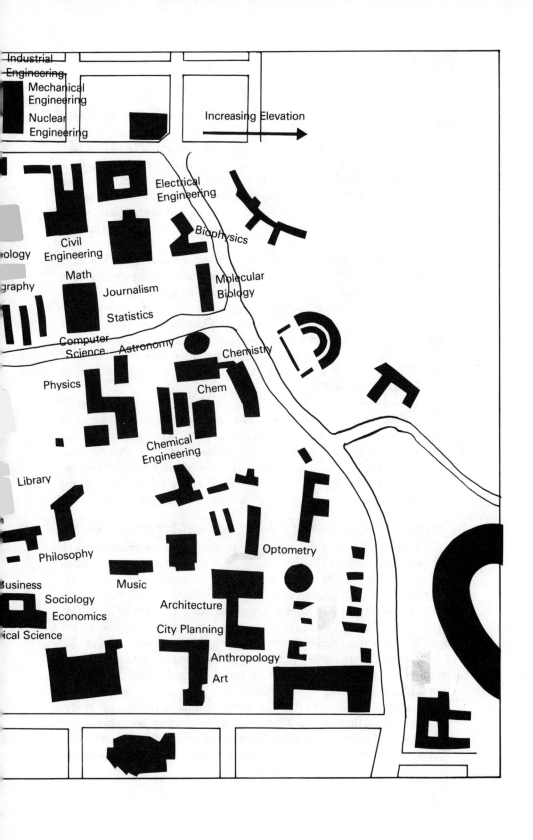

Industrial
Engineering
Mechanical
Engineering
Nuclear
Engineering

Increasing Elevation

Electrical
Engineering

Biophysics

...ology
Civil
Engineering

Math

Molecular
Biology

...graphy
Journalism

Statistics

Computer
Science   Astronomy

Chemistry

Physics

Chem

Chemical
Engineering

Library

Philosophy

Optometry

Business
Music

Sociology
Economics

Architecture

...ical Science
City Planning

Anthropology

Art

indicator of organizational centrality might be the dispersion of office size, characteristics such as furniture and other decoration, and the extent to which offices are private. Our prediction would be that organizations that have more centralization, as measured by Whisler's measure, are also likely to demonstrate more centralization when the various symbols of power and their distribution are considered as well. It would be useful to further relate these indicators of centralization to other measures of the relative dispersion of influence on critical organizational choices.

The provision of social actors with the symbols of power both ratifies their power position within the organization and provides them with power because of the symbols. In a situation in which social power may be difficult to assess, the provision of clear signals of power conveys to others the fact that the social actors who possess these symbols have come to be valued and revered in the organization. This social definition of power becomes, through its physical manifestation in the form of symbols, a shared social reality which serves to convey power to those possessing the symbols.

It is naive to think that such symbols are perfect correlates of power. Offices are not moved wholesale as power waxes and wanes in organizations. Carpets are not taken up and put down as individuals rise and fall in the informal power structure. There are lags and imperfections in the use of such symbols as guides to the power distribution. Nevertheless, these symbols of social influence provide cues which are both visible and positively correlated with distributions of social influence.

REPUTATIONAL INDICATORS OF ORGANIZATIONAL POWER

Another way of finding out where the power lies in organizations is to ask people. Perrow (1970), in a study of twelve industrial firms, asked respondents to rank the four departments of production, marketing, finance and accounting, and research and development in terms of how much power they had within the organizations. Hinings et al. (1974) used a similar though more elaborate questionnaire and interview procedure to assess the relative power of subunits of breweries in Canada. Pfeffer and Salancik (1974), in a study of the power of academic departments at the University of Illinois, asked department heads how much power they thought the various departments possessed. A similar procedure was used by Moore (1979) in his replication of the Illinois study.

Although there has not been much controversy concerning this procedure and its use in studies of power in organizations, there is a great deal of controversy surrounding the reputational measurement of power in community power studies. Hunter (1953) was one of the first to use the practice of asking respondents who had power in his studies of Atlanta, a practice which was followed by other sociologists (e.g., Pellegrini and Coates, 1956; Schulze, 1958). Polsby (1960) has criticized this research procedure by arguing that it presumes an answer to the question of whether or not there is a concentration of power in communities.

> If anything there seems to be an unspoken notion among pluralist researchers that at bottom nobody dominates in a town, so that their first question is not likely to be, "Who runs this community?" but rather, "Does anyone at all run this community?" The first query is somewhat like "Have you stopped beating your wife?" in that virtually any response short of total unwillingness to answer will supply the researchers with a "power elite" along the lines proposed by stratification theory (Polsby, 1960: 476).

The method applied in studies of organizational power is conceptually similar. Asking department heads to rank or rate the power of other departments presumes that a system of differentiated power exists in the organization. In fact, the asking of the question may produce answers that provide the appearance of a stratified system of power where none really exists. The pluralist solution to this is to study actual community decision making. In the organizational analogue, the parallel would be to study the decision making of organizations to see empirically whether or not an elite set of social actors can be identified. Alternatively, one might see if the reputational indicators of power within the organization correlate with other measures and if power, as assessed by this method, does predict the outcome of organizational decision making. Most of the studies cited did correlate these measures, either with presumed determinants of power or, as in the case of the study of budget decision making at the University of Illinois, with both determinants and decisions reflecting power.

The reputational method for assessing organizational power assumes that: social actors are knowledgeable about power within their organizations; informants are willing to divulge what they know about power distributions; and such a questioning process will not itself create the phenomenon under study, power. The first two concerns are troublesome. Given the normative value of the rational model of choice, many organizational actors may be insensitive to the operation of organizational politics and may be relatively naive about distributions of power within the organization. Those who do know the distribution of influence and are skilled in political strategies have nothing to gain by sharing this knowledge and, in fact, are probably more effective because this knowledge is not widely shared within the organization. Informants may be unwilling to tell you what they know about power within the organization. And, because of the norms concerning politics and rationality in organizations, the very asking of questions is likely to be perceived as illegitimate and upsetting. It is one thing to ask about size, structure, or job attitudes; it is quite another to ask questions about organizational power and politics. Such behavior can get one labeled as a Machiavellian person or someone who has little concern for the normative structure and sensibilities of the organization. Consequently, the reputational method for assessing power can be particularly troublesome when the normative structure of the organization stresses the illegitimacy of power and politics.

This difficulty in assessing power through the use of questionnaires or interviews is illustrated by the following example. In a study of power and resource allocation in two University of California campuses, department heads were interviewed concerning their ratings of the power held by other departments studied, as well as their own. One humanities department chairman, after receiving a copy of the questionnaire in advance of the actual interview, refused to cooperate with the study:

> . . . if I saw the university enterprise in the terms implied by your questionnaire I would be seeking, frankly, some other way of making a living, instead of practicing the profession I've been engaged in for the last three decades. In fact, my opinion of the premises on which the questionnaire rests is such that I cannot bring myself to devote more than a few moments to this letter . . . (Anonymous, 1978).

Asking questions about power and decision making clearly violated normative beliefs about the nature and character of universities and academic life. But, such questions may also violate the religion of rationality and profit maximization that pervades business organizations.

When informants can be convinced to reveal what they know about power within organizations, the reputational measure of power does provide some evidence that there are socially shared judgments within organizations concerning influence distributions. In the study of power at the University of Illinois, department chairmen were asked to rate on a seven point scale, the departments in question, as to the amount of power each possessed. As noted previously, only one person asked for clarification of what was meant by power. Although some were not familiar with the power of all the departments, there was enormous consistency in the answers provided. No department which overall was rated in the top third in terms of power was rated by any single chairman as being lower than the top one-third. And no department which averaged in the bottom one-third was rated by any chairman as being higher than the bottom one-third. There was, then, enormous consistency in the ratings, particularly for the most and least powerful departments. This consensus and consistency in power ratings provides some evidence for at least a shared social definition of the distribution of power.

REPRESENTATIONAL INDICATORS

Reputational indicators of power rely both on the knowledge of organizational informants and their willingness to share that knowledge. Such cooperation may not be forthcoming either because of normatively held views of power and politics or for strategic reasons. Furthermore, reputational indicators can be collected only to assess current distributions of influence. If power in organizations is to be studied historically to determine trends in influence, then reputational measures, with their necessarily contemporaneous quality, are insufficient.

Representational indicators of power assess the position of social actors in critical organizational roles such as membership on influential boards and committees or occupancy of key administrative posts. Representational indicators, then, are available as long as position and committee occupants and their affiliations can be identified from organizational records. These data can be collected in a less obtrusive fashion, without violating organizational norms and myths. These indicators are useful supplements to other ways of assessing power in organizations.

Some positions in organizations provide their occupants with power because of the control over information, resources, or other decisions that is inherent in these positions. Some positions in organizations are given to those social actors with the power to signify and ratify their power to others. In most cases, positions which are given to powerful social actors as a consequence of their power also provide those actors with additional power due to the information and decisions that are within the purview of these positions. If these roles can be identified, then by observing the affiliations of the role occupants, one can diagnose the distribution of influence within the organization.

In the study of power of university departments at two University of California campuses, the representational indicator employed was departmental membership on major campus committees. The committees identified had influence over the allocation of a resource, such as faculty positions or research funds, or had influence over an important educational policy or domain. In Table 2-3, the correlations among the average departmental representation on the various committees over a ten-year period are presented. It is clear that there are moderately strong correlations between most of the representational indicators of power. One way of using the information on committee representation is to combine the committees and assess proportional departmental representation on all committees taken together. Committee representation can serve as an indicator of power because the committee positions themselves convey power to their occupants. Powerful departments are also more likely to have larger representation on key committees as a consequence of their power.

TABLE 2-3
Correlations of Department
Representation on Various University Committees

(n = 40)

	Committees	Research	Educ. Policy	Educ. Dev.	Grad. Council	Fellowships
Budget	.63^e	.24^a	.36^c	.31^b	.27^b	.43^d
Committees	---	.23^a	.48^e	.28^b	.19	.34^b
Research	---	---	.12	−.01	.25^a	.23^a
Educ. Policy	---	---	---	.43^d	.29^b	.26^a
Educ. Dev.	---	---	---	---	.28^b	.64^e
Grad. Council	---	---	---	---	---	.23^a

^{a} $p < .10$ Budget = departmental representation on the budget committee

^{b} $p < .05$ Committees = departmental representation on committee on committees which selects other committee members (elected committee)

^{c} $p < .01$ Research = departmental representation on committee on research

^{d} $p < .005$ Educ. Policy = departmental representation on educational policy committee

^{e} $p < .001$ Educ. Dev. = departmental representation on educational development committee

Grad. Council = departmental representation on graduate council, the committee that works with the Dean of the graduate division

Fellowships = departmental representation on the fellowship and scholarships subcommittee of the graduate council

In business firms, a similar procedure can be employed to assess power. Critical executive positions can be identified, and the departmental affiliations of executives who have risen to these positions can be determined, as a way of seeing which subunits are more powerful. Important committees within the firm, such as capital budgeting committees, strategic planning and policy committees, the executive committee, and in some instances, hiring and personnel policy committees can be identified and representation on such committees can be assessed. Departmental, occupational, and individual representation in important roles and on critical committees can provide evidence useful in diagnosing the relative occupational, departmental, and individual power of social actors in the organization.

A SYNTHESIS

It should now be clear that there are a variety of ways of assessing power distributions within organizations, and each has its own strengths and weaknesses. The most reasonable approach in diagnosing power then is to look for a convergence of power indicators within social systems. There should be a correlation between the ranking of the determinants of power, the consequences of power, the symbols of power, and the reputational and representational indicators of power. An index constructed from all of these factors is likely to provide a reasonably good approximation of the distribution of power in the organization at a given time.

Unfortunately, there have been few quantitative, comparative studies of power in organizations conducted up to this time. Indeed, one of the purposes of this book is to synthesize the literature on power in organizations, in the hope of stimulating additional investigation. Two of the more systematic and comprehensive studies were conducted at universities in Illinois and California. Both studies found reasonably good convergence between the reputational and representational power indicators. At Illinois, there was a correlation of .61 ($p < .001$) between the reputational measure of power and total representation on important committees in the university (Pfeffer and Salancik, 1974). In the California study, the correlation was .57 ($p < .001$) between the same two measures (Moore, 1979). In both cases also, there were high correlations between these indicators of power and presumed determinants of power, such as student enrollments and outside grant and contract dollars obtained. There were also high correlations between outcomes or consequences of power such as budget allocations and the allocations of other resources such as research funds and fellowships. Thus, at least in these two studies, there is an indication that some of the various methods of assessing power do converge, providing the ability to diagnose organizational power distributions.

In the past I have asked my organizational behavior class to think of indicators for diagnosing the power distribution of the subject matter groups within the school of business and, on other occasions, to come up with indicators for diagnosing the power distribution in an organization in which they are going to work. In Table 2-4, some illustrative answers are provided. The indicators all represent some manifestation or outcropping of a source or determinant, consequence, or indicator of power in the organization. Each indicator is imperfect, since each may be affected by numerous things other than power, such as history, rules and regulations, and so forth. The point, however, is that the set of indicators taken together can, just as in the case of the two universities, provide some indication of power distributions.

Power distributions may or may not be well defined and stable. One obtains from the process just described some indication of the state of

TABLE 2-4
Sample Indicators of Power in Two Organizational Contexts

Subject Groups Within a School of Business	Functional Departments Within a Business Firm
Number of required courses in the subject	Functional representation among general management positions
Proportion of the faculty at various ranks, controlling for age or length of service	Functional representation among positions on the board of directors
Student/faculty ratio	Salary of executive in charge of each respective function
Amount of fellowship money in the subject field	Number of persons in each function
Group representation on departmental elected policy and planning committee	Level of functional department in organizational structure
Group representation among Dean and Associate Dean positions	Starting salary of new employees in various functional departments
Office locations of group faculty	Physical location of function and its head in the corporate office
National reputation of the subject group	Representation of function on committees such as capital budgeting or executive committees
Proportion of group faculty with joint membership with other subject groups	The relative representation of departments in internal and outside training activities

power within the social organization being examined. If there is little or no convergence among reputational, representational, determinants, and consequences of power indicators, then this probably indicates that the power within the organization is widely dispersed and not organized. Alternatively, it may be that the distribution of influence is in the process of change and the new structure of influence has not yet clearly emerged.

Again, the assessment of power benefits from some analytic discipline. My students and colleagues have often found it useful to explicitly list the various social actors across the top of a piece of paper, and then list all the indicators of power that they can think of down the side of the page. Then, by scoring each actor on each indicator and summarizing the data, an overall picture of the distribution of power in the organization can be obtained. The discipline of writing things down in a structured format helps to ensure that important indicators useful in assessing power are not overlooked; an attempt at some formal weighting system helps to assure that some indicators are not given undue influence in the formation of assessments of social power. Experience indicates that it is feasible, using the various indicators detailed above, to diagnose power systems with reasonable accuracy. At the same time, it is clear that substantial additional research is necessary to further develop these indicators and to examine their interrelationships in a variety of organizational settings.

Case Examples

The preceding discussion about the identification of political actors and the assessment of their power can be illustrated by the use of a few examples. These examples are based on actual data, though the specific organizations will remain anonymous.

DIAGNOSING POWER BY OBSERVING IT IN USE: THE CASE OF ENGINEERING ELECTRONICS

The Engineering Electronics company was located on the San Francisco peninsula. It was a relatively young and fairly small company, with sales of about $10 million. Like many companies in the electronics industry in the area, it was founded and staffed largely by engineers. However, that did not necessarily assist in the diagnosis of power, as some engineers were technology-oriented, others were market-oriented, and still others, particularly those who had been to business school, were financially-oriented.

Engineering Electronics was faced with making a decision concerning into which of two projects they should invest the bulk of their extra

TABLE 2-5
Characteristics of Projects at Engineering Electronics

	Project 1	Project 2
Return on investment	50%	50%
Risk	average	high
Customer Base	millions	12
Competition	scattered	heavy
Amount of downside risk	$200,000	$3,300,000
Size of required investment	$600,000	$3,300,000
Upside potential	good	fair
Amount of know-how to complete project already in company	some	very little
Sponsoring department	marketing	engineering

capital. Both could be pursued, but it was clear that some priorities would have to be set. The two projects' characteristics are detailed in Table 2-5. These characteristics were provided by a student who had worked on the analysis as part of a summer job. When these data were presented in class, with the identification of the backing department omitted, approximately 90%–100% of the class concluded that Project

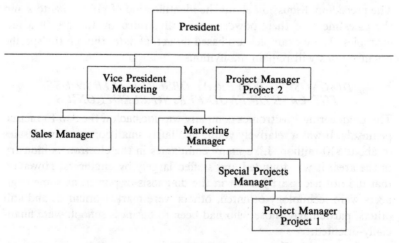

Figure 2.2
Organizational Position of Project 1 and Project 2

1 should be chosen. It has equal investment payoff with substantially reduced financial and market risk.

Interestingly enough, this particular firm chose to put its emphasis on Project 2. Indeed, Project 2's favored position is apparent from the organization that evolved, as shown in Figure 2.2.

Seldom is the use of power and influence so stark and dramatic. The project sponsored by the marketing department lost out almost solely because of their sponsorship. At the same time, the project sponsored by the engineering department won out over financial considerations and over the alternative provided by marketing. The power of engineering, and specifically engineering with a technical emphasis, was clear.

USING REPRESENTATIONAL INDICATORS: THE CASE OF WESTERN ELECTRIC

Access to actual decisions and the kind of detailed information available in the preceding example is often not possible; and, as noted, the use of power is seldom so clear cut. Yet, most organizations have committees, executives, and administrators, and their backgrounds and training are seldom private. Indeed, corporations are required by law to provide information on their highest executives, and sources such as *Dun's* and *Who's Who* also afford a wealth of information. This information can be used to get a picture of the power structure of the organization, using representational indicators.

Consider the case of Western Electric, the manufacturing subsidiary of the Bell System. One might suspect that as a manufacturing subsidiary which sold much of its output to the parent company, the primary power would be held by people with manufacturing and engineering backgrounds. One might also suspect that this power structure is changing, as the Bell System as a whole is forced to compete and as the importance of governmental and other regulatory activity increases.

In Table 2-6, we present some illustrative background information on twenty-five of the top executives of the subsidiary. The domination of the manufacturing function in these data is quite evident. It seems clear that for those with an engineering degree, the road to power in Western Electric has been through manufacturing.

If the shift away from manufacturing and engineering has begun, it is not yet discernible. However, one might expect in about ten or twenty years to see the domination of manufacturing diminished at least in part. This is evidenced by the fact that of those who have been sent to lengthy internal or external training programs, 36.8% are assigned to

TABLE 2-6
Backgrounds of Western Electric Executives

	Degree		Where Career Began		Dominant Work Experience	
	Engineering	Other	Mfg.	Other	Mfg.	Other
Executives	19	6	17	8	20	5
Executive Policy Committee	7	1	7	1	7	1
Corporate Personnel Policy Advisory Committee	4	3	4	3	5	2

manufacturing and 45.3% are assigned currently to either Bell System Sales or other sales operations. Of course, if the employees' backgrounds are primarily in manufacturing, this is just another way of maintaining control over other parts of the operation.

While reading proxy statements and other publications to discern the training and background of corporate officials and members of various organizational committees may not be everyone's idea of a good time, a great deal can be learned about the distribution of power and how it has changed and is still changing.

SEVERAL INDICATORS TOGETHER: A SCHOOL OF BUSINESS

The diagnosis of power distributions is enhanced, of course, when several indicators of power are used together. In Table 2-7, the number of faculty members, administrative positions that are of importance, and the number of chaired full professorships held by various subject fields in a school of business for the years 1969 and 1979 are displayed. A chaired professorship is a specially endowed professorship which always is honorific in nature and in some circumstances, though not the present case, brings extra remuneration or other perquisites. It is clear from the data that the largest groups, Finance and Accounting, which also tended to demonstrate the most growth over the period, ended the period with the most chaired professorships, and were represented in the two associate dean positions. Although the power of some of the other subject groups is less clear from just these data, it seems fair to state that these two fields, finance and accounting, evidence the most power within the school at this time. The fact that the representational indicators of executive positions, the use of resources in acquiring new positions, and the symbolic indicators of power, the chaired professorships, all evidence the same

64

TABLE 2-7
Indicators of Power in a School of Business

Subject Area	No. of Faculty		No. of Chaired Professorships		Associate Dean
	1979	1969	1979	1969	
Accounting	11	9	4	—	1
Economics and Public Policy	10	7	3	1	—
Finance	14	8	4	1	1
Marketing	8	7	2	1	—
Organizational Behavior	6	7	3	1	—
Management and Decision Sciences	9	7	2	—	—

pattern of results, provides greater confidence in the validity of the analysis.

We have seen in this chapter that although the study of power in organizations is still relatively young, there are some strategies available which facilitate the diagnosis of organizational power distributions and permit the identification of and the measurement of the influence of important organizational political actors. Having begun to understand processes by which social power can be assessed, it is next important to begin to identify the conditions under which such power is likely to play an important role in decision making. This issue is the subject of the next chapter.

CHAPTER 3

CONDITIONS FOR THE USE OF POWER

The following situation was used by Gerald Salancik to illustrate the conditions under which power is employed. Two wounded soldiers are lying in a tent on some distant battlefield. A medical corpsman is with them in the tent. Each man requires precisely one pint of blood to live; if each man does not receive the pint of blood, he will die. The pint of blood, then, is both a necessary and sufficient condition for the survival of each of the two wounded soldiers. In the tent, in addition to some medical supplies, is a single pint of blood. Because of the course of the battle going on around them and the associated logistical difficulties, it would be impossible to get any more supplies in time. A decision will have to be made: one man will live, the other will die. Splitting the blood between the two soldiers will cause them both to die, so compromise is out of the question.

One man is a captain, the other a corporal. Each implores the corpsman to save his life, and each musters arguments to support his position. The captain argues that he is entitled to the blood because of his superior hierarchical rank. If the arguments of rank and formal status are not convincing enough, he further argues that captains are important in the planning and organizational work of fighting. He has many men in his command, and the pint of blood given to him will make his unit a more effective fighting force because it will enable him to recover. While the captain has impact over many men, the corporal has much less influence on the war, being only a single soldier. The corporal, on the

67

other hand, argues that captains are, after all, part of the administrative overhead of the war; it is the corporals and the other front line troops that actually do the fighting. The corporal argues that he has killed many more enemy than the captain, and if he is allowed to live, is likely to have a more direct impact on the fighting in the future. Furthermore, the captain is older, and other things being equal, the corporal will have a longer life expectancy if he gets the blood. The pint of blood given to him, in other words, will probably result in more years of human life. Each then musters tales of his family—the captain has a wife and two young children back at home; the corporal tells about his poor, aged parents who are depending on him to take over the family business after the war.

How shall the corpsman decide? Each soldier has raised legitimate, relevant, and reasonable criteria, which favor him over the other soldier. The captain has rank and organizational impact; the corporal has impact on the direct work of the organization; both have claims based on family and other reasons. The corpsman, who is attempting to provide the maximum benefit to the army, finds it difficult to determine which soldier will really have the greatest potential benefit to the service. After all, there are a lot of desk officers and fighting men are scarce; on the other hand, the ability to lead and organize is important, too.

The corporal reaches into a heap of his possessions, and pulls out a gun. Suddenly, the decision becomes clear. The captain dies and the corporal obtains the blood.

This apocryphal situation is a paradigm of a decision making setting in which the use of power may be introduced. Furthermore, the situation illustrates well how the introduction of power is both a necessary and sufficient condition for making the choice. The elements that produce conflict and the use of power, or political activity, in organizations are diagrammed in Figure 3.1. A consideration of that figure along with the example indicates when and why power comes to be employed.

The first condition of the use of power is interdependence, a situation in which what happens to one organizational actor affects what happens to others. In the present example, there is competitive interdependence, in the sense that blood which is given to one soldier will not be available to another. Other forms of interdependence exist in organizations, including the interdependence which arises from joint activity on some work product, so that what one unit does to the product affects and may be affected by what another unit does. Interdependence is an important condition because it ties the organizational participants together, in the sense that each is now concerned with what the other does and what the other obtains. In the absence of such interdependence,

CONDITIONS FOR THE USE OF POWER

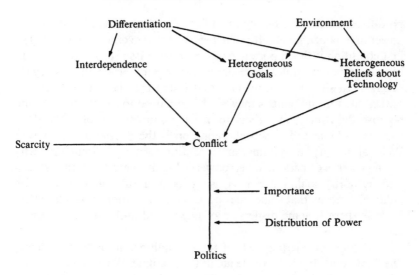

Figure 3.1
A Model of the Conditions Producing the Use of Power
and Politics in Organizational Decision Making

there would be no basis for conflict or for interaction among the participants.

The second condition of the use of power is heterogeneous goals, or goals which are inconsistent with each other. In the present case, the goal of the corporal to stay alive is inconsistent with the goal of the captain to live because of the interdependence. A related condition would be heterogeneous beliefs about technology, or the relationship between decisions and outcomes. In the present example, this was not a problem as there was agreement on the connections between actions and consequences; all parties understood that obtaining the pint of blood was both necessary and sufficient for survival. As we shall explore later, such agreement on technology is not inevitable within organizations.

The third condition producing the use of power is scarcity. If there were two pints of blood, there would be no decision problem. To the extent that resources are insufficient to meet the various demands of organizational participants, choices have to be made concerning the allocation of those resources. The greater the scarcity as compared to the demand, the greater the power and the effort that will be expended in resolving the decision.

As indicated in Figure 3.1, together the conditions of scarcity, interdependence, and heterogeneous goals and beliefs about technology

69

produce conflict. Whether that conflict eventuates in politics, the use of power in organizational settings depends upon two other conditions. The first condition is the importance of the decision issue or the resource. In the case of our example, the resource was very important—necessary for survival. In situations in which the decision may be perceived as less critical, power and politics may not be employed to resolve the decision because the issue is too trivial to merit the investment of political resources and effort. The second condition is the distribution of power. Political activity, bargaining, and coalition formation occur primarily when power is dispersed. When power is highly centralized, the centralized authority makes decisions using its own rules and values. The political contests that sometimes occur in organizations take place only because there is some dispersion of power and authority in the social system.

Before considering each of these conditions in additional detail, one final point should be made about the example. When the conditions which were specified in the figure and present in the example occur, the use of power is virtually inevitable and furthermore, it is the only way to arrive at a decision. Given conflicting and heterogeneous preferences and goals and beliefs about the relationship between actions and consequences, interdependence among the actors who possess conflicting preferences and beliefs, and a condition of scarcity so that not all participants can get their way, power is virtually the only way (except, perhaps, to use chance) to resolve the decision. There is no rational way to determine whose preferences are to prevail, or whose beliefs about technology should guide the decision. There may be norms, social customs, or tradition which dictate the choice, but these may be all efforts to legitimate the use of power to make its appearance less obtrusive. In situations of conflict, power is the mechanism, the currency by which the conflict gets resolved. Social power almost inevitably accompanies conditions of conflict, for power is the way by which such conflicts become resolved.

The model of the conditions under which power will be employed is similar to, but somewhat more elaborate than, the typology of decision situations advanced by Thompson and Tuden (1959). These authors differentiated decision situations according to whether or not there was agreement on goals or preferences, and whether or not there was agreement on technology, or the connections between actions and consequences. These two dimensions, when taken together, produce the fourfold classification of decision situations shown in Figure 3.2. The terms categorizing the type of decision making that was likely to occur under each condition are taken from their original discussion. Note that com-

Agreement on Goals

		Yes	No
Agreement on Connections Between Actions and Consequences	Yes	Computational Decision	Compromise
	No	Judgment	Inspiration

Figure 3.2
Thompson and Tuden's Categorization
of Decision Situations

putational decision making procedures involved in rational choice are used in decision making only when there is agreement both on the goals and on the connections between actions and outcomes. When there is no agreement on goals, compromise is required to reach a decision. When there is no agreement on technology, judgment is necessary to determine the best course in achieving consensually shared goals. And when there is neither agreement on goals nor on technology, an unstructured, highly politicized form of decision making is likely to occur.

Some Causes of Goal and Technology Disagreements

As indicated in Figure 3.1, differentiation within the organization is one important source of disagreements on goals and beliefs about technology. Differentiation simply refers to the fact that in most large organizations, there is specialization of the participants and subunits by task—a division of labor which enables the organization to achieve certain economies but which also entails some costs. Lawrence and Lorsch (1967) assessed differentiation along a series of dimensions in their study of ten industrial firms. After examining the marketing, production, and research and development departments in these firms, Lawrence and Lorsch argued that because of the different tasks and environments faced by the various units, there existed a variance in the units in several areas. The time horizon for planning and receiving feedback on operations ranged from very short periods for the production department, to very long horizons for the research and development department. The degree of structure of the activities within the subunits ranged from very unstructured for the research units to tightly controlled in the production units. The specific goals pursued by the various units differed, with marketing interested in sales maximization, research and development in technical

71

innovation and ingenuity, and production in cost control. Lawrence and Lorsch concluded that the most effective organizations were those that were differentiated but also able to achieve effective integration. Although differentiation clearly makes the task of integration more difficult, and is likely to lead to more potential conflict in the organization, the conclusions of this research suggest that it is not necessarily wise to attempt to reduce the dissimilarities in perspectives and goal orientations among the different subunits.

The division of labor and internal differentiation of organizations can cause disagreements about goals and understandings of technology for a number of reasons. As noted above, various subunits may have different goals explicitly provided as a part of their task assignment. These goals may inherently conflict, as in the case of marketing attempting to increase sales by minimizing delivery time and maximizing product variety, while production attempts to restrict costs by minimizing product variety and holding as little inventory as possible. In addition, different subunits receive different information as a consequence of the division of labor. Marketing may receive information about sales, market share, and market coverage; production may obtain information on unit costs, overtime, and machine utilization; research and development receives information on expenditure rates and data on scientific meetings attended, papers presented, and patents applied for. The fact that each of the different units obtains different information, which is relevant to its specific part of the task environment, tends to cause a parochialism in point of view, in which each participant sees the world through his subunit's perspective.

The problem of subunit identification is severe enough so that organizations sometimes attempt to overcome it through policies of interunit transfer. As Edstrom and Galbraith (1977) indicated in their study of the transfer of executives among divisions of multinational firms, the movement of personnel among units is a way of socializing the individual into the organization and provides linkages to the various subunits, along with some idea of the specific problems and issues faced by each. Ouchi and Jaeger (1978) have made a similar point in describing one of the keys to success in Japanese firms. As contrasted with U.S. firms, in which executives tend to stay primarily in a single function or single department and develop localized expertise, Japanese firms tend to move managers much more within the firm, sacrificing some localized specialist expertise in return for the development of a better understanding of the operation of the organization as a whole. The point of the Galbraith and Ouchi work is that although differentiation inevitably tends to cause the formation of incompatible goals and perspectives among the different subunits within the organization, there are various policies, particularly that of transfer and training, which can potentially overcome some of this effect. However, as Ouchi and Jaeger (1978) noted, these practices are not common in U.S. business organizations.

The effects of the division of labor and task specialization within the firm are accompanied by the effects of the environment on subunit goal and technology heterogeneity. By the environment we mean simply any of the many influences on the preferences and beliefs about cause-effect relations which participants bring with them when they join organizations. The subunit differences that emerge from the division of labor are reinforced by differences in the training, backgrounds, and prior socialization of individuals recruited into the different subunits. For instance, the differences between the marketing and research and development departments observed by Lawrence and Lorsch resulted not only from the differences in tasks and environments confronted by the units, but also from the fact that those hired into the different units held different types of training and experience. People enter organizations with learning histories, having developed their own patterns of information acquisition and use and perspectives on analyzing business problems. Differences in the backgrounds and training of each person brought into an organization constitute another potential source of heterogeneity among organizational members.

For this reason, the Japanese firms tend to practice lifetime employment (Ouchi and Jaeger, 1978). When persons enter the organization after college and spend, or expect to spend, their entire working lives in that firm, the amount of external heterogeneity imported into the organization is diminished. Instead of recruiting managers with a variety of different work histories, the organization recruits its employees straight from school, and then socializes them into that organization's particular culture. This clearly produces more homogeneity in perceptions and beliefs than if people are recruited into the organization at all levels and from a variety of different external organizations.

Two studies illustrate how differentiation and role specialization produce diversity in points of view and beliefs. Dearborn and Simon (1958) gave executives who attended a management training course a case to analyze. They were to assess how the participants defined the principal problem in the case. Not surprisingly, the executives tended to see the case as reflecting their own particular area of expertise. Marketing executives tended to define the problem as a marketing problem, operations people as a problem of manufacturing strategy and policy, and so forth. One would expect these executives to recommend different solutions as well, which reflected their own definitions of the situation arising from their different roles and perspectives.

An even more dramatic example of how a person's role affects his or her attitudes and perceptions is provided by a study conducted by Lieberman (1956). From a sample of employees in a manufacturing facility, he collected attitudinal data about the company, the union, and the job. At a later time, he found that some of the employees had been promoted to foremen, others had been elected shop stewards, and others remained in their old jobs. Lieberman first checked to see if there were any differences in these people prior to their assuming their new roles. Since there were not, it would be difficult to argue that they received the jobs because they were already predisposed to accept the new roles. He resurveyed the people in their new roles after some time had passed. Naturally, the foreman had developed a more pro-company attitude and the shop stewards had developed attitudes which were more favorable to the union and its perceptions of the work environment. A few months later, the company suffered some economic reversals, and some of the men who had been promoted to foremen were demoted back to their old positions in the plant. Lieberman surveyed the employees once again, and found that the persons who had been promoted and then demoted had reassumed their old attitudes and beliefs after returning to their old positions. The Lieberman data provide striking evidence for the effects of roles on people's perceptions of the world. The implication is that the more differentiated the work roles in the organization are, the more heterogeneous beliefs and goals are likely to be.

Disagreement, Conflict, and the Use of Power

The next part of the model argues that disagreements about cause-effect relations and preferences lead to conflict and, potentially, the use of power to resolve the choice. This position is well supported in the existing literature on the causes of conflict, in which the effects of disagreement are widely recognized. Dahrendorf (1959: 135) virtually defined conflict in terms of goal discrepancies:

> *All relations between sets of individuals that involve an incompatible difference of objective—i.e., in its most general form, a desire on the part of both contestants to obtain what is available only to one, or only in part—are, in this sense relations of social conflict.*

Schmidt and Kochan (1972: 361) noted that "perception of goal incompatibility is a necessary precondition for . . . conflict." Finally, examining the bases of conflict, Walker (1970: 18) noted:

> *If two members hold divergent goals . . . and if these goals motivate their behavior, then one member will be motivated to behave in a way which is inconsistent with the goals of the other.*

Because of the potential for goal disagreements to engender conflict and political activity in organizations, goal statements are made frequently at a very general level, so that all or at least most of the participants can agree with them. In attempting to explain organizational actions in terms of the stated goals, vaguely stated objectives can cause problems for the analyst. However, the very lack of clarity and specificity in these goal statements makes it possible for the various constituencies within the organization to accept them. This reduces conflict, at least at this level. Of course, as Etzioni (1964) recognized, the operative goals—the bases on which decisions and choices are actually made within the organization—are necessarily more specific. The fact that there may be agreement on general goals will not prevent conflict over the details of what the organization is to do when a specific action is to be taken. At the same time, such overall agreement can serve to potentially moderate the intensity of the conflict and provides some additional integration into the organization for the various participants.

Technological disagreement and uncertainty is also associated with increased conflict and the use of power in organizational decision making. Many of the more direct efforts to test the extent to which technological uncertainty affects the use of power and social influence in decision making have occurred in the context of decision making in science. Scientific disciplines can be described in terms of their level of paradigm development which, as operationalized by Lodahl and Gordon (1972), refers to the degree of consensus within the field concerning research problems, research methodologies, and curriculum content. These authors measured paradigm development by asking scientists, in a sample of eighty departments in four disciplines, to rank seven scientific fields according to how much consensus they perceived within that discipline on a number of issues. The overall ranking of the seven disciplines in order of the level of paradigm development was: physics, chemistry, biology, economics, psychology, sociology, and political science. There were large differences between the physical and social sciences, while the differences within the physical and social sciences were somewhat smaller.

The level of paradigm development is a concept analytically similar to that of technological uncertainty, an equivalence made also by Lodahl and Gordon. To have consensus on methodology, curriculum, and principal research issues is to share a common understanding concerning the technical requirements for research and teaching in the field. This is similar to the sharing of beliefs about the connections between operating strategies, marketing strategies, and profits in a business firm. If one follows the argument that technological uncertainty is related to the use of power in decision making, one would predict that there would be more evidence of the use of power and influence in decision making in scientific fields that are paradigmatically less developed.

This relationship has been observed in a series of studies. Yoels (1974), for instance, found that editors-in-chief were more likely to appoint other editors from their same schools in the social rather than the physical sciences. Hargens (1969), in a study of the initial jobs of new doctoral graduates, observed that persons in the social sciences were more likely to be hired by their own institution and within their own geographic region than were graduates in the physical sciences. This regional and institutional inbreeding is consistent with a more political view of the hiring process. Influence that derives from social contact is apparently more important in the job placement process in the more technologically uncertain fields.

Pfeffer, Salancik and Leblebici (1976) found that National Science Foundation grant allocations to universities were more strongly related to institutional membership on the Advisory Panel overseeing the program in the paradigmatically less developed social sciences such as sociology and political science, as compared with the more developed fields of economics and psychology. This result held even when departmental prestige was statistically controlled, and also remained after controls for departmental size were introduced. Pfeffer, Leong, and Strehl (1977) found that institutional publication in journals was more strongly related to institutional representation on the editorial boards in sociology and political science than in chemistry. This finding is consistent with the pattern of social influence as being a more important predictor of decision outcomes in the presence of higher technological uncertainty.

Our explanation for these various findings is not that when confronted with uncertainty, individuals intentionally pay more attention to social influence and attempt to behave in an explicitly more political fashion. Indeed, such a motivational assumption is neither warranted nor

76

necessary. Rather, all that one must assume is that when confronted with uncertain standards for evaluation and decision making, decision makers will tend to rely on influence-based criteria, such as similarity, because these bases of discrimination are one of the few ways to make the decision and because choosing on such a basis provides more certainty and confidence in the decision.

The effect of uncertainty on decision making in private organizations has not yet been extensively investigated, though one would expect the general pattern of results to hold. The mechanisms through which such uncertainty operates, and the pervasiveness of this effect remain important issues for further research.

THE ROLE OF PROFIT MAXIMIZATION

If goal or value dissensus is an important condition leading to the use of power and politics and to a greater effect of power on decision outcomes, then it should be evident why business organizations are, for the most part, less overtly political than organizations in the non-profit or public sectors such as governmental agencies, hospitals, and universities. The reason is not that businessmen are more rational, more analytical, or less political than administrators in these other organizations. Rather, business organizations have a reasonably agreed upon goal of profit maximization, and this goal consensus negates much of the need for the use of power that might otherwise exist. In a debate, for instance, over the addition of a piece of medical equipment in a hospital, the decision turns not just on the return on investment as compared with the hospital's cost of funds. Rather, the hospital may have to go through a certificate of need application process, thus exposing itself to regulatory delays and political review. Concerns about cost and return on assets must be balanced against physicians' demands for equipment to improve the quality of patient care. The hospital may have a reputation and self-image as providing state-of-the-art care, and this may influence the decision. A similar type of decision, the addition of equipment, in a business firm is much more likely to turn primarily on economic return considerations. Other issues are less legitimately raised, given the consensus that profit is what business firms are all about.

There are some interesting aspects to this consensual agreement on profit as an overriding goal for economic enterprises. First, this goal is legitimated both externally and internally through microeconomic theory. Indeed, the discipline of economics provides theoretical justification and support for the goal of profit maximization. Economic theory argues that, under conditions of perfect competition, Pareto optimal allocation decisions are made when each of the economic actors behaves so as to maximize his own utility or profit. Pareto optimality refers to the condition in which no reallocation can be made that would make any actor better off without making at least one actor worse off. It is a condition that is typically used to evaluate the optimality of allocation results. Thus, profit maximization, or the seeking of the maximum return for the firm, is argued to be an objective which can lead to the maximization of social welfare as well. As a consequence, profit maximization becomes a legitimated standard for decision making.

Internal to the firm, economic theory and economic concepts such as return on investment and the maximization of shareholder wealth translate into profit maximization as a decision strategy, and provide argumentation that those more immediate constituents of the firm, such as shareholders, employees, and suppliers, are best served by the firm's steadfast pursuit of profit.

What is interesting is not that profit seems to be widely shared as a goal for business firm decision making, but that this goal is so completely taken for granted by business firm managers and by others in contact with the firm. This generalized acceptance attests, it seems, to the power of business institutions and economic theory as socializing devices. Clearly, profits are not universally accepted as the sole criterion for choice by actors outside of business. Claims for social responsibility, among other demands, are made on the basis that business firms must respond on dimensions other than profit.

It appears that the study of the diffusion and adoption of profit maximization, as the major agreed upon objective and normative standard for business organizations, is itself worthy of investigation. The adoption of this objective permits the use of power to be more constrained within firms, allows the legitimation of business in the larger social context, and facilitates a unanimity of outlook and response which is beneficial in pressing the case of business organizations as a group. Conversely, the extent to which profit maximization, and the economic orthodoxy that supports it, begins to be weakened or diluted with other objectives, determines the rapidity of the politicization of business, along with the loss of legitimacy of the organizations.

The objective of profit maximization can serve as an archetype of what a consensually shared goal can accomplish, in terms of legitimating and organizing collective action. Indeed, the development of language that facilitates this process of consensus building is an important administrative activity, and will be considered in more detail in Chapter 6. It is important to remember, however, that profit is not the only possible objective that could fill such a role of legitimating and organizing behavior. Rather, it fills the role solely because it has come to be shared and believed within this country at a particular period of time.

Scarcity and Power and Conflict

Interdependence among subunits and differences in goals and in perceptions of technology are not sufficient, by themselves, to produce conflict and the resulting use of power and politics to reach decisions. It is only when these conditions are coupled with resource scarcity that conflict and power arise in organizational settings. Schmidt and Kochan (1972: 363) note that shared resources are one of the precursors to conflict. But unless these resources are in short supply, there will be little need or incentive for the various organizational actors to engage in a political struggle over them.

Decisions are contested, it is suggested, because choices must be made which will determine who will benefit and how much, from the organization's activities. When benefits and resources allocated within organizations are scarce, the funds allocated to one subunit may make another subunit unable to fulfill its objectives or maintain sufficient support to remain viable, due to its lack of funds. A promotion allocated to one individual forecloses the position to other potential contenders. If there are as many positions as contenders, it will matter much less than if many must contend for a very few promotional opportunities. It is because resources are scarce, because choices have to be made among courses of action, beneficiaries, and others interested in the organization and its activities, that conflict arises and power comes to be used in making decisions.

The effect of scarcity on the use of power in decision making has been observed in several studies. In a study of four resources allocated at the University of Illinois that varied in terms of their scarcity and importance, Salancik and Pfeffer (1974) found that power was used more in allocating the resources to the extent that they were scarce. The four resources were graduate fellowships, Research Board grants for faculty research, appointments to the Center for Advanced Study, and Summer Faculty Fellowships. These last resources were not scarce at all. In one year, for instance, there were only sixty applications for the fifty summer faculty fellowships that were to be awarded. In Table 3-1, the results reported by Salancik and Pfeffer concerning the correlation between subunit power and the allocation of the four resources are presented. The data clearly indicate that power has a much stronger impact on the allocation of those resources which are in scarcer supply.

TABLE 3-1
Correlations of Indicators
of Subunit Power with Allocations of Four Resources

Resource	Measures of Power		
	Membership on Research Board	Membership on All Committees	Interview-Based Measure of Power
Simple Correlations			
Graduate fellowships	.90*	.44**	.58**
Research Board grants	.85*	.35***	.56**
Appointments to Center for Advanced Study	.74*	.32***	.36****
Summer faculty fellowships	.31***	.01	.15
Partial correlations, controlling for objective criteria			
Graduate fellowships	.83*	.38***	.25****
Research board grants	.72*	.22	.32
Appointments to Center for Advanced Study	.57*	.10	.18
Summer faculty fellowships	-.21	-.37***	-.60*

*p < .001
**p < .01
***p < .05
****p < .10

From Salancik and Pfeffer (1974: 468).

This analysis concerned four resources which varied in terms of their scarcity as well as in their criticality to department heads. In an alternative look at the scarcity argument, Hills and Mahoney (1978) investigated the extent to which budget allocations to university departments at the University of Minnesota were accounted for by subunit power. These authors found that budget increments to the departments were more strongly predicted by power, as contrasted with other factors such as enrollments, during those periods when total budgetary resources were more scarce.

The competition for positions in any organization increases when the positions are scarce. This competition tends to involve the use of power more as scarcity increases. One reason for this is that as scarcity increases, there are more and more legitimate claimants for the limited resources or positions. It then becomes more difficult to use objective criteria to make the decision. This occurs because the criteria become less able to distinguish among the numerous worthy contenders for the resource. Also, as resources become scarcer, contenders for those resources are more likely to be willing to expend the energy and effort required to attempt to influence the decision through the use of whatever influence they might possess. If one is likely to get the position, one will not expend effort and power in attempting to influence the decision. It is when the outcome becomes increasingly problematic that the contest becomes more heated.

When the Proposition 13 property tax reduction initiative passed in California, representatives of various interests who received public funding literally descended on Sacramento, the state capital, in hordes. The lobbying activity and attempts at political influence were much more frenzied than they had been in the past, in large measure because of the increased resource scarcity.

The fact that resource scarcity produces more power and influence attempts, as well as more conflict over the limited resources to be allocated, is one important reason that formal organizations have a strong preference for growth. As Katz and Kahn (1966), among others, have noted, growth in size provides the organization with more positions, and more budget resources, to allocate each successive year. These positive increments permit all participants to obtain more, to some degree, each year, and limit the intensity and amount of conflict engendered. When the organization faces a constant, or worse yet, shrinking pool of resources, conflict and power struggles become more intense. Because few participants enjoy the conflict and the requirement of making very difficult decisions among numerous worthy contenders for the limited resources, there is a strong preference for growth—a situation in which conflict is reduced and in which power and political activity are less prominent features in decision making.

One other point should be made about scarcity and its effects on the use of power in resource allocation. Scarcity is, by definition, a concept that is defined in relative terms. Resources are scarce only in relation to the claims made upon them. Capital budgets, graduate fellowships, or positions for promotion are scarce or plentiful only in relation to how many claimants there are and how much each wants.

The psychological aspect of scarcity has several interesting implications. First, resources that come to be defined as scarce are perceived as being relatively more valuable. The psychology of price has been investigated within the business (Leavitt, 1954) and social psychology literature (Worchel, Lee, and Adewole, 1975). In marketing, the research has indicated that, particularly with products which are difficult to evaluate, price will be taken as a positive indicator of quality. In such a situation, price will be positively, rather than negatively, related to the demand for the product or service, with the higher the price the greater the demand, at least within limits. This effect can be observed in legal services, medicine, and consulting, in which clients boast about how expensive their particular professionals are. Presumably, going to an expensive doctor or an expensive lawyer will enable the client to obtain better legal or medical service. If an appointment is hard to come by, so much the better. In psychology, experiments have indicated that the perception of the scarcity of a resource produces a more favorable evaluation of the quality of the resource and more consumption of it. In this context, it is not surprising that Salancik and Pfeffer (1974) found some relationship between the perceived importance of the resource and its scarcity. Scarce resources are more likely to be more valued in any event, if other factors remain equal.

Since scarcity is seldom able to be determined objectively, particularly by outside observers, the organization or social actor possessing a resource can increase the value of that resource and their own power by claiming scarcity, and behaving as if the resource were scarce. Such behavior includes employing elaborate allocation mechanisms and formal, ritualized procedures to distribute the resource, as well as by making claims about the relative supply compared to the demand. The well-known number of applicants per position for places in university departments at once both indexes the value and prestige of admission to the department but also has a causal effect on subsequent perceptions of departmental quality. A department with thirteen applicants for every opening is clearly going to be perceived as better than one with 1.5 applicants for every opening. An interesting field experiment would involve changing the reported number of applications per opening and tracing that information's effect on the number of applications received in the future. At some point, of course, potential applicants become discouraged. However, within moderate ranges, it is likely that the lower the probability of acceptance (the greater the number of applicants per position), the greater the likelihood of application because the positions become more highly valued due to their scarcity. Such an effect may account for the relatively lower prestige accorded to schools with more open and less selective admission, even when these admission policies are mandated by law.

Scarce resources can be created by defining a resource in such a way that scarcity is ensured. In this fashion prestige and status are managed. For a real life illustration of this strategy, consider the following example. In 1975 Professor James Naylor of Purdue, along with some colleagues, founded an organization called the Society of Organizational Behavior (SOB). The organization was established with a membership limitation of fifty and a list of fifty initial invitees was drawn. New members could be brought into the organization only when an old member dropped out. Members were required to attend annual meetings at which research was discussed; any member who missed two meetings in a row was automatically dropped from membership. An executive committee was established to select replacement members from a list of nominees submitted by the general membership. The organization was almost immediately accorded a degree of prestige, much like a similar organization in social psychology. By limiting the membership to fifty, scarcity was assured, since there are many more than fifty people active in the area of organizational behavior. By so limiting membership and creating scarcity, the organization created its own valued resource to be allocated, membership. If the organization had further engaged in publicity indicating how scarce and honorific was membership, the process would have been complete. This simple example illustrates how organizations can arbitrarily define a position or status as scarce, and this definition of scarcity tends to confer value on the resource, regardless of its other characteristics.

Brehm's (1966) theory of psychological reactance also has some implications for the effects of scarcity on behavior and attitude. Reactance theory suggests that persons have some preference for freedom. When they are tightly constrained in their behaviors or choices, they will react against such constraints by becoming dissatisfied and attempting to remove the constraints. What this suggests about scarcity is that labeling a resource as scarce, and therefore implying that people cannot obtain it, may cause reactance against the constraint of unavailability, and produce more vigorous action to obtain the resource and more dissatisfaction with its apparent unavailability. Of course, by increasing an individual's desire for the resource or product, the very labeling of it as unavailable will increase demand and probably increase the actual scarcity of supply.

This effect may account for some otherwise unexplainable phenomena associated with the "gas shortage" of 1979. The revolution in Iran curtailed gas supplies somewhat. However, after some delay in production, petroleum was produced and shipped again from Iran. Of somewhat more relevance, statistics published in the United States indicated that the amount of petroleum both imported and produced domestically increased from 1978, at least for the first several months of the year. Nevertheless, the government proclaimed a fuel shortage, and immediately prices rose substantially, lines appeared at gas stations, and the amount of driving *increased* in the very short run, although it subsequently decreased. The increase in driving in the face of scarcity may have been a behavior produced by reactance against the appearance of the constraints against driving of higher prices, longer gas lines, and the government proclamation of shortage. This government proclamation may have induced hoarding and increased the desirability of the resource, thus producing the very crisis and shortage it had predicted.

The final thing to note about resource scarcity is that organizations are fairly adaptable, particularly over a reasonably long time period. Resources which are scarce and which are difficult or impossible to obtain may, over time, come to be defined as unnecessary for the organization's operations. This can occur because changes in technology make a particular resource no longer necessary, or because changes in the organization's products or goals make the resource less necessary, given the new focus of operations.

As an example of this, in the study of decision making at the University of Illinois (Pfeffer and Salancik, 1974), department chairpersons were interviewed about their perceptions of resource scarcity and importance. In one department, we determined from the chairperson that graduate education was an important and central activity within the department. The department prided itself on the large number of doctoral students produced; indeed, there was some evidence that close to 40% of all persons teaching in other universities in that particular field had graduated from this specific department. The department was large, prestigious, and research-oriented. However, the department received no graduate university fellowships and not much other assistance in graduate education. And yet, the chairperson reported that such university assistance for graduate education was neither scarce nor critical. How could that be? The department, confronted with a situation in which critical resources were scarce or virtually unobtainable from one source, had developed outside funding that provided the resources necessary to operate its graduate programs. If this funding had not been obtained, our prediction is that the department would simply have redefined the importance and centrality of graduate education in its operations. Confronted with persistent scarcity, organizations adapt, either by developing alternative sources and technologies or by changing their operations so as to make the scarce resource less necessary.

The Importance of Decisions

When resource scarcity is coupled with interdependent units and heterogeneous goals and beliefs about technology, conflict is produced within organizations. Two other conditions determine whether or not this conflict will become expressed in political activity organized around the development and use of power in order to obtain the preferred decision. One such condition is that the decision being made or the resource being allocated must be perceived as being important or critical. The use of power requires time and effort. Moreover, power typically is not inexhaustible. Votes or favors called in on one issue may not be available for use in other decisions. Thus, the use of the resources that provide power, and power itself, is husbanded. Just as there is no need to use power in the absence of scarcity, there is no desire to use power to affect decisions that are not perceived as being important or critical to the organization's operations.

This relationship between criticality and the use of power can be used to see what issues an organization defines as critical. A colleague was elected to the academic senate in a university, and had to decide whether or not to attend certain meetings. Many meetings were routine, boring, and a waste of time. At other meetings, important issues were discussed and decided. My colleague wanted a way to quickly index whether or not the meeting was going to be consequential, in order to determine whether or not he should stay. He learned which departments were the most powerful on the particular campus, and which members of the senate were from these departments. The people who were in attendance at a meeting became his deciding factor in determining whether or not the meeting was important. If powerful subunits were represented, then he stayed at the meeting, assuming that important issues were going to be discussed and decided. If these representatives were not there, he left, knowing with reasonable certainty that nothing consequential would be determined that day.

Peters (1978) has described how a similar effect can be used to signify change and facilitate implementation in business organizations. The presence of the chief executive officer or some other important corporate figure at a meeting conveys symbolic meaning that the meeting is important and that critical issues are to be discussed. Thus, the issues which are discussed at such a meeting become labeled as critical or important. Note that in these instances, since there is a presumed association between power and the criticality of decisions, the presence of powerful interests causes decisions or activities to become labeled as critical.

In the empirical study assessing the effect of criticality on the use of power (Salancik and Pfeffer, 1974), criticality was confounded with resource scarcity, and thus it was impossible to estimate their separate effects. However, the community power literature suggests that powerful interests become involved in decision making only to the extent that these decisions are consequential (Gamson, 1968). There is no reason not to expect to find a similar relationship within formal organizations.

Centralization and Political Activity

The second condition which determines whether or not political activity will be the method by which choices are made in conditions of conflict is the extent to which power is centralized within the organization. In this dimension, the present analysis departs from the Thompson and Tuden typology, in which the extent to which power was concentrated in the organization was not considered to be a feature which affected the form of decision process that was employed.

This condition is important in explaining why decision making in many organizations appears as it does. Many observers report that most organizational decision making seems to be orderly, systematic, and to employ bureaucratic or rationalistic decision procedures. Yet, it is agreed that few decision situations in complex organizations are characterized by consensus over both goals and technology. Using Thompson and Tuden's argument, one would be left with a paradox—the use of apparently computational decision making procedures in settings which are not characterized by the requisite amounts of consensus and certainty.

The explanation of this paradox is straightforward. In many organizations, particularly in business organizations, power is relatively highly concentrated at the top of the organization. This concentration of control is sometimes accomplished through concentrated share ownership. In other circumstances the concentration of power may occur because of managerial control over the election of directors, the choosing of auditors, and the consequent release of information. In still other contexts, concentrated power may result from the tremendous rewards and sanctions that may be available to those at the highest executive levels. Furthermore, the socialization accomplished in schools produces an expectation of hierarchical power, so that power which is concentrated at the top of the organization is legitimate and acceptable. When power is concentrated, potential conflicts in goals and in definitions of technology are resolved by the imposition of a set of preferences and a view of technology which reflects the position of the dominant coalition controlling the organization. The decisions which are made are enforced through various control procedures. The decision making process appears to be orderly and rational only because technological uncertainty and goal disagreements have been submerged in the organization's choice processes through the use of concentrated power and influence.

Conversely, politics, the less rational-appearing interplay of power and political strategy, occurs when power and control are dispersed. The resolution of conflicting beliefs and goals then occurs on a more equal basis. An analogue can be drawn to make the argument clearer. There is more political activity in democratic countries with relatively equal political parties than there is in countries which are run by strong dictatorships. When power is centralized, decisions are made and imposed by the central authority. When power is dispersed, decisions become worked out through the interplay of various actors with more equal power in a political process. This argument does not mean that power is not critical in determining decision outcomes in either case; regardless of the degree to which power is dispersed, power still affects the extent to which a given social actor's preferences will prevail. The argument, rather, is that when power is highly concentrated, the other participants in the system have little ability or motivation to engage in a contest for control which provokes the visible conflict and political activity observed when power is more equally distributed.

There are, then, two ways of making decisions in situations in which goals are not shared and technology is uncertain: the centralization of power and the imposition of control mechanisms to enforce centrally made choices or the use of political decision processes. Given social expectations concerning the appropriateness and value of orderly and systematic decision procedures, it is reasonable to predict that many organizational participants will prefer the more ordered and more apparently rational choice processes accompanying centralized control over the alternative, the disorder that is sometimes observed in political activity. Two issues are raised by this argument. What is the extent to which the centralization of control is likely to lead to organizational maladaptation in the long run when preferences are not shared and technology uncertain? Centralized, institutionalized control can easily lead to decisions which are out of phase with current environmental contingencies. Second, is there a tendency in organizations to observe something analogous to Bettelheim's *escape from freedom* on an individual level? When confronted with decision processes which are somewhat less predictable and more troublesome, and are predicated on power and political skills rather than on facts and rationality, will organizational members be likely to prefer and support the imposition and development of centralized decision making and control systems that restore the appearance of rationality, if not its substance?

This latter point provides another illustration of the relationship between organizational processes and the surrounding social environment. If social expectations and norms exist which support orderliness and the appearance of rationality, then there will be increased social support for the kind of centralized control and power that can prevent the appearance of overt politics in situations where there would otherwise be conflict. This association between rationality and centralization is fundamental and important, for it speaks to one of the problems of rational choice processes in situations of conflict. Submerging conflict through the centralization of control provides the appearance of rationality and satisfies social expectations concerning order, but it does so at some expense to those within the organization and, potentially, to the organization's own adaptability and long-term survival.

Making Decision Making Less Political

The identification of those factors that tend to lead to the use of power and political activity in decision making also indicates what might be done in organizations to reduce the use of power and politics. It is worth considering the costs of such strategies, to clarify some of the advantages of retaining political decision processes.

SLACK RESOURCES

Slack or excess resources in the organization can reduce the use of power and politics in two ways. In the first place, as Galbraith (1973) has noted in his discussion of organization design, slack reduces the amount of interdependence among subunits. Interdependence is an important prerequisite for conflict (e.g., Schmidt and Kochan, 1972). By reducing the amount of interdependence among units in the organization, the potential for conflict is also reduced. Slack reduces interdependence by permitting the activities of the various units to be relatively uncoupled. To illustrate the point, consider one form of slack observed in most organizations: work-in-process inventories. We will consider the copy editing and production departments of a publishing company. If the organization permits large in-process inventories, the two subunits will have little contact and little cause for conflict. The copy editing department will do its work on the manuscript, and then add the book to the inventory of manuscripts ready for production. For its part, the production department will work on the manuscripts as it has time, according to whatever priority rules the organization has set. The existence of the inventory essentially uncouples the two departments. If there were no inventory, then the production department would be arguing with the copy editing department about manuscript preparation, or, the copy editing department would be fighting with the production department about producing finished books. By decoupling the process, interdependence is reduced and so is the potential for conflict.

Slack also reduces conflict by affecting the existence of scarcity of resources. The existence of slack or excess resources implies less scarcity, and less scarcity means that there will be less conflict. With plenty of resources, there is less need to contest for allocations since there will be enough for all subunits to get what they need.

The cost of slack, of course, is the cost of keeping excess resources on hand, a cost that may entail inventory costs and costs of excess capacity. These various costs of slack have led Galbraith (1973) to suggest that this strategy is not very useful in solving coordination problems. By the same token, it may be a rather costly way of reducing the incidence of power and politics in decision making. However, it is clear that slack or excess resources is one way of reducing the use of power in organizational choice. As we will argue throughout this book, one of the advantages of organizational growth is its ability to generate excess resources at least in the short run, and this reduces the use of power and the incidence of conflict within the organization.

One of the more prominent slack creating tactics used in organizations is the creation of additional administrative positions and titles. Williamson (1975: 120) has argued, "The expansionary biases of internal organization are partly attributable to its dispute settling characteristics. ...Persistent conflict...results frequently in role proliferation." Instead of choosing among subunits for a new position incumbent, the vacant position is filled with a person from one subunit *and* additional positions are created to keep at least some of the other subunits moderately happy. If new positions are not created, then titles can be manufactured. In addition to chief executive officers, there can be presidents, chairmen of the board, chief operating officers, chief financial officers, vice-chairmen, and so forth. If position creation is a means of producing slack in an attempt to reduce conflict and its consequences for the use of power, then one would expect to see more position creation in systems in which power and conflict might otherwise be endemic. For instance, if resource scarcity produces conflict over the allocation of some kinds of resources, then position creation may proceed apace in order to pay off the subunits that lose in the struggle over those resources. Certainly, the creation of administrative positions in universities has increased as these organizations began to face more and more resource scarcity. Position creation would be expected to increase in situations where there is great interdependence between subunits and great heterogeneity in preferences and beliefs about technology among organizational participants.

HOMOGENEITY AND AGREEMENT

In addition to slack, the use of power can be diminished through the production of a homogeneous set of organizational participants, homogeneous with respect to their goals and preferences and in their beliefs about cause-effect relations. Such homogeneity can be produced through selectively recruiting persons with very similar backgrounds and training, socialization of persons once they have been recruited into the organization, or the use of rewards and sanctions to produce at least outward conformity to the dominant set of beliefs.

The production of homogeneity has its own costs for organizational decision making. Davis (1969), in reviewing the literature on group decision making, noted that groups tended to make better decisions than individuals because of the different information and different points of view that were brought to bear on the situation by the various group members. Homogeneous groups, facing certain kinds of tasks, performed less effectively than more heterogeneous groups. Clearly, the advantages of different sources of information and different perspectives on issues can be lost in an organization in which homogeneity in goals and technological beliefs has been produced.

This problem is likely to be the most troublesome for those organizations that face a changing set of environmental conditions. If the organization faces a stable environment in terms of demands and constraints, then the solutions developed at one point in time will probably suffice long into the future. In this situation, there is less need for change or adaptation, and thus, less need for new and diverse informational inputs into decision making. By contrast, an organization facing a more rapidly changing environment may require frequent changes in strategy and direction; such change is less likely to emerge from a homogeneous group. Janis (1972) has illustrated the problems of conformity to a single point of view in his discussion of groupthink and the decision making that occurred in the Kennedy administration. Janis argued that even in the absence of homogeneity, a crisis situation tends to produce demands for loyalty and conformity within the group that cause the group to make faulty analyses and to miss obvious problems and other alternatives. These problems are certainly going to be worsened if the group is already homogeneous in preferences and outlook and has been chosen specifically to minimize the potential for conflict.

REDUCING THE IMPORTANCE OF DECISIONS

The final strategy to be considered in the reduction of the incidence of power and politics involves reducing the importance, or at least the perceived importance, of the decision being made. This can be accomplished in several ways. In some instances, a decision that is perceived as being critical and about which there is disagreement may simply be avoided. Although this may not seem to be an optimal way of running an organization, the avoidance of conflict is not at all uncommon, and does result at times in the refusal to make a decision. In a firm in California which manufactured and constructed large, highly engineered projects, a conflict arose as to whether or not something should be added to the product line which would involve the use of more standard parts and sub-assemblies, but which might open up new markets to the firm. The firm, dominated by engineering in the past, wrestled with the decision. Production and marketing favored the addition. Marketing would have more to sell and possibly an easier job in selling. Production would gain substantial power in the firm, because the manufacture of standardized parts and components would now become a more important activity within the firm. At the same time, engineering, which previously had power because of its control over the critical contingencies in the design of the projects, would lose some control. In this particular instance, the decision was simply put off—for additional market research, financial analysis, production facilities feasibility analysis, and so forth. It was clear from observing the key executives that by putting off the decision they were able to avoid a severe conflict. Because of the generally favorable orientation toward analysis and data gathering, the postponements could be made to appear to be a reasonable part of a rational decision making process.

A second strategy is somewhat more common. Critical decisions are labeled as being relatively unimportant in order to avoid the involvement and concern of organizational participants. This can be accomplished by stating that the decision is relatively unimportant. Relatively little formal analysis can be done and few people, or few people of importance, can be involved in the decision process. Attention can be kept away from the decision and on other matters occurring in the organization. This strategy is somewhat risky and not always successful, in that the criticality of the decision may be so widely known that it is impossible to make it appear otherwise. Nevertheless, power and political activity can be reduced substantially if the choice can be made to seem relatively unimportant.

A related strategy involves taking a decision and breaking it into smaller pieces, each one of which is likely to appear to be less important for the organization. Peters (1978), in describing techniques for implementing change, recommends precisely such a strategy. Its benefit is that change occurs slowly, and in pieces, as part of an ongoing process. Because few may realize the totality of what is occurring, it is less likely that power will organize to contest the decisions.

This strategy is frequently used to change the direction of an organization when the person in charge does not have the direct power to do so. The dean of a school of business which had been primarily research-oriented and firmly grounded in the basic social science disciplines was confronted with the task of changing the orientation and activities of the school. One way to proceed would have been to announce that a decision would be made about the future direction of the school. This would undoubtedly have been perceived as an important decision, and the various constituencies would have organized and mustered their power to affect the choice according to their preferences. There would have been a lot of conflict and a lot of political activity over what would be perceived as a crucial decision. The alternative, and what was done in fact, was not to make an announcement about a new direction, but rather, to make a series of small and relatively trivial decisions that, in their total effect, resulted in the accomplishment of much of the change that was desired. A decision was made to incorporate a placement center in the school for its master's graduates. This decision was treated as a relatively trivial matter of moving the facility from one part of the campus to the building where the business school was located. Certainly, no one could care much about that. In a similar fashion, alumni relations, corporate fund raising, and external affairs activities were added; the advisory board, comprised of business executives, was involved more heavily in the decision making in the school; and, some changes were made regarding the importance of teaching and in minor aspects of the curriculum. Treated individually, the changes were not worth even thinking about, much less fighting. Taken together, the changes had the effect of moving the school toward a new strategy. Most importantly, the course of action avoided the conflict and exercise of power that would undoubtably have been engendered, had the total change been announced and effected at once. This strategy too has costs. In the case of avoiding important but contested choices, the costs involve failing to act when action may be required, and the possibility of missing opportunities or failing to act in time to avoid threats. In the case of trying to make an important decision appear unimportant, as well as in the strategy of breaking an important decision into a series of small, unimportant ones, the costs include the possibility of discovery, resulting in even more intense conflict. In addition, the disguising of the true consequences of decisions may fail to produce the kind of thorough analysis and discussion that such important actions warrant. Implementation may be achieved, but the wrong action may have been implemented.

In Table 3-2, we summarize the discussion of strategies for avoiding the use of power and politics and some of the costs of those strategies.

TABLE 3-2
Strategies for Avoiding the Use of Power and Politics
in Decision Making and Their Costs

Strategy	Costs
Slack or excess resources, including additional administrative positions or titles	Inventory costs, costs of excess capacity, costs of extra personnel and extra salary
Homogeneity in goals and beliefs about technology produced through —recruitment practices —socialization —use of rewards and sanctions	Fewer points of view, less diverse information represented in decision making; potentially lower quality decisions
Make decisions appear less important	Decision may be avoided; subterfuge may be discovered; analysis and information may not be uncovered

It is clear that it is possible to avoid political decision making, but that the manager must strike a balance between the costs of doing so and the benefits to be obtained through the avoidance of conflict.

Implications for Implementing Normative Choice Procedures

The conditions predicting the use of power and politics in decision making can also be employed to develop hypotheses about the circumstances in which the implementation of normative choice procedures will be problematic, and the circumstances in which the implementation will be more appropriate. By normative choice procedures we refer to the general class of decision making techniques which are modeled after the rational decision making process and which are designed to facilitate the implementation of rational choice. Such techniques include the various optimization algorithms such as linear programming, dynamic programming, etc., which have been introduced by management scientists, as well as the less mathematically sophisticated, but still rationally-based, decision making procedures such as zero-based budgeting, Planning-Programming-Budgeting Systems, and similar decision making apparatus which are designed to force choice to follow a rational procedure.

There is a growing literature on the implementation of management science in organizations (e.g., Radnor, Rubenstein, and Bean, 1968; Radnor and Neal, 1973). The implication of this literature, as well as the literature on public sector decision making, is that these new decision techniques should be implemented. The focus of the literature dwells on how to make the implementation of the techniques more successful. The tone of much of this literature is that organizations are recalcitrant and shortsighted and if only they would adopt these decision making aids, the results would be substantially improved.

The implementation of these decision making systems will be difficult if scarcity is present, the decision is important, power is not centralized, there is subunit interdependence, and there is disagreement about goals or technology. When these conditions are not present, the implementation process will proceed more smoothly, and the use of such techniques is appropriate. These factors can help explain why the use of the various techniques has diffused at varying rates and with varying success in different organizational contexts.

Consider, for instance, the difference between public sector and private sector organizations. There is a continuing effort to import decision making strategies from management practice in the private sector for use in public sector organizations. As Hoos (1972), among others, has documented, such attempts have more often than not met with failure. A distinguishing factor between public sector and private sector organizations is the extent to which there is consensus within the organization on goals and technology. Profit maximization, as argued earlier in the chapter, provides a unifying theme and an agreed upon metric which is shared by almost all working within private sector organizations. There is no such unifying paradigm in most public sector units. Consequently, it is not surprising that the implementation of techniques proceeding from a premise of rational choice is difficult; the conditions are simply inappropriate.

Interestingly enough, the push to implement such management practices is often intensified during times of financial problems or resource scarcity. Thus, just at the very moment when the decision making process is likely to become even more politicized because of the increasing level of scarcity, an attempt may be made to impose a procedure requiring assumptions of goal consistency. What this analysis suggests is that these practices have their best chance of implementation success during periods of more munificent resources or in organizations that face a richer resource environment. The relative success of such procedures, initially, in the Pentagon may be in part attributable to this relatively greater level of resources. However, as the budget tightened considerably at a later time, many of these practices failed to survive.

Similarly, one would expect to see easier implementation of such decision making practices in universities which have a higher level of resources as contrasted with those confronting more resource scarcity. One would also expect to see more implementation with less difficulty in less prestigious and research-oriented universities. This is due to the greater centralization of power in the administrations of those types of colleges (Cohen and March, 1974).

It is ironic that in situations where conflict is the greatest and decision making most difficult, that the introduction of rational decision making procedures is most likely to be resisted and be unsuccessful. For it is in precisely those situations that choice is most difficult. What this suggests, however, is that instead of working on the implementation of techniques in contexts in which they are not particularly appropriate, it might be more useful to be concerned with the development of decision making aids consistent with the political model of choice in those situations. Such techniques might include procedures such as a multiple advocacy decision system (George, 1972), which will be explored in more detail in the concluding chapter.

Summary

March (1966: 170) has used the term *force activation models* to refer to a model which assumes "that not all the power of every component is exerted at all times." The concept of activation is important for understanding the use of power in organizations. Power follows from situations in which there is conflict. Conflict is produced to the extent that there exists interdependence among organizational subunits, a condition of resource scarcity, and disagreements concerning goals, preferences, the technology of the organization, or the connections between actions and consequences. These conditions produce decision situations in which the use of power and politics is more likely. For power to be employed, it is necessary that the decision involve a critical or important issue. Power will not be activated unless the choice is consequential. When power is highly concentrated or centralized, there will be little political activity observed. Power will be used to make the choice, but it will be the power of the central authorities. Without some dispersion in power, other participants will not have the capacity to engage in substantial political activity.

The conditions predicting the activation of power and political activity in organizations can also be used to determine what kinds of strategies can be employed to reduce the incidence of power in choice processes. Each of the various possible strategies—the use of slack or excess resources, the creation of a more homogeneous organization, the avoidance of the decision, its de-emphasis, or breaking a critical decision into a series of smaller choices—has costs in terms of organizational adaptability and decision quality. Finally, the conditions predicting the use of power can also be used to forecast when the implementation of normative, rationally-based decision procedures will be problematic and possibly inappropriate.

Predicting when power will be used in decision making is important for those seeking to analyze organizational processes as well as for those seeking to intervene in such processes. It is necessary to know when politics is likely to be employed in order to adopt appropriate strategies for intervention in the decision situation. This understanding is also useful in the diagnosis of organizational political systems. In attempting to assess organizational influence distributions, one would want to analyze those decisions in which power was likely to be employed.

96

◄CHAPTER 4►

SOURCES
OF POWER
IN ORGANIZATIONS

Where does power come from? Why is it that some subunits are usually able to have their views of the world, their goals and definitions of technology, prevail over others? Why are there consistent patterns in succession to executive positions, which give evidence to the maintenance of power by certain subunits and perspectives in the organization? In Table 4-1, the list of chairmen of General Motors since 1917 and their backgrounds is displayed. The domination of finance, which as we shall see later in the chapter has actually increased over time, is evident. Why?

Having considered what power is, how it can be assessed, and the conditions under which power and politics are likely to be more important, the next issue to be confronted is the origin of power, or the analysis

TABLE 4-1
Names, Background, and Tenure of General Motors' Chairmen

Name	Years	Background
P. S. DuPont	1917-1929	Finance
L. DuPont	1929-1937	Engineering/Finance
A. P. Sloan	1937-1956	Finance
A. Bradley	1956-1958	Finance
F. G. Donner	1958-1967	Finance
J. M. Roche	1967-1972	Operations/Engineering
R. C. Gerstenberg	1972-1975	Finance
T. A. Murphy	1975-	Finance

of the determinants of power in organizations. An understanding of the sources of power helps to establish the explanatory utility of the concept, for one test of validity is to determine whether or not the concept can be reliably explained and predicted. Also, understanding the sources of power in organizations is a necessary step toward understanding how to develop strategies for the acquisition and use of power in organizations. One way to assess the distribution of power is to examine the distribution of the determinants of power (Gamson, 1968). An understanding of the sources of power is, therefore, useful in the diagnosis of organizational influence distributions.

The power of organizational actors is fundamentally determined by two things, the importance of what they do in the organization and their skill in doing it. One characteristic of most large organizations is the division of labor or task specialization. This specialization was one of the reasons discussed in the last chapter for the emergence of different goals as well as for different perceptions of the connections between actions and consequences. This specialization, which permits the achievement of various kinds of economies of expertise as well as overcoming the limits of bounded rationality and limited information processing capacities (Thompson, 1967), also leads inevitably to the creation of power differences within the organization. As soon as various actors do different parts of the whole task, the possibility arises that the various functions and activities may not be equally critical to task accomplishment and organizational survival. Those units responsible for accomplishing the more important tasks and activities come to have more influence in the organization. Thus, the differentiation of actors by the amount of power each possesses is an almost inevitable consequence of the division of labor in large organizations. The amount of power each actor possesses is derived, first, from the importance of the activity performed. It is in this sense that it can be said that power is structurally determined.

Power also derives from the skills of the various actors and their ability to perform their tasks in the organization. To have an important and critical function, but to fail at it, will not provide much power. But it is not only task accomplishment which is important. Power can also derive from the ability of the participants to convince others within the organization that their specific tasks and their abilities are substantial and important. In this sense, power is at once structurally determined but also is more than structurally determined; power is affected by the capacity of organizational participants to enhance their bases of power and to convince others in the organization of their necessity and value. Both sources of power will be considered in this chapter. We will begin by considering the basic framework for understanding structural power with a view stressing the effect of the objective conditions of exchange which occur within the organization.

Power and Dependence

Most treatments of the source of power emphasize the critical role of dependence in creating power. Emerson (1962: 32) wrote:

> *Thus, it would appear that the power to control or influence the other resides in control over the things he values, which may range all the way from oil resources to ego support. In short, power resides implicitly in the other's dependence.*

Emerson went on to define dependence as:

> *Dependence (Dab). The dependence of actor A upon actor B is (1) directly proportional to A's motivational investment in goals mediated by B, and (2) inversely proportional to the availability of those goals outside of the A-B relationship. (Emerson, 1962: 32)*

Subsequently, Emerson (1962: 33) formally defined the power of A over B as equal to the dependence of B upon A. Thus, power is defined in terms of dependence, and dependence in turn is seen to be a function of the importance of what one actor gets from the other and an inverse function of the availability of this outcome or performance in other places or from other sources.

Power, according to this formulation, is quite simply understood. Power derives from having something that someone else wants or needs, and being in control of the performance or resource so that there are few alternative sources, or no alternative sources, for obtaining what is desired. Most definitions of power offered by other authors (Blau, 1964; Thompson, 1967) are virtually identical to Emerson's original formulation. The relative power of the one social actor over another is thus the result of the net dependence of one on the other. If A depends on B more than B depends on A, either because what A gets from B is more important to A or because B has more alternatives than A has, then B has power over A. Stated quite succinctly, one U. S. Representative defined power thus:

"What is power?" asks that splendid iconoclast, Republican Representative Millicent Fenwick of New Jersey . . . "Power is having something that somebody else wants" (Farney, 1979).

Pfeffer and Salancik (1978: Ch. 3) have argued that dependence, although important, is only one of the elements necessary for power to be actually exerted by one social actor over another. In particular, the social actor who has an advantage in the net power from the relationship must have the discretion to control the allocation and use of the resources that the other party depends upon in order to translate the potential power resulting from the dependence into effective influence. It may be either illegitimate or illegal for one social actor to use its relative power over another to obtain its demands. This illegality or illegitimacy is only one way in which discretion over resource use may be hindered. The ability of the actor with power to measure and observe the other's compliance with the demands made also affects the ability to translate dependence into actual power over the other's activities.

The conditions promoting dependence, and therefore the power of one social actor over another, have also been the focus for the development of strategies for reducing the power of the more powerful party in the relationship. Emerson (1962: 35), for instance, noted that the following would reduce the net power advantage of one actor over another:

1. If B reduces the motivational investment in goals mediated by A;

2. if B cultivates alternative sources for gratification of those goals;

3. if A increases motivational investment in goals mediated by B;

4. if A is denied alternative sources for achieving those goals.

Other strategies involve making the use of power illegal or illegitimate by altering the law or social norms governing the use of power, and making surveillance of one's activities and compliance with demands more difficult.

The application of notions of dependence to the empirical study of power and its determinants has taken one of two forms: an examination of resources and the subunits or actors that bring these resources into the organization as a source of power, or an examination of the ability of subunits or other social actors to cope with critical organizational uncertainties. Note that both of these formulations used to explain power focus either on the dependence of the organization as a whole or of other subunits on the particular resources or certainty provided by other social actors within the organization. Thus, as Pondy (1977) has argued, both the resource dependence perspective and the uncertainty coping perspective on power are variants of each other, and both emphasize the source of power as being derived from the ability to solve objectively defined organizational problems.

Power from Providing Resources

The resource dependence perspective on power has been used in studying power both between and within organizations (Pfeffer and Salancik, 1978). It argues that organizations, as open social systems, require a continuing provision of resources and a continuing cycle of transactions with the environment from which these resources are derived. Organizations require personnel, money, social legitimacy, customers, and a variety of technological and material inputs in order to continue to function. Some of these resources are relatively more critical to the organization's operations than are others, and some are relatively more difficult to obtain than others. Those subunits or individuals within the organization that can provide the most critical and difficult to obtain resources come to have power in the organization. In this formulation, the emphasis is on social power which is derived from the ability to furnish those resources on which the organization most depends. There are numerous resources which potentially can be the focus around which power is organized. These include money, prestige, legitimacy, rewards and sanctions, and expertise, or the ability to deal with uncertainty. The latter capability has been the focus of its own separate investigation, under the rubric of strategic contingencies theory. The operation of the other four resources is similar conceptually, but money has been the resource most frequently empirically studied.

POWER THROUGH THE
PROVISION OF MONETARY RESOURCES

There is a New Golden Rule becoming popular, which goes something like: *He who has the gold makes the rules.* Money is an important source of power in many organizations because it is readily convertible into other resources such as manpower, materials, and information. Furthermore, money, unlike other sources of power, can be stored and is relatively divisible in terms of its use. Because of its convertibility and divisibility, it is a resource that is easily transferred across specific organizational contexts.

In the studies of power and resource allocation in universities (Salancik and Pfeffer, 1974; Pfeffer and Moore, 1980b), one of the more important predictors of the power of the various academic departments was the amount of grant and contract funds brought in by the department. In universities, grant and contract funds provide two benefits to the organization. First, these funds provide resources to facilitate research and support graduate education within the department. Since strong graduate programs are significant sources of power in universities in which research and national prestige are important, the support of graduate education is a critical and valued resource. Of perhaps even more significance is the fact that universities take overhead from the grant and contract dollars obtained. In some universities, and for some federal agencies, this overhead amount can be as much as 50% of the amount brought in for salaries and fringe benefits. This overhead money comes off the top of the grant and is not used to pay direct costs such as telephone, computer expenses, or salaries, but rather goes to a general fund in the university. In the universities, a varying proportion of this overhead money is left at the university administration level; in private schools it is 100%, in public schools the percentage ranges downward from 100%. These funds then become slack or discretionary resources which the administration can reallocate to support internally funded research and other kinds of discretionary expenditures. Such discretionary resources are critical for enhancing administrative control and for providing resources to meet needs and opportunities on an immediate, short-term basis. Thus, these resources are critical and valued in the organization, and subunits which are responsible for bringing in more of these grant and contract funds tend to have power because of their ability to provide this critical and valued resource.

In the study of power and decision making at the University of Illinois (Salancik and Pfeffer, 1974: 460), there was a correlation of .72 (p < .001) between the proportion of all restricted funds brought in by a department and the interview based measure of power, and a correlation of .36 (p < .05) between restricted funds and representation on all the university committees that were studied. In multiple regression equations predicting the interview based measure of power, membership on the Research Board which was the most powerful committee, and representation on all committees, the standardized coefficient for the variable measuring the research funds that were brought in was larger than the coefficient for either the proportion of graduate students taught, or for national rank of the department in the American Council on Education's studies of prestige. In a study of power at two University of California campuses, Moore (1979) observed a correlation of .46 (p < .01) between the proportion of outside funds obtained and an identical interview based measure of power, and a correlation of .39 (p < .05) between grant and contract funds and departmental representation on important university committees. At California, a smaller proportion of overhead monies were left with the specific campus, with a majority going to the general university system and some to the general fund of the state. Not surprisingly, then, the net effect of resources on power, when controlling other variables, was statistically significant but somewhat smaller than the effect at Illinois.

The evidence of the relative magnitude of the effects of outside fund raising on power at Illinois and California is consistent with the argument that the more critical and important the resource provided, the greater the power of the social actor who is instrumental in providing the resource. Another, more direct way of testing such an argument would involve examining the effect of outside resources on subunit power over time as the criticality and scarcity of these discretionary funds vary. For example, one might expect a greater influence of student enrollments on academic departmental power as student demand for higher education decreases, due to adverse population demography, and the competition for student enrollments among universities intensifies. Thus, although the available evidence is consistent with the position taken, that power is a function of the importance of the outside resources brought into the organization by a given social actor, the empirical evidence supporting this statement is far from complete.

THE IMPORTANCE OF SLACK RESOURCES

In understanding the acquisition of power in organizations, it is critical to understand the many important advantages and functions played by slack resources. These are resources which at a given point in time are in excess of what has already been committed and promised to other organizational participants in order to maintain their participation in the organization. It is also important to recognize how quickly slack resources become an integral part of the organization's regular operating budget. This absorption of slack into regular organizational operations makes it possible to capture organizations with a relatively small amount of resources, as long as these resources are, in fact, the only discretionary portions of the organization's budget. We will discuss the creation of resource dependence in the next section. First, we must fully understand why slack or discretionary resources are so critical to organizations.

Most allocations are made using a principle of incrementalism. As Wildavsky (1979) has demonstrated with respect to governmental budgeting, for reasons of equity and because of limited information processing, budget allocations in any given year tend to be based on the pattern of allocations in the preceding year, plus some increment which reflects growth, inflation, or the incorporation of new activities by the organizational unit. Organizational subunits come to look upon the current level of resource support as the minimum level of support that is barely sufficient to keep the unit operating. Cuts from that level are resisted bitterly. Each year's budget becomes the base, in the real sense of the word, for the formulation of requests and demands for succeeding years.

The process, as described, has much in common with March and Simon's (1958) more general discussion of aspiration levels. Success or failure, and happiness or dissatisfaction, are assessed by comparing what the social actor actually obtains to the aspiration level. The aspiration level, in turn, is determined in large measure by what the same social actor has received. Aspiration levels adjust upward if increasing resources are obtained, and they presumably adjust downward if less is obtained. However, there is evidence that the upward adjustment comes much more readily and easily than the downward adjustment.

A personal analogy will illustrate the point nicely. Pretend that you are suddenly given from some source an extra sum of money which is equal to 30% of your current income, and you are led to expect that such a sum will probably be available in the future as well. At first, the extra resources will seem like a lot. You may not even know how to spend them all. However, over time, your pattern of resource use will adjust to the new level of income. You will move to a larger house or apartment, eat out more, travel more, drive a nicer car, and undertake a number of financial commitments (house, car) predicated on the higher level of income. Within a short period of time, probably a year or two, what once appeared to be a large infusion of funds that were clearly slack or excess in the system, suddenly have become the minimum amount of money needed to support your current standard of existence. Slack no longer exists, as the level of operations in the household has adjusted to absorb such slack into regular, ongoing activities. If someone then came along and tried to take away the incremental funds, the dislocations involved would be perceived as traumatic, and there would be great resistance and reluctance to readjust the level of operations back to its previous state.

This aspiration level and absorption of slack process is one reason

Katz and Kahn (1966) argued that there were strong organizational preferences for growth. With consistantly increasing resources, all the various participants in the organization can be satisfied. Furthermore, it is only from the incremental resources that change can be readily accomplished. New activities are more easily added on top of providing the rest of the organization resources necessary to operate at previous levels; it is much harder to accomplish program changes and innovations that require taking resources from subunits or activities already being conducted, in order to begin new or different activities. Inspection of budgeting at the federal governmental level indicates the validity of this observation. Similar difficulties in accomplishing change through the redirection of resources can be observed in almost all organizations.

Thus, incremental resources at a given point in time have two important properties. First, such incremental or slack resources make change and the addition of activities relatively more feasible. Since organizations typically are interested in change, adaptation, and the expansion of their domains of operation, slack resources become important in such undertakings and thus, slack or discretionary funds are critical to most organizations. Second, slack soon becomes a necessary part of the organization's operation, and thus quickly loses its characteristic of being slack. What are excess, incremental resources at one time later become integral parts of the organization's functioning. In order to accomplish further change, additional discretionary or slack resources must be found. Slack, once allocated, is no longer perceived as incremental or discretionary in the organizational system.

The critical nature of slack resources in organizations means that many organizations or subunits are willing to pay a high price for such incremental resources. Consider, for example, the observation that many academic subunits (such as schools or departments) are willing to take on tremendously increased enrollments for a much smaller increase in faculty or teaching positions. For instance, many persons in the School of Business Administration at Berkeley were willing to take on an additional 250 part-time students in an evening MBA Program in order to add five new faculty positions. This implied a student/faculty ratio of twenty-five to one (on a full-time equivalent basis) which was much higher than that in the School's formal plan or than the school as a whole experienced. Such a response is typical, and has been observed both in other universities and in other contexts as well. The reason for this willingness to pay a high price for the incremental resources is that if new programs of study or new directions were to be undertaken, they would be much more readily accomplished by using these incremental, new

105

resources than by attempting to reallocate resources already in the system. One can predict, then, that a particularly high price will be paid for slack or discretionary resources in systems in which program change or adaptation is a more highly valued or necessary objective. The critical nature of discretionary resources in most organizations means that those social actors that can provide such resources come to have tremendous power.

CREATING RESOURCE DEPENDENCE

As noted previously, one of the critical elements in the capability to translate the dependence of others on a particular social actor into power lies in the actor's ability to control access and use of the resources on which others depend. In other words, it is not sufficient to merely provide valued monetary resources to the organization; it is necessary that the social actor control the flow of money in the sense of being able to exercise discretionary increases or decreases in such flows of funds. In fact, if discretionary control over a valued resource is held by some social entity either inside or outside the organization, and this resource flow is the only or one of very few contingencies in terms of resource acquisition, then that social actor will come to possess enormous power over the organization. This power will accrue regardless of how small a proportion of total resources the given actor actually accounts for. Furthermore, with a relatively small amount of resources, if utilized in a strategically appropriate fashion, resource dependence can be created. This will provide the social actor with discretionary control over the resource with tremendous power over the organization. *We have sometimes referred to this effect as the 10% rule, which states that organizations can be taken over by discretionary control over not more than (and frequently much less than) 10% of the organization's total budget.*

The mechanism works as follows. Consider a situation in which there are two components to some organization's budget. There is a large, relatively fixed component that is based, perhaps, on last year's budget plus some increment. This component could be a function of the number of clients served or students taught, products produced and delivered, or some other formula which is fixed and non-discretionary. The second component of the budget represents a small, discretionary allocation of resources which is not based on statute, formula, previous experience, or any other such stable foundation. Rather, this allocation is based on the decisions made by some other social actor with respect to either providing or not providing some amount of these incremental resources. Initially, the organization is offered the additional budgetary resources with few or no constraints or strings attached. For the reasons we have just detailed, the incremental resources appear to be quite appealing, as they permit change, adaptation, and new activities can be more easily undertaken; they provide the margin for excellence, the incremental resources that will make it possible for the organization to perform and operate at a more satisfactory level. Thus, in almost every case, the incremental resources will be accepted. Such acceptance is virtually guaranteed by the fact that initially, few conditions are placed on the organization as a consequence of accepting the slack resources.

Very quickly what was slack becomes necessity. If at this point the social actor with discretionary control over these incremental funds comes back and threatens to withdraw the resources if the organization fails to comply with a request, the organization is likely to comply. Faced with the painful prospect of reallocating and cutting back a level of operation and activity which is now ongoing, compliance with a request, particularly if it is initially a small request, appears to be a reasonable course of action. Of course, such requests and demands can gradually be escalated over time, so that the external provider of the discretionary resources comes to exercise substantial power over the social actor who originally accepted the slack resources. In precisely this fashion, control over an organization can be obtained with relatively small amounts of resources. The key factor is not the relative amount of the budget controlled by the social actor seeking power over the organization, but rather the proportion of contingent or discretionary funds controlled by that actor. If the rest of the budget is fixed, a party with discretionary control to withdraw resources will have tremendous power, almost regardless of how small the amount of resources. It is important to note, however, that the strategy involves first building organizational dependence on the resources *before* an attempt is made to exercise control.

The federal government has been a master at using this strategy but whether or not such use has been intentional is not clear. Intentionally, or unintentionally, the results are the same. The federal government, through its grants and contracts awards, has come to have tremendous influence over almost every major institution in the country including universities, cities, hospitals, business firms, and social service agencies. In each case the scenario is the same. Some incremental funds are budgeted and allocated to some worthy agencies with relatively few strings attached. Various federal programs for education, National Science Foundation funds for university research, the various housing, training, and manpower programs in the cities, and construction funds for hospitals are some examples. An example in business firms would be the

107

federal government awarding the firm some contract for the purchase of goods and services. In all these cases, the initial increment in resources is at once unexpected and provides the organization with the capability of expanding staff, services, and facilities. The federal programs for schools are used to hire more administrative staff (Freeman, 1979) and more special educational resources including reading specialists, art and music directors, and so forth. Labor and housing money is used to hire planners, extra city workers to perform various tasks, and to build and help supplement housing funds. Research funds from NSF are used to support graduate students, buy books and equipment, and support faculty research. The organizations quickly find uses for what was at first incremental money, and the recipients of the funds then develop claims on their use.

Then the government decides to call in its markers. If the organization is to continue to receive the money, it will have to comply with federal rules for hiring and promotion that prohibit discrimination on the basis of sex, race, and physical handicap. It will have to develop special accounting routines to fully account for how and where the money is spent. The organization will have to write proposals indicating how the funds are to be spent, justifying the use of the money to the agency sponsors. This proposal writing becomes a way of having the external agencies dictate the direction and use not only of the federal funds, but also related funds generated within the organization. In many cases, the organizations involved wind up spending more resources, including time, obtaining the funds than the original amount of funds obtained. These commitments are built up slowly over time, and by the time the organizations realize what has happened, constituencies have built up within the organizations, including grant and contract officers, accountants, and special administrators hired to deal with the government, who are in a position to maintain themselves and to advocate their further expansion. It was big news when Sears, in 1979, said it would not do more business with the government. It was big news when various medical schools in the United States in 1978 threatened to stop taking the government's money to get out from under the government's myriad regulations. The fact that such events were newsworthy is evidence of how seldom organizations, once captured through the incremental resource strategy described, even attempt to regain control and power.

Thus, the use of money to gain power is dependent first on the importance of and amount of money at one's disposal. Equally critical is the strategy of the use of money. It is the provision of discretionary funds and the control over the gaining or removal of these funds which are the critical elements in providing power.

Of course, there are some organizational ploys for resisting these strategies to obtain power. One of the more effective actions is to segment the funds and those things supported by the funds in such a way that they can be easily cut from the organization, should the occasion warrant. The entity supplying the funds, however, may demand that the programs or staff being supported be integrated into the principal operations of the organization as a condition for the granting of funds. After all, manpower training or educational activities are going to be more effective when they are linked to real jobs or real educational programs already within the organizations. The cycle of attempts to gain more power on the part of the unit supplying the resources, and then the organization's response, is nicely illustrated by Salancik and Lamont (1975) in a study of the National Science Foundation's grant to examine the effects of lead in the environment at the University of Illinois. One strategy used by the Foundation to gain power was to put the project on successively shorter review cycles, so that it was necessary to almost constantly request funds from the agency and continually provide justification and explanation for what was being done. The organization's response was to put the project under the direction of someone who was not a regular faculty member and to physically isolate the project from academic departments as a way of making it easier to resist demands that intruded on autonomy. The agency's response was to argue that interdisciplinary research needed to be incorporated into the regular research processes in the university, and so the cycle continued.

It should be clear that the extent to which the resources being provided are truly critical to the organization determines the limitations of the organization's ability to resist becoming dependent on such funds, and thus provides those who control the funds with power. Thus, a more refined version of the new golden rule would state: *He who has the gold makes the rules, but it takes less gold if you know the rules.*

Power From Coping with Uncertainty

A related perspective on power is represented by those who have argued that the power of a social actor within the organization comes from that actor's ability to cope with uncertainty. This perspective is related to the resource dependence perspective outlined above, in that uncertainty coping capability can be defined as a critical resource in the organization. At the same time, the perspectives differ somewhat in their operationalization and empirical testing.

The emphasis on uncertainty coping grows out of the work of Cyert and March (1963) as extended by Thompson (1967). As Hickson et al. (1971: 217) noted, "organizations are conceived of as interdepartmental systems in which a major task element is coping with uncertainty." This perspective has been pursued in the literature on organizational design as well, as in Galbraith's (1973) emphasis on information processing requirements and capacities as critical variables in the design process. Uncertainty coping is seen as a critical task or activity within organizations in part because organizations are viewed as social entities in which uncertainty is reduced through the use of standard operating procedures, forecasting, buffering, and other activities that permit the rationalization of organizational activity, while at the same time keeping the organization adaptive to external constraints.

Hickson and his colleagues then used Emerson's notions of dependence to further specify the conditions for the differentiation of power among organizational subunits:

> *Thus, intraorganizational dependency can be associated with two contributing variables: (1) the degree to which a subunit copes with uncertainty for other subunits, and (2) the extent to which a subunit's coping activities are substitutable. But if coping with uncertainty, and subsitutability, are to be in some way related to power, there is a necessary assumption of some degree of task interconnection among subunits. By definition, organization requires a minimum link. Therefore, a third variable, centrality, refers to the varying degree above such a minimum with which the activities of a subunit are linked with those of other subunits (1971: 218).*

Hickson, et al, further argued that power was a function of the three variables operating in a multiplicative fashion. Subunit power was a function of uncertainty coping capability multiplied by the substitutability of that capacity multiplied by the centrality of the subunit to the organization's workflow. If coping with uncertainty could be readily done by other subunits, power was reduced. If the uncertainty being dealt with was not central or critical to the organization's activities, power was diminished. The critical factor affecting subunit power given centrality and non-substitutability was its ability to cope with uncertainty in the organization.

The strategic contingencies theory developed by Hickson and his colleagues is consistent with the observations of Crozier (1964) on French tobacco manufacturing plants. Crozier found that the maintenance engineers had an inordinate amount of power, given their formal hierarchical status. He explained their power by noting that machine breakdowns were the only major, unpredictable uncertainty confronting these plants. Thus, Crozier (1964: 154) argued, the maintenance engineers had "control over the last source of uncertainty remaining in a completely routinized organizational system." And, consistent with the theory of Hickson et al., the engineers were able to cope with the uncertainty—they could fix the machines—and furthermore the uncertainty was pervasive and important in the organization. The production process was highly mechanized so that the machine breakdowns virtually disrupted production.

The strategic contingencies theory was tested directly by Hinings et al. (1974). They studied twenty-eight subunits, four subunits (engineering, marketing, production, and accounting) in each of seven organizations. The organizations consisted of five breweries and two divisions of a container company. The authors found statistically significant correlations between the various indicators of power and virtually all the variables from strategic contingencies theory (1974: 34). Though not directly testing the interactive (multiplicative) specification of the theory, Hinings et al. reported that the two power scores were in first place only when the subunit had the top scores on all the strategic contingency variables. This would indicate that coping with uncertainty alone does not provide domination but that it must be accompanied by work flow pervasiveness and centrality and low substitutability for the coping capacity.

Salancik, Pfeffer, and Kelly (1978) examined the argument that influence is contingent on the nature of the uncertainty confronting the organization. Data from fifty-four individuals in seventeen organizations which had recently purchased a piece of offset printing equipment was obtained. They argued that "the person or subunit who emerges as influential will be the one identified in the social communication process as being most capable of reducing the organization's uncertainty" (1978: 241). For some of the organizations studied, the purchase was a new purchase, for others it was a replacement, and for others it involved adding an additional piece of equipment. They argued that the nature of the uncertainty varied with the decision context.

> Since each decision context presents a different situation of
> uncertainty, the characteristics of persons capable of dealing
> with those uncertainties should differ systematically in the
> three decision contexts. And if the critical contingencies hy-
> pothesis is valid, then those individuals who are most involved
> in communicating with other organizational members about

111

the area of greatest uncertainty also will be those who are most influential in the decision (Salancik, Pfeffer, and Kelly, 1978: 241–242).

The data supported this basic position. The correlation between individual experience and influence on the decision was highest in the case of the purchase of additional equipment. The number of sources of information consulted and internal communication activity about that information correlated most highly with the individual's influence in the case of new purchase decisions (1978: 248). Similar differences were found in the correlates of influence with type of communication in the three decision contexts. In the case of additional equipment, communication about the determination of need correlated most highly with influence. In the purchase of new equipment, it was communication about information gathering that correlated most strongly with influence. For replacement decisions, communication about evaluation was most highly related to influence in the decision process (1978: 250).

Salancik et al. concluded:

The influence of a subunit or an individual on a decision is a function of (1) the kind of uncertainty faced by an organization, (2) the particular characteristic or capability which enables reducing organizational uncertainty, and (3) the degree to which a particular subunit possesses this characteristic. As decision-making contexts vary, so do the sources of organizational uncertainty, and consequently, the bases for influence in organizational decision-making (1978: 253).

The limited available evidence seems to be consistent with the strategic contingencies approach to predicting subunit power within organizations. Moreover, the theory itself is consistent with the basic power-dependence formulations employed by other researchers on power phenomena, providing more reason to have confidence in its basic tenets.

Being Irreplaceable

In the theories emphasizing power as derived from dependence, the factors of the importance of the resource or performance and the availability of the resource from other sources serve as predictors of dependence. Similarly, in the strategic contingencies theory there is again an emphasis placed on the substitutability of the capacity for coping with uncertainty. In both formulations, the argument is that power accrues to those social actors who provide a critical resource for the organization and who cannot be readily replaced in that function. Because being irreplaceable is an important source of power in social systems, a number of strategies are often employed to ensure the continued necessity of the social actors performing the task or providing the resource.

Perhaps the archetypical example of nonsubstitutability is the case of the maintenance engineers in Crozier's (1964) study of French tobacco plants. Not only did the maintenance engineers control the one remaining uncertainty confronting the organization, the breakdown of machinery, but the capacity of the engineers to cope with the uncertainty could not readily be replaced. The engineers developed the practice of training new engineers verbally, and over time, documentation that would have made the repair of the machinery easy for newcomers had disappeared. Thus, because their specialized knowledge of the equipment was not easily replaced due to inadequate documentation, the engineers came to have inordinate power in large measure because of their irreplaceability.

The example of the maintenance engineers makes an important point about power that derives from the ability to cope with problems. This power is increased when a monopoly is held over the knowledge necessary to deal with the uncertainty. Such a monopoly on knowledge is acquired and maintained in large measure through various practices of nondisclosure and secrecy so that others cannot find out what or how the parties with power are doing. Expert power (French and Raven, 1968), which is the power that comes from possessing specialized expertise, is eroded quickly if others can obtain access to the expert's information. Similarly, power deriving from the ability to solve critical organizational problems will disappear if others can acquire the capability to cope with these contingencies. Thus, in organizations, one can observe a contest of strategies in which those with expertise and the power that derives from such expertise, attempt to keep their technology secret, while others in the organization attempt to reduce the power of this group by discovering the technology involved in their performance.

Computer programmers present another illustration of the effects of substitutability on power. When programmers and systems analysts develop and program large computer systems, the most frequently heard complaint is the lack of adequate documentation of the system. In fact, this inadequate documentation makes those involved in developing the system quite powerful. Once a large expenditure of time and money has been accomplished, then those who have developed the system are in the almost unique position of knowing how to operate it. If they should leave, the organization would confront the necessity of either starting again from scratch or incurring the cost of having new individuals learn the system designed by those who have left.

In addition to not writing down information that could make the powerholder's expertise accessible to others, another common strategy involves using specialized language and symbols that make the expertise look even more arcane and difficult to comprehend. The various professions have been particularly successful in using specialized phrases and even foreign languages (such as Latin) to make their knowledge less obtainable by one not well-schooled in the profession. MBA's in finance talk about alphas and betas, and other fields of business have their own special jargon. Jargon both facilitates communication within the field but also makes the knowledge being communicated appear to be more substantial and more difficult than it really is.

The third strategy for being irreplaceable involves ensuring that subunits or individuals with knowledge that can substitute are not brought into the organization or even to the organization's attention. The operation of this strategy on an individual level can be seen in the resistance of a powerful person to bringing in another person with similar expertise. And, organizational subunits may try to attain a monopoly on certain types of expertise and the capacity to cope with uncertainty by arguing for the centralization of the particular tasks in their single unit. Thus, for example, computer systems or operations research units may argue that it is more economical to have these functions performed in a single, central subunit that serves the entire organization. The personnel and organization development departments can make similar claims. In this way, the argument of economy can be used to have a set of skills centralized in the organization. Other things being equal, this will increase the power of the subunit in which the expertise now resides. Instead of having several sources of accounting, operations research, or personnel expertise, the capacity to cope with these particular issues will have been centralized in single subunits, and therefore there will be fewer alternatives to those subunits and the subunits will have more power.

In a similar fashion, when a consultant is brought into the organization to help it solve some particular problem, the subunit in whose domain the consultant is working may make great efforts to control the visibility of the consultant and his or her access to the rest of the organization. The external consultant provides both evidence that the internal subunit is not capable of coping with the critical uncertainties on its own and, more importantly, is an alternative source of uncertainty coping capacity. It therefore becomes critical for the subunit involved to keep control over access to the alternative source of specialized knowledge and to keep the consultant in a dependent position to the subunit so that the threat from substitutability is reduced.

The point is that the degree of substitutability is not a fixed thing, and that various strategies, including the availability of documentation, use of specialized language, centralization of expertise or knowledge, and maintenance of control of externally-based sources of expertise are all employed by individuals and subunits which are interested in enhancing their power within the organization. It is important to consider substitutability as a dynamic property that can and probably will vary over time as these strategies are played out by the various actors within the organization.

Affecting the Decision Process

Both the resource dependence and strategic contingencies perspectives take a rather static view of the determination of power and resulting decision outcomes. In both instances, the power of a subunit is based on its position of relative dependence to other subunits either because of its ability to bring in critical resources, or because of its ability to cope with critical uncertainties. This view of the determinants of power, although important, is incomplete. Decisions are made in a sequential process, and it is possible for a social actor within the organization to have power because of his or her ability to affect some part of the decision process. In particular, choices can be affected if the social actor can affect the decision premises or the basic values and objectives used in making the decision. Choices can also be affected if the actor can control the alternatives considered in the choice process, or can impact the information about each of the alternatives that is used in making the decision. Such influence over the parts of the decision process can come about in the absence of formal authority, an agreed-upon position of resource control, or uncertainty coping capability.

CONTROL OF DECISION PREMISES

In making any choice, there are two elements involved: the presumed goals or objectives that are to be served by the decision, and the constraints on the decision that must be satisfied by the choice that is made. Such constraints may be physical, financial, social, or political constraints. Thus, for example, in allocating a budget among departments, a city may have to meet the constraints of having its budget balance, which limits the total amount that can be allocated, given some revenue projections. In addition, there may be political constraints that affect the choice, such as the political infeasibility of cutting the police or fire department budget, and the inability to cut the expenditure of funds on programs that may be legally mandated by state or federal law. These constraints are premises which are used in the making of the final budget allocation. Within these constraints, there may be some objectives, such as the maximization of voter utility to assure the greatest chance of re-election (Downs, 1957). Other objectives which may also come into play are the norms of equity or fairness, the issue of precedence discussed above in which last year's budget is a base for this year's, and concerns of public welfare.

It is important to recognize that decisions are, in large measure, determined by the premises used in making them. As Simon (1964) discussed when he described organizational goals as systems of constraints, if a given party can determine the constraints, then they can in effect determine the decision. Similarly, decisions can be affected by the goals, norms, and rules that are advanced and then accepted by those participating in the decision making situation. Therefore, those social actors who either have or can acquire influence over the constraints and the values and norms employed in the decision making process can substantially affect the decision outcome.

Decision premises are, in part, controlled by law or well established and long standing organizational policy. However, such laws and policies may be invented or reinterpreted on the spot to influence the decision in a desired direction by individuals involved in the decision process. One of the norms that often governs behavior, particularly in business organizations or other organizations which are ostensibly nonpolitical, is that persons trust and respect each other's judgment and motives. This trust is produced by the belief in the overall goal of profit maximization, and the faith that members of the organization have accepted the organization's goal and are acting in its best interest, as they see it. In such a context, if someone claims that a certain constraint must be satisfied because of some binding social reality, this assertion is seldom challenged. There are dangers and risks involved in exceeding constraints, and there are even dangers in challenging the validity of a specific constraint. First, a lack of trust and belief in one's compatriots is displayed. And second, if the constraint is, in fact, binding, the actor making the challenge will appear to have been uninformed about common organizational knowledge and not in possession of enough good sense to take another's word for it.

Thus, for instance, in making a capital investment decision, one party may assert that the board of directors would never accept a decision that exceeded a certain set of financial parameters. It is highly unlikely that this individual would be challenged as to the source of that information, and it is unlikely that anyone would strongly push a proposal that did not fit these constraints. The point is that most social actors in a decision situation will preemptively accept almost any reasonable assertion, particularly about constraints and feasibility issues, without challenging the source or validity of the information. Therefore, there are two ways to affect the premises of decisions. The first way involves actually having laws, regulations, or pressure from some powerful actor imposed to impact the constraints and values used in the choice process. The second, somewhat riskier but also more readily accomplished method, involves asserting these constraints or value preferences. In order to do either, however, the social actor attempting to affect the decision must have access to and involvement in the decision process.

The use of assertions of constraints to affect decision outcomes can be seen in the following example. There was a discussion concerning the reorganization of a division that built engineered structures using some standard parts which was part of a large conglomerate. The suggestion was made to move from a functional organization to one with more project management emphasis, either by incorporating elements of matrix organization design (Davis and Lawrence, 1977) or by appointing formal project managers. This suggestion was made to overcome difficulties that had arisen in project coordination which left construction efforts over budget and seriously behind schedule because there was no single department or person with the overall responsibility for getting the work done.

The present organizational structure provided substantial power to the vice president in charge of the engineering department. The development of engineering drawings and solutions was the most critical contingency in the completion of the project. Engineering had to work with marketing in selling the job, and production could not manufacture standard parts without engineering's designs and approval. In fact, what was a critical problem of project management had been defined, in this firm, as a problem of engineering. Engineering controlled the research and development function, and was the largest single department in terms of permanent employees in the organization.

Clearly, reorganization to a more project-oriented basis would cost the engineering department some power. Its designs and timetables would now be under the supervision of someone from outside the department. The inclusion of this additional authority in the structure would inevitably erode the power which was already possessed by engineering. Engineering's response was interesting. In a meeting in which the reor-

117

ganization was to be discussed, the vice president of engineering did not debate the need for more project control and project emphasis. Indeed, he disarmingly noted that many of the division's problems were arising because of that lack of control, and that more effective management of the projects was clearly required. However, he informed the group, he had talked with corporate headquarters, which would have to approve any major reorganization. The vice president in charge of corporate personnel and organization development told him that the firm did not believe in or have confidence in matrix management or project management schemes. Therefore, it was unlikely that they would approve the reorganization being discussed. Rather, the vice president suggested, the solution would be to give project management responsibility to the engineer in charge of the project. This would provide project management control but would not embarrass the division by proposing a reorganization inconsistent with corporate-wide theories of organization and management.

The strategy worked. Even the division president was reluctant to test the veracity of this report by proposing a reorganization that might be rejected and would make him and his colleagues look stupid and out of touch with corporate headquarters. Since the present structure was clearly approved by corporate headquarters, the executive committee of the division agreed to try to make the present arrangement work to accomplish the increased coordination. What is interesting is the fact that the introduction of the statement that the reorganization would not have been approved stopped the proposal right there.

CONTROLLING THE
CONSIDERED ALTERNATIVES

Most theories of choice begin with a set of alternatives and seek to predict the decision among the alternatives. This has always seemed to miss much of the variance in decision outcomes. The typical *Wall Street Journal* advertisement for a position brings hundreds of responses. The interesting issue is how the final few candidates are selected. Similarly, advertisements for faculty positions bring many replies, and again most of the decision alternatives are rejected by the time the final interviewing and final choice process takes place. Of the hundreds of potential merger possibilities, only a few may be brought to the attention of the board by the management and the firm's investment bankers. In instance after instance of decision making, the choices are substantially narrowed in the process of search, so that by the time the final few alternatives are considered, much of the potential variance in decision outcomes has been eliminated.

This fact was recognized by Cyert and March (1963) and March and Simon (1958) who emphasized the importance of a theory of search in describing the decision making process. Cyert and March argued that search took place according to where in the organization the problem was discovered. A problem uncovered by the marketing department would become defined as a marketing problem, and then the search would involve those alternatives that the department had the most experience with. If the same problem were uncovered by the production department, it would be diagnosed in terms of its being a production problem, and the search for alternative solutions would consist of options familiar to and defined by the production department.

It is clear that the final choice among alternatives will be heavily dependent on the alternatives which are considered at all and which survive the initial winnowing process. This is why astute organizational actors attempt to obtain positions on search committees, study committees, and policy and planning committees. The work of these committees in uncovering and defining alternatives is where most of the action in terms of affecting the decision outcome may occur. Pfeffer (1977a) noted that a situation in which all the organizational members have the opportunity to vote on the final alternatives is actually a situation in which centralized control may be effectively exercised. Because of the formality of the final voting, the illusion is created of a participatory decision process in which the views of many organizational participants are considered. However, few participants may be sensitive to the fact that the alternatives they have to consider have already been screened and defined by one or a few persons who are much less visible in the decision process. The voting that takes place in the Soviet Union for political candidates is an extreme and unusually obvious example of the type of alternative limitation that, in fact, occurs in virtually every decision situation. Those in a position to define the alternatives to be considered have tremendous impact on the final decision outcome, regardless of the voting or decision rules used to make the final choice.

CONTROL OF INFORMATION
ABOUT ALTERNATIVES

The third part of the decision process in which influence over the outcome may be exercised, and in a rather unobtrusive fashion, is with respect to the information made available to evaluate the decision alternatives. Typically, search committees or study committees set up to look at an issue not only present alternatives, but also develop information about each of the alternatives. In the course of developing this information, the decision outcome is affected, given the tendency of most participants in the decision to use the information provided to them by others. Thus, the control of information about alternatives is another source of power in decision situations as it affects the outcome of the decision process.

This source of power is nicely illustrated by Pettigrew's (1972) study of an English firm's decision to buy a particular computer system. In the organization in question, the board of directors had the formal authority to make the decision. The head of management services, Jim Kenny, was under the board and then under Kenny was the systems department and its manager and the programming department and its manager. It was the task of the management services group to recommend, with appropriate supporting information, which of six computer manufacturers should receive the order.

> *As it turned out, the decision process within the Management Services group developed into a competitive struggle for power between Kenny and his systems manager, Reilly, and between Reilly and the programming manager, Turner... within three months of the onset of the decision, Kenny, Reilly, and Turner had each identified with a particular manufacturer... Kenny possessed a major strategic advantage in the power conflicts because of his placement as a gatekeeper along two communication channels. Firstly, the channel between his technical subordinates and the ... board; and secondly, between the computer manufacturers and the ... board. By sitting at the junction of the communications channels between his subordinates, the manufacturers, and the board, Kenny was able to exert biases in favour of his own demands and at the same time feed the board negative information about the demands of his opponents (1972: 190–191).*

Pettigrew further demonstrated, using an analysis of actual documents during the decision process, that Kenny mentioned his favored manufacturer more often, and that the ratio of positive to negative mentions was much higher for his favored manufacturer than for any of the others. Thus, the decision was affected in the desired direction by Kenny's ability to control the information used to evaluate the alternatives.

One might expect, and indeed, Cyert and March (1963) have argued, that given this phenomenon, other organizational participants might be aware of what was going on and take steps to counter strategies relying on information control. This, however, is probably not the case. Lowe and Shaw (1968) found that even though they were suspected of being inaccurate, sales budget forecasts were accepted in a decision making situation. Such acceptance can occur for several reasons. First, the collection of information about alternatives takes time. The social value of the rational choice process ensures that information, once collected, must be attended to, so that the only real alternative is to have other social actors collect data. But they may not have enough interest in or concern with the decision to engage in this additional information gathering. Even if they did have sufficient interest, the problem of trust and cooperation then arises. To duplicate the work of an appointed individual or committee implies, naturally, a lack of trust in the work of that other party. In organizations in which the avoidance of conflict is valued, and in which the reality of organizational politics is suppressed because of its incongruity with rational, objective choice values, actions that call into question mutual trust and belief in the value of information and the overarching goal of the organization are likely to be socially illegitimate and not taken unless under extreme circumstances.

At each stage in the decision process, the definition of constraints and preferences, development of alternatives, and gathering of information about those alternatives, there is a presumed legitimacy of the process in place. To challenge the process—and conducting the activities in parallel would clearly be perceived as a challenge—is to openly express distrust of the process and those actors involved in the process. Such an action is at once an invitation to conflict and is likely to be perceived as illegitimate and harmful to the organization's solidarity and the fundamental beliefs in organizational goals and organizational rationality. Thus, although such counter measures are on occasion taken, they are not probable.

This fact leaves those in the position to define and develop information about alternatives with enormous power. Certainly, no academic reader can miss the fact that those who choose from whom letters of recommendation are to be solicited, concerning a candidate's hiring or promotion, have tremendous impact on the final result. The letters in the file are the ones that will be used by those making the decision. The likelihood of either soliciting additional material or being able to discredit material gathered is low.

The point of this discussion of the decision process is that the outcome can be affected by being in position to impact the definition of decision premises, which alternatives are considered, and the information gathered about those alternatives. Such capacity to affect the process may not have arisen because of the particular participant's ability to provide critical expertise. Rather, such outcomes may have occurred as a consequence of the particular structure adopted for making the decision, with those adopting the structure not even fully conscious of the implications for power and control which resulted.

The Power of Consensus

Thus far, the properties discussed, substitutability, uncertainty coping capacity, resource dependence, and ability to affect the decision process, can be defined for either individuals or subunits within organizations. In examining the power of subunits or other aggregations of individuals, another potential problem in the exercise of power and thus, another determinant of power becomes relevant. Subunits are comprised of many individual actors who, at one time or another, may be in a position to affect decisions relevant to the subunit. The issue becomes to what extent do these individuals share a common perspective, set of values, or definition of the situation, so that they are likely to act and speak in a consistent manner. Clearly, subunits have an advantage in the political struggle that occurs within organizations if they have a consensually-shared (within the subunit), easily articulated and understood position and perspective.

In the sociology of science, Lodahl and Gordon (1972) defined the level of paradigm development of a scientific field in a way that makes the concept applicable to this discussion. By surveying faculty in eighty departments in four fields about the degree of perceived consensus concerning course and curriculum content, research problems, and research methodologies in seven fields, these authors were able to demonstrate that there were differences in the degree to which the fields were characterized by consensus and that this difference in the level of paradigm development affected the operation of the departments. Fields that were highly developed had widely shared exemplars, methodologies, and consensus concerning the knowledge and technology of the field. Such was not the case for fields with less developed paradigms. Lodahl and Gordon (1972) compared highly developed paradigms to more certain technologies, in the sense that what needed to be done and how to go about doing it was clearer to all concerned and the results of the research activity were more predictable and expected.

Such consensus and technological certainty can have a number of effects enhancing the power of the subunit. First, the ability to argue that results are more certain and predictable encourages other social actors to rely on the subunit and to allocate more resources to it. Thus, Lodahl and Gordon (1973) observed that the physical sciences, with their higher levels of paradigm development, received much more money both from federal agencies and through internal allocations within universities than did social science departments. It can be argued that the more certain and more consensually shared technology of the physical sciences makes the return on research funds more predictable. This greater predictability encourages those who need to know that their money is being well spent, to allocate funds toward those areas of greater predictability.

Second, consensus facilitates cohesion and a common position within the subunit, which can have beneficial effects in any political struggle with other subunits. As Beyer and Lodahl (1976: 114) noted:

> . . . the higher predictability of greater paradigm development tends to increase consensus over means to goals and facilitates communication (Lodahl and Gordon, 1972). This serves to reduce conflicts within departments, and may also reduce the potential for conflict and misunderstanding with the administration. Second, faculty members who have more consensus can form stronger and more effective coalitions than those in fields rife with internal conflicts (Coleman, 1973).

Consensus on preferences and on definitions of the situation means that the subunit and its members will be more likely to speak with one voice and to pursue a consistent course of action in a number of different forums. This consensus, in an otherwise uncertain world, provides the subunit with additional power.

Of the social sciences, economics has the relatively more developed paradigm. The unanimity derived from consistently held economic theory, particularly microeconomic theory, means that economists are more likely to be heeded (even though they are often wrong) because there is such unanimity of positions. If everyone says the moon is made of green cheese, after a while it may become believable. Asch (1958) demonstrated the importance and power of uniformity in his famous conformity experiments. The presence of even one person who disagreed with the group's false estimate of the length of a line, reduced substantially the subjects' tendency to conform to group judgment. A subunit's power, in a similar fashion, is affected by the consensus and cohesion that characterizes its position on issues and its preferences and definition of the connection between actions and results.

In the study of resource allocation at two University of California campuses (Pfeffer and Moore, 1980b), the level of paradigm development of the departments contributed a statistically significant increment in explained variance even when other factors such as enrollments and subunit power were statistically controlled. These results indicate that in addition to the power that comes from the provision of critical resources, subunits can have power because of their degree of consensus and shared paradigm, which permits them to advocate their interests with more clarity and consistency.

Although defined and analyzed primarily with respect to academic organizations and scientific disciplines, the idea of consensus and a well-articulated point of view is applicable in many other contexts. In electoral politics, a critical dimension of success is the extent to which parties and candidates share a consistent world view and can articulate that view and theory of the world in a convincing fashion. The persuasiveness of the position is probably a function of both the consensus with which it is held and also the degree to which it can be demonstrated in numerous examples and can lead to predictable or certain conclusions. In business firms, both the firm itself and the subunits within it benefit in political struggles, to the extent that there is internal cohesion, and to the degree that the unit's position can be readily and predictably explained. Indeed, the importance of a shared paradigm or world view is such that elsewhere it has been suggested that the development of such consensus is one of the critical tasks of administrators in organizations (Pfeffer, 1981).

Processes of Power Acquisition: A Complementary Perspective

Thus far, we have examined what might be termed as an objective, functionally determined perspective on the sources of power. This position maintains that organizations, as open social systems, require certain environmental inputs in order to survive. Those subunits that are best capable of providing those inputs or of resolving the uncertainty concerning how to obtain those inputs come to have power in the organization because of their important and irreplaceable contribution to the organization's survival. Although for short periods of time other subunits may acquire power or may remain in power after the organization's contingencies have changed, the overwhelming reality of the need to transact with the environment operates as a constraint limiting the extent to which the distribution of power can become and remain out of line with the organization's requirements for survival. This functional perspective on power is evidenced in the model of organizational adaptation advanced in Pfeffer and Salancik's (1978: Ch. 9) treatment of executive succession and is consistent with evidence demonstrating that power is determined by objectively defined requirements for organizational survival.

An alternative view, taking a social construction or social definition of reality perspective, would make a very different argument (e.g., Pondy, 1977). This view would maintain that there are few, if any, unchangeable, immutable requirements for organizational survival. Organizations can change domains, constituencies, technologies, and by so doing, can change the pattern of resource transactions that are required. Moreover, survival or failure occurs only in the long run, and in the present, what is or is not appropriate for organizational success is problematic. Therefore, what comes to be considered a critical resource, or an important contingency or uncertainty in the organization is a matter of social definition. The fact that power at the University of Illinois was predicted by departmental contributions of prestige and research resources (Salancik and Pfeffer, 1974) occurred only because certain subunits were able to construct a definition of the organization and its relationship to the environment that made these resources critically important and favored the subunits that provided them. Similarly, Perrow's (1970) findings that in a sample of manufacturing firms the subunit responsible for disposing of the firm's products was the most powerful, and Hinings et al's (1974) results on the power of production departments, reflect not only the interdependencies facing the organization but also the ability of various subunits to advocate the criticality of the activities within their purview. In each case, other subunits could have argued for a different view of the organization and its mission and relationship to the environment that would have produced a different distribution of power. In the university example, for instance, it is possible for different subunits to have argued that the real mission of the university was undergraduate education, and it was the number of students taught rather than the size of the research programs that was the critical factor in the organization's success and survival.

To see the issue concerning the resource dependence and strategic contingencies view of power, consider the following example. In January, 1980, the retirement of Lewis W. Foy, chairman and chief executive of Bethlehem Steel, was imminent. Speculation occurred concerning who would replace him. The reader is invited to try to use his or her knowledge of the determinants of power to predict who would be selected; the answer is provided in the next chapter.

In reporting on the speculation, the *Wall Street Journal* used terms and a description of the situation that mirrored the discussion presented above:

> *It's easy to figure out who will succeed Lewis W. Foy.... Just pick the most crucial of the three big challenges facing the steel industry, and then assume the best company man in that field*

125

will get the job. . . . Is the biggest problem modernizing aging plants? If, so, then Walter F. Williams, senior vice president, steel operations, is the man. Is the problem raising money to expand and diversify? Try Donald H. Trautlein, executive vice president and a former partner in the accounting firm of Price Waterhouse & Co. Improving government relations? Then its obviously Bethlehem's president, Richard F. Schubert, who was Labor Under Secretary in the Nixon administration (Sease, 1980a: 5).

The three major contenders each represented a different strategic contingency. Schubert was Bethlehem Steel's government affairs chief and principal Washington lobbyist.

Mr. Schubert draws on his previous government experience to promote government cooperation on a number of issues, including environmental regulation, foreign trade and tax policy. Indeed, analysts . . . give him much of the credit for getting some industry views before leading Congressmen during the formulation of the recently approved trade bill. . . . Critics contend he was given the president's title as a public relations ploy to bolster Bethlehem's lobbying effort (Sease, 1980a: 5).

Mr. Williams came up through the ranks at Bethlehem, knew steel manufacturing and the steel business, and was the person to cope with the contingency of plant modernization and production efficiency.

. . . the industry assumes that a world-wide steel shortage will develop by the mid-1980s. Getting Bethlehem's facilities in shape to take advantage of that shortage has been one of Mr. Foy's goals as chairman, and Mr. Williams's credentials in that area are solid. He was chief engineer of construction of Bethlehem's huge Burns Harbor plant in Indiana, and he oversaw design and construction of the giant "L" blast furnace at Sparrows Point, Md. (Sease, 1980a: 5).

Finally, Trautlein was an expert in finance, financial analysis, and control. If Bethlehem were to raise the capital to modernize, or if it were to diversify into other areas as some other steel companies already had done, financial controls and access to capital would be critical.

... E. F. Hutton & Co.'s Peter Ingersoll favors a finance man. He stresses the high cost of needed new equipment, noting that the L furnace alone cost more than $250 million. Raising that kind of money, he says, requires a financial expert like Mr. Trautlein. (Sease, 1980a: 5).

The difficulty in making a choice illustrates the fact that there were many important contingencies in the situation:

That there isn't a clear choice for chairman of the nation's second-largest steelmaker suggests the relative importance of each issue confronting the company. The desire for government cooperation on tax, trade and environmental matters points to a need for strong government relations. Rising energy and labor costs call for continued modernization to take advantage of labor-saving and energy-saving technology. And financing an expensive modernization program with the limited returns of the steel business demands great financial skill (Sease, 1980a: 5).

This situation reflects the fact that both perspectives on the determinants of power in organizations have some validity. Clearly, the contingencies and resource constraints confronting Bethlehem Steel had narrowed the focus and the choice to someone who could deal with one of the critical issues. At the same time, the definition of which issue was the most critical, and therefore, what aspect of the company's operations was to be emphasized, was open to maneuvering and negotiation. It is because of the potential for redefining situations and using language and other forms of symbolic politics in acquiring power that strategic actions, as well as personal skills, can be important in the process of acquiring power.

THE CASE OF GENERAL MOTORS

The role of finance in General Motors and its change over time illustrates the importance of strategic contingencies, as well as the maneuverability that exists within those constraints and contingencies. General Motors was put together near the turn of the century by an entrepreneur, William C. Durant.

On September 16, 1908, he formed the General Motors Company. Two weeks later, he brought Buick into GM. A month-

127

and-a-half later he added Oldsmobile, and in 1909, Cadillac and Oakland (Pontiac). Within a year, four of the eventual five General Motors car divisions were inside the organization. By 1910, Durant enlarged General Motors Company to include 25 smaller companies which . . . built automobile parts and accessories. They were loosely organized, each company practically running itself (Wright, 1979: 184).

However, Durant found himself seriously overextended and GM had a financial crisis. At this point, Durant was forced out and by 1915, GM was under conservative management.

Undaunted by the turn of events in 1910, Durant teamed up with inventor Louis Chevrolet who wanted to build a light-weight somewhat less-expensive car than was generally being offered. The two formed the Chevrolet Motor Company. . . . By offering Chevrolet stock for General Motors shares, Durant slowly worked his way back into General Motors until on June 1, 1916 when Bill Durant was once again running General Motors as its president and chief executive officer. . . . The next four years, especially from 1918–1920, produced a whirlwind round of acquisitions and expansion which added Chevrolet, Sheridan (later phased out) and General Motors Trucks to the automotive products. . . . once again General Motors under Durant grew too fast for its resources. When the recession of 1920 hit, GM was overstocked in inventory and overbuilt in product for the slowing marketplace (Wright, 1979: 185–186).

The resulting financial crisis resulted in Durant's second resignation from General Motors in 1920. Pierre du Pont, chairman during this period, assumed the presidency, and with his lieutenant, Alfred P. Sloan, Jr., set about reorganizing General Motors so that it could be both controlled and successful. The management system put in place was designed to balance the power of the operating executives, who typically occupied the president's position, with the controls of the financial side of the organization. Finance typically occupied the chairmanship as well as the vice-chairmanship, and had persons in all of the divisions who reported both to the operating side of the organization and to finance. In this way, finance was able to obtain information on all aspects of the organization, and over time came to be increasingly involved in all the decisions which were made in the organization.

Thus, a contingency or problem—GM's financial pinch in 1920—

provided the opportunity for the power to shift somewhat from the operating and entrepreneurial parts of the organization to finance. It is important to recognize that the objectives of financial control and fiscal prudence may be and frequently are in conflict with operations' desires for expansion, product innovation, and acquisitions. Over time, the balance of power shifted, as might be expected. Finance had a well-developed paradigm, financial analysis, and a language and system of analysis which facilitated communication within the finance function and looked arcane to outsiders, particularly the engineers. The way was set for finance to assume even more domination.

> *In the person of Fred Donner, the financial side had the strong-willed leader it needed to muscle its way into control of the corporation. It was not going to let an operations man domi-nate. . . . The selection of Gordon, who was not a particularly strong president, over more obvious choices established that objective. . . . Since Donner's rise to power, General Motors Corporation has sufficiently curtailed the responsibilities of the president's office to insure that the authority of the corporation rests with the chairman and financial staff (Wright, 1979: 208).*

Eventually, the vice-chairman, a finance man, assumed control over foreign operations.

> *Thus, the power of the presidency in 1967 had reached an all-time low in General Motors. While it had been the number one slot for most of GM's nearly 70-year history, it was now the number three slot, behind the chairman and vice-chair-man (Wright, 1979: 208).*

Donner transformed potential into reality. Moving from a basis of the financial controls instituted by Sloan as a consequence of General Motors' early history, Donner was able to solidify control through strategic appointments and reorganizations. Finance remains firmly in control. The chairman (always from finance) typically has stayed on the board of directors after retirement, and then has assumed a leading position on the compensation committee on the board. Contingencies have been supplemented by strategic political moves.

Political Skills as Determinants of Power

As evidenced by the preceding illustrations, power comes both through the subunit's structural position and relative dependence in the organiza-

129

tion as well as through the capability and willingness of actors to engage in strategies which enhance or more fully employ these structurally derived resources. There is little point in debating the question of whether or not structural position or personal skills and attributes determine the power of organizational participants because both are important. The structure and relative power-dependence provides some constraints, within which individual skills and abilities affect the observed results.

STRUCTURAL DETERMINANTS OF INDIVIDUAL POWER

If power derives, in part, from the ability to resolve uncertainty or through the capability of impacting the decision process, then one's position in the communication network is clearly an important predictor of individual power. From the time of the earliest communication network experiments (Leavitt, 1951), it was clear that given a structure of communication, power was determined by position in that structure. In the star structure, the person in the center connected to all the others was more likely to be seen as the leader, and to behave as the leader, and in fact, had substantial power because of the control over information and its flow through the organization. Subsequent research on technological gatekeepers (Allen, 1969) has indicated their critical importance to the flow of technology through the organization, though Allen assumed that they would act in the organization's interests and that the only issue was to ensure the effectiveness of the communication structure. Barber took a somewhat less naive view of the role of communication when he wrote:

> . . . around and beneath the technical considerations another set of meanings, involving the interplay of communications and power, is to be found. Insofar as knowledge is power, communication systems are power systems (1966: 65).

Clearly, the power that comes from information control (Petti-grew, 1972) derives largely from one's position in both the formal and informal communication networks. The critical importance of communication centrality has led to substantial conflict within organizations about the design and implementation of information systems. For example, Whisler (1970) has examined the introduction of computers in insurance companies. He noted that the issue of which department controlled the computer was often hotly contested. He argued that this was because organizational members recognized the power that would accrue to the subunit that controlled the computer and thereby the information system, and the contest involved a contest for that power.

A second structural determinant of power is the power of the subunit in which a person is located. Stagner (1969) studied the power of a large sample of executives in a variety of organizations, and concluded that power was largely a matter of subunit membership. Executives from powerful subunits within the organization were more powerful and more often able to get their way than were otherwise similar executives from less powerful departments. The subunit's position in the organization in terms of its ability to bring in scarce resources or cope with critical contingencies confers a certain degree of power on all those social actors associated with the subunit. This is what is meant by the term, "power base," a term which recognizes the fact that, other things being equal, influence is more easily exercised from a strong subunit within the organization than it is from a less powerful subunit.

Another indicator of the importance of structural position is that studies of budgetary resource allocation such as those conducted in universities typically have not considered the particular characteristics or strategies of the various department heads but have only considered subunit characteristics in developing very effective predictors of allocation outcomes (Pfeffer and Salancik, 1974; Hills and Mahoney, 1978). If this is true with respect to the exercise of horizontal power, it is even more true for vertical power. One of the consequences of differentiated authority systems as exist in vertically differentiated formal organizations is that some persons are conferred more power than others, and this conferral of power is accepted by virtually all in the organization. It seems apparent that power in the organization is determined by structural position. Structural position impacts the amount of formal authority one possesses, as well as access to decision processes and the ability to absorb and cope with uncertainty. Cyert and March (1963) noted the importance of uncertainty absorption, and this ability to distill, filter, and provide information is vitally dependent on the role assigned and the position of that role in the communications network.

PERSONAL CHARACTERISTICS

Within the structural constraints described in this chapter, there are clearly individual differences in ability, political skill, and in the willingness to use those skills and abilities in contests within the organization. Individual resources and abilities can impact the power exercised by the occupant of a given structural position.

Individuals differ in their assessed reputations for judgment, brightness, and ability. As Bucher (1970) has noted, these differences in stature or reputation can impact political processes:

The major consequence of assessed stature is that it affects a person's ability to negotiate and persuade successfully, and it is primarily through negotiation and persuasion that the decisions that carry forward the work of the organization are made (1970: 30).

How is such stature assessed? Performance in one's formal role may be an important component, but in some situations, role performance may be difficult to ascertain. One aspect that is not as difficult to ascertain is how one appears, one's verbal skills or articulateness. Politics and the wielding of power are, after all, activities which involve argumentation, presentation, and debate. It is thus not surprising that Bucher, examining power in a medical school, noted, "Articulateness is not often explicitly commended, but it seems to me that it is a sine qua non of effectiveness in interdepartmental arenas" (1970: 37). In fact, Bucher indicated that her analysis showed that articulateness could even compensate for one's formal structural position:

Does participation in an extensive network of relationships both inside and outside the department constitute in itself a source of power? The data suggest that extensiveness of role-set is a necessary but not sufficient condition for power, and that assessed stature is the more critical variable (1970: 37).

In Chapter 2 we have already argued that knowledge of the power distribution may be important in exercising influence in an organization. Skill in diagnosing power can help one line up on the winning side of issues, thereby giving the appearance of being powerful by being associated with victories. Knowledge of the distribution of influence can provide insight into which issues hold a chance of winning, and therefore, where effort should be expended, as well as which issues are hopeless and thus should be ignored. The formation of coalitions also requires knowledge of power distributions within the organization.

As important, perhaps, as knowing the distribution of power is understanding the decision processes and rules of the game operating in the organization in question—not the formally prescribed, legitimate processes, but the actual ways in which decisions are made in the social system in question. This knowledge is, in some sense, cynical knowledge (Goldner, Ference, and Ritti, 1977) and, therefore, is not likely to be freely dispensed. Moreover, the very ideology of cooperative effort, goal maximization, and working together in the organization's interests tends

132

to make acquisition of this knowledge only semi-legitimate at best. Also, such ideology and legitimation will tend to dull the insight of persons in the organization, and hinder the discovery of the rules of the game.

An additional variable that may effect political skills is the individual's belief in his or her own position so that one is able to be a forceful advocate for one's views. Advocating self-interest is another variable associated with the exercise of power in social systems. Fortunately, persons tend to become committed to their positions by their own behaviors in any event (Salancik, 1977a), so that the more one advocates a given position, the more one in fact comes to believe in it. In part, this can occur through a process of self-perception (Bem, 1972): "If I am arguing for something, then I certainly must believe in it, and the more forcefully I argue, the stronger must my belief be." Because of this process, conscious self-dealing is seldom necessary. In fact, most social actors come to believe in the validity of their own positions and their own actions, and come to believe that these are the best for the organization. What's good for one's occupation, department, division, profession, and so forth must be good for the organization, and if only your own group had more power . . .

There have been relatively few studies of influence strategies, and these studies have typically focused on vertical influence. Even fewer have examined the effectiveness of the strategies employed and the role of personal skills in the process. Pfeffer and Salancik (1977a) examined the effects of three variables on resource allocations at the University of Illinois, after controlling for the effects of subunit (departmental) power and a bureaucratically rational criteria for allocation. The three variables investigated were: the accuracy of the department head's perceptions of the distribution of departmental power in the university; the extent to which the department head advocated basing resource allocations on criteria on which the department scored relatively well; and the accuracy of the department head's assessment of his department's position on the various criteria for resource allocation, such as number of students taught, amount of grant and contract money brought in, and so forth. The authors argued that these administrative variables would have their greatest effects on the allocation of less critical and scarce resources. They noted:

> *The more important and contested a decision or resource within an organization, the less likely it is that the decision can be affected by any administrative strategy or by knowledge of the administrator concerning the politics of the decision situa-*

133

tion. Put another way, if power is more important in determining outcomes for critical and important decisions, there is less remaining for administrative strategies or administrative knowledge to accomplish (Pfeffer and Salancik, 1977a: 645).

The results of their study supported their hypotheses. The three variables of accuracy of power perceptions, advocacy of favorable criteria, and knowledge of department's standing on the criteria had significant effects on resource allocations, particularly for the less critical and less scarce resources. Knowledge of the power distribution was more important for less powerful departments, while advocacy had a greater effect for higher power departments. Interestingly, Pfeffer and Salancik observed no correlation between knowledge of the power distribution and the department's power. Subunit power was determined by the basic position of resource interdependence within the organization.

Allen et al. (1979) have presented a table detailing the results of a survey of managers concerning perceptions of the personal characteristics of effective political actors. Their results are displayed in Table 4-2.

These results are consistent with Bucher's emphasis on articulateness and the previously-described characteristics of being skilled at diagnosing situations and being willing to use that knowledge. At the same time, the reader should be cautioned that these are perceptions of characteristics, and may reflect widely-held stereotypes and myths as much as any empirical reality.

TABLE 4-2
Reported Characteristics of Effective Political Actors

Characteristic	Percent of Respondents Mentioning
Articulate	29.9%
Sensitive	29.9%
Socially adept	19.5%
Competent	17.2%
Popular	17.2%
Extroverted	16.1%
Self-confident	16.1%
Aggressive	16.1%
Ambitious	16.1%
Devious	16.1%
"Organization man"	12.6%
Highly intelligent	11.5%
Logical	10.3%

From Allen, et al. (1979: 80)

We began this chapter by asking the question, what determines power? The answer that has emerged is both structural position and the ability to deal with critical problems and contingencies as well as the personal skills and characteristics that facilitate the use of those power resources:

> . . . *two components of subunit effectiveness must be distinguished: (1) the effects of the power of the subunit, and (2) the effects of the administrative strategies and knowledge possessed by particular subunit leaders. Both the power base of the administrator and the particular strategies pursued are possible determinants of organizational decision outcomes (Pfeffer and Salancik, 1977a: 655).*

Power is at once a consequence of the constraints and resource contingencies facing the organization, the ability of those in the organization to advocate their skills and capacities for handling those problems, as well as to shape the definition of the situation, and the knowledge and advocacy skills that help in the exercise of structurally-derived power. Definitions of the situation are part and parcel of power strategies and must compete with others which are advocated by other interests. In this competition, the realities of the environment ultimately intrude, even if with some delay.

━━◆CHAPTER 5◆━━

POLITICAL STRATEGIES AND TACTICS

In discussing the determinants of power in Chapter 4, the argument was made that although power was largely a function of position in the social structure and the social actor's net dependence with respect to other actors in the organization, there were still some strategies and tactics that could enhance the power of the actor within those constraints. In this chapter, we will describe some of the political strategies and tactics that are used in the acquisition of power and which are employed in the exercise of power and influence in organizations.

As an overview, the following statements can be made about the development and exercise of influence in organizations. Power is most effectively used when it is employed as unobtrusively as possible. The exercise of power and influence is facilitated by the legitimation of the decision process, decision outcomes, and the power and influence itself. Most strategies for the exercise of power involve attempts to make the use of power less obtrusive, and attempt to legitimate and rationalize the decision that is to be made as a result of the exercise of the social power of an actor in the organization.

The third type of power strategy involves increasing the support or power favoring the position advocated by the particular organizational participant. This involves either acting so as to increase the actor's own power or else obtaining the support or at least acquiescence of other powerful actors in the organization. These three types of strategy and tactics, the exercise of influence unobtrusively, the legitimation of decisions and actions, and the building of additional support and power behind a favored position, form the basis for the discussion of more specific strategies which will be developed.

The Selective Use of Objective Criteria

Almost all decision situations confront the decision makers with the necessity of not only choosing among multiple alternatives but also among the multiple criteria that could be used in the evaluation of these alternatives. Capital investment decisions could be evaluated on the basis of the expected return or on the riskiness or uncertainty associated with that return. Organizational strategic choices must consider both long and short term profit and possible competitive or regulatory responses. Numerous other considerations include the organization's own capabilities, risks, and the responses from the various groups such as unions that impact the organization. Indeed, as Pfeffer and Salancik (1978) suggested, organizations are inevitably confronted with multiple interests with multiple objectives, and thus the assessment of the effects of organizational choices is a difficult and uncertain task.

Given the availability of multiple measures for assessing alternatives, one use of power involves advocating the use of criteria which favor one's own position. In a decision situation, it is difficult and not very legitimate to argue for the validity and choice of a given course of action on the basis of the power of the social actor favoring that particular choice. Rather, choices must be legitimated and power is better exercised unobtrusively. One strategy, then, involves the selective stressing of certain criteria that favor the position advocated by the particular social actor in question.

The use of this strategy was quite apparent in the study of resource allocations at the University of Illinois. Pfeffer and Salancik (1974: 462–463) reported:

> There is support in the data for the idea that when asked what the criteria for budget allocations should be, respondents replied with criteria that tended to favor the relative position of their own organizational subunit. . . . To the extent the department head perceived a comparative advantage in terms of his department's obtaining grants and contracts and to the extent his department actually did receive more restricted funds, the department head tended to favor grants and contracts as a basis of budget allocation. . . . Preferences for basing budget

allocation on the number of undergraduate students taught was correlated .34 (p< .05) with the proportion of undergraduate instructional units taught . . . . Preferences for basing budget allocations on the national rank of the department were correlated .43 (p < .05) with the national rank of the department in 1969. . . . The data indicate that departments with a comparative advantage in a particular area favored basing budget allocations more on this criterion.

In another context, a number of studies have found that persons tend to favor the hiring or selection of people who are similar to themselves. Baskett (1973) found that subjects in the role of evaluating a person for the position of vice-president of a company who were furnished with information about both competency and attitude similarity, made job and salary recommendations which reflected the impact of both factors. Frank and Hackman (1975) found that in two of three cases, statistically significant correlations were observed between an index of similarity on a number of characteristics and the ratings made by college admissions officers. Salancik and Pfeffer (1978b) found that the choice of a similar person was affected by the degree of uncertainty in the decision situation, the release or non-release of information about the decision, and the anonymity of the person making the judgment. The interesting issue for the exercise of power raised by these studies is not the conditions under which similarity is used as a choice criterion or if similarity is used, but rather how such a decision might be justified.

Salancik and Pfeffer (1978b) reported that content analysis of the written recommendations used by subjects in their experiment did not reveal the explicit use of similarity as a criterion for choice. Rather, they noted:

In all conditions, choices were justified using the socially-sanctioned criteria of grades, experience, and recommendations. When these criteria conflicted, the subjects made an argument about why one of them was more important in the selection process. In no case was similarity mentioned as a criterion, nor was there use of personal characteristics to justify the choices (1978b: 254).

Just as in the case of the department heads, decisions were made in a self-reinforcing and uncertainty-reducing fashion, by selectively advocating the use of certain ones of conflicting legitimate decision criteria. In other words, arguments could be made using these criteria to favor whatever position the subject wanted to advocate. The data presented indicate that this was especially likely to favor a choice of someone similar when the information was not released, which gave the persons making the decision even more discretion in structuring the selective use of the information.

The differential attention to, retention of, and use of facts that favor one's position is part of the literature of selective perception (e.g., Zalkind and Costello, 1962), and is relevant to the use of power in organizational decision contexts. What the perception and cognition literatures suggest is that the process just described may not be entirely strategic or intentional. Rather, social actors may attend more to facts that support their position, and remember these facts or arguments better. Thus they may convince themselves of the correctness of their position, regardless of its impact for their immediate self-interest. In other words, rather than self-interest working directly to affect advocacy of certain criteria for choice, self-interest may also work through processes of selective perception and retention, to affect the arguments used and made in an identical fashion. Therefore, the selective use of criteria favoring one's own position may not even be a conscious action. Although it is possible that a given actor is selectively advocating the use of certain criteria that favor the position of the subunit, it is also equally possible that those criteria are being employed because they are more salient and are the ones the actor thinks about and can recall readily.

The use of information to justify a decision, as contrasted with making the decision, was illustrated in Cyert et al's (1956) description of the decision to purchase a computer. In contrast to the prescriptions of normative decision theory, these authors found that information was selectively collected and used in the decision process to provide support for the decision that was already favored. That such a strategy was feasible was the result of the ambiguity and multidimensionality that is almost always present in data used in decision making.

The following incident, related by a former student, illustrates both the use of information and the necessity of understanding the politics of choice. The student, well-trained in all the modern analytical techniques, accepted a position in which he served as staff to the organization's chief executive. Shortly after arriving on the job, he was asked to prepare a report evaluating various alternative expansion and growth strategies for the firm. Determined to please his new boss and to demonstrate his proficiency and skill, the individual prepared a brilliant report, studded with the most sophisticated forms of forecasting and quantitative analy-

140

sis, demonstrating a thorough comprehension of the issues and attention to collecting facts. The executive called him in after looking over the report and raised some additional considerations that he wanted him to investigate. So the staff member prepared an even more brilliant report, with more data and greater analysis. This cycle of report preparation, review, and the raising of new, unconsidered facts and concerns continued for a while longer. The new staff member was becoming increasingly frustrated, and was unable to figure out what he was doing wrong, or how to bring the project to a satisfactory conclusion. Finally, he received advice to unobtrusively discover what the executive wanted as a favored policy and to prepare a report supporting that position. With his heart no longer in the effort, and not even believing in the validity of that advice, he did precisely that. He learned from a confidant what the favored course of action was, and then prepared a sloppy, poorly-documented report with few of the analytical niceties of the previous efforts. This job was met with lavish praise and a nice raise from the chief executive, who then proceeded to implement the policy that had been selected after long and protracted analysis.

As Peter Drucker has remarked, anyone over the age of twenty-one can find the facts to support his or her position. Indeed, there are many facts in most decision making situations, as many sets of facts as there are parties interested in the decision outcome. It is not implied that the facts are intentionally distorted, although this has been known to happen. Rather, in a complex, multifaceted world, all issues have many points of view, and each side can muster evidence to support its chosen position. Those social actors with relatively more power are better able to get their perception of the problem and the environment accepted. As a consequence, their position on the decision is more likely to prevail.

The selective use of objective criteria and the virtual inevitability of this behavior, if for no other reason than because of socialization, education and selective perception, provides information about how decision making is accomplished and what some of the potential pitfalls are. Given that facts are going to be mustered by each interest to support its position, then one way of arriving at a better organizational decision is through a process in which advocacy is used and in which some mechanism of deciding among the advocated positions in a neutral fashion is employed. This, of course, is precisely the description of the legal system in the United States. In contrast to some alternative systems, the supposition is that the truth will emerge in the process of argument and advocacy, with each side mustering the facts and the law to support its position. The importance of advocacy and having opposing points of view was well recognized by Alfred Sloan of General Motors (1963) who, as a matter of practice, refused to make a decision unless and until both sides of the issue had been thoroughly developed and presented.

The selective use of information and the selective advocacy of criteria provide an instance in which we can see how attempts to make organizational decision making less political may have dysfunctional consequences. A common response to the situations just described is that they are in some sense wrong, and that they evidence a lack of proper commitment to the total organizational goals as well as a lack of attention to analysis and information. If only more information were available, the people involved were less political and more committed to the organization, then these perverse decision situations would not arise and rational choice processes could be employed. The norms and values of rationality tend to submerge differences of opinion and place great reliance on the ability of facts and analysis to solve decision problems. But information is inevitably limited, and selective perception will inevitably mean that there is a certain amount of information filtering, conscious or unconscious, that occurs. Sloan recognized that decisions were made more effectively when these processes were explicitly recognized, and decision procedures, such as advocacy in a quasi-legal setting, could be instituted to ensure the development of a comprehensive picture. Under the guise of rationality, consensus and commitment, all too often a position is being advocated which is not cognizant of the politics of the situation. When the procedures of rationality are introduced into situations in which there is uncertainty and dissensus, they are more likely to produce the subtle and unobtrusive use of politics, rather than the elimination of power and politics from the decision situation. Whether or not this submerging of actual conflict is useful, is open to some serious question.

The Outside Expert

The use of outside expertise, particularly management consulting expertise, can be seen as serving a function similar to that of the selective use of objective criteria. First, the outside expert can permit power to be used to affect decisions in a somewhat less visible way. Second, outside expertise can serve to legitimate the decisions reached and to provide an aura of rationality to the decision process.

It is fair to state that most organizations have within them the knowledge and expertise necessary to solve their own problems, particularly their administrative problems. It is a rare case when a consulting organization submits a report that is strikingly novel or unfamiliar in its

142

analyses or recommendations. Indeed, if the report were that discrepant, the firm would probably not accept or understand the content. Most often the suggestions made will encompass, albeit in a slightly more systematic or developed form, suggestions and recommendations that have already been floating around the organization. If these observations are essentially correct, then one might ask why consultants are brought into organizations so often or paid such handsome fees. Why are they necessary at all?

There are numerous answers to this question which are related to the issues of the unobtrusive use of power and the legitimation of decisions. It is occasionally the case that power is so widely dispersed in an organization that for a given critical issue, it is impossible to organize enough support or muster enough power internally for any one position to prevail. In this instance, power is so well balanced and the interests and points of view are in such conflict that the organization is immobilized, and it is impossible for any of the actors involved to bring the decision to a solution favoring their position. An actor who, at this juncture, can obtain agreement to bring in a consultant and who can participate in the selection of the consultant, can often sway the decision through the introduction of this new element into the decision situation. Consultants are presumably objective, expert and expensive. The two former beliefs ensure they will be legitimate and the latter tends to foster commitment to their recommendations. The same recommendation made by an outside expert carries more weight than if it were made by a party within the organization. The outsider is presumably more reliable. There is less visible self-interest in the recommendations, and with the expert's broad base of experience, the recommendations and analyses are perceived as being more valid.

Thus far, we have argued that consultants can be used to get a decision made when no action might otherwise be taken. But can consultants be used as part of the power strategies within the organization? Unfortunately, there is little research on the choice, use, and practice of consulting, but anecdotal evidence suggests that this idea is not far-fetched. Consultants are, of course, interested in continuing relationships (i.e., business) with the client firms. A consultant brought in by one party in a struggle for power may find it easy, because of the source of his information, as well as useful, to favor the side of those bringing him in. Once the decision is made and one group or another wins, the consultant may receive continuing business from those who are now in positions of increased power due to the consultant's actions. Certainly, if an outside expert recommends a reorganization that enhances the power of an individual or group, the social actors so benefited are likely to think well of the consultant's advice and to be more inclined to use the same outside source in the future.

This process, which is less visible in business firm consulting, becomes obvious in the arena of evaluation research. Various social programs hire consultants to provide evaluations which are favorable to their own programs; others, who are interested in hurting the programs, will also hire outside experts to give credence to their perspective. The politics and sociology of evaluation research is a subject beyond the scope of this book; however, the same processes of hiring experts to provide answers that are legitimate and accepted within the organization probably also occur in outside consulting.

This parochial use of outside expertise is also visible in the legal arena in trials where each side may provide its own expert witnesses. Note, however, that here again the advocacy process is institutionalized, and it is expected that each side will attempt to out-expert the other. In formal organizations, the role of advocacy is less legitimate and less visible. Seldom are two firms brought in at the same time to investigate the same issue or decisions and to act independently with argument over who is right when each has completed its analysis. Such a process smacks of disorder and disorganization and, more importantly, makes explicit the power and political aspects of organizational decision making, which are in contradiction to the prevailing values of rationality. The fact that advocacy and the use of experts are not institutionalized, as they are to some extent in evaluation research and to a great extent in the legal process, does not mean that the use of such experts does not occur. It merely means that the use of the outside expert in such a fashion is more difficult to discern and more problematic to challenge.

On the basis of the preceding discussion, we can begin to make predictions about the conditions under which consultants will be employed, and how such outside expertise will be introduced into the organization. Outside experts will be used more if power is more widely dispersed in the organization. If power is concentrated, it is less necessary to bring in an outside expert to buttress one's position; internal power is sufficient to carry the battle. One might expect to see less frequent use of outside management consultants by closely held firms in which one or a few stockholders have a major equity position in the firm. The more internally differentiated the firm, and the more equal the power of the differentiated subunits, the more likely it is that outside expertise will be brought in to resolve decisions about critical or contested issues.

The second conclusion that follows is that consultants are more likely to be employed in more critical issues, where the criticality of the issue is defined largely in terms of its potential to alter, in a more or less permanent fashion, the power of groups within the organization. Thus, it is not surprising that consultants are used frequently in the critical areas of organizational restructuring and the design of information systems. Typically, both types of changes involve the structural realignment of persons in such a way that some obtain more information and formal authority and, hence, more power than others. Over time the following cycle may occur. Consultants are brought in to resolve the most critical and contested struggles over design and information systems and may, as a consequence, come to see the world as being largely determined and defined by structure and information. Thus, in subsequent consulting engagements these are the variables worked on, and the use of consultants for these problems is reinforced. In this way a cycle of interaction is established so that most of the major management consultant firms now specialize in organizational design and the design of information systems. They are called in for these problems, their solutions are defined in these dimensions, and in this process the outside expert becomes part and parcel of the contest for control and power that occurs within organizations.

Because of the power that is derived from the outside expert, and the potential for a unique, symbiotic relationship between the outside expert and the internal sponsor, one would expect that the ability to call in consultants would be one of the more closely guarded prerogatives in the organization. Indeed, in many firms the consultant may be brought in only with the approval of the chief executive, which affords that individual with the ability to ensure that he or she is not "experted" out of a job. The relationship between line executives and outside consulting firms may be cultivated as a way of enhancing the power of the executive and his or her subunit within the organization. The movement of consultants from firms to organizations provides not only a source of clientele for the firm, but also provides for the new executive an outside ally with perceived expertise which can be important in the internal politics of the newly joined organization. Thus, both parties can benefit from a continued relationship.

It is also likely that the sponsoring executive will try to keep control of access to the outside expert. Informational social influence works both ways, and if a favorable report is desired, the informational environment may be managed. However, even more importantly, the personal relationship between the internal contact and the outside firm can be used to ensure the internal contact of the consultant's loyalty and willingness to support the favored position. The outside expert can be viewed as a gun, and those within the organization may all want to have a hand on the gun. Thus, the extent to which contact by other high-level executives with the consultant is minimized or managed determines the likelihood of the unit bringing the consultant in to be able to keep control of the relationship. That unit will therefore be more likely to be able to use the expert in the contest for power within the organization.

The use of the outside expert provides legitimacy to changes that might otherwise be advocated. The expertise itself provides the assurance that decisions are being made using rational, organizationally relevant criteria. The conditions and strategies for the use of outside expertise can only be hinted at, given the paucity of research and writing on this issue, but some hypotheses can be developed to suggest when and how such relationships are employed.

Controlling the Agenda— Decisions and Non-decisions

Both of the previously described strategies represent attempts to employ power unobtrusively and to legitimate decisions in contexts in which a decision must be made and in which there is disagreement concerning both the definition of the situation and the favored course of action. Both involve the mustering of resources and argumentation, and both run the risk of being unsuccessful. One of the best and least obtrusive ways of exercising power is to prevent the decision issue from surfacing in the first place. This strategy is particularly applicable to those interests within the organization which favor the present condition. Instead of developing argumentation and hiring experts to support one's view of reorganization, it may be easier and less risky to keep the reorganization issue from arising in the first place. Thus, the exercise of power frequently involves controlling the agenda of what is considered for decision.

Bachrach and Baratz (1962: 121–122) recognized this use of power when they wrote:

> Of course power is exercised when A participates in the making of decisions that affect B. But power is also exercised when A devotes his energies to creating or reinforcing social and political values and institutional practices that limit the scope of the political process to public consideration of only those issues which are comparatively innocuous to A . . . to the extent that a person or group—consciously or unconsciously—creates or

reinforces barriers to the public airing of policy conflicts, that person or group has power.

The issue of controlling the agenda for decision making arose first in discussions of the analysis of community power structures. In addition to asking which of various interests were best able to get their way once an issue, such as fluoridation of water, zoning, or municipal redevelopment arose, Bachrach and Baratz perceptively noted that one of the most effective exercises of power was to prevent the issue from becoming a focus of decision making in the first place. Most political interest groups recognize that it is more difficult to get their way on an issue once it is on the ballot or on the agenda than to defeat it by keeping it off the ballot. Thus, in San Francisco in 1979, real estate interests were willing to compromise on rent control measures and measures which restricted the height of buildings in the downtown area, in order to keep initiatives which covered those topics with provisions much less favorable to business off the ballot. In these cases the compromises failed, but the principle was the same, to keep the issues submerged and out of the political arena if at all possible.

In formal organizations, a comparable attempt to keep an issue at the non-decision status involves union representation of the work force. Most employers try, either through law or through employment practices, to forestall the necessity of having to go through a representational election. It is less expensive and less risky to avoid confronting the problem at all rather than risk a battle with a labor union for control over the workforce. Similarly, the issues of whether or not pay should be kept secret, whether or not career planning programs should be introduced, and what levels should receive certain perquisites may all be issues which are better left out of the public agenda.

Just as it is frequently in the interest of those profiting from the status quo to control the agenda to keep certain items from arising as decision issues, it is in the interests of those in the contest for power to get some of these issues on the public decision agenda. The raising of issues in public has the symbolic significance of representing a challenge to those with power in the organization. More importantly, the public raising of issues, or the moving of formerly ignored issues onto the decision agenda, permits the possible development of coalitions and political bargaining with groups that might be interested in the new issues. In these ways, control of the agenda becomes a focus of the struggle for power and is an important instrument used in organizational politics.

Three examples will illustrate the factors that influence a decision getting formal recognition and the importance of this variable in the exercise of power in organizations. The first example concerns a large grocery store organization. As is the case of many retailing organizations, power in this particular company was held only by those who came up through the stores and store manager route. Persons from warehousing, real estate, manufacturing (the firm made some of its own branded products), or any of the staff functions had substantially less power than the retailing portion of the operations. Indeed, persons from the store management career path were frequently placed as head of some of the other, less powerful, functions. Many of those who came through the store manager ranks did not have college degrees. The organization as a whole tended to devalue formal education and training and had few, if any, management development activities. The company had fair to poor labor relations and was the target of frequent strikes and shutdowns by the various unions that represented warehouse and store clerk personnel. In addition, the organization had been the target of various equal employment actions, particularly focusing on its treatment of female employees.

Personnel, industrial relations, or employee morale issues were not a threat to the domination of the traditional retail types because there was no forum for these issues to ever get on the top management's agenda. The board of directors typically reviewed financial performance, growth and diversification issues and strategic plans, such as future expansion and capital investment decisions. The agenda was controlled by those in power from the retailing part of the operation, and issues of organizational design and employee development were not introduced. Thus, the ability of those in power to set the agenda for the board of director meetings—the only context in which persons outside the organization really had an opportunity to talk about new problems or directions—meant that control was maintained and no new issues were brought up.

All this changed when a large affirmative action case brought the organization's attention to personnel and industrial relations matters. An enterprising and energetic personnel professional made a presentation to the board about the corporation's case and what might be required under a consent decree. The case got personnel and employee relations on the agenda, and this staff member used this opportunity to argue that it would be increasingly expensive for the corporation to continue to neglect the technical aspects of hiring and evaluation of employees. The company was then confronted with a particularly violent and protracted strike by one of its affiliated unions. The next time the personnel staff member appeared, one of the board members asked about industrial relations in general. The staff member suggested a survey, part of a systematic data collection effort. This was undertaken. To make a long story short, the evaluation of the company's employee relations and personnel activities became a part of the regular management agenda. The personnel function in general, and this specific individual in particular, increased their power in the organization dramatically. Although the evolution of the firm is still very much in progress, it seems clear that the power in the organization was shifted once long-neglected issues were brought to the attention of, and finally became a focus of, top management.

The second example concerns a professional school and its response to faculty requests to go on a part-time basis so they could continue to teach and maintain an affiliation with the school, but be relieved of many committee responsibilities and have more time to devote to their consulting and other business interests. Professional schools in general, and this one in particular, face an interesting dilemma. On the one hand, consulting diverts time from the faculty members' teaching and research, as well as from their administrative service. On the other hand, this activity brings the school to the attention of the professional community in general and makes it possible to raise money more readily. Thus, the school would probably like to have the flexibility to permit these arrangements when they appear to be in the long-run interests of the institution and to proscribe them when they do not. Such flexibility is manifestly impossible if a general faculty policy is instituted and, furthermore, this policy would have limited the discretion of the dean, who at the time was interested in building up the school's professional contacts. Of course, the faculty wanted the issue decided and some kind of formal policy adopted.

Faculties in general, and this case is no exception, are reputed to have a great deal of power as compared to academic administrators such as deans. But in this instance the dean was able to prevail and retain the flexibility to make individual arrangements on an individual case-by-case basis without any other kind of review within the school. He was able to do this because it was difficult to get items on the agenda for the school's faculty meetings. Bachrach and Baratz (1962: 122) noted hypothetically a situation which was similar to that which occurred in practice. They argued that the individual faculty member's reluctance to bring the issue forward might be explained by understanding his fears. The person might be fearful that he or she was in a small minority, that

149

the raising of the issue would evidence disloyalty to the administrator, or that the remedies proposed, since they hadn't gone through formulation and committees, would appear to be foolish. Without a way of controlling the agenda, obtaining committee attention, and in other ways raising consciousness concerning the problem, there was only the recourse of informal politics. Clearly, as Schattschneider has argued, "some issues are organized into politics, while others are organized out" (1960: 71). Control of the agenda is an important component of this process.

Our third example concerns one of the mechanisms through which staff personnel have come to have tremendous influence on organizational decisions. In a fairly large but closely-held financial organization, the assistant to the president determined with the president what would be discussed at the meetings of the executive committee, which was comprised of the chief operating and staff personnel. This control over the agenda assured that reorganization would be discussed only when the president and his assistant were ready with prepared reports and that strategy and planning would be discussed when similar staff work had been done. This meant that the president carried even more power than might be suggested by his formal position because the content and timing of items for discussion were under his control. Topics were brought up when and only when he was prepared with a position and supporting documentation. At the same time, it was difficult for other executives to raise items for discussion. The ordered agenda, like many mechanisms institutionalizing power, was instituted as a device to rationalize the decision process. It was considered to be in bad taste and not normatively sanctioned for another executive to insist on attention to some special issue. Under such circumstances the staff member who assisted in formulating the agenda, and thus made salient various issues and topics, had more power over the organization's decisions than most of the operating executives with their formally higher ranks. The president and his assistant thus exerted substantial power over decision outcomes.

It is just as important to consider how whole decision issues become activated or deactivated in the processes of organizational choice. It seems evident that control over the agenda of issues is both a source of power in organizations and an important mechanism through which power gets used unobtrusively.

THE ORDER OF CONSIDERATION

In addition to the issue of getting a decision item raised for discussion at all, there is growing evidence that the specific order of voting on decision items can affect the final results. Plott and Levine (1978) have argued that when an agenda is fixed, it can influence decision outcomes in two ways:

. . . first, it limits the information available to individual decision makers about the patterns of preference in the group. The primary means available for preference revelation is voting, and the content of each vote is specified by the form of the agenda. . . . Second, the agenda determines the set of strategies available to the individual. He always has the opportunity to choose among outcomes, but which outcomes he may choose among at any point is determined by the agenda (1978: 147–148).

These authors developed a formal, mathematical representation of the effect of agendas and tested the model experimentally, and found support for their argument on the effects of agenda order on decision outcomes. Some features of their experimental system and formal logic are not always matched in life. These features include the premises that the decision rule is majority rule and the agenda is specified in advance and followed closely; that there is little opportunity for premeeting caucuses; and that there is little or no uncertainty among the meeting participants concerning their preferences (Plott and Levine, 1978: 150). We would argue that there is likely to be even a larger effect of the agenda on the final decision to the extent that these conditions are not met. In the case of pre-existing preferences, if participants enter the meeting situation relatively uncertain of their opinions, then the order in which items come to the point of decision will affect what they perceive others' positions to be. This will in turn affect their own subsequent preferences and choices. If the decision rule is the typically observed maximum possible consensus, again the agenda will determine what participants believe the emerging consensus to be. Agendas have two other effects on decision outcomes which were not discussed by Plott and Levine. First, given a fixed amount of time for discussion, the agenda determines the amount of time, within limits, that will be allocated to the various issues. Issues coming toward the end of the meeting will receive less attention and discussion than those raised at the beginning of the meeting. Agendas represent a sequence of decisions, and these decisions, when taken publicly and with choice, may entail commitments (Salancik, 1977a) in the sense of causing change in individual attitudes and perceptions. The agenda can be used to build escalating commitment to a course of action that would otherwise be difficult to attain if the order of the presentation of the issues had been different.

The following examples will serve to illustrate the effects of the order of presentation of issues. Assume that a larger group is to meet and consider two issues—the issues could be promotion to tenure of two assistant professors, two capital budgeting proposals, etc.—the only constraint is that both items be in the same general topic domain (hiring, promotion, budgeting). Furthermore, assume that the same social actor is making both proposals, and that one proposal is somewhat stronger than the other. Finally, even the strongest of the two proposals is not a sure bet, and the weaker one is quite questionable in terms of obtaining group agreement. In what order should the two proposals be presented, and will it make a difference?

If the weaker proposal is presented first, because of its relative lack of merit, a lot of discussion and controversy will be generated. Various members of the group will speak in favor or in opposition, and one would expect a long and heated discussion. If at the end of the discussion, the weaker proposal fails, that does not necessarily impact the likelihood for failure of the stronger proposal. First of all, the stronger proposal will appear to be stronger and therefore different. Thus, individuals will not feel bound by or committed to their vote on the first proposal with regard to their decision on the second because it is different and better. In addition, having given the first proposal a very rough time and much discussion, the group may feel more disposed to going easier on the second proposal. Time will be getting short, and norms of fair play and fair treatment argue that the actor doing the proposing should get at least something from the meeting. This will be easy to rationalize, as the second issue clearly has more merit.

What if the stronger proposal is presented first? The stronger proposal, you will recall, was not a sure thing. Coming first on the agenda, it will also engender a great deal of scrutiny, debate and controversy. If it fails, the second proposal is sure to fail too. If the stronger alternative failed, then the group, having made that decision, will be committed to following the standards previously set in evaluating the next issue. If it passes, that does not necessarily portend good things for the second issue. Because the second proposal is weaker, the group may adopt the standards used in deciding the first case, and if the first vote was fairly close, they may reject the second, arguing that it fails to conform to the group standards that were just determined. Furthermore, after giving the actor one weak proposal, the group may not feel obliged to treat the second, weaker proposal well.

Thus, the argument is that the weaker proposal should be presented first to maximize the probability that both or at least one proposal will be approved. Indeed, the principle involved here sometimes leads to the floating of bogus or dummy proposals or ideas, to serve as stalking horses. Not only do such proposals get everybody's views out in the open, but they permit the venting of opinions and beliefs so that when the issues that are of more concern arise, there has been catharsis in the group. There is little time left, and having shown how tough and how high their standards for acceptance are, the group can now proceed to give a consolation prize by accepting this much superior proposal.

Consider the case of a school of business faculty which is going to be faced with votes on the following issues: cutting student enrollment per faculty member, increasing student course load per quarter, and broadening the curriculum. To get these three proposals accepted, it makes a great deal of difference in what order they are presented. Faculty are much more likely to vote for breadth in the curriculum *after* they have expanded the size of the curriculum by voting for more courses. This is what was meant by our discussion of slack. Once the curriculum is expanded, there are open slots which are not yet allocated. At that time, you can get faculty from various functions to vote for breadth in the program of study. Once they have developed course sequences which take up much if not all of the elective time of the students, however, breadth requirements are almost impossible to implement. Similarly, it is easier to get the faculty to vote for more courses per student per academic time period *after* they have voted to reduce the number of students per faculty member. If the faculty had to vote on the issue of more courses first, they may have worried about what would happen to the extra students demanding classes if the proposal to cut students was not subsequently passed. Thus, the order to best assure passage of these three issues is the order first specified. In the particular case in question, it was also the order used and all three proposals passed.

Finally, I have seen numerous instances in which meetings are filled with announcements and largely ceremonial discussions, leaving the critical decisions until near the end when deadlines limit discussion and force a relatively quick vote on the issue. In general, one might expect a higher rate of passage for things introduced toward the end of meetings. Certainly such a phenomenon is visible in governmental legislatures, where in the rush to adjourn, all kinds of things have been known to happen.

The nice thing about agendas is that few people regard them as elements of political strategy. Thus, the decision process and decision outcome can be affected, but altered by means which are relatively unobtrusive and nonreactive.

Coalitions

Having considered some of the processes through which power is used in an unobtrusive fashion and in such a way as to legitimate and rationalize the decision results, our attention will focus next on some processes through which additional power and support is mustered for political contests within organizations. Organizations are, above all else, systems of interdependent activity. Because of the division of labor and specialization of tasks which occur within formal organizations, interdependence is created among subunits and positions. By interdependence we mean that in order for one subunit to accomplish something, it requires the efforts and cooperation of other subunits. In order for the sales department to sell the product, it may have to rely on production for satisfactory delivery times and product reliability. In order for production to keep its costs down, it may have to rely on the purchasing department to provide high quality input supplies on an assured basis. This interdependence within organizations means that there is often a great deal of contact across subunit boundaries. And, this interdependence means that the potential for both conflict and cooperation exists. The interdependence creates conflict because the goals and values within each of the various interacting organizational units may not be consonant. The potential for cooperation and coalition formation exists because organizational participants are used to working with and through others in order to get things done.

Thus, organizational politics may involve the formation of coalitions with others either inside or outside of the formally designated organizational boundaries. In some sense, the use of the outside expert can be viewed as a coalition formation strategy with an external party. In that case, the inside subunit or groups form a coalition with an outside expert or set of experts to advocate their position on a set of decision issues. Since the expert is presumably value neutral and objective, the visibility and explicitness of the coalition formation process is lower than in the instances to be described later.

Although there is an extensive theory of coalition formation and coalition size developed in the literature on political science (cf. Riker, 1962; Leiserson, 1970), there are two difficulties in transferring that literature directly to the issue of analyzing coalition formation in formal organizations. The literature in political science has been virtually exclusively developed in one of two contexts: the study of voting blocs and coalitions in legislatures (e.g. Rosenthal, 1970) or the study of coalition formation in small, experimental groups (e.g. Gamson, 1964).

Neither context is representative of the situation confronted within formal organizations. In the legislature context, it is individuals who are bargaining, log-rolling, and forming coalitions, whereas one of the distinctive features of formal organizations is the fact that much of the activity takes place on the level of the organizational subunit. Additionally, the degree of socialization, interdependence, and consequently, solidarity is somewhat different in the two contexts. Most organizations have much more elaborate control and socialization systems, which means that there exists an ideology of an overarching organizational goal and there is probably more trust and commonly shared values than in legislatures. The small, experimental groups have suffered until quite recently from the fact that they were constructed so as to have no history and to play a very short sequence of games. In contrast, in an ongoing organization, there is a history and a future to social interaction which constrains the strategies participants will use against each other and which provides some moderation and stability to the action.

The second problem, which is in some sense even more troublesome, is that most theories of coalition formation and operation proceed from assumptions of rationality and calculation which are not completely consistent with either observed events or theories of social behavior from psychology or sociology. We could pick on many such premises, but one of the most prominent will serve to illustrate this point. One of the theoretical ideas emerging from coalition research is that participants in the political struggle seek to form coalitions that are of the minimum winning size (Riker, 1962). This is because of the assumption that although actors want to win in order to share in the rewards acquired by the winning coalition, they want to share these rewards with as few others as possible; hence, a coalition of the smallest size necessary to win is the most desirable. Importing these ideas into an organizational context, one would predict that a decision would be made whenever enough support was mustered behind one position or the other to ensure that a decision could be made.

But this is not what is observed in many instances. Many times, long after the preponderance of support in an organization has come down on one side of an issue, the discussion, debate and decision process continues in an attempt to build a broader base of support for the decision. Indeed, the goal of building consensus behind some policy or decision is one that is empirically observable in many choice situations. The desire for widely shared consensus at times means that making the

155

decision rapidly or as soon as it is politically possible to do so is sacrificed in the interests of getting as many organizational interests as possible behind the decision. One difference from the theory of the minimal winning coalition is that the situation addressed by the traditional, political science theories of coalitions is one in which the decision making ends the action, and a policy is decided and the rewards are divided. In ongoing organizations, implementation of and commitment to the decision may be as important, if not more so, than the decision itself. Making a decision in a context in which there is enough opposition so that implementation in an interdependent set of actors is problematic, is probably an almost useless activity. Many excellent decisions have been doomed by implementation problems. Thus, in formal organizations instead of the observation of the principle of the minimum winning coalition size, what is observed more often is the maximum possible coalition size principle. In this case, the making of a decision is delayed until all the interests that can possibly be lined up in support of the decision have been approached and courted. It is only when it becomes clear that almost no additional concessions or political action can produce additional support for the decision, that the decision will be finally made. Although this principle presumes some lack of immediate time pressure, this practice of consensus building is frequently followed even when there is some pressure for fairly rapid action. As Bucher (1970: 45) has noted, "most of the opposition to an idea is worked through . . . or else the proposal dies."

Yet another difference involves the zero versus increasing sum nature of the game being played. Studies of coalition behavior in experimental groups or legislatures take a situation or construct a situation in which the total rewards to be distributed among the participants are fixed at the outset. By contrast, competition and conflict among those interacting in the situation in organizations are on occasion somewhat more like a varying sum game in which one party's gain may not be the other's loss. Even when, as in the case of budget allocations or promotion decisions, there is a relatively fixed sum to be distributed, because of the values and norms stressing the goals and success of the total organization, the losers can be given symbolic assurances that the choice maximizes their long-term welfare and increases the overall well-being of the total organization. We will consider the symbolic use of political language in detail in the next chapter. For the moment we assert that the myth of organizational goals serves to transform the decision situation into somewhat less of a zero-sum game than what typically is faced in the arena of legislative politics or experimental games.

What this means is that although the analysis of coalition formation and coalition behavior in organizations can start with ideas from political science, it will have to develop its own theory and empirical base because of the differences between organizational contexts and legislative and small-group contexts. We have already suggested one difference in the argument about the size of the coalition desired. One could refine that argument to further suggest that the attempt to maximize the size of the coalition will be observed more in situations in which commitment and motivation in the organization has a stronger normative (as contrasted with utilitarian) basis. Thus, the consensus building and coalition size maximization which is described is more likely to be observed in universities or social service agencies than in business firms; within business firms, is more likely to be observed in organizations which rely heavily on shared values, socialization and inculturation as forms of control (Ouchi and Jaeger, 1978).

We have also implicitly suggested that coalition formation activity will be more prevalent to the extent that there is more task and resource interdependence within the organization. The creation of self-contained subunits or the provision of slack resources, both of which reduce interdependence among subunits (Galbraith, 1973), will tend to reduce the coalition formation activity. An extension of this argument would maintain that coalition formation activity would increase and revolve around those decisions within the organization that involve task or resource interdependence. So, the most political activity in terms of attempting to garner support and allies for one's position can be observed in situations in which there is a higher degree of resource interdependence within the organization. The amount of coalition formation activity will be reduced to the extent that units face environments of more resources or are less interdependent.

BUILDING EXTERNAL CONSTITUENCIES

There are two foci for coalition formation activity. The first focus is outward to groups in contact with the organization, and the second focus is within the organization to other social actors whose support may be obtained. Both types of supporters are sought, and each has its own advantages and disadvantages. Allies external to the organization are less likely to be in direct competition with the subunit in question for resources, power or decision outcomes within the organization. It is, in some sense, more feasible to expect to find a symbiotic rather than competitive relationship with an external group or organization. By the same token, however, allies within the organization are closer to the actual decision process and therefore are somewhat more valuable in influencing decision outcomes. An external ally may have less conflict of interest with the internal subunit. However, because of its distance and lack of direct involvement in the decision process, the external group can apply pressure to the organization but can less easily intervene in the decision process to advocate and selectively use information. Allies more proximately connected to the decision sequence are potentially more helpful in affecting the decision outcome.

Another cost of building and using alliances with participants outside of the organization is that such an activity can be viewed as being disloyal to the organization and its goals. As argued previously, the ideology of most organizations suggests the existence of a common goal or set of goals sought by those within the organization. To build alliances with external groups suggests a rejection of the organization's interests for selfish interests of the subunit, a view which is likely to be seen as going against the norms of internal cooperation and goal sharing. For this reason, it might be hypothesized that the building of external alliances and constituencies will be done somewhat more circumspectly, particularly in contexts in which the concept or belief in shared goals and values within the organization is particularly strong.

At the same time, it is clear that in many organizational contexts subunits attempt to develop relationships with external groups as a way of enhancing their power within the organization and increasing the likelihood of getting their way in organizational decisions. This process can be illustrated with several examples.

At a small electronics firm in the Southwest, the purchase of components and raw materials had been centralized and delegated to a purchasing department. This department had instituted procedures to select vendors and evaluate their quality as well as to ensure that price and quality control standards were met. The manufacturing operation within the firm, then, dealt through the purchasing department to obtain necessary supplies. Over time conflict developed between the two units. Manufacturing was most concerned about having enough materials of high enough quality on a timely basis. The manufacturing unit was much less concerned with the cost of the materials, and whether or not the suppliers had favorable or unfavorable credit terms. The unit was particularly unconcerned with the bureaucratic niceties of the procurement process, the filling out of requisitions, obtaining bids, evaluating vendors, and placing of orders. Finally, manufacturing went to the president of the company and argued that it should be allowed to purchase directly. This would fulfill its requirements more satisfactorily and also permit the corporation to save money by eliminating the purchasing department.

Having gone through the process of establishing relationships with certain vendors for various supply requirements, purchasing had, of course, developed close and at times personal relationships with these vendors. The vendors could not be sure that if the acquisition process were changed, they would still be able to generate the same volume of business. In addition, they had grown accustomed to the procedures and people in purchasing. To change and develop a new set of relationships would be time consuming and uncertain. Thus, the external constituency, those currently selling to the firm, was there to be mobilized.

The purchasing personnel informed the current vendors about what was going on within the firm and, furthermore, implied that if manufacturing took over the ordering, it was not too likely that the same business relationships would be maintained. The various vendors then wrote to the president of the firm, noting that the procedures and practices followed by the purchasing department in this firm and by similar departments in other firms enabled the vendors to plan production rates, quality standards, and specifications for the product. If the firm were to use another acquisition process, it was possible that order delivery, product reliability and willingness to work with the firm might be harmed. The firm, as previously noted, was relatively small. Input quality and delivery were important factors in controlling manufacturing costs, in ensuring product quality and, therefore, in affecting the success of the firm. Rather than risk offending these necessary and powerful suppliers for the sole reason of satisfying a subunit within the firm, the president maintained the present organizational arrangements. The future of purchasing thus was more secure than ever and the department had even more power than before.

As another example, consider the power of many accounting groups within business schools. In some instances, accounting has been able to institute its own separate master's degree program. In other instances accounting has been able to offer the largest number of doctoral courses. Typically, accounting faculty are paid somewhat more than other faculty within the school. Accounting students and faculty may receive more financial support from the school. This has tended to come about in those cases in which the accounting group has been able to build strong relationships with the professional accounting community, and this professional constituency has become active in donating money and other forms of support to the school. Once this relationship is established, every time a suggestion is made to cut down accounting enrollments, equalize resources across groups, or in some other way shift power within the schools, the accounting faculty quickly call up their external supporters who place pressure on the school to continue to favor accounting. The implied threat is that if accounting is not maintained in its favored position, the donated resources, which are of use to other groups as well, will dry up.

Finally, no setting is better for illustrating the development of external constituencies than governmental agencies. Agencies that deliver social services, money, or other benefits to various groups typically develop effective contact with those groups so that these external constituencies can be mobilized if funding is about to be reduced or the program cut back in some other way. Although this constituency building is done throughout government, it was quite evident in the various poverty, housing and training programs that were the legacy of Lyndon Johnson's War on Poverty Program. One of the things mandated by these programs was the development of community-based organizations to help with the delivery of services and with the policy formulation and management of these various activities on the local level. Ironically, these community action boards, manpower planning agencies, and housing and development boards were then politically organized and potent supporters of the various programs that were the domain of their related government bureaucracies. Any attempt to reduce funding for a given program would trigger an immediate outcry of protest from the local groups that had been established by the program itself. In this case the agency did not have to try very hard to establish an external constituency which would support it in internal struggles for resources; such organizations were decreed by the very content of the legislation which established the programs in the first place.

Building external constituencies requires contact with some organizations or groups outside the organization that are interdependent with the organization and that can be mobilized to support related internal subunits. Thus, although this strategy is certainly used, it is one that is not as readily open to every participant within the organization. However, all organizational actors can engage in building coalitions and alliances with others within the organization.

INTERNAL ALLIANCES

Just as in the case of building external constituencies, internal alliances are founded on common interests among the various participants. Internal alliances are likely to be particularly sought by the less powerful actors in the organization. Because of their limited power, the best way to ensure that these less powerful actors can achieve their interests in the organization is by finding common interests with others, particularly those with more power. Pfeffer and Salancik (1977a), for example, noted that knowledge of the internal power distribution was more highly related to resource allocations, controlling other factors, for those departments that were themselves less powerful. They argued that it was particularly necessary for the less powerful university departments to know the distribution of power because it was these departments that would find it most necessary to form alliances and find powerful sponsorship for their interests. Thus, one can predict that organizational coalitions are more likely to be sought more vigorously by the less powerful social actors within an organization.

Coalitions with other groups on issues where common positions can be identified make it possible for each group to obtain its desired outcomes. Two examples will serve to illustrate this point. We have already described the grocery store corporation in which personnel did not have much power and in which issues of employee relations and management development had for a long period been ignored because they were excluded from the agenda of high level meetings. That same corporation and example also illustrates the importance of allies within the organization.

As noted before, none of the staff groups had much power, for the power in the firm was held by retailing, the store management function. The most powerful of the groups, however, was the legal department. Lawyers held a certain expertise and a mystique regarding that expertise that brought power. In addition, some of the members of the board of directors were themselves lawyers. With the increasing amount of litigation, not only concerning employee relations, but also dealing with advertising, product quality and product liability, legal constraints and contingencies were slowly being recognized as being more important to the firm.

The personnel staff individual had come into contact with the legal department on some fair employment litigation. The personnel staff member had performed statistical analyses and had participated in a very helpful and competent manner in designing hiring and evaluation procedures to solve the current problems and help prevent new ones. As a consequence of that contact, the personnel and the legal departments formed an alliance. This alliance was based on their common interest of increasing the corporation's concern with compliance issues and a respect for the type of technical expertise represented in both departments that was helpful in dealing with these issues. It was, if you will, these two departments allied against the retailing department. In the various meet-

161

ings that occurred concerning the litigation, the personnel staff member would point out how well the legal department had handled the negotiations and managed the case and how the department should be consulted earlier and more frequently on these issues before they came to litigation. The head of the legal department came out quite strongly in favor of the kinds of training and survey and analysis activities that the personnel unit wanted to undertake. In fact, when the key personnel staff member threatened to quit, the legal department went to the president of the corporation and argued that to replace his expertise by using outsiders would be substantially more expensive and the department offered him an alternative of various consulting relationships and affiliations. It is clear that the two departments' reinforcement of each other was mutually beneficial. However, personnel, the lower power function, particularly benefited from the support for its objectives provided by the chief corporate counsel. Later, when personnel's attempts to introduce new procedures, training and evaluation were resisted by the tradition-bound retailing section, there was recourse to the legal necessity and legal support for these activities. With this outside expertise in support, personnel activity was greatly expanded in both power and scope at the corporation.

The second example has to do with the introduction of a workload measurement system at a professional school. The school was comprised of various disciplines because, as is the case for many professional schools, the school was interdisciplinary. One or two of the groups in the school were heavily burdened by the task of supervising graduate projects. These were specialties that were quite popular with the students, and many chose to do their required projects under the tutelage of persons from those disciplines. One or two of the other groups were heavily burdened by the necessity of teaching a large number of hours. Even though the formal teaching load was the same for all, some courses met only three hours a week while others met four and one-half hours, or 50% more. Because of the distribution of elective and required courses, two of the groups had much more than their share of longer courses.

A proposal was floated to provide explicit teaching credit and thus, course relief for the supervision of these graduate projects. Such a proposal, however, was favored only by the two groups that did most of this work. At the same time, the two groups that did most of the four and one-half hour course teaching were interested in adjusting the workload measurement and allocation system to recognize the fact that an n-course load teaching all classes that met three hours was not the same as an n-course load teaching classes that met for four and one-half hours. There was not a lot of support for that idea as again only a small portion of the entire school was affected. What finally happened was that the two sets of groups formed a coalition. The group burdened with project supervision supported the measurement and assignment of workload on the basis of classroom hours rather than courses, while the other group supported, in turn, the measurement and provision of teaching credit for the supervision of graduate projects. In the end, both had their workloads reduced. With the passage of the combined proposal, each group was able to benefit by its joint action with the other.

This last example illustrates an important point about coalitions, that they are unstable and shift depending on the particular issues involved. Bucher (1970: 34) has noted:

> *Most coalitions are shifting alliances, depending upon the issues. As issues come up, faculty within the department who are concerned shop around seeking out those who might be allies in relation to the particular issue.*

Politics indeed makes strange bedfellows. As long as there is enough commonality on a set of issues so a deal can be made, the other characteristics of the coalition participants may not be relevant. The type of analysis used in Chapter 2 in the discussion of interests at New York University is an example of one kind of methodology for identifying potential coalitions that can be formed around particular concerns.

COALITION BUILDING
THROUGH PROMOTIONS

The preceding discussion of coalition development has been couched in terms of issue trade-offs. Subunit A supports B on one issue of concern to B, and B in turn supports A on some other issue that is of concern to A. Such log-rolling requires the identification of a set of issues of mutual concern and working out the terms of the exchange. Both parts of the transaction may be tricky, particularly for those not well-schooled in political activity.

An alternative way of building support within the organization is through the judicious use of promotion opportunities. In John De Lorean's account of his time as a General Motors executive, he provides evidence for the use of this strategy by Fred Donner in his efforts to consolidate the power of the finance group at GM:

From him (Donner) developed what I call "promotion of the unobvious choice." This means promoting someone who was not regarded as a contender for the post. Doing so not only puts "your man" in position, but it earns for you his undying loyalty because he owes his corporate life to you. . . . A study of the past ten years of General Motors top executives and an examination of their business biographies makes it obvious that some men with undistinguished business careers moved to the top and in many cases occupy positions of power within the corporation today. An understanding of their benefactors makes their ascension more explicable (Wright, 1979: 41).

In a similar vein, Perrow (1972) has argued that nepotism practiced within the organization may not produce high quality employees but will probably produce loyal supporters. Coalitions are formed, then, by placing allies or supporters in key positions in other departments. This ensures the support of those other units when it is needed. When such placements are unjustified on meritocratic grounds, there is even more insecurity and loyalty engendered in those promoted, making them particularly reliable allies.

Although this strategy is most often discussed in terms of building personal power, it clearly also impacts the power of organizational subunits. In the large retailing organization previously described, the fact that persons were appointed from retailing to head departments of personnel, public relations, industrial relations, and so forth, who had absolutely no background in those areas, ensured that the power and reach of the retailing point of view would be maintained without opposition in the higher management ranks. People got the jobs because they were from the retailing department and loyal to it, and they and everyone else knew it. Professional competence or even experience in the area being managed was not only not a requirement, it was frequently seen as a detriment.

EVERYBODY'S A WINNER

One of the nice aspects of coalition formation in organizations is that the rewards are frequently not zero-sum, in the sense that one's gain comes at another's expense. One of the strategies that may be used to build consensus and a large coalition within the organization is to attempt to make all participants winners, to give all the major groups or interests something from the decision.

This strategy in use can be seen in the Bethlehem Steel example introduced in the last chapter. Recall that the corporation had to choose a new chief executive officer from among three leading candidates: Traut-lein, a financial man, Schubert, the public relations and lobbying person, and Walter Williams, the steel operations man. The choice, because it reflected the company's concern for what were to be the strategic issues in the immediate future, took on enormous symbolic significance. Steel manufacturing types were worried that control was about to pass to either an accountant or a governmental relations type. Finance forces within the firm were concerned that control would remain with steel manufacturing and the company would be unable to raise capital and manage diversification. What the company did, of course, was to promote everyone while giving the chief executive title to Trautlein:

> Donald H. Trautlein, a 53-year-old former Price, Waterhouse & Co. accountant, was named chairman and chief executive officer of Bethlehem Steel Corporation. . . . The move clearly reflects concern . . . about maintaining and improving Bethle-hem's financial health. . . . Two other highly touted candidates —Richard F. Schubert . . . and Walter F. Williams . . . also were promoted. Mr. Shubert will become one of Bethlehem's four vice chairmen and Mr. Williams will take over the presi-dent's office with the additional new title of chief operating officer (Sease, 1980b: 6).

Note that a new title was created, that of chief operating officer, to provide a sense of balance between the financial side of the firm, represented by Trautlein, and the operations side, represented by Wil-liams. Williams also got Schubert's old title of president, but Schubert was promoted to vice chairman which apparently satisfied him:

> Mr. Schubert . . . said he had never viewed himself as the leading candidate. Mr. Schubert added that the "clear intent" of Mr. Foy's choices for promotion "is to develop the strongest possible team concept" (Sease, 1980b: 6).

This is scarcely the only instance in which positions and titles have been created in order to bring into a coalition various interests within the organization. The win-lose aspects of organizational politics can be downplayed and more support and commitment generated for the adopted policies either by proliferating positions or by rotating subunits through them in a predetermined fashion.

There is a clearly tremendous need for the systematic investigation of coalition behavior within organizations. It seems evident that coalitions and alliances are important in the exercise of power and in the making of decisions within organizations. For the analyst of organizational power and politics, it would be useful to know more specifically under what circumstances these alliances form and when and how potential coalitions become activated. The formation of coalitions requires the information that one participant's interests are coincident in some important respect with another's. Indeed, it is probably the lack of knowledge about the preferences and beliefs of others within the organization that constitutes a major barrier to the formation of coalitions. One of the functions of informal social communication networks within organizations is the exchange of this type of information so that when decisions arise, the process of searching for allies is facilitated. If this is the case, then another component of political skill is a knowledge of subunit perceptions and positions on decision issues within the organization. It is not only important to know the distribution of power; it is also critical to know how the various participants stand so that alliances can be formed.

Cooptation

The development of coalitions takes the position of the parties on the questions at hand and attempts to build and mobilize support on the part of those who agree with the particular organizational participant involved. By contrast, cooptation involves an attempt to change the position of powerful social actors so that they favor the particular subunit's interests. Cooptation is an old and time-honored strategy which occurs across organizational boundaries. Thus, for example, bankers are brought onto the boards of firms that face financing contingencies (Pfeffer, 1972), and media representatives are brought onto the board of public utilities (Pfeffer, 1974). Cooptation is useful, however, to obtain support within organizations as well as across organizational boundaries. The typical way of coopting interests within organizations is through establishing committees. We shall consider the issue of committees in organizations in a subsequent section, but first it is necessary to understand why and how the process of cooptation works to build support.

Cooptation involves giving a representative of the organization or subunit whose support is sought a position on a board, committee, or other body of the unit seeking the support. At the organizational level of analysis it typically involves placing the representative on the organization's board of directors or on an advisory board or board of trustees. Studies of boards of directors (Pfeffer, 1972; Pfeffer, 1973) have indicated

166

that their size, composition and function can be explained by considering the organization's requirements for obtaining various types of environmental support. Within the organization, cooptation may involve establishing a committee and placing persons from groups or interests to be coopted on that committee.

As an example, at a large, prestigious state university in the early 1970's the administration came under increasing pressure over its treatment of women. The university had actually lost a relatively small equal pay case because of its differential compensation of janitors and janitresses. It was under investigation for its hiring and compensation of women faculty members, and concern was also being expressed about the equitability of the funding for women graduate students. Under pressure from a variety of groups over the same issue, the university established a Committee on the Status of Women, complete with stationery, office space and a quarter-time research assistant. The attempt was clearly to coopt the various interests making demands on the university and gain some access to high-level university administrators. In this case the strategy was reasonably effective. The group, which was comprised of students, women faculty and women non-faculty employees had enough differences in emphasis among themselves that they were often diverted by their own internal politics. Of even more importance, they were reluctant to risk their new-found position of legitimacy by pushing too aggressively to have their demands met. Although the pressures did not disappear, the protest was in many ways bureaucratized, which made it much less strident and easier to handle.

Cooptation is so often effective because it exposes the coopted representatives to informational social influence, and confronts them with conformity pressures and the necessity of justifying their actions. Cooptation provides labels and expectations that increase identification and commitment to the organization, gives the representatives a stake and legitimate position in the organization, and motivates them to be interested in the organization's survival and success.

INFORMATIONAL INFLUENCE

The position of a group member on a decision making committee will, if nothing else, bring to the person's attention different information than if the person were not on the committee. To continue with the Committee on the Status of Women example, persons once appointed to such a committee began to become familiar with information which indicated the limited pool of qualified applicants in many of the scientific disciplines. They became familiar with the actual search activities that had been undertaken and with the various applicants that had been uncovered. They became familiar, on a personal basis, with many of the key decision makers in the university. Through this they came to see that these gentlemen were reasonable, intelligent persons who were trying to manage the university to maintain its quality and stature, while still attending to a variety of other interests and demands.

Informational influence is an important way of changing an individual's perceptions and attitudes. This is particularly the case when the individuals are brought together not with like-minded persons, as in the instance described, but rather into a group of others who possess somewhat different beliefs about the world. As Festinger (1954) argued, when physical reality was not present, persons developed their perceptions and beliefs through a process of informal social communication. Beliefs, attitudes and judgments are anchored in reference groups (Smith, 1973), and through cooptation, a new reference group and a new source of information and judgments were provided to those so coopted. When exposed to others with a different set of views on the organization and its operations, one is likely to be less sure of one's own position. If the coopted individual is somewhat lower in status than the others with which he or she is dealing, it is even more likely that the person will tend to identify with and respect the new reference group and come to share at least some of its views. This influence process can proceed even more rapidly to the extent that the representative is relatively isolated from the group being represented. Constant contact with those not coopted will tend to keep the representative more in touch with their original positions. One of the functions served by isolating union-management bargainers during labor negotiations is that the negotiators have to deal with each other and come to understand each other, without the influence of their principal organizations. A similar type of phenomenon can occur in the process of cooptation.

CONFORMITY AND SELF-JUSTIFICATION

Pressures for conformity in group settings are related, but at the same time somewhat different from informational social influence. Many individuals find it difficult to maintain very discrepant opinions in a group setting, particularly if they are the only individuals with such beliefs (Asch, 1958). Such conformity to group pressure, observed in line-estimation tasks, is even more likely when the issues involve beliefs and attitudes that are much more socially and less physically anchored. There are pressures to conform to the group, and the tendency to avoid conflict and argument would also lead the coopted representatives to downplay their differences with the majority for the sake of harmony and peace in the decision situation. These pressures, coupled with the informational social influence deriving from the fact that the individuals are being exposed to new information which is consistently being interpreted by others as supporting another position, are likely to lead the individuals involved to moderate their positions in the group setting.

Once more moderate actions are taken in closer agreement with the position of the others, then the individuals have to make sense of their new behaviors. Bem (1972) and others have argued that attitudes and beliefs frequently follow action, with the behaviors being used as a way of determining what the individual's perceptions must be. Of course, the use of behavior to infer beliefs and attitudes is more likely to the extent that the behavior was taken voluntarily and publicly (Salancik, 1977a). Decisions and discussions within the committee or board are public within that group and thus constrain the individual involved, at least in that context. As for the sufficiency of the external justification, although the person could potentially admit that he or she went along because of group pressure for conformity and group influence, such an explanation is certainly not ego-enhancing and has some negative implications for one's behavior. Rather, it is easier and more likely to argue that one now has new information and has seen the old actors in a new light; having acquired these new insights, one's position on the issues has been changed because of this new information.

Having gone through this process of behavior and commitment to the behavior, the coopted individual is now, in fact, a believer in the position adopted. Therefore, the distinction between public conformity and private agreement which has troubled researchers on conformity for some time (e.g., Kiesler and Kiesler, 1969) may not be empirically significant; once public conformity has been obtained under minimal explicit external pressure, private agreement will probably follow.

LABELING AND EXPECTATIONS EFFECTS

When a person is appointed to a committee or board, the affiliation may be publicly announced and, in any event, the individual becomes associated and at least partly identified with this new affiliation. Thus, one becomes a member of the Committee on the Status of Women, a member of the personnel committee, a member of a given organization's board of directors. This affiliation, particularly to the extent that it is made public and visible, helps to shape the expectations others have for the person's behavior as well as the individual's own expectations. The fact of labeling, by creating certain perceptions and expectations, can create changed behavior, attitudes and beliefs as a consequence of the labeling.

Miller, Brickman and Bolen (1975), in an experimental context, demonstrated that the attribution of neatness to classes of school children was more successful than attempts at persuasion in producing behavior that was neater. These same authors report similarly significant improvements in mathematics test scores after the attribution that the students were facile in mathematics. There is an extensive literature on the self-fulfilling prophecy and its effects (e.g., Livingston, 1969; Archibald, 1974). Although the literature is now less clear in its findings and interpretations than it once was, the effects of expectations, labeling and role definition acting together can be reasonably argued to produce a change in behavior of the person in the new role.

When one is on the board of directors of a corporation, or the personnel committee, etc., others behave differently toward you. This, in turn, leads to new behaviors from the individual which are consistent with the new role, Behaviors can be viewed as interlocking cycles (Allport, 1962; Weick, 1969), in which each action calls forth a certain interaction and the cycle continues so that over time behavior patterns become stable and hence predictable. At the same time, a new role leads to new types of role demands and role expectations (Kahn et al., 1964), and in turn these role pressures also tend to alter behavior to make it consistent with the role. The very newness of the role is likely to arouse the individual's uncertainty, leading to a receptivity of informational social influence concerning what are appropriate and inappropriate behaviors in the new position.

In these ways, the very positioning of an individual with a new title in a new organizational context immediately sets in motion forces that will tend to produce changed behavior and behavior that is consonant with the new role and the new labels and expectations. A person on the Committee on the Status of Women can scarcely be expected to engage in militant demonstrations, for such activity would be inconsistent with her official position in the organization and the various accoutrements than follow from that position. A person on the board of an organization could scarcely be expected to oppose the interests of that organization, for the individual is personally identified with the organization, and by extention, its success and failure. Thus, cooptation binds the person to the organization by providing new roles, new expectations, and a label that produces behavior consistent with the newly acquired affiliation.

COOPTATION AND RESOURCE COMMITMENTS

The final thing that cooptation does is to provide the coopted individual with a stake in the organization and his position in it through the provision of various kinds of resources. A person receives director's fees for serving on a board of directors, as well as status from the association and the title. An individual receives status from being on the personnel committee, as well as perhaps a feeling of power and control over the organization's hiring and promotion. And as noted earlier, the Committee on the Status of Women received stationery, office space and a research assistant, as well as official recognition. Both symbolic and monetary rewards, as well as other resources, may accrue to the individual coopted.

These resources, the status, fees, feelings of power and influence, raise the individual's aspiration for more and become a base from which the person judges his or her progress and success. Then the individual is not likely to risk offending the organization for fear that the position will be lost and with it the various symbols and resources that have made the individual so comfortable. Thus, the Committee on the Status of Women was reluctant to risk offending the administration for fear of losing its access, official position, stationery, office and research assistant. If it seems impossible to understand how individuals can be coopted and be trapped by relatively small benefits, recall the discussion of developing dependence in Chapter 4. Moreover, the symbolic value and the feelings of power reflected in these resources may be the critical elements binding individuals to the organization and making them reluctant to risk the displeasure of those with more power.

COSTS OF COOPTATION

Like most organizational strategies, cooptation has its costs as well as its benefits. The two primary costs are the loss of secrecy and the loss of control. Those coopted in an organization will acquire, as a consequence of their new position, more detailed information on the organization and its workings than they previously had access to. A person placed on the board of directors suddenly learns many more details about the organization's financial condition, its market position and its strategies. A person placed on the personnel committee may acquire previously secret information about salary levels, evaluations, and background data on organizational members.

We have already argued that information is an important source of power in organizations. This is clearly going to be the case with information that is so important that it must be kept secret. Thus, there is an implicit bargain made in the coopting relationship. The coopted interest is given information and hence more power, but in return there is the expectation as well as the activation of the mechanisms noted before that the individual will act in the best interests of the organization.

171

Indeed, the very act of providing access to the previously unknown may have as much symbolic importance as anything else. The person may be awed by the responsibility of knowledge and may be even more susceptible to the influence mechanisms of cooptation due to the fact of being taken into the confidence of others with power in the organization. It is as if the possession of certain information forms a common bond serving to unite others who might in different circumstances be opponents rather than allies. Yet, it must be recognized that as effective as it is, cooptation is not inevitably or invariably successful, and the coopted participant can have substantial impact on the organization through the release of secret information.

In the early 1970's, at the time of the Cambodian incursion during the Vietnam War, students broke into the administration offices at Stanford University and ransacked the files. Among the items they came up with was a distribution of salaries by rank and department, which they promptly proceeded to publish in the student newspaper. Needless to say, there was considerable turmoil caused by the comparison of salaries by departments and by the ability of persons within departments to see where they stood on the salary ladder. It is this kind of disruption caused by the release of secret information that is a threat when an outsider is brought onto a board or committee within the organization.

The second cost involves the actual relinquishing of some degree of control over decisions to the coopted party. After all, although the representative may be influenced by others, he or she can also influence them. Membership brings with it voting and decision making power that may not have been possessed before. Selznick's (1949) analysis of the Tennessee Valley Authority illustrates nicely how in an effort to coopt interests to gain increased support, the coopting organization can itself be transformed. The TVA was a New Deal agency established in a conservative, agrarian part of the country. In order to obtain the support of the local agricultural interests, boards were established to advise the authority on various development programs. Selznick reported that these boards were successful in obtaining the support of the local elites, but in the process the mission and operations of the TVA became somewhat diverted, and served the economic interests of those who already possessed power and money, and became somewhat displaced from its original objectives.

The loss of control is, of course, greater the more individuals from outside the dominant perspective are brought onto a committee or board within the organization. Thus, to some extent the size and composition of the coopting vehicle can be managed to lessen the extent of control loss. Nevertheless, the loss of some voting and decision making power is almost an inevitable consequence of pursuing a strategy of cooptation.

Just as is the case for many processes in organizations, cooptation represents a process of mutual influence. Those brought onto the board or committee are influenced by the dominant position already in power in the organization. However, at the same time these new interests obtain information and voting that gives them increased power and control as well. In most cases, cooptation tends to be effective in bureaucratizing and diminishing protest against the current power structure. And the development of representative boards and committees ensures the symbolic legitimacy of the decision process and outcome as well as helping to obtain the commitment of those within the organization to the decision. In this way, cooptation is an important mechanism through which coalitions and consensus become developed within organizations.

Committees

One frequently used vehicle for coopting various internal interests and building legitimacy and support of decisions is the use of committees. Although committees are ubiquitous in organizations, there has been little systematic analysis of their use, size or composition. The existing literature relevant to committees is, however, consistent with the perspective adopted here.

Lippitt and Mackenzie (1976) defined what they termed authority-task problems as incongruities between the authority system and the task role system in an organization. Their investigation sought to examine the conditions under which administrators confronted with an authority-task problem would adopt one of the following strategies: passing the buck; hiring a consultant; forming a committee; using an existing committee; or solving the problem themselves. Nineteen administrators at the University of Kansas worked on ten hypothetical cases to produce information on the conditions under which committees would be formed. Committees tended to be used when there were problems of decision acceptance, informational problems, when it was not feasible to hire a consultant, pass the buck, or when no standing committee existed. Interestingly, though not referenced in the Lippitt and Mackenzie article, their conditions used in a mapping function for committee formation (1976: 650) parallel quite closely the Vroom and Yetton (1973) work on individual versus group decision making. Much like the university administrator study, Vroom and Yetton argued that consultation or group decision making was required primarily to overcome problems of limited information and to gain an acceptance of and commitment to the decision reached. A critical variable in the Vroom and Yetton formulation, not considered in the Lippitt and Mackenzie study, was whether or not those participating in the decision process could be trusted to act in the interests of the overall organization. In the Vroom and Yetton model, group decision making tends to be used only when the decision is relatively inconsequential, in the sense that there are many acceptable outcomes, information is limited, acceptance of the decision is problematic and those participating in the decision situation can be trusted to act in the organization's interests.

From our point of view the critical variable in both formulations is the emphasis on the use of group decision making or committees to increase decision acceptance. Both formulations suggest that committees are used when decision acceptance is problematic. Decision acceptance is likely to be troublesome, it could be argued, when the problem being worked on is not one susceptible to technical rationality; when there is no clear right or wrong answer, something besides the obvious correctness of the analysis must convince those involved to accept the decision. One such condition would be if the interests of all the participants would benefit from the decision. However, in many cases some will benefit while others will lose. Thus, decision acceptance is likely to be problematic and as a result, committees are used when there are multiple interests which are not coincident when working on a problem for which there is no clear, correct or incorrect answer—in other words, when the issue is political.

In turn, the committee must be large enough to represent the various conflicting interests and must be comprised of representatives from the various constituencies potentially affected by the decision issue. Since size is often associated with the development of differentiated perspectives arising from role specialization (Meyer, 1972), one would expect to, in general, observe a positive association between organizational or subunit size and the use of committees within the unit. Committees become necessary also because it is impossible to have all of the individuals in the unit participate as a collectivity; the committee provides a way of feeling that their interests are being represented without direct involvement.

If the preceding arguments are correct, then the reason why committees are frequently slow to act and frustrating for their members becomes clear. Committees are created in those situations in which there is no clearly agreed upon technology for finding a generally acceptable or correct solution. Thus, committees are created and used in just those decision situations in which it is going to be the most difficult and problematic to arrive at a decision. In such a circumstance it is hardly surprising that the committee would take a long time to reach any kind of decision, or that the discussions and disagreements evidenced at the meetings would become uncomfortable for those involved. This feeling of frustration is particularly likely given the belief in rationality that pervades most work organizations. As a consequence, persons come to committees not only joining a difficult decision making situation but, furthermore, with a set of beliefs about the operation of decision processes which are likely to be violated as a very necessity of the purpose of the committee.

Committees serve other functions besides the representation and cooptation of interests. Committees are forums for the pulling together of expertise (Davis, 1969), as well as mechanisms for coordinating interdependent activities within organizations (Galbraith, 1973). In developing a theory of committee use, size and composition, these other factors must be accounted for. Nevertheless, committees are frequently used, it seems, as mechanisms for attempting to build consensus, or if not consensus, at least legitimacy for the decisions and actions undertaken in the organization (Pfeffer, 1977a).

Anything that increases the heterogeneity of interests within the organization will tend to increase the use and size of committees. In academic departments, the extent to which there is a well-developed, scientific paradigm characterizing the discipline, and the extent to which faculty are homogeneous in background and training can decrease both the size and need for committees. Since common cultures come also from socialization and time together as a collectivity (Ouchi and Johnson, 1978), committees are also likely to be smaller and less prominent in organizations in which the members are longer-tenured; the shared understandings and beliefs that develop from interaction over a long period of time make the need for the formal representation of interests, as through a committee, less necessary. Heterogeneity and length of time together are variables that can be defined in various forms and kinds of organizations. And, as suggested elsewhere (Pfeffer, 1981), the concept of paradigm, too, can have corporate analogues.

Given that committees are established to legitimate decisions and provide outlets for the expression of various interests, the important aspect of committees in organizational politics is not their function as much as their very existence. It is the process of cooptation, the process of interest representation, and the process of meeting and conferring which is critical in providing acceptance and legitimacy of decisions.

These processual aspects may be as important as the substance of the decisions actually reached.

The use of committees in organizational politics raises another important, but unexplored issue: to what extent does the use of committees actually change decisions from what would have been predicted by considering the power-dependence relations existing within the social structure? The literature on participative decision making has wrestled with the issue of the extent to which participation involves an attempt to produce commitment to previously chosen courses of action or whether the participation involves an effort to affect the nature and presumably the quality of the decisions reached. In the organizations literature, clearly the issue of whether or not committees affect what is ultimately decided is critical for understanding the role and function of committees in organizations. Equally important is the question of the extent to which committees actually develop more commitment to the organization and its decisions through their cooptive and symbolic representational functions.

Though these questions cannot be answered very definitively on the basis of present research, two clues can be provided. First, in the studies of university resource allocations described in the preceding chapter, one did not need to know whether the decisions were made by committees or by the administration in order to predict the results. In both instances departmental power, along with bureaucratically rational criteria, affected the final choice. And second, the very ubiquity of committees in organizations may speak to their utility as mechanisms for legitimating the use of power and politics in organizations. Thus, paradoxically, the criticisms of committees so frequently heard in organizations in the context of their continued use, speaks both to the fundamentally political nature of many organizational decisions and to the important function of committees in coping with and managing the organizational politics involved.

In this chapter, we have reviewed some political strategies and tactics that have two major purposes: to make the decision making process appear to be rational and, thus, legitimate, and to obtain additional support for the subunit's position on important and contested organizational issues. The social value attached to rationality and the rational process requires the selective use of objective criteria in the contest over positions. At the same time, the usually unwavering belief in knowledge, information, and expertise makes the use of outside expertise an important political weapon in political contests. In considering how additional support is mustered, two types of tactics were seen:

176

cooptation, through the use of participation, committees, and other forms of involvement in the decision process; and exchange, in which policy commitments or, at times, positions are bargained either explicitly or implicitly for future support. As in other exchange systems, power comes from the relative dependence positions of those involved. Therefore, the strategy of promoting the unobvious choice, or someone who is at best marginally qualified for a job, ensures those doing the promoting of a faithful follower.

In describing the legitimation of decisions and the mobilization of support, the role and use of language, ceremonies, rituals, and symbols becomes increasingly important. Indeed, the management of meaning in organizations, through processes of paradigm or shared belief creation, is one of the critical tasks confronted by managers in organizations. We explore this issue in more detail in the next chapter.

CHAPTER 6

POLITICAL LANGUAGE AND SYMBOLS: MOBILIZING SUPPORT AND QUIETING OPPOSITION*

I n 1980, after much debate, lobbying, and hue and cry, the Congress passed and President Carter signed into law the "Windfall Profits Tax," which at the time was estimated to raise about $227 billion over the next ten years. A year before, a tax increase of similar magnitude had been approved to provide funds for the Social Security System. The oil tax was ostensibly designed to return to the government some of the money the oil companies would receive through the decontrol of oil prices on domestically produced oil. In fact, as virtually every analyst pointed out, the tax had nothing at all to do with profits. It was a form of excise tax, as it was based on the price of oil. There is some substantial debate in the economics literature as to whether or not all forms of corporate tax are shifted to the consumer, but there is widespread agreement that excise taxes almost inevitably fall on the consumer. How had it been possible to get support for such a massive tax increase, at a time when there were tax-cut and tax reform movements growing around the country?

Suppose the tax had been called an Excise Tax on Gasoline, or the Oil Products Sales Tax, or the Oil Price Increase Tax, any of which might have been of equal accuracy. How can anyone object to taxing the profits of the big oil companies, particularly if the profits are "windfall"

---

*This chapter is drawn heavily from Pfeffer (1981).

179

profits, as contrasted with "hard-earned" or "deserved" profits. The labeling of the tax as a tax on windfall profits, even when most of the people involved knew it was no such thing, had a powerful effect. It helped to create an atmosphere in which the tax could be passed, in spite of substantial industry opposition.

This example from the national political scene is illustrative of what occurs all the time in organizations; language, symbols, rituals, and ceremonies are used to manage the process by which actions and events are given meaning. The process is managed in such a way as to provide legitimation and a supporting structure for the desired behaviors and actions which are to be carried out within the organization. I have suggested elsewhere (Pfeffer, 1981) that one of the most important functions of administrators is the development of common understandings about the world within the organization. This function serves to legitimate the organization to its external environment (Dowling, 1978) and to increase the commitment of those within the organizational coalition. Political language and political symbols are instruments for use by all who contest the organization's decisions.

To understand the role of political language in organizational politics, it is necessary to understand the following things. What is the relationship between beliefs, norms, and attitudes generated around activities and decisions, and the activities and decisions themselves? Are they as loosely coupled as is implied by the oil tax example? How is it possible for organizational participants to be taken in by the labels or symbols associated with events? Can't organizational members understand why and what is going on? How is symbolic action taken in organizations? What language, symbols, settings, and ceremonies are used? It should be emphasized at the outset that the study of symbolic activity and the use of political language in organizations is not very advanced. Thus, we will offer more in the way of examples, hypotheses and suggestions than hard evidence.

The Relationship Between Outcomes and Attitudes

Decisions are made, resources allocated, people promoted, and strategies begun in organizations all the time. It is important to distinguish between these substantive outcomes, with actual referents and consequences, and the attitudes, beliefs, norms, and values which are generated around them. The two may be loosely coupled, and probably are in most organizational contexts. This means that decisions can be rationalized with little regard to the actual specifics of the decision. For instance, Chaffee

(1980) found that in spite of the emphasis on rationality and the use of program quality criteria, resource allocations at Stanford were predicted from many of the same variables, such as departmental power and student enrollments, that had accounted for allocation outcomes at Illinois and the University of California. Yet, because of the decision making process and apparatus in place, the process was perceived as being much less political by the participants at Stanford.

Organizations are social systems which are populated by individuals who come with norms, values, and expectations, and with a need to develop an understanding of the world around them. These understandings are necessary to provide enough predictability for individuals to take action, and enough legitimacy and rationality associated with the action, to make it justifiable and meaningful.

The requirement for legitimacy affects the context of the causal explanations for organizational events. Because of the norms, values, and expectations that individuals bring with them from the larger society into the organization, they are not indifferent to the type of explanations which are given to make sense of the organizational world. For instance, in the attribution theory literature, Kelley (1971) has noted that persons seek to develop theories which are not only accurate but also provide a feeling of control over events. A preference in favor of interpretations of individual power or efficacy colors the explanations for events developed within the organization. Gergen (1969), in commenting on the criteria for the acceptance of social theories, noted that although consistency with the data was desirable, theories have continued to exist in contradiction to the data, and that tastes, preferences, and values also governed the theories of behavior. Organizations thus can be viewed as systems of patterned activity in which the participants attempt to develop and convince others of rationalizations and explanations for these patterns of activity. The explanations which are developed are constrained to be acceptable in the social context, and there is, in addition, a preference for explanations that provide feelings of control and justice.

In the political process within organizations, the task of the various political actors is to develop explanations, rationalizations, and legitimation for the desired activities and choices which are themselves frequently resolved through the use of power. Some of these concepts have been defined previously in the development of a social information processing perspective on the determinants of attitudes toward work:

The term "rationalize" refers to any situation in which a
person's action is described with reference to some supporting

181

*reason or cause. The term "legitimate" refers to one criterion
by which rationalizations are selected from the many possible
explanations for action. Justifications or rationalizations are
selected primarily when they are acceptable explanations in a
given social context. This means they fit with the facts as
known according to the rules of behavior generally followed
(Salancik and Pfeffer, 1978a: 231).*

Political actors provide justifications and rationalizations that justify
proposed decisions. These justifications serve to ensure support both
inside the organization and from external groups, in that they are consistent with social norms, values, and expectations for organizational
activity. The task confronting political actors has been described as one
of justifying and legitimating choice. The choice itself may be principally
the result of the power and dependence relationships present in the
situation. Substantive organizational actions, by which we mean actual
decisions and choices with observable, physical referents, are largely
predicted from circumstances of power and dependence. The task of
those who benefit from these decisions is to legitimate and justify them,
to render power less visible and to provide justification for others acced-
ing within the organization.

Commenting on political analysis, Edelman noted (1964: 12):

*Political analysis must, then, proceed on two levels simultane-
ously. It must examine how political actions get some groups
the tangible things they want from government and at the
same time it must explore what these same actions mean to the
mass public and how it is placated or aroused by them. In
Himmelstrand's terms, political actions are both instrumental
and expressive.*

The argument advanced here is that political actors use language on the
expressive level to impact the attitudes and beliefs of organizational
participants. Substantive, instrumental results are determined by the
distribution of power in the situation.

The symbolic and instrumental aspects of organizational political
activity are clearly linked, but they are only imperfectly related. Choices
or decisions may precede the development of explanations or justifications, just as behavior frequently precedes the development of the attitude consistent with that behavior (Bem, 1972). Also, the link between
the justifications and explanations for choice and the choices themselves

can be loose, just as there is a far less than perfect correspondence between attitudes and behavior, even after the behavior has occurred. Of course, under external prompting (Salancik and Conway, 1975), behaviors can be explicitly made salient and one can thereby force a closer correspondence between attitudes and behavior. If the contradictions between the content of the justifications and legitimations and the content of the decisions are made more apparent, then those who are engaged in the political process may invest more effort in making sense of and explaining the decisions and choices.

In Figure 6.1, the relationship between symbolic and substantive outcomes and political language and power-dependence relationships is displayed. The argument is that political language operates largely with and on symbolic outcomes and sentiments, such as attitudes, beliefs, and social perceptions. At the same time, the conditions of power and interdependence, which characterize the social context, operate to affect the allocation of positions, budgets, and other substantive resources and decisions. In each case the linkage between the adjacent concepts is loose. There is some link between substantive allocations and the sentiments about those decisions and choices, but the linkage need not be strong. Similarly, the political language employed to justify and legitimate the effects of power and dependence may not only be imperfectly correlated with the actual results, but may, in fact, be intentionally designed to obfuscate the actual operation of power.

The argument is that there are two distinct levels of analysis of organizations. One level involves the prediction of actions taken within the organization, such as decisions that have observable, substantive

	Substantive Outcomes (allocations or decisions with physical referents)	Sentiment Outcomes (feelings, attitudes, beliefs, perceptions or values)
Power-Dependence Considerations	Large effect	Small effect
Political Language and Symbolic Action	Small effect, except as strategies affect the mobilization and use of power	Large effect

Figure 6.1
The Relationship Between Substantive and
Sentiment Outcomes and Power and Political and Symbolic Activity

183

outcomes. The second level involves the perception, interpretation, and sentiments which surround these organizational choices. Considerations of social power are relevant for predicting organizational outcomes on the first level, the pattern of resource allocations and strategic choices that are made. However, because of norms and values that exist in the organization, it is the task of the various political actors to make these outcomes of power meaningful and legitimate.

The task of political language and symbolic activity is to rationalize and justify decisions that are largely the result of power and influence, in order to make these results acceptable and legitimate in the organization. In fact, without this legitimation and rationalization, the exercise of power is hindered.

Consider, for instance, the following example. My colleague George Strauss was serving on the budget committee at Berkeley during the period Bill Moore was doing his dissertation research on power and resource allocation at the university. One day George said to me, "Why should I waste all these hours in deliberation with this committee on the allocation of the budget, when we can just plug the figures into your regression equation and predict almost perfectly what we are going to come up with anyway?" Reflect, for a moment, on the difference between budget allocations which emerge from a long, deliberative process in which there has been heavy involvement of a faculty committee, and the same allocations which are produced by running a mathematical model which includes departmental power as one of its terms. It is clear that in the first case, the results will be accepted much more readily, and cooperation and interaction within the organization will be much more readily maintained than in the second case. The fact that the two sets of numbers are identical does not matter. The process, the ideology, and the symbolism surrounding their production is what affects how they are perceived.

The view developed here and elsewhere (Pfeffer, 1981) is that language and symbolism are important in the *exercise* of power. It is helpful for social actors with power to use appropriate political language and symbols to legitimate and develop support for the decisions that are reached on the basis of power. However, in this formulation, language and the ability to use political symbols contribute only marginally to the development of the power of various organizational participants; rather, power derives from the conditions of resource control and resource interdependence. It is possible that those who have emphasized the role of language and political symbols have confused the exercise of power with its foundations. Two points relevant to this issue can be made.

Edelman (1964; 1971; 1977) emphasized the role of language in the broader societal political process. Edelman believed that political language and symbols are useful for mobilizing support and quieting opposition among those who are not proximately connected to and have relatively smaller stakes in the political process. His argument implies that the political participants with more resources and more access get largely what they want from the process, and use language and symbols to provide expressive outcomes to others in the society. This argument is parallel in structure to the one made here with respect to the outcome of organizational political processes.

It is also necessary to consider under what conditions political language and definitions of situations will be accepted. In some sense, anyone can assert that a given resource is more critical, a given constraint or contingency more important, a given technology, or action-consequence sequence, more appropriate and more accurate for the organization, a given set of implicit objectives more consonant with the values and beliefs of the larger social context, and so forth. Indeed, assertions such as these are made all the time in the course of political activity within organizations. Academic departments with larger enrollments assert the primacy of the teaching function, its consonance with environmental beliefs about education, and its criticality within the organization. Departments with distinguished research reputations make the same claims about their specialized competencies. Anyone can assert claims for competence and importance. What language-based analyses of power fail to answer is how these competing claims become resolved. Clearly, the organization's history and culture are important. However, those units which can provide resources, or resolve problems that are more critical for the other subunits and for the organization as a whole, are more likely to have their definitions of the organizational situation accepted. The conflicts in advocated organizational paradigms are resolved through the use of power; it is difficult to see how conflicting belief systems can be also sources of power in the organization, except as they serve to legitimate positions and link them to other sources of support.

The Social Nature
of Organizational Realities

The ability of political language and symbols to provide legitimation and reassurance in decision outcomes, as well as to legitimate and justify these outcomes derives, in large measure, from the inherently social nature of organizational reality. In other words, it is possible to affect feelings about decisions and actions independently of the actions themselves, because of the socially constructed nature of organizational reality. This means that while events have physical referents, such as patterns of promotion, budget allocation, and so forth, the meaning of these events is open to a social interpretation. It is this interpretation that determines how the outcomes of organizational politics are perceived and what various actors feel about the justice, as well as the legitimacy of the decision results.

Numerous authors from a variety of disciplines have noted the inherently social nature of much of organizational reality. Although the physical factors of the organization, such as work hours, pay, the location and content of task activities, promotions, and the distributions of resources and perquisites within the organization, constrain the extent to which events can be reinterpreted and reconstructed, these realities are far from binding in the determination of beliefs and attitudes. Salancik and Pfeffer (1978a) noted that the content and dimensions of jobs, for example, were partly the result of perceptions that were subject to social influences. In an experimental test of this idea, O'Reilly and Caldwell (1979) gave students two conditions of a task involving the processing of admissions files. In the unenriched task condition, the students merely recorded information. In the enriched condition, students had more decision making authority. The authors demonstrated, with a set of control subjects, that the two tasks significantly differed according to the traditional dimensions used to describe jobs (Hackman and Oldham, 1975). In the experiment, subjects randomly assigned to either the enriched or unenriched condition were exposed to information that indicated that the task was either interesting and challenging or was not. O'Reilly and Caldwell reported that job perceptions and affective reactions to the job were more strongly affected by the presumed social information than by the task itself. In a replication of this study, White and Mitchell (1979) obtained similar results.

The literature on pay equity (Adams, 1965; Goodman and Friedman, 1971) has argued that perceptions of fair, overpaid, or underpaid conditions result from a process of social comparison, so that definitions of equitable treatment are socially anchored, if not socially derived. Theories of aspiration level (e.g., March and Simon, 1958: 183) have maintained that one determinant of a person's level of aspiration, which in turn determines the experience of psychological success or failure, is the amount received by others in the individual's environment. The extensive literature on relative deprivation (e.g., Stouffer, et al., 1949) also indicates the importance of the social context for anchoring and defining individuals' perceptions of their own situations.

186

Festinger (1954) has made the general argument that when the situation is ambiguous and there are not clear physical cues to resolve the uncertainty, persons will seek to communicate informally with others. Through this process of informal social communication, a shared and more stable set of perceptions about the events taking place will be developed. Smith (1973) has noted that this process of informal social communication produces a process of informational social influence, in which what each person believes becomes dependent on the emerging consensus regarding the content and meaning of events taking place. In this fashion, the meaning of the various decisions made within an organization becomes defined and shared by the various organizational participants.

As noted in the task design or job enrichment literature (Salancik and Pfeffer, 1978a), the social environment can provide several forms of influence over perceptions of the legitimacy and justification for decisions. First, the environment may provide cues as to which dimensions might be used to characterize the decisions which are made. The determination of whether one focuses on the equality of the distribution, the relationship between decisions and goals, or the relationship of the choice to social norms, is partly under the control of a social environment in which some values and decision properties are discussed, and others are ignored, and are thus less salient. Second, the social environment provides information concerning how the various dimensions of the decision should be weighted, whether equality is more important than equity, one set of values or goals are more important than another, and so forth. Third, the social context provides cues concerning how others have come to assess the decision on each of the selected dimensions. The determination of whether or not a decision is equitable, or whether or not it really facilitates attainment of certain types of goals, may be as much a function of social perception as of the specific content of the choice. Finally, it is possible for the social context to provide direct evaluation of the decision along either favorable or unfavorable dimensions, thus leaving it to the organizational participants to construct rationales which make sense of these generally shared affective reactions.

It is the task of those exercising power within organizations to employ social processes such as these to ensure that the results of power will be received as legitimate and justifiable. Although this is not discussed as frequently with respect to the exercise of horizontal power, the literature on leadership, or the exercise of power vertically in the hierarchy of the organization, makes clear the importance of the construction of meaningful and sensible rationales for activity. Weick (1979) has

187

noted that managerial work can be viewed as managing myths, symbols, and images, and that the manager may be more of an evangelist than accountant. Pondy (1978), in his discussion of leadership, explicitly developed the argument that the exercise of hierarchical influence or power involves a large component of symbolic activity. One of the tasks of the manager or leader involves providing a label and explanation or rationale for the activity of the organization:

> . . . *the effectiveness of a leader lies in his ability to make activity meaningful for those in his role set—not to change behavior but to give others a sense of understanding what they are doing and especially to articulate it so they can communicate about the meaning of their behavior.* . . . *If in addition the leader* can put it into words, *then the meaning of what the group is doing becomes a* social *fact.* . . . *This dual capacity* . . . *to make sense of things* and *to put them into language meaningful to large numbers of people gives the person who has it enormous leverage (Pondy, 1978: 94–95).*

The task of those who wish to exercise power in organizations is to present the advocated decisions and activities in a meaningful and sensible way to the organizational participants, so that a social consensus and social definitions around these activities and decisions may be developed. Thus, political activity in organizations involves both labeling and sense-making as well as the development of a social consensus around the labels and definitions of the decisions and actions.

This task is an inextricable part of the influence process in organizations. It is directed both internally, to produce organized and committed collective action, and externally, as part of a process of legitimating the organization in its larger social context (e.g., Dowling, 1978). In the process, external support is gathered. One of the ways of generating external support and developing external allies for a given perspective is to make that perspective appear to be consonant with the prevailing social values or with the goals of those from whom support is sought. Such external coalition building can be accomplished through explicating a paradigm of action or choice in such a way that makes the decision consonant with prevailing social expectations.

The discussion to this point about legitimation, sense-making, and coalition building has been fairly abstract, as the argument is a general one. However, three examples will be provided to illustrate how language and legitimation are used in political contests within organizations. The first two examples involve a school of business administration that has perceived itself, and is perceived by others, as being more research oriented, more quantitative and theoretical, and somewhat less professional and applied than many other such schools. The school, because of a previous decision to remain as one of the social sciences on campus, does not have a separate salary scale and thus suffers in comparison with the salaries offered at other schools of business.

The first example deals with the change in the orientation of the school. Because of the need to attract more resources from alumni and the business community, it was perceived as desirable for the school to shift, to some degree, its curriculum, values, criteria for hiring and promotion, and activities, so as to appear to be more responsive and consonant with the desires of business firms. Business firms and business alumni were deemed to be important sources of supplementary support. It was perceived to be valuable to shift orientation and emphasis away from the academic community as a reference group, toward the newer, more important constituencies from which the support was to be sought.

It should be clear that in a large and diverse faculty with various subject matter groups, this shift in orientation was likely to alter the distribution of both personal power and subunit power within the school. First, those subject matter groups that were more strictly theoretical in orientation (for instance, economics) would lose power relative to present and emerging groups such as real estate, business policy, and accounting, which had more of a professional orientation and a more immediate, monied external constituency. Second, since fund raising was centralized in the administration (it was the Dean, not individual faculty who solicited funds), there would probably be a centralization of power that accompanied these new funds and resources.

The power-dependence relationships within the school had changed as funding and resource contingencies changed in the environment. The school was to move in a new direction. But, these new thrusts needed to be legitimated. To talk about changing fundamental academic orientations for something as crass as mere money was unthinkable; in changing the direction of the organization, it was necessary to develop a legitimation that would justify the organization to its external environment as well as provide a rationalization and explanation for the change internally. Several symbols were developed. One professor developed the term, "theory based professionalism," to describe the school. Note that this conception retains the historical emphasis on theory and scholarship, incorporates the notion of professionalism, and serves to make sense of activities within and outside of the organization. The phrase, "theory based professionalism," was also used to argue that what was unique about the school was that it was both professional and theory based, in distinction to some other schools which had gone too far in one direction or the other. Thus, the external constraints and contingencies became translated into a language and rationale which justified movement in new directions. The development of the justifications and legitimation for the new activities, which included committees and reports on new subjects and new hiring criteria, as well as this political language, were critical in the process of realigning the organization with its environment. The language and symbolism provided a way for the change to occur in a more subtle fashion, and for power to shift in a less explicit and direct way.

The second example deals with how the salary situation was managed. Given a relatively cosmopolitan faculty and severe salary differentials, it was scarcely feasible to argue that the school's salaries were not, in fact, lower than those in other schools. The fact of lower salaries can have many meanings. One set of meanings revolves around the school's power position in the larger university, the decisions that created this power position, and the competence of those running the school to enhance the school's position vis à vis the rest of the organization. Needless to say, interpretations that the school had acted unwisely in the past to remain another social science department, and that the present administration was unable to remedy the lack of power in the organization, had the adverse effect of discrediting both past and present governance in the organizational subunit.

The social consensus emerged that the school had a uniquely favorable intellectual environment which stimulated research and creative thought. This environment was a product of the school's unique relationship with the rest of the campus, enhanced by its comparable, low salaries, and by its emphasis on research and scholarship to the neglect of consulting and fund raising. This social definition was developed through the continual articulation of stories and myths which illustrated its reality and by a constant repetition of the theme. In the best traditions of the insufficient justification literature (Pfeffer and Lawler, 1980), the argument was made that if persons were joining and remaining in an organization that offered fewer extrinsic rewards, then it must be the unique, intrinsically rewarding atmosphere which served as an attraction. Note that the interpretation provided might be a conscious and strategic reinterpretation (or, perhaps, misinterpretation) of cause-effect relations. The real cause of the lower turnover might have been the geographic area and not any intrinsic quality of the school.

With this shared definition of the situation, the power of those currently in the administration or allied with that dominant coalition could be better maintained. One justification in attacking the competence or the strategies and values of those in power was the relatively resource-poor position of the school. However, with the shared perception that the resource-poor environment was actually causally related to the school's intellectual environment, the issue was nicely finessed, and a cause of complaint was turned into an advantage. One other thing should be noted. It is easier to socially construct perceptions about an intellectual environment as opposed to salary levels, as the former is less precisely defined and assessed than the latter.

The third example illustrates what happened when a set of administrators failed to effectively explicate an organizational paradigm or shared perception. The organizational subunit in question became easy prey for those who opposed it and sought its resources. In the early 1970's there was a great deal of controversy surrounding the School of Criminology at the University of California at Berkeley. After discussions, debates, and demonstrations, the recommendation was made in 1974 to close the school, and after further demonstrations and protests, the school was closed. Many reasons were given for the closing, including the failure of the school to develop a professional constituency, its radical faculty and students, and the fact that in a time of decreasing resources, faculty and administrative positions were eagerly sought for reallocation to other subunits. Of the three reasons which were provided in a report on the closing of the school, one clearly relates directly to the failure to develop a defined and shared language which described the school and justified its activities:

> Second, the faculty of Criminology has been unable to agree on its educational objectives or to provide a stable and systematic curriculum that reflects a broadly shared view of the field. These weaknesses may be attributable to the state of criminology generally, but it appears that continuing disagreement within the faculty has prevented the establishment of common goals and would continue to do so (Committee on Educational Policy, 1974: 2).

The failure to develop a shared language which rationalized and justified the subunit's activities made the school vulnerable when it was perceived as being weak in scholarship and without outside constituency support. The point is that in the presence of strong external support and a reputation for outstanding scholarship, the school would probably not have come under attack, particularly if the resource environment had not also become more difficult. When the attack came, the issue of an articulated justification and legitimation for the program became an important determinant of the final outcome. Without explanations and justifications for the activities that were widely shared and well known in the social context, the program was left without a defense against the more powerful and more academically oriented departments which claimed that criminology was an illegitimate area of study as practiced at Berkeley at that time.

The argument is that power, born in large measure from considerations of resource interdependence, becomes used in political contests in which the definition of the situation itself is problematic and in which the legitimation and justification of advocated positions becomes crucial in the contest. This approach departs somewhat from the perspective of those who have argued that the resource-dependence and social constructionist views of power are unrelated at best (e.g., Pondy, 1977). The position taken here is that power, which is derived from strategic, resource-based considerations, is employed in part in the definition of social realities and justifications for activities that are consistent with the position of those with power. The development of alternative perspectives, paradigms, rationalizations and justifications for activity represents an additional arena in which the play of power and politics can be observed.

The Role of Political Language

In the political activity of developing justifications and rationalizations for activities and points of view, the use of language is critical. As noted in an often quoted passage, "Sharing a language with other persons provides the subtlest and most powerful of all tools for controlling the behavior of these other persons to one's advantage" (Morris, 1949: 214). Pondy has written, "Language is after all one of the key tools of social influence" (1978: 91). In the examples just described, the importance of language and labeling is evident. The development of the term, "theory based professionalism," was critical in justifying to those within and outside the organization the sense of the business school's new activities. And, the labeling of a resource-poor environment as intellectually stimulating, facilitated maintenance of both employee commitment and faculty support of the administration. Indeed, if politics involves the exercise of power, then language is one of the critical elements of political activity.

Perhaps no other analyst has devoted the amount of attention to the role of language in the political process as Edelman has. Although his work treated language in the broader political arena, the view of organizations as coalitions in which power and politics are critical determinants of decisions, which is taken in this book, makes his work on politics generally applicable. Edelman (1964: Ch. 6) saw language as a catalyst for focusing and developing interests and points of view. He wrote, "Political argument, when it is effective, calls the attention of a group with shared interests to those aspects of their situation which make an argued-for line of action seem consistent with the furthering of their interests" (p. 123). If politics involves the rationalization and justification of those courses of action desired by the power holders, then language is the vehicle through which this justification occurs. Language can mobilize support by convincing others of a commonality of interests, thus enhancing the coalition building process. Language provides the justification for action necessary for the legitimation of political choices.

Edelman made two other points about language which are crucial for understanding the role of language in organizational politics. First, language is an important substitute for the use of raw power or brute force. "Force signals weakness in politics, as rape does in sex. Talk, on the other hand, involves a competitive exchange of symbols, referential and evocative, through which values are shared and assigned and coexistence attained" (1964: 114). Language is used to provide meanings and justifications for desired choices so that the use of power is not as necessary and when it occurs, it is much more subtle and indirect.

A second, and related point, is that Edelman saw political language as clouding analytical processes. Political language was seen as symbolic language, which was evocative and motivating, but did not produce an accurate assessment of self-interest. Edelman argued that political speech was a ritual which dulled the critical faculties rather than sharpening them (164: 124). Thus, the use of language in the political process was viewed as a way of providing symbols rather than substance to participants who were not closely involved in the political process and who had relatively little power. This theme emerges quite clearly in his treatise on the war on poverty programs (Edelman, 1977), in which the argument was developed that social policies served primarily symbolic value while substantive activities continued to serve those with substantial power. Edelman saw the political process in terms of two sets of actors, those with a dominant position and clearly defined self-interest, and those who were more removed from the centers of authority and control who had limited interest in and knowledge of political activities.

The substance of decisions served the former group, while the latter was placated with symbolic language and ritualized actions. The parallel to formal organizations is direct, with the dominant coalition (Thompson, 1967) being the vested interests, and employees, shareholders, customers, and the public being those with limited power who receive primarily symbolic outputs from the organization, although in any specific instance, some portion of these groups might have substantial contact and power.

PLANNING AND RATIONALITY AS THE RELIGION OF FORMAL ORGANIZATIONS

The arguments developed thus far suggest that political language is necessary and useful to justify and legitimate organizational decisions and thereby make the exercise of power less overt and more effective. In the development and use of political language, the intention is often to make the use of power unobtrusive, and to make a political decision process appear to conform to the widely shared social values of rationality and justice. The use of rational analysis and planning in formal organizations can, in many instances, be viewed as the development and use of political language to accomplish the justification of decision outcomes, while at the same time making the politics producing the decision less salient. Indeed, it might be suggested that beliefs in the value and efficacy of analysis and planning constitute ideologies, which are like religions in formal organizations. These ideologies are held with conviction and are not empirically examined, much as one would not attempt to empirically demonstrate the existence or non-existence of God. The belief in the value of rational decision procedures and planning, coupled with the belief in their use as the foundation of organizational decision making, provides a common ideology linking together members of a given organization and uniting participants of formal organizations. These ideologies help to hide the use of power and legitimate decision outcomes.

This is not the first time that this point has been made. Kramer (1975), in writing about the analysis of public policies, made a similar argument:

> *Apparently, analysis is used primarily to justify actions that are based on political predilections . . . the techniques used and the emphasis on quantification give the results of analysis a "scientific" appearance—an appearance of value-free rationality at work (Kramer, 1975: 509).*

According to Sargent (1972: 1), an ideology is "a value or belief system that is accepted as fact or truth by some group." It is an inter-related collection of beliefs that provides those who believe with a comprehensive world view or perspective. These beliefs are, in Brown's (1978) terms, reflective of different organizational paradigms. One of the important functions of such an ideology or world view is to provide a way of simplifying a complex reality, of providing a "feeling of orderliness and rationality that is valued" (Kramer, 1975: 511). Certainly, the use of rational decision procedures and planning provides those in the organization with a feeling of orderliness and control. More importantly, these procedures are consistent with dominant ideologies and serve to legitimate the decisions reached *and* tend to obscure the use of power and politics that may underlie the decisions.

One can consider, on a broader scale, the response of the U.S. government to the escalation in medical costs. Through a series of bills, a large planning apparatus (and, indeed, a planning industry) was established as a legal requirement. When confronted with a problem, the response was to establish planning. At that point, although it was never stated quite this abruptly, one could argue that the actions and policies taken were "good" and "effective" because they were planned. Planning was established so that actions could be said to have been planned by the planners, and therefore, carry the imprimatur of technological rationality and hence, legitimacy. A similar situation exists with respect to city and county planning, where the planners busily write plans to accommodate the growth and development policies that result from the interplay of local politics. Yet, this activity is necessary so that decisions, when they are reached, can be justified by recourse to the plan, the planners, and the planning process.

Though some business organizations may not be quite this political, it is clear that in many instances strategic plans are developed to rationalize and legitimate the embarked-upon strategic course. However, with the plan, the planning and the planners, the strategic decisions with their resource allocation results are less open to question. Some authors have noted that, in times of increasing resource scarcity or organizational retrenchment, the size of the administrative component does not decrease as fast as those parts of the organization which are more proximately connected to the delivery of goods and services, and may actually increase in size (Freeman and Hannan, 1975). One reason given for this is that those in power are not likely to be quick to cut their own staffs and their own positions. This is clearly an important part of the explanation, but is only a part of it. The other argument is that in times of

195

retrenchment and scarce resources, political contests and struggles are likely to be more intense than when resources are more plentiful. Then, more administrators, planners, and analysts are required to produce the documents and political language needed to justify the decisions being made. When resources are more munificent and there is less politics, there is less requirement to veil the use of politics with rational analysis and planning, because there is less politics to hide. It is when power and politics come into prominence that the tasks of legitimation and rationalization increase in both scope and importance, creating a need for more analysts, planners, and administrators.

The implications of this line of argument are reasonably clear: "There is no way to expunge . . . ideology from policy analysis, but we must take off the mask of objectivity that often covers the face of analytic work" (Kramer, 1975: 514). In the analysis of decision making in organizations, it is necessary to empirically consider the possibility that rational decision procedures and planning are part of a ritualized ideology, used to legitimate and partially obscure the actual choice processes that are taking place. Considering these activities from such a perspective provides new hypotheses and insights into the use and extensiveness of them. If nothing else, it suggests reading the sociology of religion literature rather than normative economics and operations research in order to understand decision and planning techniques.

Why Political Language and Symbolic Action Are Effective

The argument was developed earlier that reality was, at least in part, socially constructed and that one part of the political process within organizations involved the development of legitimation for decisions that provided both justification for the actions and a common frame of reference within which these policies were discussed. Legitimating the results of organizational power and politics involves the taking of symbolic action and the use of political language. As Edelman has more generally suggested in the case of political programs, some persons receive tangible benefits and others receive only symbolic outcomes from and within organizations. Much of the organizational action which is associated with decision making is ritual and ceremony. For this to be both true and effective, it must be the case that at least some portion of the persons involved in the decision process must be unable to discern with any certainty what they are obtaining from the organization. In other words, symbolic outcomes will suffice if those in contact with the organization are unable to discriminate between reality and symbols. It is in this case that symbolic action is effective in legitimating decision outcomes and quieting opposition.

A symbolic outcome or the use of political language involves some action taken or a statement repeatedly made, even when the underlying facts and decisions remain unaltered. Of course, sometimes the symbolic changes and the use of new terminology accompany changes in actual allocations or strategies, in which case one can say that substantive as well as symbolic changes have occurred. Some years ago, the employment service in the state of California changed its name to the Human Resources Development Department, to reflect the national Labor Department's emphasis on training and imparting job skills to the hard to employ. When that phase became outdated, the Department changed its name again, to Employment Development Department (EDD). Consulting studies done for the department during this period reveal that in terms of the department's actual operations, there was virtually no change. Rather, if Human Resources was the label needed to attract federal and state funding, then human resources it would be. After human resource development became passé, the department took a title which reflected its development of employment, rather than merely serving as an employment service (State Employment Service). In several U.S. firms, ethics committees comprised of directors and/or executive officers of the corporation have been established, and in some instances, codes of ethics have been issued. In at least some of the firms, the amount of attention and enforcement given to these ethical policies is minimal. Rather, the symbol of the corporation's involvement and interest in ethics is presumed to be sufficient. Interestingly, one firm that is associated with providing funding for the study of business ethics, Levi Strauss, has been the subject of several price fixing complaints, associated with illegal resale price maintenance practices. Casual observation suggests that Levi's public relations around the corporate ethics issue dominates the public's perception of the firm.

The language of meritocracy is hallowed in most firms when discussing the determinants of promotions or raises. One is assured repeatedly that performance matters, seniority is not that important, and currying favor with the boss and other forms of ingratiation are not rewarded. Most accept these statements when they are made repeatedly enough without further investigation. I can recall a personnel director who was shocked to find the overwhelmingly high corre-

197

lations between years of service in the company and pay and the very low relationship between pay and any indicators of performance such as employee evaluations. All this took place in a company where pay for performance was one of the critical mottos.

Political language and symbolic action can be effective for several reasons. Individuals or groups within the organization may have uncertain, unstable, or undefined preferences. Organizations may engage in practices which, consciously or unconsciously, make those in contact with them susceptible to informational influence. Actions may be taken to systematically avoid providing data that would facilitate assessment. Those engaged in the political process may be unable to discern what outcomes they are obtaining or the value of these outcomes. Symbolic outcomes may also be all that are desired by those making demands of or within the organization.

THE NATURE OF PREFERENCES

One reason why symbolic political language may be both appropriate and sufficient is that parties in contact with the organization may have unclear preferences for organizational decisions. March (1978) expanded the critique of the rational decision making literature from a concern with cognitive information processing limits to rationality to a concern with the nature of preferences. In contrast to theories of choice that dominate the economics and decision sciences literature, March argued that preferences may emerge as a consequence of action rather than guiding action *a priori,* a point which was also developed by Weick (1969) in the discussion of retrospective rationality. Preferences may be uncovered and discovered through actions. Analogously, preferences may be discovered through what one obtains from organizational decisions. A person may not know how much of a resource he or she wants, how rapid promotion will be evaluated, how one will respond to the hiring of a given colleague, or the embarking on a new line of business, until these decisions are made and their outcomes perceived. If preferences are relatively unstable or unformed, then it will be difficult for social actors to assess whether or not they are being satisfied by the outcomes of the political decision process occurring in the organization. Satisfaction or dissatisfaction with decisions, and the legitimacy and justifiability of these decisions, can be much more readily assessed if and when preferences are formed in advance of the decision. Given an unclear idea about what is wanted, it may be difficult to discriminate symbolic language from substantive outcomes.

SUSCEPTIBILITY TO
ORGANIZATIONAL INFORMATIONAL INFLUENCE

As discussed previously, informational social influence is particularly potent in uncertain circumstances, and describes the process by which individuals seek to find referents for their attitudes and actions from their social environment. Unsure of what to do, persons look to those around them for guidance. By their very nature, organizations separate individuals from previous reference groups and provide them, at least initially, with very uncertain and tension provoking stimuli.

Most organizations are physically separate, if not in another building, at least in a separate office. To enter Stanford University, for example, is to physically withdraw from the surrounding Palo Alto community. The organization may be reasonably self-contained, in the sense of having a cafeteria, rest rooms, library, reading room, and even recreation facilities. Thus, during one's working time, there is little contact with others outside the organization, except for employees in boundary-spanning roles such as field sales. As Dornbusch (1955) has noted in his discussion of the socialization of Coast Guard recruits, physical separation is an important factor in the process.

Most organizations are also unfamiliar, in the sense that the surroundings, space, and required activities and interaction patterns may be different. To some extent this novelty and unfamiliarity is increased by things such as specialized language, abbreviations, codes used within the firm, uniforms or customary modes of dress, unusually spacious or imposing office facilities, and so forth.

Thus, it is reasonable to presume that new entrants to the organization will be uncertain about what is required of them, as well as somewhat anxious because of the novelty of the surroundings, and their separation from the rest of the world. In such circumstances, the likelihood is great that the person will be reasonably susceptible to informational social influence, and to seeing the world as it is defined by those in the immediate environment. It is not surprising that at the time of entry, there may be particular susceptibility to believing the various stories, symbols, and political language which exist within the organization. Once the person is in the organization, future perceptions will be shaped by those initial impressions. Although cynical knowledge is certainly shared within organizations, it is important not to overlook how the very novelty and uncertainty of entry into the organization can create a predisposition to informational social influence which would tend to make the use of symbolism and political language even more effective.

199

AVOIDANCE OF ASSESSMENT

Even if preferences are well formed, political language may be sufficient to satisfy some social actors if assessment of the decisions is difficult. One of the interesting aspects of many organizations is the effort undertaken to systematically avoid assessment or the release of information that would make it easier for participants to perceive their status in relation to that of others in the organization.

Meyer and Rowan (1977) have noted, for instance, that educational organizations in the U.S., such as public school systems, have attempted to avoid the assessment of the educational product. Publication of test scores by schools on standardized reading and mathematics tests was, at least in California, initiated by the legislature over the opposition of the educational establishment. As of this writing, assessment at the level of the individual teacher or classroom has still been resisted. Schools are not the only organizations that have taken pains to avoid the collection and dissemination of data that would make the assessment of decisions or outcomes feasible or easy. Hospitals avoid the publication of mortality or morbidity figures, universities steadfastly avoided the collection of placement data for doctoral students in the humanities and social sciences, and police departments seldom publicize the proportion of serious crimes that they solve.

Non-profit or governmental organizations are not the only ones that engage in such behavior. One could do an interesting case study of the implementation of various Securities and Exchange Commission reporting requirements for business over time, with business often opposing these disclosures at each stage. Things such as line of business reporting, making 10-K reports available to shareholders, the publication of historical and quarterly data in annual reports, the inclusion of lease and other long-term obligations, fuller disclosure of adverse legal actions, and more explicit and detailed information about executive compensation, are relatively recent inclusions in required financial disclosures.

The issue of pay secrecy illustrates one instance in which the non-release of information can help forestall opposition and create support for organizational policies and values, primarily because their actual implementation is not known. In many organizations, the amount paid depends not only on the individual's hierarchical level but also on the person's departmental affiliation, as will be discussed in the next chapter. There are two comparisons that can potentially lead to feelings of dissatisfaction and questions of the legitimacy of organizational pay systems. There may be a perceived illegitimacy or inequity in the pay accorded to different hierarchical levels (Martin, 1981), and there may be concern over the discrepancies in pay across departments. The publicness of these pay differentials makes them more salient and useable as arguing points about the justice and justification of organizational decisions. By keeping pay secret, one can never be sure about the hierarchical differentials, and thus, one is less likely to argue about their fairness. Because of the secrecy, these differentials are not as likely to be salient and therefore important to the organizational participants. Instead of continually contending over the validity and legitimacy of various kinds of reward differentiation, many organizations have adopted a policy of making it difficult to find out what other individuals and subunits receive. This helps to forestall conflict within the organization and challenges to present organizational reward practices and those that implement them.

One strategy for avoiding assessment, then, is simply to keep secret the information necessary or useful for evaluating organizational decisions. However, since some assessment of the legitimacy of organizational decisions is likely to be desired, a related strategy involves the selective release of information which is defined along criteria chosen by those making the decisions, measured along criteria which are more readily controlled by those in the dominant coalition, and still acceptable to those interested in the organization and its decisions. One such strategy is to release information with numerous indicators of inputs and not to release information about process and outcomes. For instance, hospitals, although refusing to divulge risk-adjusted mortality and morbidity, are willing to disclose figures on staffing ratios, capital equipment ratios, the proportion of board certified physicians, the number of services provided, and other indicators of input resource intensity. Schools report decisions in terms of their effects on the proportion of teachers with advanced degrees, the average per pupil expenditure, equipment per pupil, and average class size. Note that in these cases, it is easier to manage the input resources than to actually affect results, which may require a knowledge of the technology, or the connection between actions and results, which is simply not possessed. These indicators of input resources come to be defined as levels of effort, and are substitutes for more specific knowledge about either process or outcomes. In the absence of clearly measured outcomes or defined preferences, decisions are assessed by their goals rather than by results. Edelman has written, "Willingness to cope is evidently central. Any action substitutes personal responsibility for impersonal causal chains and chance" (1964: 79). And George Gallup, quoted in Edelman (1964: 78), noted, "People tend to judge a man by his goals, by what he's trying to do, and not necessarily by what he accomplishes or by how well he succeeds." Organizational choice processes are treated similarly and are judged by their apparent goals and values, not by the political process that produced them or by their actual results. So, an organization that tries to provide the best input resources can scarcely be faulted, or even assessed, by how those resources are allocated or what they accomplish.

The use of secrecy and restriction of access to some information, while at the same time providing other, more controllable and more favorable information, is a practice that is supported through the development of various rationalizing mythologies which justify the practice. Myths have been defined as generally unquestioned, widely taught, and shared beliefs about the world. The myths that justify the non-release of decision or results data are numerous and are tailored to the situation. The release of student achievement data or the use of such data in evaluation, it is maintained, will tend to direct the educational process to teach for proficiency on the tests, rather than to produce broadly trained young citizens. The release of salary data might engender unnecessary internal competition. The release of medical outcome data may fail to take into account the uncertainty of medical service delivery technology. In the practice of organizational politics, the usefulness of keeping secret information that might facilitate social comparison processes is great enough so that resources are devoted to the development of ideologies justifying such policies.

UNCERTAINTY ABOUT RESULTS

Related to the issues of undefined preferences is the problem of ambiguity concerning the decisions made and the results of those decisions. This uncertainty may result from a social definition of expertise and professionalism which maintains that the client, customer, or organizational participant is not qualified to determine either what he or she wants, or to evaluate the quality of the decisions that are made on his behalf. This professionalism is fundamentally a political process which accrues power to those in the organization so designated as professional, as the very designation places the definition of satisfaction in the hands of those being assessed (Benson, 1973). Expert status can convey to those so annointed the right and the duty to define acceptable decision criteria. By doing this, experts define for others in contact with the organization what their beliefs should be.

Such a process may be used in the maintenance of power by those higher in the organizational structure, in a strategy which turns Weber's (1947) theory of bureaucracy on its head. Weber argued that one basis

202

of promotion should be technical expertise, so that those higher in the organization have the knowledge to evaluate and coordinate the work of their subordinates. This presumed association between hierarchical level and expertise is used to assert expertise as evidenced by hierarchical level. This expertise, once asserted and accepted, is used to argue that those in the organization who challenge the control of the administrators do not have the requisite competence, understanding, or perspective to make such claims. On a horizontal level of analysis, socially conferred and legitimated expertise, such as that possessed by lawyers and accountants, causes them to have more power in the organization because of their ability to use that socially conferred legitimacy to argue for a definition of decisions and results that can serve their own interests.

Even in the absence of such professionalization, evaluation of what is received may be difficult because organizational decisions have multiple attributes. A product design decision may have price as well as quality implications, and quality itself may be measured along many dimensions. Education costs resources and has, as its results, levels of reading, mathematics, and skills in other subjects, as well as socialization into widely shared values and patterns of conduct. The multi-attribute nature of the assessment process makes the assessing of who has gained what from decisions difficult. This uncertainty concerning the evaluation of decisions is increased by the presence of undefined or ambiguous preferences, and by the ability of some individuals to selectively define and present information relevant to the decision. Even in the absence of these latter two factors, the multi-attribute nature of organizational choices may make the assessment of substantive consequences more difficult than the average person or group, with limited contact and limited dependence and time, can or will deal with.

THE VALUE OF SYMBOLIC LANGUAGE

If the assessment of decisions is problematic because preferences are unformed, information is hard to obtain, and even if obtained, requires complex multi-attribute trade-offs, then a reasonable position may be to rely on surrogate measures of the organizational benefits derived from organizational choices. Such benefits may include the symbolic actions and symbolic language taken in response to the claims of some organizational participant. These symbolic responses may be desirable either because that is all those in contact with the organization really desire, or because they are incapable of discerning symbolic action from substantive decisions, due to limited time and information.

Downs (1957), in an effort to explain why small but committed interests could get policies implemented that were inconsistent with the preferences of the majority, argued that for most people, the choices in question were of little enough importance so that voting and other expressions of political preference would not be primarily affected by politicians' responses on that single issue. However, this was not the case for the smaller but more interested group for whom the specific policy might have substantial consequences. Downs was able to derive, using a rational economic approach, the result that it was not just the number of people who favored or opposed an issue that determined the outcome, but also the intensity of concern. Edelman, using a different mode of analysis, came to the same conclusion. "The fact that large numbers of people are objectively affected by a governmental program may actually serve in some contexts to weaken their capacity to exert a political claim upon tangible values" (Edelman, 1964: 43). Both Downs and Edelman maintained that a large number of persons who share limited concern in the outcomes received are probably going to be unwilling to invest the time and energy required to monitor outcomes and to attempt to exert influence. For these social actors, symbolic responses may be sufficient to assure quiescence, as there is little incentive to look beyond the symbol or the language, given the limited concern over the outcome in question.

A similar argument is applicable in an organizational context. Symbolic responses may be sufficient because, in the absence of the ability to specify precisely what is desired or to assess the multiple dimensions of organizational choices, interests in the organization may only desire some reassurance that their concerns are being taken seriously. In this case, a symbolic response conveys the information that the organization is responsive, and the gesture itself may be reassuring. Most students, for instance, have neither the time nor the inclination to get heavily involved in the running of universities. When they protest against investment policies, resource allocation practices, or faculty evaluation procedures, a symbolic response which reaffirms their power in and importance to the organization can convey a sense of efficacy that reassures them of their power in the organization. The symbol of response and power may be the surrogate for the substance, and may suffice to provide reassurance about the power of an organizational actor. The ratification of one's position and power in the organization may be the primary objective of the political activity in the first place.

In a large manufacturing firm, the personnel and industrial relations department felt relatively powerless. Among the things that persons in the department complained about was that even though they were ostensibly responsible for internal training and personnel development, the operating departments regularly put training expenditures in their budgets, and sent managers to off-site training programs without the advice or approval of the personnel department. The operating departments, for their part, tended to feel that they could best select those courses that were most relevant to the specifics of their operations, and were reluctant to lose the discretion they had enjoyed over training funds and their use. The response of the chief executive was to delegate to the personnel department the task of developing and updating a catalogue of training opportunities which included information on cost, evaluations, and specific program content. The operating divisions were left with the actual discretion to choose the ones they would attend (and, in fact, very little change in past practice was observed). The activity of developing and publishing this internal documentation of training provided the personnel department with the feeling of involvement in the planning and direction of training, as well as giving them some informational influence. This involvement was sufficient to provide reassurance about their power in the organization. Interestingly enough, those persons interviewed in the personnel department not only did not know if the publication of their document affected the operating departments' decisions, but made it clear that in a number of subtle ways, the employees in their department avoided finding out.

Thus, symbolic language may be effective in organizational politics because preferences are undefined or ambiguous; assessment may be avoided through secrecy of relevant information; there may be uncertainty about the dimensions of choice; and symbolic responses may be all that are desired, given the limited aims of various organizational actors. These factors, taken together, suggest that political language can be effective in quieting opposition or mobilizing support in many instances. "It is not uncommon to give the rhetoric to one side and the decision to the other" (Edelman, 1964: 39). Political language helps to not only legitimate the decisions reached, but also to give those that have fared less well in the decision process beliefs about the process and its results which produce a commitment to the decisions and support of the organizational political process.

Mobilizing Support and Quieting Opposition

The effects of political language on mobilizing support and quieting opposition have already been described in several instances. The development of phrasing that made sense of new directions in educational policy served to quiet opposition to the change in a school of business, while the failure to develop a rationalizing language helped in the demise of a School of Criminology. The point is that political and symbolic language can have real consequences. Actors respond on the basis of perceptions and sentiments, even when these perceptions and sentiments have been produced through evocative symbolic language. Symbolic action can have consequences for the motivation and mobilization of support, the diversion or satisfaction of demands, and the implementation of policies in organizations. These ideas will be expanded to provide some additional detail on the use and consequences of symbolic action in the context of organizational power and politics.

MOBILIZATION AND MOTIVATION

Political language may serve to motivate and mobilize individuals within the organization as well as those outside the organization. In a study of job enrichment versus job enlargement programs, King (1974) observed that the consequences of the programs on employee attitudes depended much more on the language and expectations surrounding the change than on the substance of the change itself. In the job enrichment conditions, jobs were actually changed to incorporate more autonomy, variety, and challenge in the tasks. In the job enlargement conditions, the jobs were expanded but the additional duties did not significantly alter the discretion, variety, or challenge already present in the job. Cross-cutting these two changes were two expectations manipulations. In the high expectations manipulation, there was a great deal of talk about the likelihood of success of the new program and how beneficial it was. The low expectations condition had less overt language describing the likely positive benefits and the good things that were to come out of the program. King's results, albeit derived from a relatively small sample of treatments, provide support for the position that it is the language describing change that can affect the results of the change. Furthermore, this language and the expectations produced by it can have substantive outcomes as well as affect sentiments and attitudes.

The so-called "Hawthorne effect" is another example of the mobilizing and energizing potential of symbolic action. The effect refers to the phenomenon of individuals who, when subjected to observation, change, and special treatment, responded with higher levels of performance, regardless of the content of the changes implemented. The effect was first observed in the classic Western Electric studies in which productivity improved regardless of the changes in illumination level that were tried. Although there is some question about the scientific validity of the conclusions that were most often drawn from these original studies (e.g.,

206

Carey, 1967), it does appear that the Hawthorne effect is a real phenomenon present in many situations. Change signals that individuals are to be considered and treated differently. This signal of increased attention and importance can motivate more action and different actions on the part of organizational participants.

Participatory decision making and cooptation provide more general examples of the effects of symbolic action. As discussed in the last chapter, one of the consequences of placing a representative from a group or organization on another organization's board is that this signifies the affiliation symbolically and thus presumes the support of one organization for the other. This mutual identification can lead to expectations and labeling effects that serve to reinforce the ties between the organizations. Involvement of some constituency in decision making, even if the involvement is symbolic rather than actual, can have effects on developing commitment to the decisions that are reached (Salancik, 1977a). Unfortunately, most studies of decision making participation do not distinguish between the effects achieved through provision of real involvement in the decision process and the effects obtained through the symbolic identification of some participants with the decision process. The argument can be made that it is the symbolic identification with organizations or decisions, as much as real choice and participation, that produces commitment and action on behalf of the organization and its decisions.

SATISFACTION OF DEMANDS

Symbolic language may serve to mollify groups that are dissatisfied with the organization, thereby ensuring their continued support of the organization and diminishing opposition and conflict. A symbolic gesture can be productive in generating social support for the organization, to the extent that these results are obtained.

Edelman (1964; 1977) has described the creation of administrative agencies in these terms. The creation of a regulatory organization may convince some individuals that action has been taken to monitor and control organizational activities. Groups that formerly were adversaries of the particular organization are quieted through a belief in the efficacy of that administrative apparatus. Complaints about the conduct of lawyers leads to the establishment of bar association committees on judicial ethics which have the formal responsibility of disciplining errant lawyers. Similar problems and responses are observed in the medical and accounting professions. General political support for a profession can continue, as the problems of professional malpractice and misconduct are presumed to be remedied by the boards or agencies created and labeled as coping with the problem. The fact that few lawyers, doctors, or accountants were ever disciplined, almost regardless of the grievousness of their misconduct until very recently, indicates that it is the symbolic action rather than the substantive outcomes of the action that may suffice to ensure continued political support.

Analogous responses can be seen within organizations. Universities establish ombudsmen to handle student complaints about grading and classroom procedures, privilege and tenure committees to protect professors from administrative capriciousness, and grievance mechanisms for students to deal with issues ranging from sexual harassment to program content. In each instance, the aggrieved group may be quieted by the appearance of an administrative structure to deal with a problem, regardless of whether or not the administrative procedure really can provide protection for the group in question. Indeed, because of the importance of these various political symbols for maintaining legitimacy and satisfaction, administrators in organizations are likely to invest a great deal in the maintenance of the appearance of the use of these administrative bodies. An example in a university context illustrates this point.

In the early 1970's, an assistant professor in the School of Criminology at Berkeley was denied tenure. The professor had been active in the People's Park demonstrations in the late 1960's and in other protests and reform efforts. The professor claimed that in the tenure decision he had been denied due process and that his various political, extra-university activities had been held against him. In an investigation conducted by the campus Privilege and Tenure Committee, there was evidence that there were news clippings of his various involvements, including a false arrest which subsequently resulted in his winning a cash suit for damages from the university in his personnel file. The committee, on the basis of this, concluded that the possibility existed that the professor's rights had been violated. The response on the part of the administration was to appoint a special ad hoc committee to investigate the issue further. The committee was appointed by the campus administrators (the other was appointed by the Committee on Committees, a faculty body) and concluded that there had been no denial of due process. With that, the denial of tenure stood. The important thing to note is that even though the power clearly lay with the administration at the campus level, care was taken to provide the appearance of faculty involvement and faculty governance. To ignore without some symbolic response the work of the faculty committees would be to show how completely ritualistic and powerless these committees might be in the final analysis. This, in turn, might have aroused the faculty to attempt to take power back from the administration. Thus, the procedures used were employed to maintain the appearances of the propriety and usefulness of the administrative structures, which were carefully established to provide the symbolic reassurance of shared power. There was a willingness to spend more time and effort in the resolution of the issue rather than to destroy the credibility of the administrative structures and processes which had been carefully established in order to quiet and reassure sources of opposition.

Business firms, too, make similar responses, by establishing consumer affairs departments (Fornell, 1976), consumer hotlines, affirmative action offices, and offices of public affairs (social responsibility). All of these subunits can be used to provide evidence that the demands of various constituent groups are being heeded. After all, the very establishment of a department to handle a given problem can be taken as evidence that the problem is being taken seriously, and steps have been taken to resolve the issue in an effective fashion. In this way, symbolic responses become used and accepted as evidence of more substantive compliance with demands. There have been virtually no empirical studies on the effects of symbolic responses on quieting demands and ensuring continued support, or at least, quiesence from organizational participants; such studies are clearly both possible and desirable.

The firing of managers, such as in professional sports (Gamson and Scotch, 1964), provides a classic example of a ritual political activity which has consequences for public perceptions of organizational responsiveness and concern for performance. One interesting test of the effectiveness of this response in a sports context would be to see whether or not attendance improves upon the firing of a particularly hated coach or manager, and especially whether or not this improvement in attendance is greater than might be predicted from team performance after the change. In business, Chrysler's stock price rose immediately after the previous managers were replaced and Lee Iococca was brought in from Ford to run the company. There was much discussion in the press about how Chrysler dealers were content and would now be more likely to stay with the organization, and how employees in the various divisions and plants felt better about the company and its chances after the change. Clearly, disaffection and unrest were quieted by the change in leadership, at least for a while, and it is likely that initially, higher commitment and effort on the part of some may have occurred. In general, it is difficult to obtain support with the same organization and individuals that were previously the objects of criticism. A change, particularly at the top, can convey symbolic affirmation of the hoped-for improvement which can generate new support, while quieting previous complaint and opposition.

209

IMPLEMENTATION

The use of political language and symbolic action in the process of implementation has been recognized in an analysis by Peters (1978). He argued that symbolic behavior was not only useful in accomplishing change, but that such an approach to implementing change might be more effective than traditional techniques such as management or organization development, strategic planning, or organizational redesign. Cohen and March (1974), in an analysis of university presidents, derived some rules of action for operating in a political environment in which rules and procedures are unclear and power is shared. Peters built from these rules to develop a perspective on the implementation of change in organizations. Some of these techniques of implementation and their use of symbolic action are detailed in Table 6-1.

TABLE 6-1
Symbolic Administrative Actions and Why They Work

Action	Explanation for Effect
Spend time on activity that is to be emphasized or defined as important	Time spent is one measure of the importance of a goal and goals and objectives become the reality defining managerial action; also time spent conveys to others the importance of the focus of the time.
Change or enhance the setting	A new setting conveys that something new is going on; an enhanced setting will convey the meaning that the activity now occurring is more consequential and important.
Exchange status for substance	Symbolic outcomes may be sufficient to ensure support of a relatively uninvolved group for the proposed action, if the conditions facilitating symbolic action are present.
Interpret history	Events have meaning only through interpretations; interpreting events as consistent with the definition of the problem or the solution can help develop a social consensus around the chosen course of action.
Provide a dominant value expressed in a simple phrase	Language can evoke support or opposition, can serve to organize social consensus, and can provide an explanation and rationalization for activity.

Adapted from Peters (1978)

210

The interpretation Peters provided of successful managerial action taken to change organizations is consistent with the emphasis on political language and symbolic action developed in this chapter. He maintained that ". . . managing the daily stream of activities might be said to consist of the manipulation of symbols, the creation of patterns of activity, and the staging of occasions for interaction" (1978: 9).

Political language and symbolic action, as we have seen, can have consequences for the mobilization and motivation of support, for cooling off or placating opposition either inside or outside the organization, and for organizing activity within the organization around the issue of implementation. The focus on political language and symbolic action is useful in helping to explain how the processes of power and politics become legitimated and accepted in organizations, and how political behavior comes to have effects and legitimacy within organizational contexts. As Peters has argued, ". . . symbols are the very stuff of management behavior. Executives, after all, do not synthesize chemicals or operate lift trucks; they deal in symbols" (1978: 10).

The Methods of Symbolic Action: Language, Ceremonies, Symbols, and Settings

We have described the role of political language in legitimating decisions, obfuscating power relationships and political strategies, and helping to produce shared meanings and definitions of organizational reality which serve to mobilize support, diminish opposition, and assist in the implementation process. This chapter concludes with a discussion of four complementary ways in which symbolic action is taken and political language expressed. One productive research task involves taking each of these general strategies, and delineating specific examples of each. Then hypotheses could be developed and tested concerning the conditions associated with the strategies' use and the circumstances under which each is likely to be effective in mobilizing support and quieting opposition to decisions. To this point, there has been little empirical comparative study of these forms of symbolic action and political language, but this type of comparative analysis is clearly feasible and necessary to further understand the use of political language in organizational politics.

The four general forms of symbolic action are language, ceremonies, the use of symbols, and settings. In each instance, the examples presented should be considered illustrative rather than exhaustive of the type of behaviors possible. The four categories themselves are heuristically useful as a way of cataloguing the forms of political behavior observed in organizations in the attempt to create shared beliefs and legitimated meanings within the social structure. No claim is made for the comprehensiveness of the classification, but only for its diagnostic utility.

LANGUAGE

In the legitimation and justification of decisions, power structures, and organizational practices, evocative symbolic language is an important technique. Though not recognized or at least not frequently publicly admitted by its principal practitioners, much of organization development operates through the use of language to connote therapeutic change taken in the interests of those whose commitment is being mobilized or whose opposition or powerlessness is being quieted. Ouchi and Price (1978) recognized the importance of organization development for using language to develop a shared set of meanings or understandings within the organization. They noted, ". . . a philosophy of management provides a form of control at once all pervasive and effective because it consists of a basic theory of how the firm should be managed. Any manager who grasps this essential theory can deduce from it the appropriate response to any novel situation" (1978: 42). Consequently, Ouchi and Price argued that organization development should be focused on developing a shared philosophy or culture within the organization, and further implied that organization development tended to be successful only when this direction or result was observed.

These shared philosophies and cultures are created through the development of shared systems of meaning and belief, or shared organizational paradigms. In this endeavor, the development of a common language which sets the organization apart, and conveys in an evocative and emotional way the uniqueness of the organization, is useful if not critical. One might predict that major, successful organization development practices or programs would be successful to the extent that they were successful in using the strategies described in this chapter, and in particular, legitimating and describing their activities in ways which justified those activities and developed commitment to them.

Salancik and Pfeffer (1977a; 1978) have argued that the very theoretical model underlying many organization development activities—the need satisfaction model of human behavior—evokes language which is useful in the politics of organizational governance. It is presumed that people have needs, and that these needs are capable of being measured. It is further argued that employees are satisfied and motivated to the extent that they have the opportunity to fulfill their needs through the nature of the work itself. Then, efforts at organizational change which involve job restructuring can be described in terms of need satisfaction. Instead of arguing that changes are being made to coopt employees to increase their efforts and commitment on behalf of the organization, changes can be justified in terms of their capacity to increase the satisfaction of basic human needs. Needs assessments are conducted; jobs are analyzed in terms of their need-satisfying properties, and then changes are recommended to increase the amount of potential need satisfaction present in the work place.

This is a brilliant example of political language at work, so brilliant that I suspect some of its very practitioners may not be fully conscious of the game being played. To understand the politics of the situation and the role of language, consider the outline of three change efforts described in Table 6-2. In each case, there is an unfreezing phase in which data on the source of problems and the need for change are gathered. In each case, there is an attempt made to recommend a change that satisfies the problem uncovered. In each case, if the process has been consistent in the use of evocative language and symbols relevant to the focus of change, then the process is likely to be successful in increasing commitment and convincing those within the organization that they are being heeded and are important. The only difference is that in some cases the results of the change are more costly in terms of money or control than others.

TABLE 6-2
Stages and Language in Organizational Change

Stages	I.	II.	III.
1. Diagnosis and Unfreezing	Human needs assessment	Wage and salary allocation assessment	Hierarchical power and discretion assessment
	Need satisfaction measurement	Pay satisfaction measurement	Measurement of satisfaction with decision making power
2. Change	Redesign work to meet needs	Restructure and change salary levels to meet expectations	Restructure decision making power to meet demands
3. Refreezing and Evaluation	Do new jobs better meet needs?	Do new salaries result in more feelings of equity and satisfaction?	Does new distribution of decision making authority provide more satisfaction with decision power and discretion?

Questionnaires are an important vehicle for creating and transmitting language in this process. If the questionnaires are used in conjunction with outside experts, then they have all the advantages of legitimacy and presumed unbiasedness which are associated with the strategy of the outside expert as described in the last chapter. The questionnaires introduce terminology and cause those in the organization to begin to think in those terms and focus on those aspects. As Salancik and Pfeffer (1978a) have argued, questionnaires not only assess individual preferences and expectations, but also are important vehicles for helping to create those very preferences and expectations. The questioning process provides symbolic assurance that changes are to be made and that employee opinions are important in this process. There has been little study of the dramaturgy by which the changes are introduced into organizations. Clearly, however, the announcement of change, a change in some aspect of the organization, and the pronouncement that data from the employees as analyzed by outside experts were used in developing the change, can serve to provide the symbol of involvement, importance, and reform.

Survey-research-feedback has many of these elements. Questionnaires symbolize the importance of the individual employee while helping to define and focus the dimensions of concern. Meetings bring into being new settings which signify reform. The development of a language around the survey results focuses attention on the articulated and advocated dimensions. Salancik and Pfeffer's argument about the effects of information saliency as an explanation for the efficacy of these change approaches captures only a part of the process. It is not merely the cognitive focusing of attention that is involved; it is also the language and symbolism used which reassures organizational participants and evokes positive sentiments which are followed by commitment from them.

The importance of the choice of language in this political activity cannot be overestimated. For another illustration, consider Ouchi's (1980) description of organizations as markets, clans, or bureaucracies. In Table 6-3, we have provided some illustrative language describing positions and relationships in organizations that might be used and appropriate for the three types of settings. It is evident that an individual's reaction to a person with more authority may differ, depending upon whether that person is called a boss or supervisor or is referred to as an elder, a counselor, or a sponsor. Similarly, the rules that delimit one's freedom can be viewed differently when they are described in the language of norms, or shared beliefs about technology. Finally, one is likely to view others on one's same hierarchical level differently if they

TABLE 6-3
Language Describing Organizational Actors
and Relationships in Markets, Clans, and Bureaucracies

Market	Bureaucracy	Clan
Competitor, supplier, or customer	Co-worker	Colleague, peer
---	Boss, supervisor	Sponsor, counselor, elder
Evaluation	Contol	Feedback, direction
Laws, contracts	Rules, procedures	Norms, ways of doing things
Specifications	Objectives, standards	Goals, values, aspirations

are labeled as competitors for promotions and resources, or as co-workers, peers and colleagues.

In taking symbolic action and in the justification and legitimation of decisions, the language that is used becomes all important. Recourse to shared goals and values is a more effective way of legitimating decisions than references to the individual or subunit interests that are enhanced by some specific policy. It is important to recognize, however, that the use of political language is not limited to those on one side of an issue. In the contest over the control of the organization, all of those involved in the political process will attempt to compete for legitimacy through the use of evocative political language and legitimating symbols.

CEREMONIES

There are numerous ceremonies in organizations that provide occasions for the mobilization of support and the quieting of opposition. The occurrence of executive succession provides many opportunities to create symbolic meaning which is useful in mobilizing support and providing symbolic outcomes to various participants in the organizational coalition. For instance, the fact of involuntary succession provides symbolic ratification of the intention to change organizational operations and, presumably, the effectiveness of those operations. Scapegoating (Gamson and Scotch, 1964) occurs in organizations other than sports organizations. It is interesting to note how complaints about illegal corporate political contributions were readily diffused by the firing of the chief executive at Gulf Oil and Northrop. In the case of Gulf, it subsequently became clear that various questionable activities continued after the departure of Robert Dorsey, indicating that these practices were embedded in the corporation and were not completely Dorsey's fault. Never-

215

theless, although organizations are large and complex systems in which the control exercised by a single person is limited, demands for change and for retribution are typically satisfied by one or a few involuntary successions. These successions provide symbolic reassurance that the organization as a whole does not tolerate the deviant behavior or poor performance.

Two further points should be developed about the ceremony of replacement. First, it is conceptually possible to empirically estimate the effects on mobilizing support and quieting opposition from the act of replacement. In the case of a corporation, one could examine changes in stock and bond price behavior, controlling for the movement of the general markets and other factors, after the announcement. One could examine the short-term effects on turnover and absenteeism, particularly among those high enough in the organization to be symbolically identified with its wellbeing. It would be possible to estimate, if not to precisely measure, the hours worked by managerial employees before and after the change, with the expectation being that the symbolic act of replacement would serve to remotivate the managerial ranks, thus causing less voluntary turnover, less absenteeism, and longer working hours. Attitudinal measures might be collected which assess commitment to the organization and sentiments about the future and the organization's prospects.

Second, the ceremony of replacement is indeed a ceremony, and there are a number of steps that are typically observed. Gephart (1978) detailed the ritual of replacement of an officer in a graduate student organization, and many of the features are the same for the replacement of corporate executives or sports managers as well. Initially, there is an attempt to make the individual to be replaced more salient and more visible as a symbol of the the past problems associated with the organization. Stories may be provided to the press in which various individuals in the organization attribute problems confronting the organization to the person to be replaced. The individual may be the feature of an article in a business publication, in which the strategy pursued may be dissected. There may be public appearances before financial analysts, and in a number of ways, a person who may have been relatively anonymous becomes known and salient. Then, there is a ritual of discrediting the individual or the strategy pursued by him or her. This involves, on occasion, the production of a report or an analysis by some outside agency, committee, consulting firm, or some objective analyst or set of analysts which demonstrates to all concerned the error of the decisions that were made. Then, with a fair amount of publicity, the individual or individuals involved are dismissed. Typically the dismissal, and its accompanying presumed degradation, receive a lot more attention than the amounts to be paid under the contractual arrangements which are provided to ease the pain of the departure. Thus, the person responsible for the organization's problems is banished ignominiously from its ranks, and the publicness of the process, along with the attempt to identify symbolically the deposed individual with the past policies and performance of the organization, can provide the assurance that things will now change.

The voluntary or involuntary departure of a chief executive provides the occasion to select a replacement. The act of choosing a successor becomes an occasion for ceremony, with the appointment of search committees or the retention of an executive search firm, and with the expenditure of time and other resources on the search effort. These efforts reaffirm the importance of the position to both its potential new occupants and to others in the organization. The creation of the belief that the position is consequential is particularly important when the possibility exists that the position incumbent will need to be used as a scapegoat for organizational difficulties in the future. These ritualized activities may also be particularly necessary when the position in fact has little power or effect. The activities taken to create meaning become more critical when such meaning or belief would not otherwise emerge.

The inauguration of the successor may involve investiture rituals that further ratify the importance of the position and the incumbent and signify the new direction the organization is taking. Care is often taken to call attention to past successes associated with the new position occupant, and to distinguish the new person in background, style, and appearance from the predecessor. Again, there will be the attention to the media, newspapers, magazines, and if possible, television, and often a series of meetings within the organization in which the new individual becomes known to organizational participants. These ceremonies of firing and replacement can help to placate groups from which the organization needs support, as well as to signal change to those who work within the organization. These ceremonies are important in the symbolic reaffirmation of the power of various interests within the organization.

Meetings, also, may take on a ceremonial character, and be used to provide symbolic reassurance to an important interest, that it is indeed considered seriously within the organization. As Peters (1978) has commented, meetings provide a manager taking over an operation, particularly if he or she is from the outside, with a way of quickly setting the tone for the operation in the future. When De Lorean was promoted from Pontiac to head the Chevrolet division of GM, he recognized and used meetings to help manage the system of beliefs and expectations around his new position:

> *In trying to get hold of the Chevrolet tiger, I concluded that the best way was to examine the division personally. So I set out on a three-month study. . . . First I met with Chevrolet managers and their staffs in the problem areas—finance, product, manufacturing, sales and marketing. I wanted their personal assessment of their problems. And I hoped that, by seeking their counsel, I would show them that I was truly interested in getting at the source of Chevy's problems and in the process combat the natural hostility toward me as an outsider who was coming in to tell the people how to run their business. If the meetings were with home office personnel, as often as I could, I tried to meet in the employees' office rather than mine (Wright, 1979: 107).*

The meeting established several things very quickly: first, that this was a take-charge guy who wanted to get at the problems and solve them quickly; second, that the new manager was concerned about his subordinates and was sensitive to their power and knowledge of the operations; and third, by talking to all aspects of the operation, no group could feel left out. Very quickly, the meetings provided an introduction to the division in a way that left a favorable impression.

One can think of few meetings that serve the ceremonial function so clearly as the annual meeting of stockholders. Here is a group with potential power because of their ownership of the firm and the formal rights conveyed by this ownership, and the power to sue managers and directors for neglect and disregard of their fiduciary duties to the stockholders. At the same time, stockholders, particularly when they are relatively small in terms of share ownership and geographically dispersed, have little effective control over the operation of the organization except under extreme circumstances. Thus, individuals are asked to invest money in an enterprise in which they formally have ownership rights and claims on the loyalties of the managers and directors; these rights are almost impossible to exercise, as is the measurement of the activities of those who are presumably acting in their behalf. The annual meeting provides a nice ceremony and creates the illusion of control. Stockholders have, at this occasion, their chance to ask the tough and embarrassing questions that show who is boss; they have the right to vote for the directors who, in turn, choose the management; they have the right to receive financial reports and proxy statements detailing the compensation and transactions with insiders, as well as the legal problems confronting the corporation; and, they have the privilege of being addressed, catered to, and treated as important on this one day of the year. Regardless of whether or not the annual meeting and the associated reports and proxies have substantive effects on corporate governance, the symbolic value is substantial in reassuring the presumed owners of the corporation about their importance in it.

Indeed, the ceremony surrounding the annual meeting and the annual report is so potent that other organizations, not required by law, engage in similar activities. Schools of business have begun to prepare annual reports, and have annual alumni days in which the alumni, which are an important constituent group, can ask questions of and have contact with the administration of the school. Schools and school districts publish annual reports and have meetings in which parents can become involved. Charitable organizations, hospitals, and social service agencies have similar types of meetings and rituals. In each instance, a constituent group is convinced of the care and attention paid to it through a ceremony in which the importance of this group to the organization as a whole is carefully displayed. One might argue that the very requirement of engaging in such ceremonies and rituals belies the importance of the organizational participants so honored.

There are other examples of ceremonies that could be discussed. There are ceremonies of involvement, as in work reform efforts in which elections may be held for representatives to participate in meetings of quality of working life committees. Many committee meetings serve ceremonial and symbolic functions. Academic senate meetings in universities may be analogous to stockholder meetings in corporations, providing reassurance and symbolic affirmation of faculty power. There are ceremonies to honor loyalty and commitment to the organization, in which long-tenured employees are presented with pins and badges, or honored with luncheons or dinners. In each case the question is not just what the substantive effects of the ceremony are, but also how the ceremony is or is not useful in producing support for organizational activities by groups that have some potential power over the organization.

SYMBOLS

Ceremonies and language typically are associated with each other, and both are associated with the use of symbols, another form of political language. Organizational structures serve symbolic as well as substantive functions, and therefore become a focus for change in political contests within organizations. Although Peters (1978) argued that redesign was a cumbersome tool for organizational change, organizational restructuring shares many of the same virtues of the other change techniques he advocated. There are several ways of thinking about the organizational redesign process. One way involves taking a technical approach, and trying to produce a new organizational structure that is better able to meet the problems that have arisen in the organization. This might include additional coordination among some subunits, additional adaptability and responsiveness to market changes, or some other structural solution to an operating problem. To successfully implement such a redesign, knowledge is required about what levels of interdependence and interaction are necessary, what levels of flexibility and responsiveness are desirable, and what organizational innovations or changes can produce the desired results. Such knowledge may not be available, and if it is, it may not be widely agreed upon within the organization.

A second way of thinking about organizational redesign sees it as a symbolic, attention-focusing process. The very act of restructuring signifies a change in the organization's operations, which may satisfy the demands of clients or customers, owners, or some other group which was previously unhappy with the outcomes being received from the organization. The creation of new subunits with new titles permits emphasis to be given to new aspects of the organization's operation. A restructuring which creates a new product development department, a new consumer affairs department, or a public relations department provides a visible manifestation to those inside and outside the organization that the activity just annointed through the creation of a subunit has become more important to the organization. In this way, the creation of a subunit comes to symbolize change as much as replacement and succession symbolizes change. The appointment of a person to head a new consumer affairs division provides almost unquestioned evidence that consumers now have more power in the organization. The act and fact of the subunit's creation becomes proof of the change. We can be sure that equal employment is being seriously considered and worked on because the corporation has an EEO department headed by an EEO expert who works on EEO. The fact of the activity, as noted previously, comes to substitute for the assessment of the results or impact of the activity. The creation of organizational subunits with appropriate titles and staffing, particularly when these new units are loosely connected to the rest of the organization, provides one form of response to those with enough power to demand more say in the organization, but without enough power to be taken too seriously.

Change and restructuring provides symbolic reassurance that action is being taken. This restructuring can alter the symbolic value which is given to different aspects of the organization's operation. Through such symbolic action, it is possible to both motivate and placate various interests in contact with the organization. At the same time, the new subunits come to have some influence because of their existence, and the symbolic value of their creation can have consequences on the power of various political groups within the organization. Thus, it is important to recognize that what can begin as a symbolic response to quiet an interest group, may set in motion the creation of a subunit and the creation of a set of understandings of the new importance of an interest group, that results in the change of the political power of organizational participants.

SETTINGS

As Peters (1978) noted in his discussion of the implementation process, the symbolic value of physical settings is important. The ceremonies, the language, and the symbols are more or less effective depending upon the physical settings in which the symbolic activity takes place. The size, location, and configuration of physical space provides the backdrop against which political activity takes place, and thereby influences the interpretation and meaning of that activity, as well as its effects. Although the design of space is clearly important in the management process and in organizational politics, there has been surprisingly little research done on this issue in an organizational context. There has been some research on the effects of physical design in classrooms, airports, and mental hospitals (Sommer, 1969), but there are few attempts to examine the effects of settings in formal organizations. Steele (1973) has recognized the importance of physical design as a component of organizational change efforts. Physical design has real consequences for the amount and content of the social interaction which occurs within an organization. Settings have effects on how organizational participants perceive the organization and their role in it. It is this symbolic use of physical design, rather than its effects on social interaction patterns, that concerns us here.

In a contest for power, the physical setting one occupies provides a resource because of its symbolic effect on how others relate to the occupants of the space. This can be seen clearly in the competition for prominence among organizations. In San Francisco, the Bank of America built not only one of the taller buildings in the city, but put it on a hill so that its height advantage would be intensified. Thus, in a literal as well as a figurative sense, the Bank of America's world headquarters towers over the other banks in the financial district. The competition for power and status among organizations becomes represented in the construction of ever more grand and taller headquarters buildings. These buildings have effects on how those within and outside the organization perceive the firm. In a discussion at McGraw-Hill, the impact of building a new headquarters—a fifty-story structure in Rockefeller Center at a cost of $84 million—was described as follows:

> *The McGraw-Hill building was Fisher's pet project. The shift from the old green building on West Forty-Second Street, in Hell's Kitchen to the Avenue of the Americas next to Exxon was, to Fisher, "moving into the big time." Though the building cost much more than projected, he is convinced it paid off. He recalls that right after McGraw-Hill moved in, while he was prowling around checking things, he encountered a publisher staring out of a window. Says Fisher proudly, "The man turned and said, 'Shel, I'm already thinking bigger than I did last week'" (Holt, 1979: 104).*

The competition for power and status within organizations becomes evidenced in and reflected by physical settings. In the case of at least two major banks in the San Francisco area, the personnel and executive development departments are located in separate buildings; in both cases they are located in older, smaller, and less lavishly appointed spaces than the principal administrative offices. The physical separation makes contact with important operating units on a regular basis more difficult, and the physical separation and condition of the buildings provides a continual, visual reminder of the relative status of the various functions.

Internal struggles and disagreements can take on physical referents which serve to help maintain the saliency of the conflict. The Berkeley department of economics was split some years ago by a division between the mathematical economists and those who stressed economic history, development, and more policy-relevant and less theoretically-sophisticated approaches. The mathematical economists moved to Evans Hall, the home of the computer center, while the others stayed behind with the other social sciences in Barrows Hall. Recently, there have been reports that the whole department will move to Evans, which may provide some clue as to which side won in the ensuing conflict over paradigms.

A designer and builder of cooling towers moved into facilities vacated by another firm. The facilities were a series of small, relatively plain buildings arranged around a nice open area of grass and trees, much like a college campus. Of course, the marketing department occupied one building, administration and systems another, engineering a third, research and development a fourth, and production the fifth building nearest the construction yard and the plant. The physical demarcation of functions into separate territories hindered communication and resulted in problems of coordination and control. The only decent conference room happened to be in the marketing building, and most meetings were held there. The consequence of always meeting on marketing's territory provided the marketing function with some subtle advantages in the contest for whose perspective on the business was to prevail. Production, with the least imposing facilities that were also the farthest removed, fared poorly in the contest for power. Of the top management group, all except the head of production carried the title of vice-president; the head of production was the production manager. Even personnel, in the central administrative office, was headed by a person with the title of vice-president.

Hierarchical power, as well as the power of various subunits, becomes visible in the physical settings of formal organizations. The use of open offices, without the trappings of status that come from different size and location of office space, represents an attempt to remove status distinctions and to encourage the free flow of communication among organizational members. Oldham and Brass' (1979) finding of aversive reactions to these plans reflect that the open office and its symbol of equality are inconsistent with the decision making style and hierarchical structure of most U.S. corporations. Interestingly, the open office arrangement is more common in Japan, in which there is more of a consensual, group decision making style of management.

As Steele (1973) has also noted, hierarchical position in organizations is frequently indexed by things such as the amount of space, the location of the office with respect to views, windows, and other facilities, and the amount and quality of furnishings, carpets, and decorations in the office. The size and quality of desks and other office furniture indexes rank in some organizations, while in most organizations the higher the department or the individual in the building, the more power this signifies. As mentioned in the second chapter, in a western electric utility in which the power was shifting from engineering to law as the contingencies and uncertainties changed, one could observe in a very physical way the literal rise of the legal staff and the fall of the engineers as the departments shifted floors in the building over time.

The symbolic use of space and its consequences on organizational participants can also be seen in De Lorean's description of his time as a General Motors' executive. General Motors is headquartered in the General Motors Building—the name was changed from the Durant building after Durant fell from power—in midtown Detroit. Approximately 7,000 people work there. We pick up the description of the executive offices:

In General Motors the words "The Fourteenth Floor" are spoken with reverence. This is Executive Row. . . . To most GM employees, rising to The Fourteenth Floor is the final scene in their Horatio Alger dream. . . . The atmosphere on The Fourteenth Floor is awesomely quiet. . . . The omnipresent quiet projects an aura of great power. The reason it is so quiet must be that General Motors' powerful executives are hard at work in their offices. . . . It is electrically locked and is opened by a receptionist who actuates a switch under her desk in a large, plain waiting room outside the door. . . . GM executives usually arrive at and leave their offices by a private elevator located just inside Executive Row.

Across from the elevator are several bedrooms used by visiting executives or those too tired to go home. To the right, inside of the entrance, is the executive dining room. Straight ahead . . . are executive offices opening on either side. They are arranged in order of importance. . . . There is great jealousy among some executives about how close their offices are to the chairman and president. . . . The decor of The Fourteenth Floor is almost nondescript—blue-green carpeting and beige, faded oak paneling. . . . The executive offices are arranged in pairs, separated by a central office occupied by a private secretary for each executive. . . . Doors . . . open to a single, spacious, executive office. All were uniformly decorated in blue carpet, beige walls, faded oak paneling and aged furniture . . . except for those of a few uppermost executives, who could choose their own office decoration . . .

One rule on The Fourteenth Floor was that we should frequently use the executive dining room, especially at lunch. GM wants its managers to eat together whenever possible. . . . As in the offices outside, there was a pecking order even

224

in the executive dining room. To the left of the main dining area was the "executive committee dining room" where the top corporate officers met every day for lunch (Wright, 1979: 16–19).

In the description of the layout, several symbolic uses of space are apparent. First, note that to try to promote the team atmosphere, offices are paired around a common entrance, virtually no distinctions in decor are permitted, and a nearby dining room is provided to make eating in the building convenient. The committee, team-oriented tone of GM management is emphasized symbolically by the offices. At the same time, the position of the offices, the security, and the quiet contributed to the maintaining of the proper hierarchical distance from levels of supervision below. Thus, GM was symbolically seen to be run as a team, with a big distinction made between the team and the rest of the organization but with much smaller gradations on the executive floor.

De Lorean reported that there were two problems which he observed with the top management in the firm: they had too many meetings, and they forgot about the presumed separation between policy setting and operations and got involved in relatively minute details of design and marketing. Both problems can be seen to be consistent with the fourteenth floor arrangement. With all the team emphasis, meetings would be just a natural extension. Both the meetings and the meddling probably resulted from there being very little for those on the fourteenth floor to do. The gap between them and the rest of the organization was so large and awesome that they paraded around in all that quiet elegance without a lot of actual work to do. Thus, meetings and poking into operations were used to fill in the time vacuum.

This is not meant to imply that rearranging the building would change the pattern of executive behavior. On the other hand, the pattern of the physical space both reflected the organization's conceptions of power and contributed to its style of operations.

Furniture also conveys messages about power. The rectangular conference table, with the clear demarcation of a head-of-the-table position, provides a symbolic reminder as to who is in charge at meetings. Podiums and platforms serve to elevate the speaker using them and to separate the speaker from the audience. These are additional reminders of status distinctions and social distance. Peters (1978) told of a new chief executive who, upon taking the job, began going around the country to meet with employees at their facilities; this was a departure from past practice in which subordinates were summoned to headquarters. The significance was that the message was conveyed throughout the organization that headquarters was interested in learning about the subsidiaries and their operations, and that these operations were important and significant in the organization—significant enough so that the chief executive could take the time and effort to visit them. This behavior conveyed a sense of unity in the organization, and clearly indicated that the new chief executive wanted to break down some of the hierarchical distinctions and barriers that had emerged between corporate headquarters and the operating facilities. These distinctions, of course, had also made it difficult to control and manage effectively the field operations.

Arrangement of personnel in physical settings also conveys symbolic meaning that affects the content and consequences of interaction. Sommer (1969) has diagrammed how various seating arrangements are associated with co-acting, competition, and collaboration. Meeting in an arrangement that conveys competition, or an us-them orientation, may serve to help foster such behavior. Thus, several sales managers have reported that in making sales presentations to large, industrial clients in which a complex set of material is to be presented, the various persons from the selling organization are told to sit among the representatives of the prospective purchaser, as opposed to the arrangement in which one group sits on one side of the table and the other groups sits across from them. This prevents the development of a united front of opposition, and helps to break down the feelings of separateness among the two organizations.

Perhaps the best example of how physical settings and arrangements can be used strategically comes in the following instance related by an executive of a division of a large conglomerate. The division president and his controller were summoned periodically to corporate headquarters in the midwest to present results and to argue for their proposed operating and capital budgets. Capital budgets, in particular, were centrally allocated. In these meetings, traditionally the seating arrangement, diagrammed as follows, had been employed. The conglomerate chief executive, a person who relished his authority, sat at the head of the table, with his controller on his immediate right. The division president sat to his left, and his controller sat beside him. Although the setting did not imply competition, the meeting developed in most instances into an argument between the corporate headquarters persons and the division persons over the budget. On one occasion, after arriving at the meeting early, as they always did (since waiting also signifies the hierarchy of power), the division persons took the two seats on either side of the table nearest the head. When the president came in, he took his

226

Original Seating Arrangement

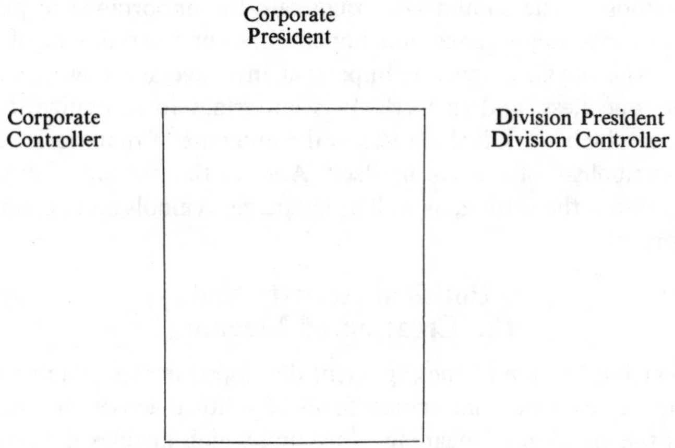

Corporate
President

Corporate
Controller

Division President
Division Controller

seat at the head, and then the controller, having no place to sit except next to the division president or the division controller, moved down the table (to disassociate himself from them). This left a new seating arrangement.Although many factors were in operation, the division president reported that this was the first time they had ever obtained 100% of the requested capital budget, and that the meeting had gone more smoothly and more to their liking than before. The controller, physically isolated

New Seating Arrangement

Corporate
President

Division
Controller

Division President

Corporate Controller

227

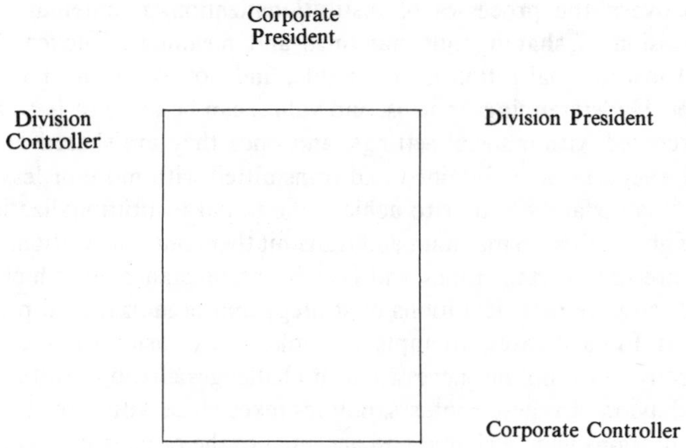

from the chief executive, was relatively quiet and could not as readily consult to oppose the proposals made by the division.

Although one should not exaggerate the importance of physical settings in affecting organizational operations and the outcome of political contests, physical space is important in conveying power, control, prestige, openness, and so forth. It is important to recognize that the setting in which work is done affects the outcome of that work because of the symbolism of the setting itself. And, in the playing of organizational politics, the setting, as well as language, symbols and ceremonies, is important.

Political Activity and the Creation of Meaning

The clear implication of the argument developed in this chapter and in the last chapter is that one critical focus of political activity in organizations is the creation of meaning—meaning which justifies the positions of power of some participants, which justifies and rationalizes decisions and actions, and which discredits the motivation or information of opponents. In this meaning creation process, language, ceremonies, symbols, and settings are important ingredients, and those effective in organizational politics know how to use these elements. At the same time, it can not be forgotten that organizational politics takes place within a larger social context, and the norms and values of that context, including values of rationality and the social definition of legitimacy, affect the strategies and tactics that can be and are used within the organization.

Two concluding comments are in order on this conception of organizational politics. First, Zucker (1977) has drawn a useful distinction between the processes of institutionalization, maintenance, and transmission of shared understandings and meanings. Zucker (1977) treated institutionalization as a variable, and not as an all or nothing concept. Understandings, norms, and values can be more or less shared and accepted within social settings, and once they are shared and accepted, they can be maintained and transmitted with more or less difficulty. It is certainly harder to achieve the initial institutionalization of a set of norms than to maintain and transmit them once institutionalized. There are only certain times and certain circumstances in which it is possible to have new definitions of strategy and organizational practice accepted. In most cases, attempts to invoke new decision rules, criteria, or objectives will not be successful as it challenges already institutionalized behaviors. In these contexts, politics takes place within the confines of justifications widely shared and accepted in the organization. Indeed,

228

the process of institutionalization makes the ability to change, including the ability to change the distribution of power and control, limited. Institutionalization is a process of enough importance that it is discussed in Chapter 8. For the moment, it is important to note that the potential for using new political strategies is itself a function of the extent to which behavior and decision rules are shared and accepted within the organization.

The second point to be reemphasized is that political language and symbolic activity take place in a competitive environment in which certain individuals are trying to discredit the symbols and language used by other participants. In this competition among symbols and languages, it is likely that the self-interest of the various actors involved will have at least some chance of being discovered and expressed. It is unlikely that through language and symbols one can be permanently prevented from coming to see other points of view, particularly when these other points of view impact the self-interest of those involved. For example, it is in the interests of those wanting to mobilize shareholder action to try to advocate symbols which stress the powerlessness and disregard of shareholder interests that emerge from present governance. Both sides of the political contest use similar strategies, relying on recourse to essentially similar norms, values, and beliefs. It is through the competition that occurs on both a symbolic level as well as with respect to interdependencies and power relationships that the outcomes of organizational power and politics are determined.

──CHAPTER 7──

POWER
IN
USE

The subject of power is of interest primarily because of its importance for understanding what occurs in organizations. Power has consequences in organizations for resource allocations, administrative succession, structures, and strategic choices. In the preceding chapters, an attempt has been made to build an understanding of what power is, how it is measured and assessed in organizations, where it comes from, and the strategies through which it is acquired and employed, as well as the conditions which tend to make organizational decisions more or less political. It is now time to consider power in action, to review some evidence and examples of power in use.

The analysis of power in use can serve several purposes. First, as noted in Chapter 2, the outcomes of power provide one kind of indicator useful in understanding power distributions in organizations. Second, support for a political perspective on organizational functioning is provided to the extent that power can be shown to have predictable effects on a wide variety of decision outcomes in organizations. Third, as power in use is considered, it will be possible to provide examples of the kind of analysis that can be undertaken by others in other organizational settings to help understand and explain organizational choices.

It is not much of an exaggeration to claim that power and its effects are omnipresent in organizational decisions. Power affects the allocation of resources both across departments and across personnel categories. Power affects the succession of executives in organizations as well as the promotion of persons at all organizational levels. Power has effects on the structure that emerges in the organization, including its information system, and is also affected by that structure, of course. The task of this chapter, then, is to explore power in use in the following contexts: the politics of budgets, the politics of succession and careers, and the politics of structures.

The Politics of Budgets

As Pondy (1970) has noted, resource allocations within organizations are important because as organizations have become increasingly large, and economic power has become more concentrated, the allocation of society's resources becomes accomplished more through allocation decisions made *within* organizations than through the operation of markets *across* them. From the point of view of studying power and politics in organizations, the analysis of budgets offers some distinct advantages.

> . . . *budgets at public organizations are visible and developed annually. Since they are found in all organizations, they provide opportunities for extending and replicating research results. Budgets are theoretically important because they represent decisions that are both critical and contested within most organizations. . . . Resource commitments have been suggested (Etzioni, 1964: 6) as one way of measuring an organization's objectives (Pfeffer and Salancik, 1974: 138).*

The budget represents the outcome of a bargaining process which occurs within organizations over the setting of priorities for action which become represented in the budget (Cyert and March, 1963). Wildavsky (1979) has explicitly argued that budgets are the outcomes of political contests, rather than the result of the application of bureaucratically rational and neutral decision rules. His analysis, which focused on the allocation of resources across governmental agencies, is equally applicable to the analysis of resource allocations within other types of organizations. He has described budgets as follows:

> *For our purposes, we shall conceive of budgets as attempts to allocate financial resources through political processes. If politics is regarded as conflict over whose preferences are to prevail in the determination of policy, then the budget records the outcomes of this struggle. If one asks who gets what the (public or private) organization has to give, then the answers for a moment in time are recorded in the bud-*

get. If organizations are viewed as political coalitions, budg-
ets are mechanisms through which subunits bargain over
conflicting goals, make side-payments, and try to motivate
one another to accomplish their objectives (Wildavsky,
1968: 193).

Because of the issue of data availability, the quantitative comparative study of the use of power in resource allocations within organizations has focused on public organizations. In three instances, universities
were the focus of the study; in a fourth, the focus was on the allocation
of funds to social service agencies within the United Fund. Although the
studies were not conducted on private corporations, the methodologies
are instructive in indicating how studies such as these might be conducted. Moreover, although "the degree of politicization is variable
across the universe of all organizations" (Hannan and Freeman, 1978:
199), anecdotal evidence suggests that corporations are not as different
as one might think, in terms of the influence of power and politics, from
these public organizations.

RESOURCE ALLOCATION IN UNIVERSITIES

The initial study of the effects of power on resource allocation in a
university was conducted at the University of Illinois at Urbana-Champaign, a large, prestigious state university with about 34,000 students, of
which 8,000 were graduate students (Pfeffer and Salancik, 1974). The
study focused on twenty-nine departments, and the budget data was
collected over a thirteen year period. The dependent variable which was
employed was the average proportion of the general funds budget—that
portion of the budget not committed by contract or bequest—that was
received by each of the academic departments during the period. Explanatory variables included the proportion of total instructional units (or
credit hours) taught by each department, the representation of each
department on the University's Research Board committee, and representation on a total of seven university-wide committees, as well as on
college executive committees. The estimated equation explaining general
funds allocations was:

$$\text{GENFD} = .0112 + .393 \text{ IU} + .090 \text{ RESBD} + .199 \text{ \#COMM } r^2 = .35$$
$$(9.10) \qquad (4.46) \qquad\qquad (4.18)$$

when each allocation for each year was considered separately, where the
values in parentheses are the T-values of the respective regression coefficients and IU represents instructional units, RESBD represents member-

233

ship on the Research Board, and #COMM represents membership on all the committees combined.

The equation indicates that both power measures (committee and Research Board representation) and workload or bureaucratic measures (instructional units taught) significantly affect budget allocations. Pfeffer and Salancik reported that this basic conclusion on the effect of power was unchanged when size was statistically controlled (1974: 146), when the national ranking or reputation of the departments was considered (1974: 147), or when dummy variables were introduced to assess the impact of the departments being in different colleges (1974: 149).

One other analysis from this study is important. One explanation for the relationships observed in the regression equation runs as follows: in some departments, instruction is more expensive than in others because of the need for specialized equipment and intensive, laboratory-based instruction. These departments are also more likely to be represented on university research committees or research boards because of their greater involvement in equipment-intensive research. Thus, the presumed relationship between power and budget allocations, and the fact that student workload does not correlate more highly with resource allocations reflects these cost of instruction factors more than the effect of organizational politics. One way of examining this argument involves computing, for each department separately, the correlation over time between the proportion of instructional units taught and the proportion of budget obtained, as well as the proportion of teaching faculty in the department. If, in fact, some departments are more expensive to operate than others, then unless these instructional costs were changing differentially, the correlations between student instructional units taught and resources used (budget and faculty positions) over time should be constant across departments. Alternatively, the effects of power would predict that powerful departments are able to increase their share of the resources regardless of what happens to their share of the students taught. Thus, there should be a negative correlation between departmental power and the department's correlation between instructional units and resources over time.

This latter argument is generally consistent with the data. In Table 7-1, the correlations relevant to the argument are presented. An example will illustrate this point. One relatively powerful department exhibited a correlation of − .60 over the thirteen year period, between the proportion of the budget received and the proportion of instructional units taught. "This indicates that the department's resource allocations were not only independent of changes in workload, but were actually nega-

234

TABLE 7-1
Relationship Between Indicators
of Departmental Power and Correlations
Between Workload and Resources Within Departments Over Time

Power Measure	Over Time Correlation Between Instructional Units and General Funds	Over Time Correlation Between Instructional Units and FTE Teaching Faculty
Interview-based measure of power	−.11	.03
Departmental representation on Research Board	−.18	−.40**
Departmental representation on university committees	−.38**	−.24*

*p < .10
**p < .05

tively related to changes in teaching demands over the period" (Pfeffer and Salancik, 1974: 148). Conversely, less powerful departments tended to exhibit positive correlations between instructional units taught and resources obtained; resources were lost when student demand fell, and at the same time, the only way additional resources were acquired was through the demonstration of substantially increased student demand for the department's offerings.

The results from this initial study were replicated and extended in a study of resource allocations on two University of California campuses (Pfeffer and Moore, 1980b). In addition to departmental power and student enrollment, the paradigm level of the department was included as an explanatory factor. This variable is consistent with the argument developed in Chapter 3 concerning the effects of consensus and the ability to demonstrate results on providing power to social actors in organizations. The possibility that enrollments or changes in enrollments might be used more effectively in the bargaining for more resources by the high paradigm departments was explored by including enrollment by paradigm interaction terms in the explanatory equations. There were two analyses which were carried out, a cross-sectional analysis, in which measures were aggregated over the period, and an analysis of change from the initial budget allocation to the final one, with paradigm and departmental power assumed to have been constant over the period. The results of these analyses are displayed in Table 7-2.

235

TABLE 7-2

Multiple Regression Equations Estimating Resource Allocations
to Forty Departments on Two University of California Campuses

---

$$\text{BUDGET} = -.0061 + .495^e \text{ ENROLL} + .216^b \text{ COMM} + .000702^e \text{ PARADIGM}$$
$$\phantom{\text{BUDGET} = -.0061 + .}(.094)\phantom{\text{ ENROLL}}(.087)\phantom{\text{ COMM}}(.000131)$$

$$+ .0100^b \text{ ENxPAR} \qquad r^2 = .76$$

$$\text{FACULTY} = -.0036 + .661^e \text{ ENROLL} + .139^a \text{ COMM} + .000446^e \text{ PARADIGM}$$
$$r^2 = .81$$
$$\phantom{\text{FACULTY} = }(.085)(.078)(.000120)$$

$$\text{BUDGET76} = .00046 + .721^e \text{ BUD67} + .194^e \text{ CHGEN} + .165^e \text{ COMM}$$
$$\phantom{\text{BUDGET76} = .00}(.051)(.055)(.039)$$

$$+ .000147^a \text{ PARADIGM} + .0112^b \text{ CHGENxPAR} \qquad r^2 = .95$$
$$(.00077)(.0044)$$

$$\text{FACULTY75} = .0018 + .688^e \text{ FAC67} + .230^e \text{ CHGEN} + .224^e \text{ COMM}$$
$$\phantom{\text{FACULTY75} = }(.058)(.048)(.045)$$

$$+ .0150^d \text{ CHGENxPAR} \qquad r^2 = .94$$
$$(.0048)$$

---

[a]$p < .10$ BUDGET76=department's share of budget in 1976
BUD67=department's share of budget in 1967

[b]$p < .05$ FACULTY75=department's share of regular faculty positions in 1975

[c]$p < .01$ FAC67=department's share of regular faculty positions in 1967

[d]$p < .005$ CHGEN=change in proportion of total student enrollment
ENROLL=department's share of total student enrollment
PARADIGM=department's score on index of paradigm development

[e]$p < .001$ ENxPAR=enrollment by paradigm interaction
CHGENxPAR=paradigm by change in enrollment interaction
COMM=proportion of total committee positions occupied by departmental
faculty

The results were consistent with those from the earlier study and
with the various predictions. There was evidence that power, as well as
enrollments, affected the change in budget and faculty resources over
time, as well as the absolute levels of those allocations. Additionally,
there was evidence for a positive effect of paradigm on the level of
resource allocations, as well as evidence that change in enrollments
interacts with the paradigm level of the department to affect changes in
resource allocations over time. Departments that had more consensus
about educational requirements and research issues, as well as the ability
to more predictably produce research results, were more successful in
translating enrollments and change in enrollments into increased re-

236

sources. As in the case of the Illinois study, there was no evidence for an effect of the department's national prestige on resource allocations.

The third study conducted in a university context was undertaken by Hills and Mahoney (1978) at the University of Minnesota. The focus of their study was somewhat different, as these authors used a different dependent variable—change in resource allocations from one year to the next net of non-discretionary components—and somewhat different measures of power. Nevertheless, the basic conclusions of the other studies were supported. There was evidence for the effect of power on allocation outcomes, particularly during periods of increased resource scarcity.

The three university studies, when taken together, provide reasonably strong support for Baldridge's (1971) perspective on universities as political coalitions. In all three instances, power acted along with student demand to affect allocation outcomes. In the one instance where it was examined, the level of development of the paradigm of the department, which was discussed previously as a source of power, acted to positively impact allocations and to alter the effects of enrollment on those allocations as well.

The studies at Illinois and California also provide evidence on the unobtrusiveness with which power is exercised and the strong norms of rationality which dominate. When I first came to Berkeley, I met with Martin Trow, a very famous sociologist of education, who had served on the faculty for many years and was in the Graduate School of Public Policy. I remember, quite distinctly, him telling me that he thought the Illinois research was interesting but that nothing like that occurred at Berkeley. The inference that emerged from our discussion was that Berkeley was a truly great university and that the faculty valued only one thing, academic excellence. It was academic excellence and nothing else which accounted for allocations. Some time later, when my friend and colleague George Strauss joined the Budget Committee, I heard a similar speech. We have reported in more detail elsewhere the comparisons of the results on two University of California campuses, cross-sectional and dynamic analyses, and attempts to control for various alternative interpretations of the data (Pfeffer and Moore, 1980b). Suffice it to say that the results are quite similar to those obtained at Illinois, and that there is a manifest evidence for the effects of power operating not only on budget and faculty position allocations, but also on the allocation of graduate student aid (Moore, 1979) and faculty career speed, an issue which will be discussed in more detail later.

Both Trow and Strauss are clever people who had been on the

campus for a fairly long time. I don't think either was intentionally trying to mislead me or to tell me something that he did not honestly believe. The lesson, therefore, is all the more powerful: The perceptions of those within the organization, even those knowledgeable and well placed, are not inevitably reliable in terms of portraying the extent to which a political process is operating. There are normative and value considerations, which also involve the maintenance of the respondent's self-identity and self-respect, which bias perceptions toward finding rationality, objectivity, and a lack of political activity.

There is one other interesting footnote. Subsequent to the publication of the University of Illinois study, two things occurred at Illinois. First, as Pondy (1977) has reported, an announcement was made specifically stating that student enrollment levels would *not* be considered as bases for budget requests. Prior to this time, there had been an assumption that one way of increasing the budget was to take in more students. Though this was not the case, it did have the interesting effect of causing the lower power departments to take on more of the students who were formerly taught by the higher power departments; this benefited the latter but not the former. The announcement was made to formally and finally deny the existence of any enrollment economy governing resources. Confronted with evidence that non-bureaucratic criteria were being used, great care was taken to justify and legitimate those criteria and to completely discredit the bureaucratic criteria.

Second, in a series of steps, some of the Research Board's power was taken away and given to the Dean of the Graduate Division, who was a member of the campus administration. This was part of a general movement which occurred during this period, in part as a response to resource scarcity, to centralize power and control in the administration. In this instance, the evidence for the power of the Research Board was used to bring that body, which was comprised of faculty, into tow.

The careful reader will have noticed that in the first instance, bureaucratic criteria were explicitly rejected by the administration as the bases for their budget allocations; and in the second, the non-use of objective criteria led to somewhat successful attempts to remove the power of a faculty committee and transfer that power to the administration. This provides just one more instance of the loose coupling between language and reality, and between actions taken at one point and actions taken at another. Power was in the process of being centralized, and the political language that was used to justify and legitimate this process was whatever was appropriate for the event at hand.

RESOURCE ALLOCATIONS
IN UNITED FUNDS

A study of allocations to local social service agencies that were members of United Funds also provides evidence on the use of power in budgeting. The United Fund, formerly called the Community Chest, was established to achieve some economies of scale in fund raising, as well as to cope with employer complaints about multiple agencies requesting permission to solicit payroll-deduction contributions at the workplace. The United Fund has as its goal the inclusion of as much of the local fund raising effort as possible. In return for receiving a share of the United Fund's annual take, the local agency, such as the scouts, a home for unwed mothers, a disease prevention or treatment society, mental health or other social service agency, foregoes any other solicitation in the community, at the workplace particularly, although other fund raising activities such as sales, lotteries, and so forth are permitted. This arrangement has made the United Fund, although private, an important source of funds for many public-sector social service organizations in the community.

Budget allocations to member agencies for the years 1962, 1967, and 1972 were examined for a sample of sixty-six United Funds by Pfeffer and Leong (1977). These authors argued that the power of a member agency in the Fund was negatively related to the agency's dependence on the Fund, measured as the proportion of the agency's budget obtained from the Fund. The power of a member agency in the Fund was also a positive function of the Fund's dependence on the agency, measured as the proportion of the total United Fund budget that went to each member agency. The agency needed the Fund allocations for its operating budget, and the higher the proportion of this budget that was obtained from the United Fund, the greater the dependence and therefore, following the arguments of Chapter 4, the less the power. At the same time, however, the Fund needed agency participation to legitimate its own activities, and also the United Fund came to define its goal as including as much of the local agency fund raising as possible. The net power of the social service agency vis à vis its United Fund, consequently, was the net result of its dependence on the United Fund and the United Fund's dependence on it.

Wenocur (1975) suggested that a political model of organizational behavior was applicable to the analysis of United Funds. Following the political line of analysis suggests that United Fund allocations to agencies will be based on agency power and not on the various demographic characteristics of the community that may index the need for different kinds of social services.

The individual agency's power within the United Fund is a function of its importance to the United Fund and its ability to articulate a credible threat of withdrawal. The ability to threaten withdrawal is determined by the agency's ability to raise funds on its own outside the Fund . . . the greater the amount of outside funds raised, the higher the allocation from the United Fund. . . . Our argument suggests that this causal relationship will be stronger (a) the smaller the proportion of the agency's budget received from the United Fund (the less dependent the agency is on the Fund), and (b) the larger the proportion of the United Fund's budget that goes to a given agency (the larger, and hence, the more important, the agency is to the Fund) (Pfeffer and Leong, 1977: 779).

The arguments were supported after examining allocations across cities to eleven agencies in 1962, fifteen agencies in 1967, and eighteen agencies in 1972. In virtually no case was there a significant association between any demographic variable and the allocations to social service agencies. The allocations to agencies serving primarily black constituencies were unrelated to the proportion of blacks in the area; allocations to agencies providing financial assistance were unrelated to median income or to the proportion of the population falling below the poverty line; and allocations to agencies serving youth (the so-called character building agencies) were unrelated to the age distribution of the population in the areas served. Seventeen demographic variables, ranging from population size, income distribution, age distribution, and occupational distribution, to the crime and divorce rate were examined. The inability of these variables to account for allocations to the various social service agencies provides some evidence that politics intervened in the resource allocation process.

A finding which was consistent with the arguments on the effect of power was that there were frequently observed, statistically significant correlations in the expected direction between the proportion of non-United Fund resources obtained and allocations received from the various United Funds (Pfeffer and Leong, 1977: 781–782). These relationships were stronger for the more powerful agencies, with agency power being determined by the net dependence between the agency and the United Fund. Thus, in this study of the United Fund, the political model found empirical support.

More recently, the Pfeffer and Leong results were replicated in a study of the resource allocation practices of a single United Fund located in the northeastern part of the United States (Provan, Beyer, and Kruyt-bosch, 1980). While extending the original analysis in some new directions, Provan *et al*. replicated the basic result that the higher the proportion of non-United Fund resources obtained (the greater the agency's power and the less its dependence with respect to the Fund), the higher the allocation obtained from the United Fund. The research extensions involved examining the impact of member agency community board of directors interlocks on the agencies' ability to extract resources from the budget allocation process. The study found that community centrality was important in enabling the particular agency to obtain resources.

Thus, the two studies conducted so far of United Fund allocations to member social service agencies support the position of the importance of power and politics in the resource allocation process. The unimportance of measures which might serve as surrogates for community need provides a striking testimony to the very political nature of budget decision making when the standards of assessment are unclear and technologies are uncertain.

The most powerful agencies in the United Fund have typically been the Boy and Girl Scouts and YMCA and YWCA. All are fairly large, but most importantly, all service the employees and their families who constitute the core of the United Fund's contributors. Agencies serving the poor and those otherwise in distress typically provide fewer direct services to the United Fund contributors. Thus, the United Fund has found itself in a paradoxical position: it collects most of its contributions basically from the working middle class, and then provides a great share of its budget to support agencies and programs such as community centers, scouts, and the Y's that service the middle class. While there is some redistribution of benefits away from the contributors, it is not as much as might be dictated by relative need, because these agencies have the power to threaten withdrawal.

Two instances illustrate this power and how it is used. In Urbana-Champaign, the two cities in which the University of Illinois was located, the pattern of United Fund contributions and budgeting was similar to that observed elsewhere. Most of the funds came from employees of the University and other major employers in the area, and the bulk of the budget went to the scouts, the Y's, and the various community centers. The board of the United Fund one year decided to rationalize its decision making process. Instead of just having agencies make budget proposals (which were typically based on last year's budget plus an increment), the board required the agencies to identify the type of services provided and the specific client population groups (identified by sex, race, and income

241

level) which were served by the various programs. Then, the board determined to provide more funding to the various agencies which provided more important services to client groups which would not otherwise be served.

The board did this with little debate or discussion. After all, if they worked out the indicators of program criticality and client group need, how could anyone object to basing budget decisions on a criterion that would better serve the social welfare of the community? When the criteria and then the new funding decisions based on these criteria were announced, the scouts and the Y's were outraged. They were the big losers in the process, since recreational services for the middle class fared poorly by the criteria when compared to health services, job training, and other forms of social welfare for much poorer parts of the population. The aggrieved agencies soon discovered their common plight and formed a coalition. This coalition formation process was facilitated by the overlapping memberships in some of the boards, and the fact that these four agencies were the ones most dominated by university faculty or their families.

After much discussion among the agencies, they determined a course of action. They went to the local United Fund board as a group and argued that unless they got their previous share of the allocation, they would withdraw and form a separate fund raising organization among themselves. After much discussion and debate and negotiating, the United Fund determined that the agencies were serious, at which point they got back their previous allocation.

However, the United Fund still had a problem. It had retained significant member agencies, but it had also just had every agency go through this new budget request process, and announced to the world its new criteria for budget allocations. There were board members and others in the community who agreed with the new directions. It would be embarrassing, to say the least, to announce that it had disregarded the very procedures and rules it had just formulated, particularly when it would have done so as the result of a pure power play. What the Fund did, of course, was to use the new rules, forms, information and procedures, but somehow the allocations came out looking much as they had in the past. It turns out that there was enough latitude even in these new procedures to permit the Fund to do just about what it wanted, which was to allocate resources in a way which was in large measure based on the political clout of the requesting agencies. Thus, the objective criteria were selectively used, and the coalition of member agencies got what they wanted from the United Fund.

In the San Francisco bay area, the charities which primarily served the black population were distressed by the United Fund's allocations. They thought that it was wrong to recycle such a large proportion of the budget to those agencies that served the relatively more affluent parts of the populace. After some years of negotiation for a larger share, a set of charities which served the black community withdrew as a group from the United Fund and formed their own organization for raising and allocating money. Although initially United Fund collections were hurt by all the attendant negative publicity, after a few years contribution levels pretty much recovered and there are probably now many people in the area who do not even know that such a splinter group broke off or that it still exists. Organizations fail to take account of power only at some peril; if they do respond to power, most of the time they seem to survive in pretty good shape.

THE SIZE OF PERSONNEL COMPONENTS

In the study of the politics of budgeting within organizations, a third stream of empirical research has examined the allocation of positions and, implicitly, funds, across various categories of personnel. This research arose from the literature which was concerned with the relative size of the administrative component, as contrasted with the production component in organizations, but has recently moved beyond that two-fold distinction to consider the relative allocation of positions to categories of employees more precisely defined. The research has, thus far, treated only the allocation of positions in school districts, but the arguments and analytical techniques are capable of being extended into other contexts.

The first study (Freeman and Hannan, 1975) employed a model which "mixed organizational politics and administrative rationality" (Hannan and Freeman, 1978). Freeman and Hannan argued that there were general norms governing teacher/pupil ratios which produced a virtually constant class size. They anticipated a relatively proportional change in the number of teachers as districts' enrollment changed, and expected this process to be roughly equal in districts that were gaining enrollments and those that were losing enrollments. With respect to the non-teaching or administrative component, the authors argued that as long as the district was growing, the other personnel components would change proportionately with the number of teachers. In times of decline, however, the power of the administrative staff would lead to a less than proportional decline in the size of the administrative personnel component. This was due to the fact that the administrative staff possessed a hierarchical power, as they had the ability to make budget adjustments. Thus, the model which was developed distinguished between declining and growing districts. In growing districts, there would be a smooth adjustment of all personnel components in an upward direction. In declining districts, there would be more administrators than would otherwise be predicted, because of the administrative component's ability to reduce decline due to its political power.

These arguments were supported. The effects of enrollments and enrollment changes (see also Freeman, 1979) were less great on the number of administrators in declining, as contrasted with growing districts. There seemed to be a difference between growth and decline in the politics of resource allocation. The arguments were extended by Freeman (1979) to include the effects of tax and bond elections, as well as the source of district funds. Freeman replicated the basic Freeman and Hannan (1975) results with the changes in funding being statistically controlled. For instance, after considering a narrow definition of administrative personnel (certified personnel who do not perform direct services for students), Freeman observed the following differences between the coefficients for predictors of the number of administrators in 1973 in growing and declining districts (1979: 128):

	Growing	Declining
Administrators in 1971	.652*	.532*
Change in enrollment	.003*	.0003
Change in federal funds	.002	−.002*
Change in state funds	.004*	.002*
Change in local funds	.003*	.002

* denotes statistical significance

In every instance, the effects are larger in growing enrollment districts than in declining enrollment districts. The change in enrollment has a ten times larger effect on the number of administrative personnel, and the change in funds has between one and one-half and two times the effect in growing rather than in declining districts.

Freeman also investigated tax elections and the effects of the passing or failure of the election. The prediction was that when there were elections, changes in enrollments and revenues would have smaller effects on the personnel components than when no election was held, and when the proposal passed, there would be stronger effects than when it failed. This argument received only weak support. Freeman (1979: 129–

130) concluded: "It seems that districts exposed to outside scrutiny responded to relief of that scrutiny by becoming less responsive to changes in enrollments."

The third stage in the analysis involved a more sophisticated model of competition among personnel components (Hannan and Freeman, 1978). This model examined two factors: the carrying capacity, or the number of various personnel that would be observed in equilibrium; and the time required, or the speed by which the system adjusted toward the equilibrium values. Hannan and Freeman (1978: 180) argued that ". . . the size of any particular category is determined by the availability of environmental resources on which it depends, on the sizes of competing components and the intensity of competition, and on stable characteristics of the organization and its environment that favor this particular category." Their new analyses of the original data revealed that the assumption of constant class size was unwarranted. They also found that the intensity of competition was increased in the case of declining districts, and that the competitive position of administrators differed between growth and decline.

> When enrollments are growing, the administrative staff appears to get only the remainder of the resource pie. However, when enrollments are declining, administration shifts to a more controlling position in the political struggle for resources (Hannan and Freeman, 1978: 189–190).

The Hannan and Freeman results on school districts have been interpreted (Hannan, 1978) as supporting a political, as contrasted with a rational or bureaucratic model of resource allocation. However, since no explicit attempt was made to measure independently the sources or amount of power of the various personnel components—by considering unionization, political support of the board of education, and so forth—the results are open to alternative interpretations. At the same time, the method demonstrated for assessing competition among resource contenders provided new insights into the dynamics of the internal adjustments which were occurring among the personnel components.

The studies of universities, United Funds, and school districts together provide support for the position that power and politics affect the allocation of budgetary resources within organizations. As noted above, it is important to extend these relatively few empirical studies and consider other forms of organizations and other contextual variables that impact the political process of resource allocation.

The Politics of Careers

Organizations allocate two fundamental resources—budgets and other monetary resources and positions in the organizational hierarchy. As Kalleberg and Sorensen (1979: 351) have maintained, "Since the majority of people in industrial society obtain income and other rewards in exchange for work, labor market processes form the central mechanisms of social distribution in industrial society." As Pfeffer (1977) argued, it is within organizations that positions, and the monetary and fringe benefit rewards that accompany positions, are determined. Thus, the allocation of rewards within organizations becomes an important arena of study for those interested in career processes among individuals, as well as for those interested in more general stratification in society.

The common belief, or at least the commonly articulated value, stresses that career rewards, such as promotion and raises, go to those who perform the best and contribute the most to the organization. Although it is not often made explicit, this prediction is derivable from classical human capital labor economics (e.g., Mincer, 1974) and more generally from the theory of competitive markets. The argument, as reviewed by Bibb and Form (1977), is that in a perfectly competitive market, employees will be paid according to the human capital they provide in their most efficient use. If they are not being used and rewarded optimally, they could be attracted away by another firm that would use their skills more appropriately. Because of competition in product markets, it would be impossible for any firm in the long run to pay workers more or less than what they contributed to the firm. If the firm paid more in the long run, other competitors would be able to undercut it in terms of costs and prices and the firm would go out of business. If the firm paid less, another firm would attract its employees away and still make a reasonable profit, given the competitive market price. Thus, under assumptions of perfect information, utility maximization on the part of firms and individuals, and mobility on the part of workers, the labor market is expected to operate to allocate each individual to his or her best use, given their human capital and the structure of the economy. Politics or other non-rational factors do not play a part in such a process.

A belief in the merit-based and non-political aspect of careers is important in order to maintain the legitimacy of the organization's internal labor market and to help assuage the feelings of those who earn less than others in the organization. The importance of legitimating organizational decisions was described in the last two chapters. In a situation

246

in which some individuals make more money than others, the quiescence and solidarity of all are maintained if there is a shared belief that each individual is being compensated justly according to an impersonal, market-determined worth. This value is articulated repeatedly, and comes to be believed by those involved in the process. For example, on the occasion of his retirement as the Dean of Stanford's Graduate School of Business, the following exchange was reported between Arjay Miller, the former president of Ford Motors, and a reporter:

Reporter: *"What advice do you give about dealing with politics inside a corporation—or academe?"*

Miller: *"The best way is to avoid them. Do your best at the job in hand. Work hard and keep your nose clean. I have seen a lot of people try to be too clever by getting involved in office politics. In the long run it never did them any good. Get promoted for what you are"* (Campus Report, 1979: 2).

The irony is that the Ford Motor Company provides a classic example of politics in the executive succession process, but we will defer that topic until the next section. For the moment, it is important to realize that the belief in the efficacy of hard work and good performance is widely held and forms a part of the ideology of organizations.

As another example, Smigel (1965) asked a sample of associates and partners who worked for several large Wall Street law firms what they thought an associate could do to help himself become a partner. The responses ranged from being a good lawyer and working hard to having the proper social background and contacts. If we categorize responses into those associated with hard work, performance, or helping the profitability of the firm, those which reflect the effect of contacts or politics, and other responses, then the distribution of answers to this question would appear as follows:

Techniques to Partnership	Associates	Partners
Working hard, job performance, enhancing firm profits	51.5%	58.6%
Politics, including going to right school, being in right department, contacts, etc.	33.1%	20.3%
Other, including luck	15.3%	21.1%

It is clear that both partners and associates believe that working hard and job performance are the most important factors. It is also clear however, that the partners believe more in the importance of performance and other factors and less in the effectiveness of office politics than do the associates. Given the set of widely held norms and values in this country this could easily reflect self-justification, as it is more flattering to regard one's position as being the consequence of effort and ability, rather than the consequence of social background or political skills.

What do the data regarding these shared beliefs, or the ideology of careers indicate? The data from both qualitative and quantitative studies consistently suggest the importance of contacts, linkages in social networks, social background, and being in the right department. In short, the importance of the factors associated with the power of various subunits and the political skills of individuals to get themselves in the right place at the right time is stressed.

In a study of 282 professional, technical, and managerial workers in Newton, Massachusetts, Granovetter (1974) consistently demonstrated the importance of personal contacts in the job finding process. He found that of the three ways of finding a job, formal mechanisms, personal contacts, and direct application, job satisfaction was reported to be higher for those who found the job through personal contacts (1974: 13). For our purposes, both direct application and formal means are likely to involve the use of more formal screening and more competition than the finding and filling of jobs through personal contact. Thus, we will call the formal and direct application modes more routinized and bureaucratic, and the personal contact, more political. Granovetter reported data which are quite instructive on the use of the various methods by the three categories of worker (1974: 19):

Job-Finding Method, by Occupational
Category of Respondent

	Occupation			
Method Used	Technical	Professional	Managerial	Total
Formal or direct application	55.0%	34.1%	28.4%	37.6%
Personal contact	43.5%	56.1%	65.4%	55.7%
Other	1.4%	9.8%	6.2%	6.7%

Two things are evident from these data. First, personal contact is the most frequently used job finding method for the sample as a whole. Second, if one assumes that technical jobs are relatively more certain and technical capacities are the most objectively evaluated, while managerial jobs are the most uncertain and managerial capabilities the most problematic to evaluate, then the data support the argument made in Chapter 3 concerning the role of uncertainty in the use of politics and power. The most political job finding strategy, personal contacts, is used the most for the most uncertain occupation, while the least political strategies, which involve direct application and formal mechanisms, are used more often for the most certain and analyzable occupation.

Finally, Granovetter found an association between the income level of the job and the job finding method. "Nearly half . . . of those using personal contacts report incomes over $15,000 whereas the corresponding figure for formal means is under one-third; for direct application, under one fifth" (1974: 14). Thus, managerial and higher income positions are more likely to be found through personal contacts. One explanation for this is that personal contacts provide better information. Better information reduces the greater uncertainty present in the filling of those jobs that are themselves more important or difficult to assess (managerial jobs) and which pay more, a factor which may also be associated with more uncertainty and importance to the organization. As Mayhew argued:

> The source of the staying power and functional capacity of ascription (in modern society) can be summed up in three words: it is cheap. Ascription involves using an existent, pre-established structure as a resource rather than creating a new specialized structure for the same purpose" (1969: 110).

In a study of graduates from the MBA and undergraduate programs at the University of California, Berkeley, Pfeffer (1977c) attempted to estimate the effects of socioeconomic origins on career success, measured in terms of salary attainment, and to investigate the organizational factors that seemed to give importance to the socioeconomic background in the salary attainment process. Pfeffer (1977c: 555–556) argued that socioeconomic background could provide three advantages to someone's career if promotion and hiring decisions were based on factors other than ability or performance. First, the respondents' social background would affect their similarity to those doing the hiring and promoting, with those from higher backgrounds having a greater likelihood of similarity. Given the research which demonstrates that interpersonal choice and attraction are significantly related to similarity (Byrne, 1969; Baskett, 1973), this social similarity could provide an advantage in the politics of promotion and hiring. Second, socioeconomic background might affect access to the type of social networks and contacts that Granovetter found to be important in the job finding process. And third, social background might be associated with personal attributes such as willingness to take risks, facility in language and self-presentation, self-confidence, and knowledge of dress and manners that would provide the respondent with an advantage in the career attainment process.

Controlling for other variables such as whether the individual was in a line or staff position, whether the person was self-employed, the number of years worked, and whether the person had a bachelor's or an MBA degree, Pfeffer (1977c: 560) observed a significant effect of socioeconomic origins on current salary for the sample of almost 300 business school graduates. Furthermore, Pfeffer found that either standardized admission test scores or grades while in school had no effect on salary. These findings are consistent with those from other studies which have found either small or insignificant effects of grades on career attainment. Harrell and Harrell (1975) found some effect for second-year elective grades but no effects for measures of mental ability for the sample of Stanford MBA students. They interpreted these results to indicate that motivation, rather than ability, was more critical in salary attainment, with the higher grades reflecting work effort and motivation more than skill or mental capacity.

Pfeffer's arguments concerning the conditions under which social class backgrounds would have effect dealt with those factors that would make the evaluation of objective performance more or less possible. The argument was that in the absence of objective, measurable indicators of performance, features such as social similarity and social skills would be more important in the career attainment process. Pfeffer observed that social class background had stronger effects on salary, controlling for other factors, in small rather than large organizations, in staff rather than line positions, and in finance, insurance, banking, or real estate as contrasted with manufacturing organizations. Large organizations were presumed to have more sophisticated evaluation and performance measurement procedures, and to have more developed internal labor markets that would lessen the effect of personal style and background relative to performance. Staff positions are more difficult to evaluate than line, because most line positions are more proximately connected to direct outcomes. And, the finance, insurance, and real estate businesses provide essentially undifferentiated services which are marketed largely through social contacts. Thus, Pfeffer's findings are consistent with those of Granovetter: both suggest that non-bureaucratically rational factors such as social similarity, social contacts, and personal style are more likely to affect career progress in those circumstances in which objective evaluations are more difficult to obtain or less likely to be available. These studies together support the arguments concerning the conditions under which politics will be used, which were described in Chapter 3 and also provide evidence for the effects of particularistic, political factors on the career outcomes of individuals.

Kanter's (1977) study of one specific corporation, Indsco (a fictitious name given to a real company), provides additional evidence consistent with these arguments. Kanter also recognized the critical role which uncertainty played in the demands for social homogeneity:

> *Conformity pressures and the development of exclusive management circles closed to "outsiders" stem from the degree of uncertainty surrounding managerial positions. . . . The greater the uncertainty, the greater the pressures for those who have to trust each other to form a homogeneous group (Kanter, 1977: 48–49).*

Selection on the basis of homogeneity tended, of course, to exclude women, and to place a premium on similar social backgrounds. In uncertain positions, which included particularly the higher managerial ranks, a premium was placed on similarity in the selection process. Performance, even in the sales part of the organization, was not as critical to promotion as was fitting in and being a good team player. Kanter wrote:

> *"Individual performers" who did a job unusually well but were not organization men could be rewarded by raises but not by promotions . . . the factors contributing to both promotions and raises were given approximately the same rank—except in the case of the item reflecting exceptional performance of the job content. This was seen as very important for a raise (ranked second) but much less important for promotion (ranked sixth). For promotion, such factors as reliability and dependability, skill with people, and seniority were considered more important. Fitting in socially was a requisite for the transition to managerial status (1977: 61).*

The implications of Kanter's argument, as well as the studies of Granovetter and Pfeffer, are that job performance is not a sufficient condition for career advancement in many organizational contexts and

251

may not even be necessary. Social similarity, social background, and social contacts are necessary and in many instances sufficient. This suggests that careers take on a political aspect, in which jobs and positions are evaluated in terms of the contacts they can provide, and strategic career moves are made to develop more social similarity and identification with those who are in the position to allocate rewards and promotions. It is in this sense that we can speak of a politics of careers.

As the power of different units in the organization changes, the career fortunes of those in those units change correspondingly. It is almost trite to suggest to persons who are choosing new jobs that they select organizations in which their skills and the unit in which they are to be hired are more critical and important. Nevertheless, the very validity of this advice suggests that the outcomes one can expect to obtain in an organization are very much a function of the power of one's subunit. This is illustrated specifically by the following item from the *Wall Street Journal:*

> *Golightly & Co. International, New York, surveyed 28 vice presidents at big Fortune 500 companies who deal directly with government regulations. The aim: to determine if their responsibilities and corporate standings have grown as federal regs increase. The conclusion: yes. Fully 86% said their positions had been upgraded because of their increased importance to top management. About 82% had increased their staffs.*
>
> *In addition, three fourths reported their positions had been upgraded to vice president in the past five years, and nearly half said their positions had been newly created in that period. About three-fourths attributed the upgrading to "a need to give more visibility to the function throughout the company" (Wall Street Journal,* July 24, 1979: 1).

Upgraded positions and titles, and larger staffs, all carry the connotation of higher salaries and more chances for even further advancement in the corporations.

The effect of subunit power on career advancement is also evident in the data collected on two University of California campuses (Moore and Pfeffer, in press). That particular university's personnel system has defined ranks (assistant, associate, and full professor for the regular faculty) and steps within those ranks. For each rank-step combination, there is a normative or normal time expected. Persons making normal career progress, for instance, stay in each assistant professor step for two years, and the time in the steps is three years at the full professor level. Given these normative times, it is possible to calculate quite precisely the amount of acceleration or deceleration (compared to normal) which an individual has experienced, and the proportion of the faculty at various ranks that have experienced a given amount of acceleration, deceleration, or normal progress for each department. A study of departments was done by a university administrative office, and the data from that study constituted the dependent variables for the analyses.

The basic hypothesis was that subunit, in this case, departmental power, affected the career progress and career speed of individual faculty in those departments. The data provide support for that assertion. There was a correlation of .46 (p < .05) between the proportion of assistant professors accelerated and subunit power, as assessed by total committee memberships, and a correlation of .47 (p < .05) between the proportion of full professors accelerated and the department's power. Only in the case of associate professors was a significant relationship not observed.

Of course, one might argue that accelerations in particular and career progress in general were affected primarily by the merit of the specific individuals involved, and that some departments, which were also the most powerful, had better faculty. This argument would maintain that power came from having the better faculty. Rather than power being the cause of accelerations, the better faculty which produced the faster career speed, also caused the subunit's power. As data were not obtained on individual performance, this argument is difficult to assess precisely. There was no correlation between departmental prestige and the indicators of subunit power, and furthermore, there was no correlation between departmental prestige, as assessed in the national rankings, and faculty career speed in the departments. Thus, if the distinguished faculty manifested itself in national prominence, the argument for the alternative interpretation is not consistent with the data.

Moreover, even if the data had been collected on individuals, it is not clear that would resolve the issue, because of problems of comparability. The norms are different for number of publications, publication type (book versus article), and length and type of publication (empirical versus theoretical) across disciplines. Comparing resumes on quantitative indicators of productivity across disciplines would certainly be problematic. Indeed, it is this very difficulty that makes it possible for power to have some effect on career outcomes. What we are suggesting is that there is probably a linear and possibly a multiplicative relationship between power and career performance. Clearly, individual productivity matters. It also matters, however, where the individual is located. High power departments can get more raises quickly for their average faculty member, and probably have the political clout to make especially effective arguments for their best faculty. The traditional literature on faculty salaries has emphasized the effects of individual level variables on faculty salary outcomes—variables such as the prestige of graduate program, age, number of articles, number of books, and so forth. The analysis suggested by these results would look at individual variables, departmental power, and the interaction of departmental power with individual performance as a determinant of individual salary outcomes.

A similar analysis might be conducted in other types of organizations. The fact that careers have political elements associated with them should not be taken to mean that performance is unimportant. Rather, one's subunit identification, contacts, social background, and political skills can contribute to advancement and interact with performance to facilitate career progress. A reasonably complete model of career achievement should take into account each of these components.

The Politics of Executive Succession

The choice of a new chief executive or new chief administrator, and the consequences of such a choice, could be examined more generally under the rubric of the politics of careers. However, the choice of the chief administrative officer of an organization has significant symbolic importance (Pfeffer, 1981), and may have more consequences for the organization's structure and decision making. Therefore, it is worthwhile to highlight a few facts. First, the replacement and selection of chief executives is as political, if not more so, than any other promotion or demotion in the organization. Second, the choice of a new chief executive typically puts in motion a series of actions which are designed to solidify and institutionalize that executive's power; these actions also have consequences for the careers of other high level executives.

In the model of organizational adaptation outlined by Pfeffer and Salancik (1978: Ch. 9), the argument was made that as environmental contingencies and constraints change, the power of subunits within the organization changes, as some subunits become more critical and important and others become less so. This new distribution of power becomes reflected in the selection of chief executives from the subunits which have acquired more power; the perspectives of these subunits and interests become represented in the structures and decision making of the organization through the mechanism of executive replacement. More generally, the selection and replacement of chief executives represent the interplay of power and politics in use, as these positions are symbols of control and powerful hierarchical positions in their own right.

Perrow (1961), in his examination of hospitals, found that the background of the chief administrators had shifted systematically over time. Initially, hospitals were places where one went to die, and were seen more as charitable organizations than as the providers of technical medical services. In keeping with such an orientation, the background of the administrators tended to be in areas related to fund-raising, community contact and charity. There was little attempt to hire someone who possessed either medical or administrative knowledge. Rather, the ability to run charitable organizations, and the capacity to interact effectively with wealthy sponsors in the community, were the critical elements of most administrators' backgrounds. The changing rules of legal liability governing the hospital's responsibility for its services (Zald and Hair, 1972) and changing expectations of the role of the hospital, which emphasized its delivery of quality medical services, brought a new set of administrators to power, doctors. When hospitals in the U.S. began to be defined in terms of the delivery of medical care, the medical profession became intimately involved in the administration of them. Typically, the chief hospital administrators during this period held an M.D. degree, and there were few hospitals of any size or quality that were not, in fact, headed by persons with medical backgrounds. More recently, the hospital's role has been redefined as part of a system of medical care. This redefinition, along with the cost containment pressures from the concentration of funding in the hands of a few private insurers and the federal government, has placed a greater emphasis on cost accounting and administrative efficiency skills. This is evidenced by the emphasis on formal training in hospital management and administration, and the replacement of doctors as chief administrators with persons who have business or administrative backgrounds. The history of hospital control indicates how the changing environment produced a shifting of power within the organization and, as a consequence, the changing backgrounds and orientations of the chief administrators.

Pfeffer and Salancik (1977b) observed a correlation between the hospital's environment and the background of the chief administrator for a sample of fifty-seven hospitals in Illinois. The relationship between context and background was observed more strongly for administrators who had been more recently appointed. Their findings are consistent with Perrow's argument concerning the effect of the environmental context on the distribution of control within organizations.

The view portrayed so far is one of ecological rationality—organizations that are successful respond to the changing environmental demands for certain decision making and structural outcomes which are consistent with the constraints and demands of their environments. Although organizational politics may, indeed, produce adaptation to environmental contingencies, it need not. As was noted in Chapter 4 on the determinants of power, there is some latitude within the organization for the use of argument and advocacy concerning the definition and solution of the critical organizational problems. Executive succession can, at times, be the result of internal organizational politics without there being any correlation with organizational adaptation.

In the 1950's, Mr. Robert R. Young, a wealthy investor, decided to displace William White, who was at that time the chief executive of the New York Central Railroad. As related by Mills (1956: 137–138), the following sequence of events took place:

> Over a luncheon table Young offered White the title of "chief operating officer" and stock options—"an opportunity to buy Central stock at a fixed price without any obligation to pay for it unless it went up." White refused, announcing that if Young moved in he would give up his contract: $120,000-per-year salary until retirement at 65; a $75,000-a-year consultant fee for the next five years; then a $40,000-a-year pension for life.
>
> Immediately White hired, out of Central's funds, a public relations firm at $50,000 a year plus expenses, turned over the $125 million advertising budget of the Central to the coming fight, and engaged a professional proxy solicitor from Wall Street. From Palm Beach, Young began maneuvering cliques among the rich and among friends with contacts to get control of blocks of the property. His side came to include three important members of the very rich—Allen P. Kirby of the Woolworth fortune; and two men each worth over $300 million: Clint Murchison, with whom Young had previously done business, and Sid Richardson, whose ranch Young had visited. The deal shaped up in such a way that a block of 800,000 shares at $26 a share ($20.8 million worth) was secured. Of course, the multimillionaires did not have to put up the cash: They borrowed it —mainly from the Allegheny Corporation, which Young is presumably able to treat as his personal property and .07 per cent of which he personally owns. And they borrowed it in such a way as to cover all risk except 200,000 shares. They were on the scheduled new board of directors. Young had 800,000 voting shares.
>
> Chase National Bank, a Rockefeller bank, had had the trusteeship of these shares and now had sold them to Murchi-

*son and Richardson. John J. McCloy, the Bank's board chair-
man, arranged for White to meet Richardson and Murchison,
who flew up the next day to New York City. The Texans, who
now owned 12½ per cent of the New York Central, attempted
to arrange a compromise. They failed, and a fight for the votes
of the more scattered owners began.*[35]

*Young's side spent $305,000. (Later the New York Central
repaid it, thus footing the bills of both the winners and the
losers.) One hundred solicitors for White from coast to coast
were reaching stockholders, as well as several hundred volun-
teer employees of the railroad. Young also engaged a professional proxy solicitation firm; he also had the services of Diebold, Inc., a firm manufacturing office furniture which
Murchison owned—250 of its salesmen were hired to solicit
proxies. If Young won, the office furniture for New York Central might henceforth be made by Diebold.*[36]

The depiction of this and other corporate proxy fights and take-
overs share many aspects in common: the fundamental issue most
often revolves around which of several competing interests will establish control over a large organization; the protagonists typically muster allies who are connected either through social or personal ties, or
through current or potential financial relationships; and the welfare
of the smaller shareholders and issues such as profit or performance
in these struggles serve either to legitimate one side or the other or
are not figured in at all. It is most often difficult to interpret these
contests in terms of some performance or other rational criterion.
The fight for corporate control, as represented by the fight over who
is to hold the chief executive position, is frequently political in nature. The descriptions, dimensions, and analyses of such contests for
control can be seen as analogous to political contests more generally.

This interpretation of the issues involved in the selection and replacement of chief executives is not solely the result of its source. It is
true that C. Wright Mills was a sociologist who critiqued the world of
corporate governance and financial interests. It is also true that the *Wall
Street Journal* and *Fortune* are basically pro-business, and fundamentally politically conservative news organizations. Reference to descriptions of executive succession events which are described by them leave
the impression that succession is political in nature, and is only loosely
related, if at all, to issues of corporate performance. This can be clearly
seen in the more recent events that transpired at International Telephone
and Telegraph.

THE CASE OF INTERNATIONAL
TELEPHONE AND TELEGRAPH

Harold Geneen had ruled ITT with an iron hand for many years. He had pursued a policy of growth through acquisition, and ITT had become a conglomerate firm with worldwide diversified operations. By 1977, Geneen was well into his 60's, and he had become increasingly tainted by scandals associated with the corporation. "In early 1977, ITT's board was concerned that Mr. Geneen's 1973 Senate testimony about the company's role with the Central Intelligence Agency in Chile could lead to a federal indictment for perjury against Mr. Geneen. Although Mr. Geneen didn't want to retire, the board insisted he step down" (Meyer, 1979: 1). Geneen was replaced by Lyman Hamilton, the company's chief financial officer and a person who had remained untouched throughout the various governmental investigations of ITT. When the government dropped possible prosecution of Geneen in March, 1978, the struggle over the succession of a chief executive at ITT began again.

Hamilton believed that the way to get ITT's stock price up was to concentrate on return on equity rather than growth per se. To that end, Hamilton began, almost immediately after taking office, to divest ITT of some of its subsidiaries, particularly a number of small subsidiaries in Europe that were not performing at what he believed to be acceptable levels. Hamilton's strategy was, of course, the exact opposite of the strategy Geneen had followed. "It was a question," according to Ulric Weil, a vice president of Morgan Stanley & Co., "of whether to achieve higher profitability through greater efficiencies like cutting back employees, or through aggrandizing by acquisition and increasing the size of the empire" (Meyer, 1979: 27). Hamilton's moves, needless to say, made the managers of the European subsidiaries very unhappy. It was also an affront to Geneen and his policies.

Geneen was able to oust Hamilton, primarily it appears, because Hamilton was not very sensitive to the politics of the situation and to maintaining good relations with the board of directors.

> At the time of Mr. Hamilton's appointment, a securities analyst close to the company recalls, "I wondered how such a man would ever survive in the political jungle of ITT." The jungle grew more forbidding with each of Mr. Hamilton's moves. "Geneen was totally paranoid about what Hamilton was doing to his company," one insider says (Meyer, 1979: 1).

Hamilton was insensitive to the fact that the board was composed primarily of people who had been selected by Geneen, and thought he had the board's support in the political struggle that was developing. But, whatever support he might have had, he lost by not paying enough attention to the cultivation of the board members:

> But the board was also becoming increasingly alienated by Mr. Hamilton's methods. For unlike Mr. Geneen, who had lavished personal attention and perks on his outside directors, Mr. Hamilton seemingly ignored them. A case in point centered on ITT's $147.5 million stock-swap acquisition late last year of Qume Corp., the high-speed printer-maker.
>
> It was ITT's biggest acquisition of 1978, but "neither Qume nor ITT sought or obtained any independent evaluation by an investment banker, of the fairness of the conversion rate," Qume said in its proxy material. Mr. Hamilton wouldn't have had to look far for such an evaluation. There are two investment bankers on the ITT board—Felix G. Rohatyn of Lazard Freres & Co. and Alvin E. Friedman of Lehman Bros, Kuhn Loeb Inc.
>
> (The firms of Messrs. Rohatyn and Friedman didn't do nearly as much business with ITT under Mr. Hamilton as they did before he came to power. During 1978, the only full year that Mr. Hamilton was in command, fees paid by the company to Lazard fell to $117,900 from $957,820 in 1977, and fees paid to Lehman dropped to $130,687 from $1.2 million in 1977) (Meyer, 1979: 27).

While Mr. Hamilton was on a three-week business trip to Asia, Geneen returned from Europe and convinced the directors, one by one, that Hamilton had to be dismissed. The board obtained Hamilton's resignation and immediately appointed in his place Mr. Rand V. Araskog, Mr. Geneen's choice as successor.

> "Who is Rand Araskog?" an executive of another company who is close to Mr. Geneen was asked. "Araskog is somebody Geneen likes; Hamilton is somebody Geneen doesn't like, and it looks like Geneen won," he said (Metz, 1979: 4).

There is one final postscript to the story, to indicate the role of firm performance and shareholder wealth behind all these machinations:

The ITT announcement came after Wednesday's market close. Yesterday, after a trading delay due to an imbalance of sell orders, ITT stock closed on the New York Stock Exchange composite tape at $28 a share, down $1 for the day (Metz, 1979: 4).

Thus, to the extent to which the securities market is an efficient assimilator of information and market valuation represents the best estimate of a company's present worth as perceived by its likely future prospects, the replacement of Hamilton by Araskog was not a move that seemed to reflect the best long run performance and profitability interests of the company.

Again, as in the case of the New York Central replacement, the role of critical allies which are bound by personal and financial ties can be seen. Again, the replacement crisis centered more around issues of personal style and control over the enterprise, than over performance or other, similar objective indicators of success.

THE CASE OF MCGRAW-HILL

Another example of the politics of executive succession can be found by considering the sequence of successions at McGraw-Hill. As reported by Holt (1979) in an article in *Fortune,* McGraw-Hill was developed from a foundation of technical magazines such as *American Machinist* and technical books. The company was founded in 1909 and when Hill died in 1916, leaving no heirs who were interested in managing the business, James McGraw assumed complete control of the company. Control has remained in the hands of McGraws since that time. By the time McGraw retired in 1935, the firm published more than twenty magazines and its foundation in the trade magazine and trade and technical book markets was firmly established.

At this point, the company faced the first of its succession crises. Jay McGraw, one of James McGraw's four sons, took over the company.

He ran the company so autocratically that even his brothers had to make appointments to see him. A chain-of-command jumper, Jay would promote editors or raise an employee's pay on the spot. . . . He could be rude and arrogant. But in 1950, his fed-up brothers got together and ousted him (Holt, 1979: 102).

It is important to note that this first succession crisis occurred not because of profit problems, but because Jay could not keep the other holders of McGraw-Hill stock happy by involving them and making them feel important. Jay had not originally been selected because of any particular managerial aptitude—rather, he was the oldest of the four sons (there was also one daughter), and assumed the chief executive position primarily because of this seniority.

The next chief executive was the second eldest of the four sons, Curtis.

> *Curtis, a likable former Princeton football star with a genius for good employee relations, stepped in to repair the morale damage. Three years later . . . he fell dead of a heart attack at the age of fifty-seven (Holt, 1979: 103–104).*

The next eldest son, Donald, took over the company and ran it until his retirement in 1968. At that time, the company was turned over to Shelton Fisher, the only person not from the McGraw family to run the company. Fisher attained and maintained his position, however, primarily because he understood the necessity of placating the various family interests.

> *. . . most agree that he handled one aspect of his job superbly —being the family regent. He was able to get the support of the family for most of what he did. Still, even though he had the title of c.e.o., he was probably not as free to act as it seemed at the time. He had to keep in touch. One family member recently expressed surprise when reminded that Fisher was the chief in those years (Holt, 1979: 104).*

It was under Fisher, an outsider, that the company began to shed its conservative financial image and embarked on an expansion program that was important to its long term success and growth. Under Fisher, the firm acquired Standard and Poor's Corporation, *Medical World News,* and four television stations, as well as built a new headquarters building in Rockefeller Center. The television stations in particular have paid off with very high returns on investment, and the expansion into financial reporting and analysis, with the acquisition of Standard and Poor's, has been another key element in the company's growth and diversification. It is interesting to note that this major expansion occurred during the tenure of the only outside chief executive. This is consistent with the views of many top executives in the firm who "believe that professional management instead of a succession of McGraws would have been more imaginative and aggressive" (Holt, 1979: 102).

When Fisher retired in 1974, the company faced its second succession crisis. It was clear that someone from the McGraw family would again assume the chief executive position, but the question was which one.

Ambitious executives began taking sides. Big, gregarious Donald Jr. was the popular favorite. Then in his early forties, he had held a variety of high executive posts in the publications company. . . . Gossip in the trade breathlessly tracked the ups and downs of Don's chances, rated John, then in his thirties, a dark horse, and barely mentioned Harold. The eldest son of the only second-generation McGraw who had never run the company, Harold McGraw Jr. was tucked away in the book company . . . magazines gave the company its public identity. Also, Harold was working for a boss, Edward Booher, president of McGraw-Hill books, who didn't think much of him and kept pushing non-family executives into prominence (Holt, 1979: 106).

Harold was able to obtain control by forming an alliance with some of the McGraw women who owned shares in the company. By 1975, Harold McGraw was president, chairman, and c.e.o. One of his first moves upon assuming power was to eliminate the position of group-president, a job held by Edward Booher, who retired and left the board of directors. Harold also forced his cousin, Donald McGraw, out of the company by denying him a position of influence or authority. Within a short period after assuming control, then, Harold McGraw had eliminated from the firm family members who might have been potential rivals and a senior vice president who had been unsupportive of his career aspirations.

Several elements stand out in Holt's description of McGraw-Hill and its management. First, it is clear that succession and advancement within the corporation was dependent in part on performance, but was even more dependent upon the ability to forge alliances with powerful ownership interests, since stock ownership was an important source of power in the company. Persons who guessed succession struggle outcomes unsuccessfully, like Booher, found themselves out of power and on their way out of the company. Fisher's success came not only from the expansion he undertook but also from his ability to serve as a family representative who was trusted and sensitive to the various McGraw family interests. Harold McGraw's succession to power came from his ability to forge alliances with other ownership interests, and was not primarily a function of previous background, training, or demonstrated administrative or executive skills.

Second, there is evidence to suggest that change in strategy and organizational adaptation tended to come about primarily through the various political struggles associated with succession. Organizational redesign (the elimination of the group-president positions) and organizational expansion could both be seen as the outcomes of succession patterns and the needs of those emerging as chief executives to solidify their power. In the case of Harold McGraw, the strategy involved reorganizing to force enemies and rivals out of the firm. In the case of Shelton Fisher, such a strategy was infeasible, since he was not a member of the family. His strategy involved a program of expansion which provided visible evidence of growth and success and helped maintain his position of stature and power within the firm.

The third lesson from the history of McGraw-Hill is that change is often accomplished by outside succession or by bringing in persons from outside the dominant management interest to run the company. This point will be developed in more detail when we consider the institutionalization of power in the next chapter.

One final point emerges from Holt's description. Although profits, sales, and growth are mentioned, they are treated almost as byproducts of a series of political struggles over succession and control within the firm. Although such a deemphasis is probably unintentional and not fully warranted, the idea that business firms are characterized by decision making that is not completely determined by profit considerations or share price maximization is a point worth remembering. It is not just public bureaucracies and universities that are the scenes for organizational power and politics; business firms also demonstrate choice processes in which evidence for the operation of power and politics can be clearly discerned. The consequences of organizational power can be observed in organizational strategies, patterns of resource allocation, organizational structures, and in the careers of organizational employees. "Booher, an intellectual who is still highly regarded in textbook publishing, has to go down as one of the more careless office politicians. 'It just never occurred to me that Harold would one day be my boss,' he says now" (Holt, 1979: 106).

Zald (1965), in describing the choice of a successor in a social welfare organization, noted that the decision was consequential for the future direction of the organization, and had the further importance of demonstrating the relative power of the various interests to all within the organization. Therefore, Zald argued, succession decisions were almost inevitably political. They provide a forum in which the power of the various participants in the organizations can operate in a way that provides symbolic ratification of that power, and leads to an outcome that can either enhance or diminish their power, depending on the success or failure of the favored candidate. It seems clear that similar observations hold for succession in corporations as well. The symbolic consequences, as well as the control accomplished by such succession, make succession a critical and contested event, and therefore a forum in which the power of various interests and their political skills are brought to bear.

THE CONSEQUENCES OF EXECUTIVE SUCCESSION FOR OTHER MANAGERS

In political organizations such as governments, when a new leader takes over, he or she typically acts to remove high level personnel from the previous administration and brings in new personnel to operate the government. This replacement of the old personnel by new personnel who are loyal and in sympathy with the aims and goals of the new leader is taken for granted in governments, but is not frequently thought of as occurring in formal, more bureaucratized organizations. Nevertheless, there is evidence that, consistent with the political model, a similar replacement of executives is observed on the occasion of the succession of a new chief executive.

Such replacement, of course, is much more widespread and likely to occur if the successor comes from outside the organization. As Carlson (1962) noted in his study of school superintendents, outside successors are usually hired to accomplish change and are less bound up with and constrained by the organizational history and its commitments. Consequently, since they are not part of the system and represent change, the need for replacing other executives and for bringing in personnel who are loyal to them is greater for executives who come from outside the organization. The new successor is also likely to obtain additional positions, and to attempt to replace the occupants of current high level positions. Kotin and Sharaf (1967) suggested that this expansion of positions was a result of the outside successor's belief that it would be easier to recruit new personnel for new positions than it would be to replace the current occupants of already created positions. Thus, there are two responses that are commonly observed when a new executive takes over: the replacement of key subordinate personnel with personnel who are loyal to the new executive; and the expansion of the number of subordinate positions so that the new executive can bring in loyal subordinates without encountering the difficulty of replacing present position occupants. The two strategies are, of course, not mutually exclusive. Because of the lack of connections and social similarity with present organizational executives, it is likely that these strategies are more likely to be employed by an outside successor or by a successor who represents more change in the organization.

Carlson (1972), in surveying 100 school districts in California and their superintendents, found that the outside successors tended to expand the number of positions in the central office at a faster rate than inside successors. Whisler (1960) found that outside successors made greater initial use of assistant administrators. Gouldner (1952) also observed that an outside successor tended to make more replacements in those positions which immediately surrounded the executive positions. Helmich and Brown (1972: 371) observed:

> ... the replacement of persons in the executive role constellation enables the outsider (1) to get rid of those old lieutenants who appear to be shirking their duties, (2) to quiet those in the surrounding work team who might oppose the leader's new policies, and (3) to bring in new lieutenants who are loyal to the successor. In short, the use of strategic replacements empowers the outside manager to form a new informal social circle which revolves around himself and supports his own status and policies.

It is important to recognize that these functions are served for either the inside or outside successor; it is only that the inside successor is already more bound to and familiar with the other executives than the outside successor, and thus needs less strategic replacement to ensure their loyalty and commitment to him.

Helmich and Brown (1972) tested the effect of inside versus outside succession on the amount of change in the executive's immediate role constellation for a sample of 208 firms in the chemical and allied products industry. They observed a gamma coefficient of association of .33 between outside successor type and the amount of change in personnel in executive positions, an association that was statistically significant at less than the .02 level of probability and that maintained its significance when various control variables were introduced into the analysis. Helmich and Brown (1972: 378) concluded, "... organizations experiencing inside succession, relative to organizations undergoing outside succession in the office of corporate president tend to exhibit less organizational change in the executive role constellation within two years after succession." Their results for a sample of corporations, taken with Carlson's for school superintendents and Kotin and Sharaf's for hospital administrators, suggest the relative ubiquity of the replacement phenomenon. Furthermore, the explicitly political nature of this process, in which surrounding personnel are removed almost regardless of performance so that the new executive can bring in persons loyal to him or her, provides further evidence which is consistent with a political model of organizations more generally, and executive succession in particular. Replacement of personnel or the expansion of administrative positions accompanies both inside and outside succession, but is more pronounced in the case of outside succession.

These results suggest that the frequency and form of succession are important explanatory variables in understanding the growth of administrative assistant positions in organizations as well as for understanding organizational change processes. The implications are clear for other executives in the organization: succession of any kind, but particularly outside succession, is likely to be threatening for those currently occupying high level executive positions. This fact can help to account for the kind of resistance Hamilton received at ITT and for the strong pressures operating in most organizations against outside succession.

Thus, ironically, the politics of succession that make change more likely with an outsider, because of the wholesale expansion and/or replacements that are likely to follow, also make the choice of an outsider more problematic and resistance to the new outside executive more intense. One would expect to see the kind of coalition building and politics observed in the ITT case more often with an outside successor than with an inside successor in any kind of formal organization. Organizational change is threatening to those who benefit, in terms of power and perquisites, from the current arrangements, and these persons are likely to try to institutionalize control and power in order to resist change and outside succession. The institutionalization of power will be explored in more depth in Chapter 8.

The Politics of Organizational Structures

Organizational structures have most frequently been analyzed as a problem in design or engineering, with the issue being how structures can be developed to maximize the organization's effectiveness. An alternate view (Pfeffer, 1978a; 1978b) looks at structure as being the outcome of a political contest for control within the organization which, at the same time, provides participants with further advantages in the political struggle because of their structural positions.

> *The design of an organization, its structure, is first and foremost the system of control and authority by which the organization is governed. In the organizational structure, decision discretion is allocated to various positions and the distribution*

*of formal authority is established. Furthermore, by establish-
ing the pattern of prescribed communication and reporting
requirements, the structure provides some participants with
more and better information and more central locations in the
communication network. . . . Thus, organizational structures
create formal power and authority by designating certain persons to do certain tasks and make certain decisions and create
informal power through the effect on information and communication structures within the organization. Organizational
structure is a picture of the governance of the organization and
a determinant of who controls and decides organizational activities (Pfeffer, 1978a: 38).*

It is inevitable, given the power and authority conferred, that one of the
foci of politics within the organization will involve the structural arrangements or the design of the organization.

Rather than being viewed as designed to produce effectiveness,
since effectiveness is a relative concept anyway, issues such as profit and
return can be viewed as constraints which delimit the ability of those in
the political struggle to design organizations without any regard for their
economic efficiency. Necessary rates of return, product market and capital market competition may constrain the extent to which organizational
structures can depart from economic efficiency concerns, but as Child
(1972) has noted, such functional requirements are seldom binding on
design decisions.

Although there is virtually no comparative empirical work which
attempts to explain organizational structures from a political theory
perspective, it is possible to develop arguments concerning the explanation and prediction of structural dimensions by following this theoretical
line. The predictions can guide both the observation and study of organizational structures in the future. After developing these predictions, we
will illustrate the politics of design with a specific example from a large
financial institution.

DIFFERENTIATION

Differentiation has typically been defined and measured as the number
of different subunits—departments, divisions, or bureaus—in an organization when it is considered horizontally, or by the number of levels in
the hierarchy when vertical differentiation is the topic of study. Differentiation has been most frequently and consistently correlated with organizational size (e.g., Blau and Schoenherr, 1971; Meyer, 1972), with the

argument being that larger organizational size facilitates the increasing division of labor which produces more numerous subunits and levels in the hierarchy. Although size is clearly and logically related to differentiation, it is not the only or even the most theoretically interesting explanation of the vertical and horizontal elaboration of organizational structures. As Meyer (1971) demonstrated, assuming constant spans of control, increasing organizational size inevitably leads to vertical differentiation, and a similar logical relationship exists for size and horizontal differentiation.

Size certainly does not explain why universities with relatively small faculties of 1,500 or so have more than eighty departments, while much larger public and private organizations have the same or fewer subdivisions, or why professional schools of approximately the same size are departmentalized in some cases and not in others. The commonly adduced explanation other than size is environmental uncertainty. The argument is that uncertainty and rapidity of change foster the differentiation of structures in organizations (Thompson, 1967: Lawrence and Lorsch, 1967). Both size and environmental conditions need to be considered in any explanation of differentiation, but some distinctly political predictors of differentiation can also be developed.

The first question to pose is, what does differentiation provide? Differentiation provides many things, but one thing is formal, recognized status for a given level or horizontal unit in the organization. Consider horizontal differentiation for a moment. The creation of a Management Development department provides legitimation and status for the activity of management development and those who work on it, just as the creation of a Marketing Research department does for those involved in that activity. The creation of a subunit with its own name and identification provides assurance of a continuing claim on the organization's resources; activities are much more readily added and subtracted when it does not entail the reorganization or closing down of a whole department. The creation of a subunit on a given hierarchical level gives that activity formal equivalence in terms of symbolic importance with other activities on that same level. It also provides a starting point for the subunit equivalent of the managerial career ladder, the climb of a function or division up the organization. Furthermore, as Leeds (1964) has suggested, the creation of a specific subunit provides those associated with the unit with a stake and legitimacy in the organization, which can serve to coopt protest that might otherwise occur. Thus, by providing status, assurance of continued resources at some minimal level at least, and symbolic recognition of the importance of a function, the subunit becomes a measure of a group's importance or power in the organization.

When is such symbolic reassurance most necessary? It is necessary when there is a great deal of conflict and heterogeneity within the organization and when such domain creation can delimit the political conflict that might otherwise occur at an unacceptable level. Thus, differentiation should be positively related to the number of different disciplines, professional specialties, kinds of educational degrees, and educational institutions and backgrounds represented in the organization's workforce. All of these factors increase the heterogeneity of the organization's participants and therefore the potential conflict over policies, technologies, and goals in the organization. Increased heterogeneity and difference in point of view is likely to result in giving each different specialty, and point of view, legitimacy by giving it its own subunit.

The heterogeneity and diversity of the organization's environment, or the environment it has chosen to cope with, should also help predict the amount of differentiation within the organization. The implication of this argument is that it is diversity and the potential for conflict, not so much change or uncertainty per se, that requires the establishment of different subunits to cope with the different environmental segments (Thompson, 1967: Ch. 6) and to provide the diverse interests represented within the organization with symbolic reassurance of their importance.

This argument also suggests why merger and consolidation is difficult, and why the way in which growth occurs—either through acquisition or internal expansion—may be important in affecting the extent of differentiation. When a merger or consolidation occurs, the new organization contains participants from both the acquired organization and the one which brought about the merger. The acquired organization's members may be particularly insecure about their position in the new organization (which is why increased turnover often results), and thus, it is difficult to achieve the forecast economies by folding them into the previous organizational structures. The acquired organization's members will want their own subunits, divisions or departments, and domains or else they will feel powerless in the new structure. If the merged organizations are of close to equal size, the new participants will have the power to obtain such recognition through the establishment of additional units representing their definition of the world and the technology of the organization. By contrast, internal growth may permit the slow accumulation of new members. These members can, potentially, be hired for their similarity in background and training to those already in the organization, and at an early stage in their careers so that socialization is possible. This socialization and acculturation leads to a greater homogeneity in perspec-

269

tive within the organization (Ouchi and Johnson, 1978), and therefore, to less differentiation of the organization's structure.

The form of control used may also affect the level of structural elaboration which is observed. Organizations that hire on the basis of homogeneity of orientation or background, or that employ strong socialization practices, create a more homogeneous culture. This homogeneous culture will result in less structural differentiation, not only because there may be less explicit task specialization but also because the greater commitment to and identification with the total organization reduces the politics and power struggles that are one of the sources of the creation of new subunits in the first place.

If differentiation is to be measured not only by the number of subunits or levels but also, as Lawrence and Lorsch (1967) suggested, by the differences in goal orientations, time perspective, and structural attributes across the various departments or subunits, the preceding arguments would still be expected to hold. They suggest that differentiation is, at best, only indirectly related to the task and technology of the organization. The indirect relationship is through the task and technological requirements for certain skills, specialties, and points of view. Collins (1979) has suggested that the educational or training requirements of modern organizations are probably overstated, not only in terms of their level, but also in terms of the effects of these skill requirements on organizational operations. The level of differentiation is more likely to be predicted by the power-dependence relations between the organization and the various groups from the environment that comprise and interact with it. The greater the diversity and number of these groups in terms of backgrounds, views of goals and technology, and importance for organizational survival, the more differentiated the resulting organizational structure is likely to be.

CENTRALIZATION

In addition to the degree of structural elaboration, another critical variable used when describing organizational designs is the degree of concentration of authority and decision making within the structure. The literature on centralization has several strands which provide somewhat complementary and not completely comprehensive explanations of the degree of decision centralization in the organization. Blau and Schoenherr (1971) argue that as organizations become larger, there will be a greater reliance on formalization, or the use of impersonal rules and procedures, and a diminished reliance on personal bases of control, if for no other reason than the fact that individual information processing limitations preclude the personal control of large organizations. Other arguments which are based on the functional necessity for different degrees of centralization emphasize environmental characteristics rather than organizational size. Thus, for example, Burns and Stalker (1961) suggest that mechanistic, more tightly controlled structures are appropriate in stable, predictable environments, while organic, more flexible structures are better suited when the environment is technologically complex and rapidly changing. These contingency theories of structure enjoy much more general acceptance than the supporting evidence would warrant. Pennings (1975), in a study of stock brokerage offices, found little support for the contingency theories of organizational structure. Child (1972) has argued that neither size, technology, nor environmental requirements are so binding in most organizations so as to remove the potential for choice of the structural arrangements by those in power in the organization.

Child's focus on strategic choice is quite compatible with our emphasis on the politics of structures, as both positions imply that to understand organizational designs, one must examine the distribution of power and the preferences of those in the organization's dominant coalition. In the argument concerning the distribution of decision making authority, it is assumed that every one in the organization wants as much decision making control as possible, and that political, as well as technical or information processing limitations help to determine the actual distribution of decision making power.

"If structure is the mechanism for control, the representation of control, and the manifestation of organizational power and influence, then it is logical to presume that structure will differ depending on the distribution and particularly the concentration of power in the organization" (Pfeffer, 1978a: 46). Thus, one predictor of the degree of centralization is simply the degree to which determinants of power are concentrated in the organization. One form which concentrated power may take is in the concentration of the ownership of the stock of a corporation. Ownership of company shares certainly represents a source, though clearly not the only source, of power in an organization. Thus, the more highly concentrated the share ownership, the more centralized control should be in the organization.

Child (1973: 10) reported a significant correlation between the concentration of organizational ownership and centralization ($r = .47$; p $< .001$). He also reported a negative relationship between the concentration of ownership and the perceived authority of higher level managers ($r = -.32$; $p < .05$). Both results are consistent with this argument.

Centralization is increased in the organization in which ownership power is also concentrated, and the power of higher level managers relative to those of the external owners is decreased in situations of concentrated ownership control.

Hage and Aiken (1969) found that the routinization of the task was correlated with the degree of centralization observed in the organizational structure. This finding is also understandable from a political or power-oriented perspective. The strategic contingencies' theory of power (Hickson et al., 1971) which was outlined in Chapter 4 argued that power was the joint result of the extent to which the subunit could cope with critical uncertainties and the degree to which such coping capacity was unique or nonsubstitutable. The routinization of tasks in organizations accomplishes two things. First, routinization reduces the amount of uncertainty present in the task, and thus the opportunity for coping with uncertainty. A routine task, which by definition is repeated many times and is programmable, is the epitomy of certainty in organizational operations. Second, the reduction in the uncertainty to be dealt with and the reduction, therefore, in the complexity of the tasks and the skills required to do the task, makes those performing the job much more replaceable. It is easier to find someone who can learn to do a relatively simple repetitive task than to find someone who can learn a more complex and elaborate set of task procedures. The combination of these two factors suggests that those performing more routinized tasks have less power. With less power, they can claim and obtain less decision making discretion in the organization.

The relationship between task routinization, the loss of power, and therefore the loss in decision making authority, can help to explain the frequently observed tendency for individuals or subunits to avoid the introduction of technology or techniques that would increase task routinization in their domains of work. This also suggests that the psychological consequences of routine jobs may involve more than just the affective reaction to the nature of the work itself. It has become customary to relate job attitudes to the variety, autonomy, and skill required in the job (e.g., Hackman and Lawler, 1971). The underlying assumption of that argument is that most persons, and particularly those with stronger growth needs, prefer jobs with more challenge and variety. An alternative explanation for the relationship between job dimensions and attitudes involves, however, the relationship of job dimensions to the power of the various social actors. Participants performing routine, repetitive tasks which require little skill have little power in the organization and thus minimal decision making authority over their own working conditions or other issues in the organization. The negative attitudes and lack of motivation which are sometimes observed may result from this powerlessness rather than from the psychological properties of the tasks themselves. This argument suggests, for instance, that the presence of a strong union with contract provisions that provide more worker control over the pace and environment of the work may diminish the relationship between task routineness and negative attitudes toward the job. Indeed, any strategy that provides more power for the workers may negate the relationship between task characteristics and task attitudes, to the extent that this relationship is partly spurious, and really captures the relationship between participant power and affective reactions to the job.

A political perspective can also help to account for some of the results reported in the literature on participative decision making. Heller and Yukl (1969), for instance, assessed the amount of subordinate influence as a component of decision behavior. In comparing three groups of industrial leaders, they found that the higher a leader was in the organizational hierarchy the less centralized was his decision making style (1969: 234). A group of student leaders were found to be less centralized in their decision making styles than even the highest level industrial leaders. Heller and Yukl also reported that decision making centralization varied across functional area (1969: 235). Production and finance had the most centralized decision making, sales and purchasing were intermediate, and general management and personnel were the least centralized. In all three management levels, the research showed the centralization increased with the time spent in the present position.

In each case, the results can be explained in terms of the relative power of the supervisor and subordinate involved. Consider first the difference in decision making centralization by functional area. Production and finance are more likely to be more routinized than are sales or purchasing. The general management task and personnel are the least likely to be routinized. This is true in the former case because of the non-specificity of the role and the wide variety of skills and tasks required. In the latter case, the function itself has not yet been defined with enough precision to facilitate task routinization in most organizations. The greater uncertainty in general management, sales, and purchasing provides subordinates in those functions with more power than they might have in the more routinized production or finance function. This increased power provides them with greater decision making authority.

Consider next the differences by hierarchical level. A similar explanation can hold in this case. As one moves up the hierarchy, the task uncertainty is likely to increase (e.g., Kanter, 1977). The greater uncertainty and diminished routinization provides more power to the subordinates at these higher levels, and thus, they have more say in decision making. The difference between student leaders and managers can be explained by the greater formal mechanisms of control such as raises, promotions, and firing or demotion which are possessed by the leaders in formal organizations. The student leaders, who possessed fewer of these control mechanisms and therefore, fewer bases of power, were more equal to their subordinates in terms of power, and therefore had to share the decision making responsibility.

Finally, time spent in the present position provides the individual with more knowledge about the job and the function being managed. This greater knowledge provides some incremental expert power for the position incumbent. This increased power affords the position incumbent a greater advantage over his or her subordinates, and thus, results in less sharing of decision making authority. In each instance, there are simple relationships between the dimension in question and the relative power of the various hierarchical levels that can parsimoniously account for the observed results. A fuller test of this argument would involve measuring relative power directly rather than inferring power differences from other variables. Our expectation is that with power included as an intervening variable, the explanation of decision participation would be substantially enhanced.

The general argument developed to explain centralization, then, is that it is a consequence of the extent to which the sources of power are concentrated in organizations. If uncertainty coping capability, resource provision, ownership, information, and technical skills critical to the organization's operation are concentrated, the organizational structure will be more centralized. This perspective implicitly adopts the position that decision making discretion is the result of a political contest for control within organizations. Decision making authority is seldom granted or given in an effort to enhance decision making quality or organizational efficiency. Rather, decision making descretion is provided to those with enough power in the organization to effectively demand and claim that discretion.

As a final illustration of this argument, consider the greater degree of centralization which is commonly found in functionally organized as contrasted with divisionally organized firms. In the functionally organized structure, each major business function is located in only one department—there is one marketing department, one production department, one engineering or research and development department, and so forth. By contrast, divisionalized structures may and typically do have multiple marketing or sales units, production units, and even research, personnel, and other staff units. In the divisionalized structure, each subunit is less critical to the overall organization because of the lesser degree of interdependence with the rest of the organization and it is more likely to be pooled rather than sequential or reciprocal interdependence (Thompson, 1967). Furthermore, each division is more substitutable, because there are numerous other divisions in the structure. Because there are more potential positions of power in the structure (Thompson, 1967), each division or each position has less power as a consequence. In a divisionalized structure, it is much less likely that a single unit can come to have the domination over the organization that a unit in a functionally organized structure can attain. In a functionally organized structure, interdependence is higher and there is no way of substituting for the uncertainty or resource providing capacity of the specific unit. Consequently, power is more widely shared and the structure is more decentralized in the divisionalized organization. The potential for centralization and domination is greater in the functional organizational form.

It seems clear that studies of centralization, and also differentiation, formalization, and other structural attributes could be enriched by the inclusion of power as an explanatory variable. Power and politics can apparently readily incorporate existing research findings, and can suggest additional arguments and hypotheses in the explanation of organizational designs. And, power and politics are critical concerns in organizational change and redesign (Pfeffer, 1978b: Ch. 7).

INFORMATION SYSTEMS

The design and incorporation of management information systems into the organization is another element of structure that can be analyzed from a political perspective. The existing literature on information systems is primarily normative in orientation, and argues about what file structures, table layouts, and degree of comprehensiveness should be incorporated in order to improve managerial decision making. Yet, as was noted in Chapter 4, information and control over information is an important source of power in organizations (Pettigrew, 1972). Thus, it is inevitable that the design and location of information systems will be entwined with the struggle for power which occurs in many organizations.

The design of a financial information system at the Golden Triangle Corporation, which was described by Markus (1979), provides evidence on this point. The financial information system collects and summarizes financial data from input covering transactions involving expenses, revenues, assets, and liabilities. The system outputs monthly profit and loss statements by division and for the whole company, as well as balance sheets.

Golden Triangle is a major chemical manufacturing concern which operates internationally, with sales in excess of $3 billion. It is organized into a staff group that includes accounting and four fairly autonomous operating groups (Markus, 1980: 7). Within each operating group are divisions which are headed by general managers. Divisional accountants report directly to these general managers, with only an indirect relationship to corporate accounting. Corporate accounting is supposed to provide "broad policy guidelines" (Markus, 1980: 8).

In 1971, Golden Triangle had a multiplicity of reporting systems in use. Seven different computerized systems and numerous manual systems were in use in the divisions. The introduction of the financial information system would serve to standardize these systems and store all transactions in a single, centralized data base. Prior to the development of the new system "divisional accountants had collected and stored transaction data however they saw fit, but had reported summary data to corporate accountants in a standardized format" (Markus, 1980: 7). Clearly, the introduction of the standardized system would profoundly change the relationship between corporate and divisional controllers, as well as between the division and headquarters operating managers.

The idea for the information system came from corporate accounting. Since 1964, Golden Triangle had grown very rapidly through merger. Some units were sold as others were acquired. Each change in organizational structure created problems in reporting and accounting. The financial information system was designed to provide better control over a very large, diverse, rapidly growing and changing company.

But there was more than managerial control and more effective deployment of resources at stake. First, with the acquisition of newer, more rapidly growing subunits, the original chemical division was beginning to fall in power. Corporate accounting was headed by a person who was a long-standing enemy of the controller of the chemical division. Furthermore, it was almost certain that the new divisions would attempt to operate independently and would resist control from corporate headquarters.

The single, centralized data base would solve several problems for the corporate accounting office. First, it would enhance its power, which it felt was lacking because of its indirect control over the various division controllers. Second, it would enhance the centralized control of the corporate management over the divisions. Prior to the implementation of the system, virtually all data on divisional operations had to be obtained from the divisions; after the installation of the new system, divisions would be unable to resist or delay in the furnishing of information. There had been accusations of misreporting figures and this would also be stopped by the centralized system.

Of course, what was good for corporate was, in general, bad for the divisions. The loss of autonomy and control over their operations information would involve a loss of discretion to corporate. Thus, in many respects the original information system design was a political choice. When it was time to implement it, corporate accounting went to an outside vendor for the system, to avoid having to rely on internal operating support. The divisions fought cooperation with the new system, attacking its design, technical adequacy, and feasibility. The process dragged on over years, costing numerous hours of effort and meetings. Attempts were made by the divisions to sabotage the system. During the conflict, the head of accounting for the chemical division was reorganized out of his job. Ironically, if that had been accompanied by some similar moves, it would have made the original design politically unnecessary. Control could have been exercised through the placement of allies in those positions (recall the discussion of the promotion of the unobvious choice in Chapter 5).

There are two lessons to be gleaned from Markus's (1979) analysis of Golden Triangle. First, the events in the organization are much more readily understood from a political rather than a rational perspective. The information system was part and parcel of a power struggle within the company as the various divisions developed a stable power relationship among themselves and with corporate headquarters. Second, because of the technical nature of many of these systems, and because of the ultimate dependence on outside vendors for the software and support and the divisions themselves for cooperation in data entry and design, a computerized financial information system is *not* the most effective political weapon to be used in struggles within the organization. In this case, reorganizations and replacements of personnel worked more effectively. Moreover, delays and cost overruns in the system substantially threatened the position of the corporate accounting chief and those associated with the introduction of the system. In playing politics, it is useful to operate from a less vulnerable position.

STRUCTURAL CHANGE
AT FEDERAL FINANCE

The operation of political factors in the design of organizations is exemplified by the sequence of events at Federal Finance, a fictitious name for an actual financial intermediary organization. Federal Finance was created through a series of mergers by the man who now serves as its president and owns 54% of the stock in the company. The company was created in the 1960's by combining, under one ownership, a set of smaller organizations which were previously in the same business. The founder of Federal Finance does not have a lot of formal education, but is an entrepreneurial type who delights in putting deals together. He does not have much interest in the day-to-day operations of the business, although because of the concentrated share ownership, one would predict the existence of a centralized structure in which he is reluctant to let very much in the way of importance happen without his involvement.

The company had not been very professionally managed. In a regulated environment (both banks and savings and loans operate with the benefit of restrictions on competitive entry and with regulated savings rates) the firm had grown and prospered, but it was becoming apparent in the mid-1970's that the firm was becoming too large to be controlled in the same informal, one-man way that it had been run in the past. The president's brother was involved in the management of the business, but the two of them, lacking formal managerial training, were having problems with maintaining the efficiency and control of the firm. The auditing firm for Federal Finance, as part of its work, recommended stronger professional management.

In 1975, they hired a professional manager from a presumably good source of management talent, a management consulting firm. The man had been on a consulting team from the firm which did Federal's audit, and which had recommended new management practices. This new manager, Dan Smith, was given the title of executive vice president of operations, and was given the general mandate to clean up the organization's operations and to provide more control and efficiency. The structure as of October, 1975, is displayed in Figure 7.1. The other executive vice president in charge of administration, Sam Jones, was Bill Jones' brother, and Bill was the president of the firm.

Smith was personally ambitious and not too politically astute, but was a reasonable diagnostician of the firm's operating problems. Many of the executives in the firm, such as the senior vice president in charge of loans, had been personal friends or acquaintances of the president, and the firm, like many in its industry, suffered from a lack of managers with real training or experience in the professional skills. In order to shape the firm up, Smith convinced the executive committee and Bill Jones to permit him to reorganize the firm, and by May, 1976, the organization diagrammed in Figure 7.2 was in place.

Several changes are readily apparent. First, Smith had assumed

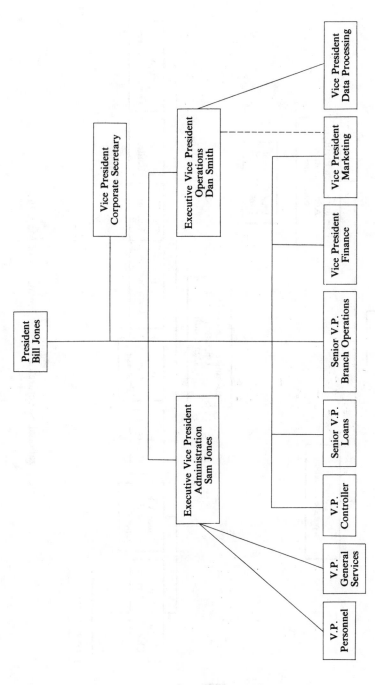

Figure 7.1
Organizational Structure of Federal Finance as of October, 1975

President
Bill Jones

Vice President
Corporate Secretary

Executive Vice President
Operations
Dan Smith

Executive Vice President
Administration
Sam Jones

Vice President
Data Processing

Vice President
Marketing

Vice President
Finance

Senior V.P.
Branch Operations

Senior V.P.
Loans

V.P.
Controller

V.P.
General Services

V.P.
Personnel

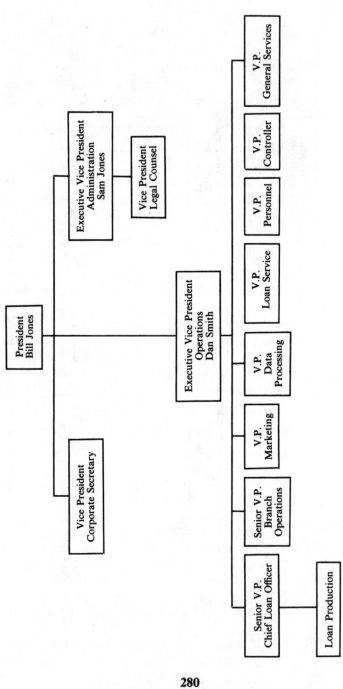

Figure 7.2
Organizational Structure of Federal Finance as of May, 1976

direct line control over virtually all of the operating departments, insert-
ing himself between the president and these departments. This was
agreed to by the president because, as you recall, he was more of an
entrepreneur and deal-maker, and never cared much for the day-to-day
operating details. When Smith promised more efficiency and less demands on the president's time, he willingly agreed to the reorganization.
Also note that the president's brother has lost one function (general
services) and has lost any operating parity with the new man, Smith. The
finance function has been renamed and reconstituted as loan service, but
otherwise, the structure was the same as before.

Smith at that point went to the corporate counsel, an old friend and
colleague of the president's, and argued that the legal function was
critical in a regulated organization governed by consumer protection
laws, restrictions on new branching, complex financial reporting requirements, as well as the usual personnel regulations and safety rules applicable to any organization. Needless to say, the legal counsel was impressed
with this argument. Together, the two went to the president and argued
for the elevation of the legal counsel's position in the organizational
structure. Furthermore, Smith thought that in the financial services
industry, competition from other financial intermediaries was already
becoming intense and was likely to become even more so, as distinctions
between banks and savings and loans were eroded and as retailers got
into the savings and loan and financial intermediary business through
check cashing and credit extension. Therefore, he wanted to institutionalize a product development and service innovation activity. By June,
1976, the organizational structure shown in Figure 7.3 had emerged.

Within nine months, Smith had been able to convince others in the
organization to redesign the structure so as to provide him with a substantial amount of power. In an organization that was closely held and
in which the president's brother as well as personal friends were managers, this outsider had accomplished the removal of most of the functions
from the president's brother's control, the removal of the president's
direct line control over the operating units, and the introduction of a
service and product innovation unit which incorporated some of the
planning and entrepreneurial activities of the office of the president.
Smith had emerged as the most powerful man in the company.

However, the rapidity of the accumulation of power was to be
matched by the rapidity of its loss. Consider the situation as of June,
1976. Contrary to the data of Child (1973) and the argument concerning
concentration of power and concentration of share ownership, this was
a firm in which share ownership was concentrated, and in fact, two

281

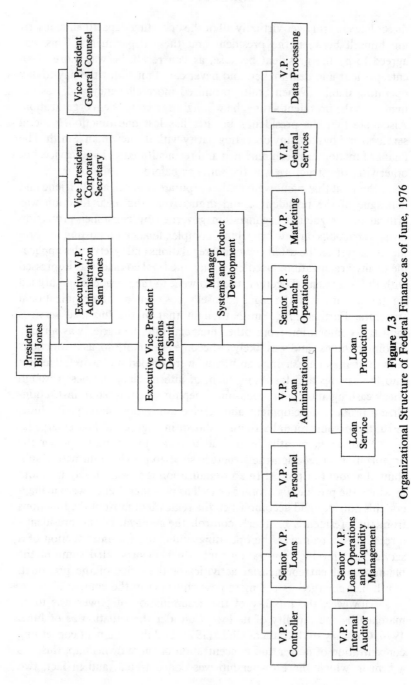

Figure 7.3
Organizational Structure of Federal Finance as of June, 1976

family members were involved in the management of the business, but operating power had become concentrated in the hands of an outsider, who owned relatively few shares, and was not a member by blood or by friendship with the inner circle that had dominated the company. In the reorganizations that had occurred since October 1975, the president's brother had lost the legal counsel, personnel, and general services functions, and the president had lost direct line control over the operating divisions of the organization. Moreover, the divisions of loans, branch operations, and the controller, which formerly reported directly to the president, now reported to Smith, so they had lost some status and power in the organization. Furthermore, the loan function, which was one of the more critical functions in the business, had been reorganized so that loan operations and liquidity management were now grouped together and loan administration, which included loan service and production, was created. The finance or treasury function, and the loan function, in other words, had become intermingled. Thus, Smith had a group of executives, including the president's brother, who had lost status, had been reorganized, and could be politically threatening.

What was the basis of Smith's power? It was technical, managerial competence in an organization which operated in a protected regulated environment in which share ownership was concentrated. In 1976, the market value of the firm was approximately $30 million. The substantial share ownership of the controlling stockholders made them all very wealthy, so wealthy that the president was heard to remark, "I am not so concerned about small gains in profit margins which increase my dividends or share wealth slightly; I am most concerned about the continued growth and expansion of the business." Although this was unstated, it became evident that he was also concerned about his ability to run the business in a way that was comfortable for him and his colleagues. Even if Smith had been successful in increasing profit margins or efficiency, the payoff to those in potential control was small. Furthermore, Smith, by focusing on internal operating efficiencies, missed one of the organization's most critical contingencies and also focused attention on the part of the operation that the president cared least about. Finally, Smith was badly overextended. By assuming line control over the whole scope of the organization's operations, he had eight senior executives reporting to him. Some of those executives resented not being able to report to the president directly. Because of the executives' ties to the president, Smith had been unsuccessful in bringing in his own people or new professional managers to run those divisions.

The inevitable happened—an operating crisis, or rather, series of crises occurred. Problems in data processing (one of the divisions originally assigned to Smith) caused several hundred accounts in one branch to become lost in the system. Problems with the data processing system also caused increased losses from bad checks being cashed against customer accounts. Smith's claim to power, administrative efficiency, was called into question. The argument was made that he was trying to do too much, and the removal of his responsibilities began. By January, 1977, the president's brother again had some subordinates. As seen in Figure 7.4, he acquired office services, savings administration, consumer loans, and personnel and training. Most importantly, he acquired the new products and business development function, one of the more critical functions in the firm, and one of the few that was run by a very technically and politically skilled manager.

Smith reacted inappropriately to this move. Instead of trying to build alliances with other powerful interests within the organization, he became increasingly alienated from the other senior operating officers. He criticized the new arrangement and the new mode of operation. At the same time, because of his increasing involvement in the political struggle and his continued inability to be able to get critical subordinates replaced, branch operations and data processing continued to deteriorate. In fact, after seeing that Smith was on his way out, the heads of those divisions may have acted intentionally to not correct problems or to work at their own maximum potential in order to hasten his demise.

By the end of the year, December 1977, Smith had essentially been stripped of his power. As seen in Figure 7.5, the organization had been changed once again, but not back to its original form. The president's brother had more power than before, controlled more departments and reacquired control over the legal department. At the same time, there were now four executive vice presidents where there had been two. Savings, loans, administration, and planning had been segmented from each other so that the control of the president was firmly re-established. No single individual had enough departments or enough control of critical resources or contingencies to seriously challenge the president. Smith had some of the least critical and least powerful units, as evidenced by the fact that he was the only one of the executive vice presidents who had only assistant vice presidents reporting to him. By 1979, Smith resigned from the company.

Smith's rise and fall reflected the operation of internal politics more than reorganizations designed to improve operating efficiency or profitability. Although Smith ultimately had performance problems, these problems, it could be argued, were due as much to the politics of the

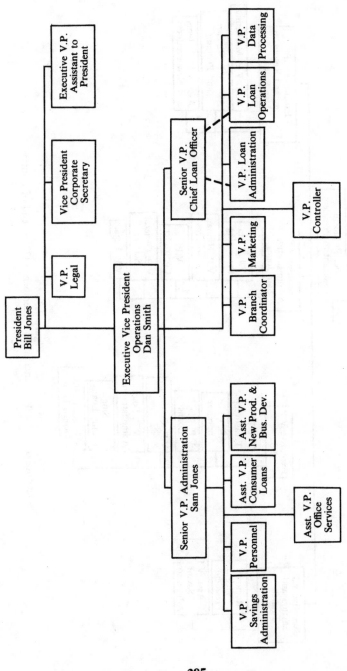

Figure 7.4

Organizational Structure of Federal Finance as of January, 1977

285

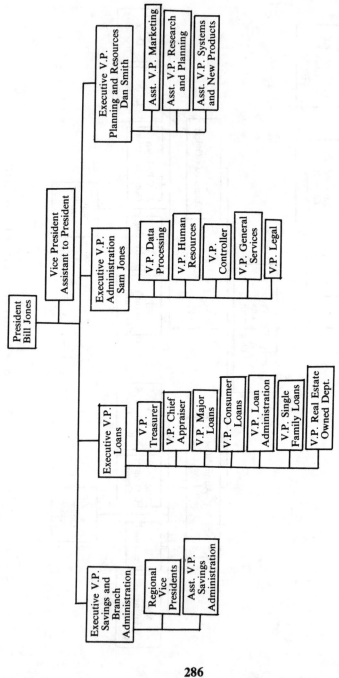

Figure 7.5
Structure of Federal Finance as of December, 1977, at end of Political Contest

286

situation and to his inability to bring in professional management as to his own lack of managerial skill or insight. Indeed, many of the innovations in operations, procedures, and planning which were begun under Smith continued after his departure and are generally well regarded within the organization, although these innovations are seldom attributed to Smith. Fundamentally, Smith tried to accumulate too much power in an organization in which ownership was highly concentrated. Equally as important, Smith did not work well with the other senior operating officers in the firm to cultivate their support. Convinced of their incompetence, Smith let them know his low opinion of their managerial skills and thus created a coalition of individuals, including the president's brother, who were ready to oppose, sabotage, and degrade his efforts at every turn. When problems did arise, they were used as arguing points by the coalition already in place, to argue for a series of reorganizations that left Smith an organizational eunuch. Smith's response, at each step, was to claim ever more loudly his competence and the validity of his ideas, causing further isolation from the other managers and a further deterioration in his political position.

The example just described illustrates power and politics and their effects on structure in a rather extreme form. A single case study clearly does not prove the validity or utility of taking a political approach to the analysis of organizational structure and structural change. However, it is only space and time that precludes the presentation of many more instances which illustrate the basis of structural change in the power of groups and individuals within the organization. Although structures must at some level provide for effective operations, there is, indeed, a great deal of room for strategic choice in the design and redesign of organizations and this choice is often governed by the operation of organizational power and politics.

In considering power in use, evidence was reviewed that not only indicated the effects of power and politics but also provided illustrations of the formation of coalitions (McGraw-Hill) and the use of political language in efforts to legitimate decisions (United Fund and university budgeting studies). Indeed, the justification and legitimation of the decisions was in some cases a crucial element in the ability of powerful political actors either to succeed or fail in their efforts. There is evidence from the range of decisions and organizations covered that a wide variety of organizational processes and outcomes, from structures to careers to budgets, can be productively examined using a political model.

CHAPTER 8

PERPETUATING POWER

erms like coalitions, political struggle, interests and strategy all convey an image of incessant pulling and tugging in organizations. Similarly, the material on the determinants of power suggests that as the major problems which confront the organization change, one may expect to see shifts in power within the organization. Power, however, is stable in most organizations most of the time. Stability, not change, is descriptive of the power distributions in most organizations as well.

It is important to consider which factors promote the stability of power in organizations. If power is critical in affecting what organizations do, then understanding the stability of power can help us understand the problems and issues associated with changes in those decisions and activities. For those seeking to alter organizations, an understanding of the sources of stability is a necessary first step in the attempt to overcome resistance to change.

The institutionalization of power in organizations derives from three effects. The first effect, which is commitment to decisions and strategies previously adopted, tends to cause administrators to persist in courses of action long after the courses of action have outlived their usefulness. Problems tend to be seen as issues of implementation, and change comes about primarily when the present administrative cadre is replaced because of increasingly severe organizational difficulties. Commitment makes it difficult for current administrators to change course, but even more importantly, it may cause them to take actions to further increase their power in the organization. The second effect is the institutionalization of beliefs and practice within the organization. This phenomenon occurs when rules, processes, task procedures, and beliefs about the world become unquestioned and taken as objective reality. It occurs in many social settings but is particularly likely to occur in formal organizations because of the presumptions about rationality, stability, and authority which are inherent in the image of formal organizations. This institutionalization of social knowledge makes it less likely that those within the organization will challenge the present power distribution, and reinforces the process of commitment by providing stability to all aspects of the organization, including its distribution of power and influence. The third effect involves the fact that the possession of power enables those participants with the power to obtain additional determinants of power. Once in power, in other words, power can be used to take action and acquire resources which will provide at least as much if not more power in the future. Power has within it the source of its own perpetuation. The combination of these three effects makes major change in the distribution of control in organizations incredibly difficult and unlikely.

Commitment

Commitment involves the binding of an individual to a decision, so that consistent beliefs develop and similar decisions are taken in the future. Or, as Salancik (1977b: 62) defined it:

> *Commitment is a state of being in which an individual becomes bound by his actions and through these actions to beliefs that sustain the activities and his own involvement.*

The interesting thing about commitment is that it causes individuals, because they are bound to a course of action and set of beliefs, to persist even when evidence suggests that action and decisions should change. It makes organizations and their administrators resistant to change, and causes persistence in activities long after the wisdom of persistence should have been discredited. As Staw and Ross (1980) argued, commitment to courses of action makes it difficult to implement trial or pilot programs, or to approach the implementation of various policies as natural experiments. The difficulty is that once decided, courses of action become difficult to reverse.

There are two aspects of commitment of interest to us in our discussion of power in organizations. First, we need to understand how commitment arises, its causes. Then, it is necessary to explore what commitment effects mean in terms of the persistence and institutionalization of power in organizations.

CAUSES AND
CONSEQUENCES OF COMMITMENT

The causes and effects of commitment have been very well documented in the experimental social psychological literature; there are now enough field examples of the causes and effects to provide some assurance that the findings are not the artifacts of laboratory experimentation. The first necessary condition for commitment to occur is choice; without choice, or at least the perceived freedom to choose from among a set of options, an individual will not become committed to the choice.

The effects of choice were demonstrated in an interesting experimental study conducted by Reibstein, Youngblood, and Fromkin (1975). Students were led to believe that they were participating in a soft drink taste-testing study. In one condition, students assigned to that treatment chose from between two flavors (which pre-testing had determined were the most preferred). Students randomly assigned to the second condition chose from among four flavors, including the same two as in the first condition. In the study, measurements were collected on how long each student engaged the soft drink dispenser, how much of the soft drink was actually consumed, and attitudes toward the soft drink. The predictions were that the students who were confronted with more choice, and hence more decision freedom, would be more committed to that choice as reflected by the behavioral and attitudinal measures. The results of the study indicated that both the length of time the dispenser was engaged and the amount of soft drink consumed was positively affected by the number of choices presented (Reibstein, Youngblood, and Fromkin, 1975: 436). However, no differences were detected in the attitudinal measures.

The importance of choice for producing commitment was emphasized by Salancik (1977b: 69), who argued:

> *Volition is essential to all commitment. It is the cement that binds the action to the person and that motivates him to accept the implications of his acts. . . . Without volition, a behavior is not necessarily committing, for the person can always assert that he really did not cause the behavior himself. He thus would not have to accept the consequences of the behavior or care very much what he has done.*

291

Commitment is also produced to the extent that the chosen behavior is made public. As Salancik (1977b: 64) argued, "Acts that are secret or unobserved lack the force to commit because an act that has not been seen cannot be linked clearly to an individual. The person can deny or forget it." The committing effects of public action are visible at evangelical services. When the minister at the end of the service asks people to come forward, it is to induce a public commitment. Making a pledge to a charity, converting or joining a religious organization, pledging support for a political candidate, all of these actions are likely to be more binding to the extent they are made publicly. Organizations manage the publicness of decisions to manage the amount of commitment engendered. When a new associate joins a law or investment banking firm, advertisements may be taken out and announcements mailed. This publicly associates the person with the firm, thereby committing him or her more firmly to it. At the other extreme, when persons are unsure of their positions and tentative about their opinions, they may feel uncomfortable about expressing their views in the context of a formal meeting. In those circumstances, informal conversations around the washroom or the coffee pot will be used to exchange views without having commitment necessarily follow those views.

The third cause of commitment occurs when the publicly chosen behavior is also irrevocable. Again, Salancik (1977b: 65–66) provides the reasoning:

> *Visibility means the individual cannot deny that an act occurred; irrevocability means the behaviors that occurred cannot be changed. This aspect of behavior . . . adds to its constraining effects. . . . The irreversibility or irrevocability of behavior is committing because in taking a step that cannot be retrieved one is left to accept the salient implications that support it. Because of this, in the future a person faces either regret over past acts or an assertion of their wisdom.*

Staw (1974) provided evidence for the importance of irrevocability in producing commitment and the effects of commitment on subsequent behavior in a study of ROTC cadets following the first draft lottery. The study was made possible "by the fact that many young men had joined an organization (the U.S. Army Reserve Officers' Training Corps), in part, to avoid being drafted" (Staw, 1974: 744). If one joined the ROTC, one would emerge from college and the ROTC program as a commissioned officer. Many persons felt that this was preferable to taking their chances with the draft. A natural field experiment was created when the U.S. government, which was dissatisfied with the endless array of deferments and with criticism of the draft, instituted a lottery based upon the individual's birth date to determine the order in which persons would be drafted. Each year in Washington a big drum filled with the days of the year would be turned. The order in which those dates were drawn from the drum would determine the order in which persons subject to that lottery would be drafted. In general, a number below 122 meant that you were almost certain to be drafted; a number above 244 meant that you were not likely to be drafted.

There were two levels of commitment to the ROTC program:

> *Two levels were distinguished on the basis of whether or not a subject had signed a military contract before receiving the treatment. The contract stated that the cadet must continue in ROTC for the remainder of his course of study at the university and that he must accept an appointment as a Reserve Officer in the Army if such an appointment were offered. . . . By signing a military contract, the cadet is formally bound to the organization. Legally, he is permitted to disenroll from the ROTC program only if he can prove extenuating circumstances such as medical disqualification, dropping out of school, or extreme hardship, and in such cases a Board of Officers is convened to investigate the matter (Staw, 1974: 744).*

Those cadets who were not committed by contract, who discovered they had high draft numbers and were unlikely to be called, dropped out of the ROTC program at a very high rate. Staw (1974: 746) reported that while about 34% of the cadets with the lowest draft numbers dropped out of the program, slightly more than 62% of those with the highest numbers disenrolled.

It is the effects of commitment that make the process so important in understanding organizational decision processes. Once an individual is committed by making irrevocable public choice from among several options, he or she is bound to that behavior. When confronted with the fact that the behavior has failed, was unnecessary, or in some other way has produced unpleasant results, a process of justification apparently ensues. This process frequently results in even more commitment to the chosen course of action, which leads to more resources, effort, and more favorable attitudes being expressed toward something that has not worked out.

Festinger, Riecken, and Schacter (1956: 3) described the process as follows:

Suppose an individual believes something with his whole heart, suppose further that he has a commitment to this belief and that he has taken irrevocable actions because of it. Finally suppose that he is presented with evidence, unequivocal and undeniable evidence, that his belief is wrong: what will happen? The individual will frequently emerge not only unshaken, but even more convinced of the truth of his beliefs than ever before. Indeed, he may even show new fervor for convincing and converting other people to his view.

The effects of commitment on subsequent behavior and attitudes have been demonstrated repeatedly and produce results that are both striking and occasionally shocking. Staw (1976) argued that pressures for justification could lead to escalating investments in a course of action that was not working out. He had students work on a business case in which research and development fund allocations were made. Results were received in terms of subsequent firm performance, and then a second allocation decision was made. Staw (1976: 38) found that when the decision consequences were negative, more funds were allocated to the previously chosen department on the second decision occasion. This effect was much stronger for students who were made to feel more personally responsible for the decision. This finding was replicated in a second study (Staw and Fox, 1977). If justification of past decisions was what created the escalation of commitment in the presence of failure, then conditions which made the administrator feel more vulnerable might be expected to intensify the escalation effects. This is what Fox and Staw (1979) found in yet another study using the same type of procedure. Administrators who faced a situation of job insecurity and policy resistance—in other words, who felt a strong need to justify their actions to others—were even more likely to escalate commitment to a course of action in the presence of information which indicated that the program was failing.

There are many plausible explanations that can be used to justify behavior, and they are heard in organizations every day. "We haven't given the program enough time," "it can't be expected to succeed with that inadequate level of support," "if we try a little more, I know things will work out" are all statements used to justify committing more resources to a course of action that is not working out. If an advertising budget of $1 million isn't moving the product, then certainly doubling the budget will offer more chance of success. Indeed, the committing effect of failure, coupled with personal responsibility and vulnerability, leads to the statement that nothing succeeds like failure, and nothing fails like success. Federal, state and corporate budgets are filled with programs that receive more resources each year precisely because they are not accomplishing all that they are supposed to, while programs which are achieving success have less need or claim for additional resources, and therefore don't receive them.

Staw and Ross (1980) have argued that one of the reasons why people persist with failing courses of action is due to a general social belief that effective leaders behave in a consistent fashion. In other words, consistency may provide its own reward. In their study, students were asked to read a case in which an administrator behaved in either a consistent or inconsistent fashion, allocated either a lot or few resources, and achieved apparent success or failure. They were then asked to evaluate the administrator and recommend the size of a raise he should receive. All three behaviors had significant effects on perceived administrative ability: the administrator in the case was rated more favorably when he was successful, when he was consistent, and when he used the minimum rather than the maximum resources.

Staw and Ross happened to use three different sets of student subjects for their study: students in an evening MBA program, who worked during the day, business undergraduate students, and psychology undergraduate students. In Figures 8.1 and 8.2, we have reproduced the graphs for the different perceptions of these groups of both consistency and success. Note in Figure 8.1 that actual performance had the smallest effect on rated performance for the evening MBA students. The evening MBA students also had the largest difference between their evaluations of consistent and experimenting behavior. The evening MBA students, whom one could assume to be either managers or aspiring managers, gave the lowest ratings of any group to administrators who changed courses of action. These data further support the argument that as one enters and moves through management, one acquires a "lay theory of leadership" in which consistency and perseverance, particularly in the face of adversity, is seen as a valued quality for administrators. If this is the case, then it is little wonder that, when faced with problems, the response is likely to be one of consistency rather than any re-evaluation of strategy.

What of Staw's ROTC cadets? Well, as you might expect, those cadets who were committed to ROTC by an irrevocable contract, who

295

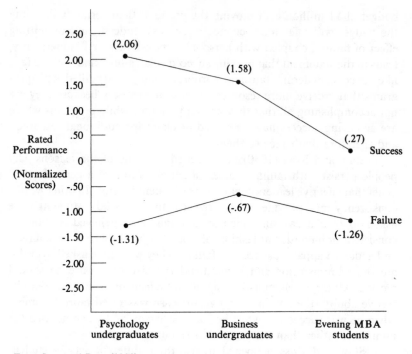

From Staw and Ross (1980)

Figure 8.1
Interaction of Performance and Subject Group

had high draft numbers—so they had no external justification for their participation in ROTC—developed more favorable attitudes toward ROTC and even performed better in their ROTC courses. Faced with a commitment that could no longer be justified in terms of external pressure, they reassessed and re-evaluated their ROTC program, finding within it new sources of satisfaction that had been previously overlooked.

COMMITMENT AND THE
INSTITUTIONALIZATION OF POWER

In most organizational contexts, decisions are taken in public; they are made from several alternatives, and are explicit in terms of their implications for the individual's beliefs about the desirable course of action for the organization to follow. Most organizational decision situations, therefore, are committing. What the literature on commitment suggests

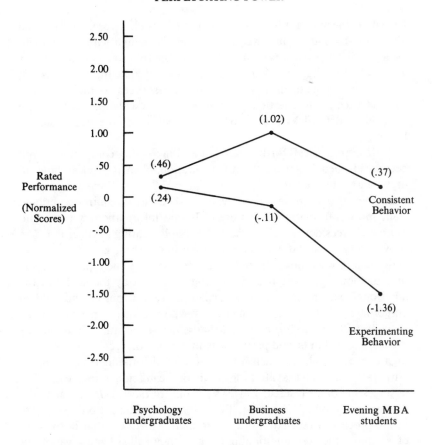

From Staw and Ross (1980)

Figure 8.2
Interaction of Consistency in Behavior and Subject Group

is that individuals are likely to become bound to decisions regardless of their effectiveness and, in some instances, because of their ineffectiveness. These commitment processes make it difficult for organizational participants to see, much less admit to, mistakes. Rather, the situation is likely to be defined in terms of needing more resources, more control, and more effort along the lines previously selected.

Organizational difficulties tend to become defined as problems of implementation and organizational control. The problem isn't that we have done the wrong thing; the problem is that we have been half-hearted about what we are doing; we haven't done it enough with enough efficiency. This response was quite apparent in the Johnson administration's actions in the Vietnam War. The problem was that the U.S. was not trying hard enough, or devoting enough resources to the task. The various attempts to question the wisdom of the escalation policies were themselves defined as being part of the reason for the occurrence of failure.

If problems call forth escalation and increasing commitment, and become defined in terms of implementation, then it is clear how an organization under crisis may react to failure by institutionalizing power. Implementation, after all, requires control. Control requires additional staff, more information and more elaborate information systems, and more resources devoted to the activities implementing the decision. The provision of more staff and more information to those already in power and making decisions will only tend to increase their power in the organization. The analytical capabilities provided by the staff and the additional information serve as further sources of power and tend to perpetuate in office the administrators who are most proximately associated with the course of action that is not successful. Although this process has its limits, and particularly in the case of electoral leaders, the high degree of public cynicism tends to diminish the increased support fairly rapidly, recall that after the failure of the mission to rescue the U.S. hostages in Iran, President Carter's popularity *increased;* similarly, the decline in Lyndon Johnson's political fortunes occurred only very late in the process of escalation of the Vietnam War. Note that in the case of Vietnam, the very questioning of the policy called forth a variety of efforts which were designed to centralize more power in the administration. Similar effects can be observed in many organizations. Failure is justified to argue for more resources and many of these resources are provided to those in power to enhance the implementation of policies already undertaken; these resources, then, serve to further institutionalize the power of those already in the dominant coalition in the organization. Indeed, nothing may succeed like failure, at least for a while.

Institutionalization of Organizational Culture

The second effect which causes the persistence and institutionalization of organizational power distributions is the tendency for ways of doing things in the organization, patterns of authority, and standard operating procedures to take on the status of objective social fact. Thus, instead of questioning the distribution of power, the making of certain decisions, or the following of certain rules of operation, these aspects of the organization become defined as part of the organization's culture and are seen and accepted by participants in the organization as a natural part of their membership in that particular social system. Organizational change, including changes in the distribution of power and control, is made more difficult by the tendency to develop shared beliefs, world-views, or organizational cultures which legitimate and institutionalize present practices, structures, and influence distributions.

Zucker (1977: 726) has written:

> . . . social knowledge once institutionalized exists as a fact, as part of objective reality, and can be transmitted directly on that basis. For highly institutionalized acts, it is sufficient for one person simply to tell another that this is how things are done. Each individual is motivated to comply because otherwise his actions and those of others in the system cannot be understood.

In this way, the distribution of power in the organization exists as a social fact, and is perpetuated because people come to believe that this is how things always were, always will be, and always should be. These shared perceptions form one of the bases which tie organizational participants to each other and integrate them into the organization.

Power distributions take on a life of their own. The distribution of control becomes a social fact which is shared and accepted by many in the organization; those who do not accept the power distribution or other organizational facts may be removed from the organization. Power becomes institutionalized by a process which perpetuates not only the social reality of the distribution of power but also the various structures, procedures, and practices which reinforce the existing power structure.

The institutionalization or legitimation of the social control process in formal organizations is illustrated quite nicely in an innovative study conducted by Lynne Zucker (1977). Zucker was interested in the transmission of values or beliefs over generations. The experimental setting which was chosen to investigate this problem was the Jacobs and Campbell (1961) modification of Sherif's (1935) original autokinetic effect experiment. Sherif studied conformity by having persons make estimates of the movement of a point of light in the presence of confederates of the experimenter, or of other naive subjects, in an effort to observe the process of mutual social influence. In actuality, the point of light is stationary, but appears to move in the darkened room when the subjects stare at it intently. Jacobs and Campbell modified the original experimental paradigm to include varying numbers of confederates who were removed one at a time on successive trials (generations) and replaced by naive subjects. The latter authors wanted to observe how long the original distance estimates—the cultural reality—would persist as the original group members were replaced.

Jacobs and Campbell (1961) found that the originally established microculture, embodied in the extreme distance estimates, decayed quite rapidly as new subjects were brought in. The original distance estimates settled back to the estimates one would obtain from averaging the judgments of a random sample of subjects doing the task without any social contact.

Zucker's research called attention to the fact that the institutionalization of various beliefs can be seen as a variable, "with different degrees of institutionalization altering the cultural persistence which can be expected" (1977: 726). She wanted to study the transmission, maintenance, and resistance to change of an established culture, embodied in the distance estimates, in situations which varied in terms of their institutionalization. In the personal influence condition, the original Jacobs and Campbell (1961) instructions were followed. The task was introduced as involving problem solving in groups. In the organizational context condition, the following instructions were used:

> *This study involves problem-solving in model organizations. You will be participating with another organizational member. . . . Most large organizations continue even though individual members, or even whole divisions, may be replaced. . . . The model organization in which you will participate also will have this feature. . . . Thus, performance of any single member may not be important to the organization as long as the job continues to be done (Zucker, 1977: 732).*

Finally, in the office condition, the organizational context condition was supplemented with the additional instructions:

> *Large organizations also place members in different positions, often according to the amount of time spent in the organization. The model organization in which you will participate also has this feature—the member who has spent the most time in the organization will be the Light Operator. . . . To simplify*

300

*the recording procedure, the Light Operator will be asked for
her judgment first (Zucker, 1977: 732–733).*

Zucker's experimental results were striking. In Figure 8.3, we have
reproduced the graph of the data from the transmission experiment. The
initially established culture, as represented by distance estimates, was
much more persistent in the organization context condition, and even
more persistent in the office condition. Furthermore, in the maintenance
and resistance to change experiments, a similar pattern of results was
observed: the culture was more resistant to change in the office condition
than in the others. In the maintenance experiment, the subjects returned
a week later to perform the same task. Again, there was more maintenance of the distance estimates in the office condition, with the organization context condition demonstrating more maintenance than the control
condition.

By telling people that they were joining an organization, and by

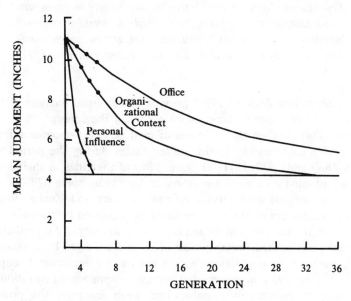

From Zucker (1977: 735)

Figure 8.3
Response Levels Extrapolated from Estimates Provided
by First Three Generations in each Condition

301

giving them a position title, the cultural traditions of the experimental group were maintained longer, in spite of physical evidence that told the subjects that the distance estimates were probably incorrect. This demonstrates in a dramatic fashion the power of organizations and positions to shape beliefs and perceptions and to cause these realities to be accepted as social facts. Zucker noted, "Any act performed by the occupant of an office is seen as highly objectified and exterior" (1977: 729).

Thus, the very existence of organizations and the shared meanings and beliefs that come to be expected as a consequence of organizational membership tends to foster the process of institutionalizing the distribution of power. Organizations are institutions, permanent, large, formal. Because organizations are settings in which regularity in behavior and rationality of action come to be expected, attributes of organizations can become institutionalized merely through their association with the organizations:

> *Settings can vary in the degree to which acts in them are institutionalized. By being embedded in broader contexts where acts are viewed as institutionalized, acts in specific situations come to be viewed as institutionalized (Zucker, 1977: 728).*

Tolbert and Zucker (1979) provide an empirical analysis of the meaning of institutionalization as we are using the concept, in a field context. They studied the diffusion of civil service personnel reform among city governments in the United States during the period between 1880 and 1930. In 1900, some 17% of the cities in their sample had adopted civil service reforms, and by 1930, some 67% of the cities had adopted civil service reforms. Tolbert and Zucker found that early adopters of the reforms could be predicted by variables associated with the size and demographics of the city. "As predicted, early adopters tended to be 'middle class' cities (i.e., to have an educated, white collar population) with a narrower governmental scope" (1979: 22). By 1930, however, civil service reforms were institutionalized, and the explanatory variables had much less predictive power. The results are summarized:

> *These results are consistent with the progressive institutionalization of civil service as part of the formal structure of cities. Prior to institutionalization, adoption was largely an individual process, rooted in the rational need for efficient/effective*

city administration. Later, however, . . . transmission became
less problematic . . . and specific city characteristics became
generally less important as determinants of adoption (Tolbert
and Zucker, 1979: 23).

Although the study was done on civil service reform across cities, the point is a general one and the basic design could be replicated in studies of the diffusion of management practices across organizations. At some point, a belief or practice becomes so generally accepted that it is no longer questioned using rational criteria; its acceptance becomes almost automatic and serves only to distinguish deviant members of the group from others. A similar process occurs within organizations. Beliefs become institutionalized when they are no longer questioned very explicitly, and when they are accepted as a normal part of the operations of the organization. It is through this process that power distributions become institutionalized. What is both interesting and impressive is the relative ease with which institutionalization occurs in organizations. Practices need not be around very long in order to become part of the standard operating procedure.

Institutionalization serves several roles in organizations. First, it binds participants together with a common set of understandings about the organizational way of doing things (Brown, 1978). It provides each person with common beliefs and a feeling of belonging. Second, institutionalization provides certainty in the conduct of social interaction. Weick (1969) has argued that interlocked cycles of behavior persist because they make interaction predictable for those involved, and this predictability causes the persistence of the cycle. Similarly, institutionalized beliefs and meanings provide certainty for organizational participants. Each shares his or her experiences with others and comes to a common understanding of the world, which provides both stability and predictability in social interaction, as well as a feeling of control that comes from the socially-derived consensus.

Weber's (1947) description of legitimate authority is consistent with the institutionalization concept. It is not only power that becomes accepted as a normal and desirable attribute of the organization; many other aspects of the organization are similarly institutionalized.

Thus, institutionalization or custom, and the commitment process, tend to produce stability in the organization, including stability in the distribution of control. Each process complements the other, with institutionalization helping to make sense of behaviors, and the psychology of commitment reinforcing the institutionalization process. As we will discuss below, although institutionalization has many other bases in organizations, the social psychological foundation of organizational stability is important.

Self-Perpetuation of Power

The third source of stability of power in organizations derives from the fact that power in use can provide those subunits who possess power with the ability to acquire resources, which in turn are helpful in the maintenance of power. Power, in other words, enables those units which possess it to get things that other units cannot obtain. Many of the things acquired, such as extra budget resources, additional positions, and information, can in turn be used to provide more power in the future, because these things can be readily translated into the determinants of power.

Some examples will clarify the point. Consider, for instance, power in a university. Pfeffer and Moore (1980b) have suggested that power in universities is determined by the department's ability to provide to the university two scarce and critical resources, student enrollments and grants. In turn, power, along with enrollments and the department's scientific paradigm, determines the allocation of various resources, including budget, faculty positions, graduate student financial aid, and faculty career speed. The model of resource allocation used by Pfeffer and Moore is displayed in Figure 8.4. We have added some feedback loops to indicate that the resources acquired through the use of power can in turn be employed to help assure the department of continued supplies of the determinants of power.

For instance, financial aid resources can be used to attract and retain students, particularly graduate students. Indeed, these resources may enable the department to compete effectively for the very best students. Similarly, students may be easier to attract to departments that offer smaller classes. Such classes are possible for departments that have relatively more faculty per students taught—these departments have the power to obtain a larger share of faculty position allocations. Also, grants may be more accessible to departments that have more faculty per students taught, implying that the faculty may have more time to apply for grants. The ability to pay better, offer more graduate student aid, and to offer somewhat lighter teaching loads, enhances the department's competition for the better faculty. Better faculty will also provide the department with some advantages in the ability to obtain additional outside resources.

A similar process can occur in a business firm. If power is accrued to those units that best cope with the organization's critical problems,

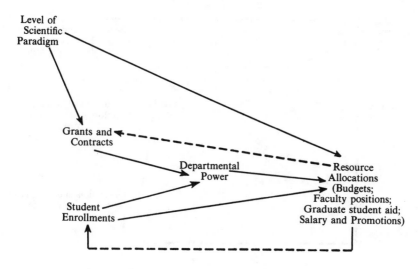

Adapted from Pfeffer and Moore (1980b)

Figure 8.4
A Model of the Sources and Outcomes of Power in a University

then once in power, these units can use their influence to ensure that they will remain with this uncertainty coping capacity. In Figure 8.5, we have diagrammed some of the things that subunits in a firm can and do accomplish once in power to maintain the security of their position.

Certainly, power provides those units who are in possession of it with a greater ability to eliminate or consolidate competing sources of expertise and problem-solving capacity within the organization. Once in control, units that might be viewed as substitutes for the unit in power can be eliminated, or better yet, consolidated within the unit, to ensure its monopoly over the capacity to solve the critical problems. As in the case of universities, power brings with it the ability to pay relatively more at both entry and senior levels. This incremental compensation provides the unit with the capacity to attract and retain the best and brightest people in the organization, thereby ensuring that other units will fare less well in the internal competition for talented executives. Power and influ-

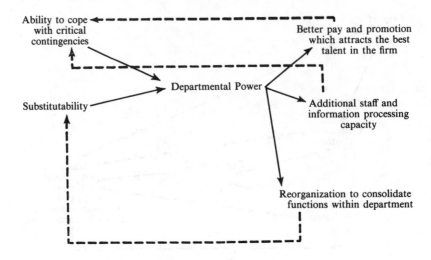

Figure 8.5
A Model of the Self-Perpetuation of Power in a Firm

ence may also facilitate the acquisition and use of additional staff and information processing resources. These informational resources provide the unit that has control of them with an ability to argue more persuasively for continued support, and to argue that it best understands the organization and the problems it faces.

The case of the finance unit in a San Francisco area industrial products firm provides evidence for these techniques in action. The firm was not very large and sold a relatively limited product line of fairly complex and sophisticated equipment to industrial users. The firm was functionally organized, with a marketing department that was responsible for the product brochures, industrial marketing, advertising, and trade show activity; a production department that handled the manufacture of the products; a purchasing department that was responsible for the acquisition of input materials at the best prices; a personnel and industrial relations department which was responsible for recruitment, training, and labor negotiations; and a finance unit which handled both the controllership function of providing management information as well as the treasurer function of negotiating bank loans and managing the firm's cash balances and financial institution relationships.

Although engineering was at one time the most powerful department in the firm, after the firm was acquired by a large conglomerate and a financial type was put in charge of it, finance began to assume increasing power. It is of interest to us how that power, once acquired, was maintained. Several factors operated to maintain the power of the finance unit. In the first place, the new chief executive's emphasis on financial controls, financial planning, and sophisticated management information systems (an activity also within the purview of the finance department) led to the belief within the firm that the way to the top was going to be increasingly through finance. This caused several of the better engineers to attend evening MBA programs or executive programs in which they could increase their skills in administration and in financial control. This was encouraged by the chief executive and his immediate subordinates. Thus, the situation developed that the best and most talented engineers sought to leave engineering and move into finance and general management. The head of engineering complained that he was losing his best people. When positions opened up at the general management level, persons with a finance background tended to get them. As the chief executive explained, "The best people tend to be in that unit." That was, in fact, probably the case. However, it was the case because the best people were recruited to that unit due to the unit's power and the perception that it was the way to get promoted in the firm.

Second, the finance unit developed increasingly comprehensive information systems and financial controls to keep track of what was occurring in the organization. Inventory of supplies and products in various stages of completion was monitored by the information system. The firm developed a very sophisticated personnel information system, which kept track not only of the usual payroll information, but also of the career histories of individuals, their evaluations and performance in different jobs, their educational background, and skills. The cost accounting and manufacturing cost control system was equally comprehensive, as was a system which analyzed the marketing data to produce forecasts as well as very complicated sales analyses. Because the information system was assigned to the finance function for overall responsibility, each of the operating executives had access to some of the data on the firm. However, only the chief executive and the head of finance had access to all the various pieces of information which together indicated the total picture of how the firm was performing. In meetings of the top level executives, this overall information gave the finance executive a distinct advantage in any discussions about the firm and its problems and prospects.

Finance was in a relatively secure position, with control of the information and managerial control system, and a reputation for being the avenue to the top, so that it could consistently attract and retain some of the best people from the other departments as well as from the outside. It would have been difficult for any other unit to develop bases for power that could have dislodged it. In many ways, the possession of power facilitates the taking of actions that serve to maintain that power. This fact constitutes another reason for the stability of power distributions in most organizations.

Indicators of Institutionalized Power

In order to empirically study institutionalization in organizations, we must develop indicators of the extent to which power is institutionalized. The Tolbert and Zucker (1979) study, and the material on commitment both suggest that institutionalization can be assessed by the extent to which an organization is apparently unresponsive to factors operating in its environment. The inability of demographic variables to predict the adoption of civil service reforms was taken as evidence that the reforms had become institutionalized. In an analogous fashion, the lack of relationship between environmental or organizational variables with each other or with organizational structure measures might suggest an institutionalization of power and behavior in the organization. The lack of a relationship between organizational performance and responses that might be expected as a consequence of that level of performance can also indicate institutionalized control.

There are not many studies that enable us to illustrate these ideas, but one example of a study of institutionalization is found in Meyer's (1978) analysis of the effects of leadership succession on organizational structure. The assumption is made that leadership turnover represents a more fluid situation of control than lack of turnover. In situations in which the leadership is stable, definitions of acceptable organizational practices are more likely to be stable, and role expectations are also more likely to remain unchanged. If leadership stability is associated with institutionalization, we should be able to observe the same lack of relationship between causal variables and their presumed consequences that was observed in the case of the civil service reforms.

Meyer studied state and municipal finance agencies, obtaining data on 215 finance departments in both 1966 and 1972. He reported several different analyses of the data for those departments where the head had changed between 1966 and 1972, and those departments which were stable in leadership over the period. In Table 8-1, we reproduce Meyer's (1978: 209) data on the relationship between the tenure of the finance department head and the correlation between various dimensions of organizational structure between 1966 and 1972, or the autocorrelation of the measures over time.

TABLE 8-1

Autocorrelations of Structural Variables by Leadership Stability

Variables	1972 Tenure 0-5 Years	1972 Tenure 6+ Years	1966 Tenure 0-5 Years	1966 Tenure 6+ Years
Size	.94	.94	.88	.98
Number of divisions	.52	.62	.50	.68
Number of levels of supervision	.60	.57	.54	.67
Number of sections	.64	.74	.63	.74

With the exception of one reversal (number of levels of supervision in 1972), the results are all in the expected direction. All four measures of the organization are more stable over time in those organizations that have had more stable leadership, which is indicated by having leaders with longer tenure.

Meyer also examined his earlier results on the causal effects of size on structure (Meyer, 1972) to see if they differed depending on whether or not leadership was stable. He concluded:

> Under leadership conditions tending toward instability—short tenure of department head and dependence on higher authority—the causal impact of size is evident. All... coefficients are positive and significant... where the department head has six or more years' tenure and where he is either elected or a civil servant—no significant effects of size on the number of divisions appear. ... Much the same pattern is in evidence ... where 1972 sections are regressed on other variables. Where department heads had held office less than six years prior to 1966 and where they are politically appointed, all eight coefficients of size are positive and significant. Where they had lengthy tenure and were autonomous of higher authority, seven of the eight coefficients of 1966 size are not significantly different from zero (1978: 222).

Meyer's data indicate that "effects of environment on size and structure and effects of size on structure are contingent on leadership allowing external uncertainties to intrude on organizations" (1978: 223).

The study of municipal finance agencies is consistent with the study of the civil service in supporting the stability in organizational measures over time and a lack of relationship between causal variables

309

and organizational variables as indicators of institutionalization. Meyer's study also suggests the critical role of leadership change in the institutionalization process, which is consistent with the literature on commitment and the consideration of the social psychology of institutionalization.

The Effects of Ownership on Institutionalized Control

Meyer (1978) found that whether the head was appointed, elected or a civil servant affected the degree of institutionalization. Specifically, the appointed head, who was subject to removal at any time with no distinct, separate constituency, was least institutionalized. Zucker's (1977) study indicated that associating phenomena with the concepts of organization and office facilitated the institutionalization process. In the study of institutionalized control in business firms, the distribution of share ownership affords another possibility for examining institutionalization and its effects.

There has long been interest in the relationship between executive performance and tenure in the executive position. McEachern (1975) observed that chief executives were more likely to change when the firm's profits declined four or more years in a row. Pfeffer and Leblebici (1973b) found a negative relationship between the tenure of the executive and the average debt to equity ratio which characterized the firms in the industry —a measure of financial risk. Grusky (1963) and more recently, Allen et al. (1979) found that baseball manager turnover was related to poor team performance. Common sense certainly suggests that an executive in a poorly performing organization should expect a shorter tenure than one who oversees an organization which is performing at a higher level.

An implicit assumption of the argument that performance would affect tenure is that there are interests inside or outside the organization that are both willing and able to change executives when the organization's performance is not acceptable. At the same time, for replacement to occur, the position incumbent must lack sufficient power to maintain control or, in other words, power must not be institutionalized. We have seen that such conditions do not always hold, and therefore, an issue of interest is the conditions under which executives can stay in office even when the organizations which they are managing perform poorly.

One such condition promoting the institutionalization of power involves the ownership of the firm. McEachern (1975) classified firms in these terms: owner managed, in which stock ownership was concentrated among its managers; management controlled, for which stock ownership was dispersed among numerous stockholders; and externally controlled, for which stock ownership was concentrated among a few individuals who did not manage the firm. Salancik and Pfeffer (1980) argued that the three ownership conditions had different implications for the effects of performance on executive tenure.

> *Among owner-managed firms, where managers are most in-*
> *sulated from opposition, one would predict either a null or even*
> *a slightly negative relationship between performance and ten-*
> *ure. . . . In management controlled firms, opposition to the*
> *current management is organized with difficulty, primarily*
> *through unfriendly mergers, takeover attempts, or proxy*
> *fights. Thus, we would predict a null relationship between*
> *operating performance and tenure. It is only in the case of*
> *externally controlled firms that the conditions exist for effec-*
> *tively holding managers accountable for the firm's perfor-*
> *mance. For firms of this type a positive correlation between*
> *performance and tenure would be observed . . . (1980: 5–6).*

In owner managed firms, the owners are the managers, and under the assumption that persons are unlikely to fire themselves, tenure would be relatively impervious to performance. In management controlled firms, the discipline on the manager comes from the possibility that depressed share prices would encourage takeover attempts or mergers. The best discipline would be imposed under the conditions of external control, in which there is a powerful, concentrated bloc of shareholders who are not involved in the management of the firm and therefore committed to current management.

Another condition that fosters the institutionalization of power in corporations is having the board comprised of a high proportion of inside directors, or directors who are also actively involved in the management of the company. The supposition is that inside directors, as part of the current management team, are more loyal to the current management and more committed to current organizational strategies and policies. Thus, a firm with a larger proportion of inside directors should be less adaptive and less likely to replace the chief executive when performance was poor because of the institutionalization of management control on the board.

Salancik and Pfeffer (1980) empirically examined these arguments using the sample McEachern (1975) had employed for his study of control, executive compensation, and corporate performance. Eighty-four of McEachern's ninety-six original firms were included in the analysis, with approximately an equal number in each of the three ownership categories. McEachern had classified control type on the basis of the concentration of share ownership, using 4% as the cut-off point to distinguish concentrated control from dispersed control. Executive tenure was the number of years spent as chief executive as of December, 1972. Firm size was measured in terms of assets in 1970. The proportion of insiders on the board was defined as the proportion of directors who were managers in 1972. Two sets of measures of firm performance were employed. One was a combined rate of return on common stock for the period 1963 through 1972, in which dividends were considered as being reinvested in the stock of the firm throughout the period. The second set of measures involved assessing the firms' net income as a percentage of sales for the period 1965–1973. Two measures of profit margin were employed: the profit margin itself, and profit margin compared to the average for other firms in the same industry.

In Table 8-2, the simple correlations of executive tenure with the size and performance measures and the ownership categories are displayed. It is evident in the table that for the sample as a whole, tenure in the chief executive position was not associated with firm size, or the proportion of inside directors, and was only very weakly associated with profit margins. Ownership, on the other hand, had a strong effect on tenure. The average tenure was 16.0 years for owner-managed firms, 5.41 for externally-controlled firms, and 4.89 for management-controlled firms.

TABLE 8-2
Correlations of Chief Executive Tenure with Other Variables

(n = 84)

Variable	Correlation
Proportion of inside directors on the board	.022
Total return on common stock, 1963-1972	.078
Total assets, 1970	.020
Average firm profit margin compared to industry, 1965-1973	.146*
Average firm profit margin, 1965-1973	.147*
Owner managed classification	.604**
Management controlled classification	−.316**

*p < .10
**p < .005

We have argued that ownership affects the institutionalization of control so that the relationship between performance and executive tenure is diminished for firms in which power is more institutionalized. Data relevant to examining this argument are presented in Table 8-3, in which the correlations of the length of chief executive tenure with the variables of performance, size, and board of director composition are displayed separately for each of the three ownership categories.

The data indicate that in the case of the owner managed firms, where power is the most institutionalized, no measure of firm performance or size significantly affects the tenure of the chief executive. In the case of the externally controlled firms, profit margins and profit margins compared to the industry average are significantly positively correlated with executive tenure, while in the case of the management controlled firms, total return on common stock is significantly correlated with executive tenure. Although we did not anticipate this observed interaction between the type of performance measure, ownership, and executive tenure, the relationship is consistent with the argument about institutionalization. Since opposition to the incumbent executive in management controlled firms is organized through the capital markets, it is reasonable that tenure for executives in these firms is related to performance in the capital markets, as assessed by the combined rate of return on investment. In the externally controlled firms, profit margins, rather than share price performance, become the focus because of the concern with immediate operating characteristics of the firms.

Although the proportion of inside directors was not directly related to executive tenure, it is possible that this variable acts interactively with performance to affect tenure; the higher the proportion of inside directors, the less tenure would be affected by poor firm performance. Inside directors, along with ownership, may help to institutionalize control and buffer the chief executive from the consequences of poor performance. This argument was tested by computing interaction terms by multiplying the proportion of inside directors by the measures of profit margin. The correlations between tenure and these terms were statistically significant at less than the .10 level of probability in the predicted direction, indicating that when more insiders are on the board of directors, the general positive relationship between tenure and performance is reversed.

The study of ownership, performance, and tenure again illustrates how the institutionalization of power provides for more stability (longer tenure in office) in the organization and also severs the re-

313

TABLE 8-3
Correlations of Chief Executive Tenure
with Other Variables for Three Ownership Catagories

Variable	Owner Managed (n=28)	Management Controlled (n=27)	Externally Controlled (n=29)	Statistical Significance of Difference Among Correlations
Proportion of inside directors	.006	−.015	−.244	n.s.
Assets, 1970	.157	−.336*	.031	p<.05
Average firm profit margin compared to industry, 1963-1973	−.181	−.153	.413**	p<.05
Average firm profit margin, 1965-1973	−.168	−.098	.428**	p<.05
Total return on common stock	−.145	.376*	−.069	p<.05

*p<.10
**p<.05

lationship between performance and organizational adaptation. Institutionalized power in corporations can come from share ownership as well as from the composition of the board, with ownership having a particularly strong effect. The problems that arise from institutionalized power are evident. If an organization, in which control is institutionalized, develops difficulties with performance, it is unlikely that the various possible corrective actions, including changing personnel, strategies, and structures will be taken very quickly. Rather, problems will have become severe before remedial actions are taken. This line of argument suggests that organizations with institutionalized control and characteristics that foster the institutionalization of power are likely to be less effective and less frequently observed in environments in which change and adaptation are required on a more frequent basis. Although this argument has not been empirically demonstrated, it follows logically from a consideration of the causes and consequences of institutionalized control, since these consequences become manifest in organizational growth and decline.

EXAMPLES OF INSTITUTIONALIZATION IN OWNER MANAGED FIRMS

Institutionalization of power occurs to some extent in all organizations. However, the problem is particularly severe in owner managed firms. In these firms, there is frequently difficulty even after the founder or owner-manager steps down. Many of these individuals have found it difficult to relinquish control. This has made life very uncertain and demanding for their successors. The problem was posed recently in an article in *Business Week:*

> *Anyone making the case that succeeding the company's founder or family manager is tough is not likely to get an argument from Lee A. Iococca, who ended up trying to save a dying Chrysler Corp. after a run-in with the founder's grandson at Ford Motor Co. . . . Nor would an argument come from Arthur Taylor, the former president at CBS, Inc., who, not long after inheriting that position from William S. Paley, soon also began inheriting the founder's wrath.*
>
> *Clearly, the job of succeeding an entrepreneur . . . can be a no-win proposition. The problem . . . seems to be getting worse, if only because transitions from entrepreneur to professional manager appear to be more prevalent (*Business Week, *1980: 62).*

315

To some extent, this was also the problem in the Federal Finance example discussed in Chapter 7, though in that instance the problem was worse because there was an attempt to bring in professional management while the founders of the firm were still involved in its management. The ways of doing things and the ethos of the firm can remain even after the founder has ostensibly stepped aside, and even after his death:

> *Successful entrepreneurs are often flamboyant and autocratic, and even after retirement their image looms larger than life to directors and employees. . . . "Whenever the new man makes the slightest misstep," observes one corporate psychologist, "employees keep thinking, 'if the old man were here, we couldn't have these problems.' "* (Business Week, *1980: 62)*

The cases enumerating the difficulties of assuming power in a firm which was formerly tightly controlled by a founder or a family are both numerous and classic. William Paley has now fired two CBS presidents who occupied that position after he began to withdraw from control of the company. He had retained his 7% stock ownership and other positions in the company, and was jealous of those who did not know their place and did not defer to the policies and strategies that he had implemented. Any show of authority on their part quickly led to dismissal:

> *Arthur Taylor's quick rise and fall at CBS was also a classic power play between a founder who would not let go and a young comer who did not have the patience to deal with slow and steady change. . . . At the time of Taylor's forced resignation in 1976, CBS had just reported a quarterly earnings increase of forty percent. . . . Paley's prized reputation as a "show business person" was jeopardized when Taylor almost immediately divested the money-losing but prestigious New York Yankees and when CBS' Nielsen ratings fell in 1976* (Business Week, *1980: 63–64).*

Paradoxically, Taylor's replacement, John Backe, was fired in the spring of 1980 after CBS had reassumed the lead in the Nielsen ratings. At that time, the attribution was set forth that he was fired because he was too successful and threatened Paley's image as the only person who could really keep CBS on top.

Similar problems occurred with succession at Schlitz Brewing Company, Firestone Tire and Rubber, and Ford Motor, among others. In those cases where the successor has managed to retain his position, it is primarily because he has been successful in maintaining the support of the founder-entrepreneur, primarily by deferring to him in a number of symbolic ways. John Bryan, on assuming the chief executive officer position from William A. Buzick, who had been forced out by the builder of Consolidated Foods, Nathan Cummings, immediately raised Cummings' annual consulting fee from $50,000 to $75,000, a move that Buzick had opposed (*Business Week*, 1980: 64).

An additional problem frequently occurs because:

> ... *the entrepreneur has set a pattern of making all the major decisions himself, leaving him with a second-tier management group that is highly capable of implementing his plans but virtually incapable of drawing up plans of their own* (Business Week, *1980: 66).*

This means that succession may involve bringing in an outsider to run the firm. The outsider, who has no previous close association with the owner-founder, and less knowledge of the company's folkways and politics, is likely to be particularly vulnerable to accidently violating some long-standing company tradition or in some other way accidentally upsetting the founder, who may then reassert himself into the picture.

This pattern of institutionalization is certainly not inevitable. Alonzo Decker of Black and Decker and Thomas Watson of IBM are among those who have stepped aside without retaining power over the firm. So did Royal Little, founder of Textron, who has kept out of the firm's business since he retired from the board in 1962 at the age of sixty-six:

> "*I knew I wouldn't be able to sit there and shut up; I'd be a pain in the neck,*" *Little explains.* "*It's a great mistake for the founder to stay on the board. It just creates confusion*" (Business Week, *1980: 65).*

Institutionalization, particularly the institutionalization of control by a founder or owner, is a problem because it inhibits the development of new perspectives and strategies, and retains control in the hands of people who may be getting older and who are no longer able to keep up with the demands involved in running a business. Like other forms of institutionalization, the adaptation of the firm to changing circumstances is hampered. Because of the personalities involved, this form of institutionalized power is often the most dramatic and provides an easier context in which to see the harm that can be done. However, all forms of institutionalized control can do the same amount of damage to organizations, which must face new problems and new constraints, while operating from the old premises and with the old strategies.

Organizational Constitutions

It seems clear that institutionalized power can pose problems for the future survival and adaptation capabilities of organizations. The ability of those in power to maintain that power, regardless of changes in performance or environmental contingencies, is affected by the formal rules of governance, succession, and operation that are adopted in the organization. As one observes organizations, one can see a constant political struggle over the changing of these rules, with those in power trying to make changes that will ensure their continued control, and those out of power trying to implement changes that will facilitate adaptation when and if that becomes necessary. Since those who are already in power have some built in advantages in this political struggle, resulting from their very positions in the organization, the most frequently observed trend is for ever-increasing degrees of institutionalized control.

These points can be exemplified by considering the issues of rules for mergers and electing directors in business firms and the use of formal terms of office in formal organizations of all kinds. In both cases, the trend seems to be toward putting in place policies which institutionalize the power of those presently in control of the organization.

CORPORATE POLICIES
REGARDING MERGERS

The capital markets provide the potential for exerting discipline and external control on firms which may face little product market competition and whose management would otherwise be insulated from the consequences of their decisions and policies. Manne (1965) was among the leading proponents of the theory that competitive capital markets could substitute for other forms of competition, in keeping management efficient and concerned with the welfare of the firm and its shareholders. The argument was that if a management did not employ the firm's assets in an optimal fashion, for instance, by engaging in self-dealing or simply by being committed to unsuccessful practices, the firm's stock price would drop. Entrepreneurs would see this depressed stock price and realize that they could pay a premium for the stock over current levels, thereby gaining control of the company. By improving the management of the firm, they could increase the price of its shares even further; this would provide the entrepreneurs with a profit incentive for them to engage in this transaction. Under this theory, management performance problems would lead to lowered share prices, external takeover or merger efforts, and consequently, a revitalization of the organization and its management. In this process, the critical element was the potential for an unfriendly merger or takeover of a poorly performing firm.

Needless to say, current firm managements do not view the potential for external takeover or merger, which is often accompanied by the loss of their jobs, with the same enthusiasm that characterizes free market economists. Thus, managements in many firms have embarked on a series of steps to make this operation of the capital market much more difficult. First, many firms have placed proxy statements in annual meetings and had their shareholders approve rules which stipulate that without the approval of a majority (in some cases two-thirds or three-quarters) of the board of directors, a merger would require the affirmative vote of much more than a majority of the voting stock of the firm. Provisions for the requirement of a two-thirds positive vote of the eligible shares are common, and requirements for as much as three-quarters or even an 80% vote of the stock in favor of a merger or takeover have been seen. What these rules create, clearly, is a dichotomy in the type of merger and the ease with which it can be accomplished. If the board, and presumably, the management, approves of the buy-out, only a simple majority of the shares need approve of the plan. When the board and the management do not approve, the merger is much more difficult to effect, and requires the approval of much more than a majority of the shares of the firm. The distinction turns on management approval, and it is interesting to see which factors cause management to approve of some tender offers and not others. Although the price offered is likely to be one consideration, the retention of the present management in at least advisory capacities may be another condition that affects the response to the offer.

Related to the formal change of corporate rules is the use of the power of the government, both state and federal, to block takeovers. In the classic case of American Express' bid for McGraw-Hill, the issues of antitrust were raised by McGraw-Hill in an effort to thwart the merger. Many states now have laws protecting companies which are headquartered in their states, from takeover by others from outside the state. These takeovers may require the approval of some state official. The target firms typically attempt to use alleged securities law violations, as well as potential antitrust issues, to bring the federal government in on the side of the present management.

In each instance, the legitimating reason provided is couched in terms of protecting the interests of the present shareholders. These shareholders are to be protected against selling out too cheaply, being taken advantage of by misinformation, or being misled by promises of increased wealth as shareholders in the new corporate entity. It seems clear that shareholders can buy and sell their stock as they assess the fortunes of the firm, and that the capital markets are reasonably efficient. Although couched in terms of shareholder protection, the public interest, and maintaining competition, it is patently clear that the changes in formal corporate charters and the use of governmental agencies are designed to institutionalize the power of the present management in the firm, and to insulate that management from the consequences of its decisions.

BOARD OF DIRECTOR ELECTION RULES

The board of directors has become an important focus of the contest for control over the corporation. First, as we have just seen, it is the approval of the board that conditions how large a majority of the stockholders may be required in order to effectuate a merger. Second, it is the board that has the formal authority to hire, fire, and determine the compensation of the highest level managers of the firm. Third, it is the board of directors, at least formally, that has the responsibility of proposing to the shareholders the various changes in the rules of corporate governance that can help institutionalize the power of the current managers. Thus, rules for the election of directors themselves become a focus of the contest for control in corporations.

The two most critical rules are whether or not the terms for the directors are staggered over time and whether or not cumulative voting is permitted. If there are a given number of directors whose terms are staggered over a three or four year period, then regardless of how many shares an outsider buys, he can elect no more than one-third or one-fourth of the board in any single year. This permits the present management to maintain control longer, control the board and its power, and thereby inhibit the attempt of any outsider to obtain control of the management of the corporation. Many corporations changed their director terms to an arrangement of staggered terms during the 1970's when mergers and take-overs were frequent. Such change is one response, amid the external turbulence, to maintain the control of those already in power in the corporation.

Cumulative voting, which is permitted in all states and required in a few, permits a minority shareholder to concentrate the votes to which he or she is entitled, to be able to elect at least some representation to the board. Straight voting, which is permitted, for instance, under the laws of Delaware, the most common state of incorporation, requires that votes be distributed over all of the director positions to be filled, thereby guaranteeing that the group with the majority of the shares or share proxies can elect every single member of the board.

An illustration from a corporate law book will make the distinction clearer:

> Let us assume a corporation with two shareholders, A with 18 shares, and B with 82 shares. Further, let us assume that there are five directors and each shareholder nominates five candidates. Directors run "at large" rather than for specific places; hence the five persons receiving the most votes are elected. If only straight voting is permitted, A may cast 18 votes for each of five candidates, and B may cast 82 votes for each of five candidates. The result, of course, is that all five of B's candidates are elected. If cumulative voting is permitted the number of total votes that each shareholder may cast is first computed and each shareholder is permitted to distribute these votes as he sees fit over one or more candidates. In the example above, A is entitled to cast a total of 90 votes (18 × 5) and B is entitled to cast 410 votes (82 × 5). If A casts all 90 votes for A_1, A_1 is ensured of election because B cannot divide 410 votes among five candidates in such a way as to give each candidate more than 90 votes and preclude A_1's election. Obviously, the effect of cumulative voting is that it increases minority participation on the board of directors (Hamilton, 1976: 344).

The number of shares needed to elect one director is:

$$V = \frac{S}{D + 1} + 1$$

where S is the total number of shares voting, D is the number of directors to be elected, and V is the number of shares needed (Hamilton, 1976: 346).

Clearly, proscription of cumulative voting makes it easier for those once in control to maintain that control against outsiders. The combination of straight voting and staggered terms of office for directors makes it very difficult for an outside group to achieve significant control of the firm regardless of how poor present performance is.

Using the same sample as that employed for the study of the effects of ownership and performance on tenure, we attempted to explain the rules on merger and directors, and changes in those rules, in terms of the functional need for protection against outside threats. However, the effort was unsuccessful primarily because most of these provisions have, it appears, reached institutionalized status themselves. Almost no firm permits cumulative voting. There are widespread attempts to make it more difficult for an outsider to purchase or otherwise obtain control of the corporation without the cooperation of the present management. Thus, it seems fair to conclude that in large measure, control has already been institutionalized in most publicly held U.S. corporations. There is stability in management, and management is able to maintain power under all except the most extreme conditions.

TERMS OF OFFICE

The term of office for the chief executive may be prescribed by law, as for the President in the U.S. Constitution, or by custom. A fixed term of office encourages turnover in the occupants of executive positions and although the position may then be passed to allies of the past occupant, at least some change in the control structure is mandated. Few formal organizations have explicitly defined terms of office. In some cases, such as Occidental Petroleum and Gamble-Skogmo stores, the founders or major shareholders of the firm were able to have even formal retirement rules waived for a period, to permit them to stay in the chief executive position longer. The ITT case cited previously illustrates how Harold Geneen was able to affect the operations of the firm even after he was formally out of office.

A fixed term of office has some distinct advantages, in spite of its limited use. In the absence of a fixed term, suggestions about succession or replacement become defined as threats to the incumbent's ego and challenges to his or her competence. This results in more resistance to the idea of replacement because of the symbolic correlates of the act of replacement. This symbolic baggage and self-image protection are not invoked if there are regular terms of office, and the expectation that there will be a rotation of personnel through the position. Second, in the absence of a fixed term of office, a tremendous political struggle is re-

322

quired to mount the effort to replace the present incumbent. In the presence of a fixed term, the conflict and bad feelings that can be residues of such efforts are not needed, as there is a rotation out of the position on a regular basis. And third, in the absence of the fixed term, one of the tasks of the position incumbent is likely to involve institutionalizing his or her control over the organization and locking in control on the position. One might argue that such efforts at institutionalizing control are not functional for the organization as a whole and represent an unnecessary diversion of resources and effort. With a fixed term of office, although efforts may be expended to lengthen the term or change the rules, such behavior is much less likely, given the legitimated norms of succession and replacement in the position.

Thus, fixed terms of office can help to discourage the institutionalization activities, political struggles, and personal commitments that inhibit change in organizations. In addition to the political system of governmental offices, university positions, particularly at the departmental level, often have fixed or at least normatively determined terms of office. Although there are clearly risks from too much and too frequent executive succession, it seems evident that in most organizations today the problems derive from too much rather than too little institutionalization of power.

Institutionalization as a Response to External Threat

Formal mechanisms which inhibit the institutionalization of power are particularly critical, because in their absence, the modal response to external threat or crisis, such as that caused by performance problems or the failure to adequately meet the demands of critical elements in the organization's environment, is likely to be a series of steps that increase institutionalization of control within the organization.

We can consider first the variable of centralization, or the extent to which decision making autonomy is dispersed or concentrated in the organization. Hamblin (1958), in an experimental study, found that leaders had more authority during crisis as contrasted with non-crisis periods. Pfeffer and Leblebici (1973a) examined the effect of competition, conceptualized as a source of external pressure, on the structures of thirty-seven small firms in Illinois. They found that, controlling for organizational size, the degree of competition was positively correlated with the frequency of reporting ($r = .42$; $p < .05$), the extent to which decision procedures were well specified in advance of the decision, a measure of formalization ($r = .30$; $p < .05$), and was negatively related to the percentage of oral as contrasted with written communication used in decision making ($r = .24$, $p < .10$). Competition or external pressure, then, appeared to "have an effect on the specification of decision procedures, with the greater the competition, the greater the specification of such procedures" (Pfeffer and Leblebici, 1973a: 275). These authors also examined the extent to which factors such as the number of different products, changes in product design, and changes in the production process had the expected effect of increasing differentiation and decentralization. They observed the predicted associations more strongly in the case of the non-competitive environments. When the organization was under external pressure, there were fewer relationships between the predictors of decentralization and differentiation and measures of these concepts.

Pfeffer and Leblebici interpreted their results to indicate that under conditions of external pressure, there was a tendency for control to tighten within the organization. This argument is consistent with that proposed by Korten (1962), who argued that at the nation state level, centralization of political authority was fostered by external threat to the nation. Thus, the evidence is consistent with the position that under external pressure, there will be a tendency for increased centralization of power in the organization. Ironically, then, the very onset of identifiable problems can set in motion a centralization of control which will tend to ensure that those who are already in power will make even more of the decisions and control the organization's operations more tightly.

The literature on intergroup conflict (Sherif, Harvey, Hood, and Sherif, 1961) discusses the effects of external pressure or a crisis in the organization on dissent or disagreement. As Janis (1972) pointed out in his analysis of the groupthink phenomenon, attack and crisis can promote a we-they atmosphere in which loyalty, as demonstrated by agreement with and compliance to the beliefs and attitudes of those in power, becomes a critical attribute. Positions harden so that those who are not in agreement with the policies in place are accused of disloyalty. Such disagreement is seen as a threat to the unity and welfare of the organization, and this deviance is much less likely to be tolerated when the external threat is perceived as being greater. The tendency of conflict with others to increase stereotyping, in-group loyalty, and to reduce contact with others outside of the group has been frequently documented (e.g. Blake and Mouton, 1961). Ironically, at the very time the organization faces a crisis which may have resulted from inattention to the demands of the environment or from failures of policy, psychological dynamics are set in motion which reduce contact with the external environment, place a premium on loyalty and commitment to already chosen policies, and define as treasonous any kind of deviation from the adopted line.

Attacks on the dominant beliefs or paradigm of the organization are likely to be met with counterargument and efforts to reinforce the paradigm. As Salancik (1977a) discussed when analyzing commitment on an individual level, one of the least effective ways of changing attitudes or behaviors is by attacking them directly. This direct attack merely causes the expenditure of effort to justify the present course of action and the present set of beliefs. As a consequence of this effort in justification, those involved become even more convinced of the wisdom and rightness of their course. At an organizational level, attacks on the organization may lead to the more frequent repetition or manufacture of stories which glorify the now-attacked organization and its past performance. Rationales which further legitimate and justify the organization and its way of operation are developed with increased vigor. Attacks on performance become defined as failures to fully understand the organization's interest in long-run performance; attacks on the organization's ability to provide for the demands of various constituent groups become defined as proof positive of the inability of those constituent groups to really appreciate what they need, thus further reaffirming the correctness of the organization's position. Up to a point, what might appear to be visible indicators of failure on the part of the organization become tests of its essential character and paradigm and the opportunity to commit additional resources to demonstrating the correctness of its policies.

Finally, organizational failures become defined in terms of failure of implementation, planning, or decision making. The typical prescriptions are for more analysis, more staff, more computers, and more control over operations to ensure that even better decisions are made and implemented. The staff, computers and analytical capabilities, however, are most often brought into the organization in some central staff capacity, so that they serve those who are already in control of the organization. Buttressed by the additional staff and data analysis capacity, those already in power become even more firmly entrenched through their additional information processing and decision making capacity. Thus, each crisis becomes an instance in which the expansion of management and management control is justified and legitimated, leaving those in management even more in control and more firmly institutionalized than before. This pattern has been observed in universities (Pfeffer, 1978b) and in other organizational contexts as well.

Institutionalization, it seems, is a very perverse process. It is seen as being in the best interests of the organization by those seeking more control. When failure and problems arise, the tendencies of escalating commitment and the structural responses of increased centralization and control act to further enhance the domination of those already in power. The more the organization might appear to need change, because of manifest performance problems, the less likely change is to occur. These processes may form part of the reason for the stability in organizational performance observed over time, and may help to explain why change in social systems is so difficult. It is possible to institute various formal rules and procedures that either inhibit or facilitate institutionalization. As Pfeffer and Salancik (1978) argued, the rules and practices that inhibit institutionalization are those that permit the processes of the political market which exists within organizations to work. Attempts to rationalize the process by the introduction of more computers, staff, and control. ironically come to help institutionalize the power of those whose decisions may have led to the problems in the first place.

Some Positive
Consequences of Institutionalization

Thus far, the discussion of institutionalization has described the negative consequences—primarily, the effect of institutionalization to increase stability in the organization and, therefore, retard organizational adaptation to changing environmental circumstances and new internal political realities. Indeed, institutionalization is associated with organizational stability, and under some conditions, this stability and commitment to past decisions and structures can be dysfunctional for organizational survival. However, it is also the case that a certain amount of stability is useful.

Organizational environments and the contingencies to be confronted change constantly. New constituencies emerge with demands and the old constituencies may change their preferences. Stockholders may demand dividends at one period, and growth and internal reinvestment in another. Customer demands for price versus quality may change. Labor demands for work force stability, pension benefits, or current wages vary as the economic environment makes some issues more salient than others. Markets for products and services vary over time. With each change in the environment, the organizational units that are more compatible with the new requirements are likely to assert claims for more power and control in the organization. If each environmental variation were met with new executive succession, new organizational structures reflecting these new power arrangements and environmental contingencies, and new evaluation and information systems, the amount of internal turbulence might be so great that the organization would be immobilized by the rapidity and frequency of internal change.

Institutionalization permits organizational stability and the predictability and potential for organizing collective action permitted by such stability. As Pfeffer and Salancik (1978) argued, organizations confront a dilemma between adaptation and implementation. The stable power structure in institutionalized organizations permits the organization and mobilization of energy to get things accomplished. A certain amount of stability is necessary to permit the organization to function with any degree of success. Too much responsiveness would leave organizational participants continually uncertain about what to do, and would leave the organization in continual internal political turmoil, unable to mobilize its resources to accomplish anything. Thus, a certain amount of commitment to the past, of institutionalized power, of institutionalized organizational structures and processes, is necessary for collective action to occur at all.

This line of argument suggests that the ability of organizations to grow and attract resources and other forms of support from their environments will be a curvilinear function of the extent to which power is institutionalized. At very low levels of institutionalization, change in the distribution of power and in structures and procedures will be so frequent that concerted action will be difficult and change so disruptive that the organizational ability to cope with environmental requirements will be harmed. At very high levels of institutionalization, there will be so much stability that changes in environmental requirements will not be registered by the organization and persistence in doing the same thing in the same way will lead to a loss of external support. It is at the point of moderate institutionalization that the organization will be able to adapt and also to mobilize resources for action. This optimum intermediate point of institutionalization will vary, depending upon the amount of change in the organization's environment, where such change involves both changes in interdependence and changes in the demands of those with whom the organization is interdependent.

The field of education offers many examples of the dilemma between institutionalization and responsiveness. Universities, for instance, are under pressure to include more relevant course material, which some have interpreted as going into field studies and social action as education. This move has, in turn, alienated old alumni, but more importantly, when the pendulum began to swing back to basic skill training, those schools that had moved too quickly in the other direction were left in trouble. A good example is Antioch, which opened a large number of urban campuses around the nation in the 1970's and found themselves, by the late 1970's, close to bankruptcy as a combination of declining enrollments and changing student demands left their newly constructed programs out of phase with the environment. Other more conservative colleges, because of a more institutionalized power structure, maintained their same educational programs, and this inner directedness turned out to stand them in good stead when educational demands shifted back in their direction.

The textbook publishers, too, have been buffeted by the simultaneous pressures for change and maintaining traditional approaches to pedagogy. Scott, Foresman brought out a new history textbook at an investment of $500,000, but found itself criticized for being too bland:

> There's something for everybody in this two-year-old American history textbook for eighth-graders, and that's by design.
>
> "We don't want to get complaints from anybody," says Landon Risteen, editorial vice president at Scott, Foresman & Co., the book's publisher. . . . That attitude, however, is condemned by many critics. "I've been teaching history to college sophomores since 1962," says Professor Barry Karl at the University of Chicago, "and it has never been as bad as it is now. I get students who just don't know any history."
>
> Many of his colleagues agree, and they blame it largely on the uninspiring blandness of the American history textbooks. The problem, they say, is that by trying to please everyone, publishers take the edge off history, eliminating the exciting stuff that the past is made of (Rout, 1979: 1).

Staw (1979) has argued that consistency and perseverance are socially held to be traits of effective leaders, and, it might be argued by extension, effective organizations. There is some social positive value placed on consistency and taking a position and holding it, as this demonstrates both strength and a sense of the value of the organization. Thus, there are clear dangers from having power so fluid in the organization that the organization is viewed as lacking any consistency or direction. There is a lot of evidence from social psychology that people value predictability and certainty, and a continually changing organization becomes viewed as unpredictable and unstable, and hence, not preferred.

Consequently, the institutionalization of power and the stability that this brings serve to provide predictability and to make the organization capable of mobilizing resources for action. While too much institutionalization in a rapidly changing environment can prove fatal to organizations, too little can prove to be equally harmful to the organization's ability to attract and retain resources and support.

How Do Organizations Change?

After this extensive discussion of the forces that promote stability in organizations, one might wonder how organizations do manage to change. Between commitment, the institutionalization of organizational cultures, and the self-perpetuation of power, one might get the impression that there were powerful factors causing organizational stability, and that change was both infrequent and difficult to accomplish. To the extent that it does not require any fundamental shift in the power distribution of the organization, change is more readily accomplished. However, changes which do entail shifts in the distribution of influence are rare events, brought about chiefly by major changes in the organization's environment which create problems or constraints which are too pervasive to ignore.

The fact that change may be difficult to accomplish at the level of the individual organization does not, of course, have any necessary implications for change when it is measured at the level of populations of organizations. As Hannan and Freeman (1977) suggested in their discussion of a population ecology approach to organizational analysis, change can come about through two mechanisms: the adaptation or transformation of a given organization, or the differential growth and survival of different organizational forms or types of organizations. Selection, as contrasted with adaptation, is the mechanism of change emphasized by population ecology. Hannan and Freeman's (1977) attempt to emphasize the importance of selection as a mechanism of change was based in part on their argument that organizations possessed a tremendous amount of inertia. This inertia in a variety of structural mechanisms and other properties meant that the assumption that organizations changed, at least rapidly or frequently, through processes of internal adaptation was unwarranted. It is some of these causes of organizational inertia that have been discussed in this chapter on the institutionalization of power.

If selection is an important mechanism producing change, and if institutionalization tends to make adaptation of specific organizations difficult, then the logical implication is that actions taken to forestall the operation of selection mechanisms tend to produce the institutionalization of organizational properties and power at the societal level. Just as conflict and power and politics can foster change within organizations, so conflict and competition among organizations can enhance change and adaptation at the level of the larger society consisting of populations of organizations. The restriction of selection processes serves to institutionalize and perpetuate those characteristics that are shared by the population of organizations at the time the institutionalization occurs.

The arguments made about the importance and pervasiveness of institutionalization imply that selection processes are critical for the adaptation and change of organizational characteristics over time. However, in many sectors of our organizational society, selection processes are not allowed to operate (Salancik and Pfeffer, 1978). This suggests that organizational change accomplished by any means is problematic. To the extent that the conditions which foster institutionalization are present, restriction in the operation of selection mechanisms will have even more deleterious effects on organizational change. Restriction on selection, coupled with institutionalization, can produce populations of organizations which are seriously out of phase with their environments. It would be interesting to explore whether or not this line of argument can account for the growing noncompetitiveness of many sectors of U.S. industry, and if it can explain the relative success of various organizations based in different countries.

The parallel between change within organizations and change in populations of organizations can be extended further. Just as conflict and political activity appear to be disorderly and inappropriate within organizations, conflict, competition, and interorganizational political activity appear to be disorderly and nonrational at the macrosocial level. Planning, centralized control, and attempts to impose rationality through the concentration of power and resources occur at the level of society as well as within organizations, with much the same effects. Orderly decision processes, buttressed with staff work, information systems, and planning, and typically involving the institutionalization and centralization of power, are implemented in an effort to ensure coordinated and more efficient organizational operations. Their effects, however, are as often perverse as beneficial. This process of reliance on planning and the centralization of resources can be seen clearly in attempts to promote efficiency in the health care system, in education, and in other forms of social services. The effectiveness of this strategy is very much open to question (e.g., Warren, 1970).

In Figure 8.6, we have diagrammed the model of organizational change which is implied by the discussion of power and organizational decision making in this book. We have added a notation to the effect that institutionalization represents, to the extent it is accomplished, a break

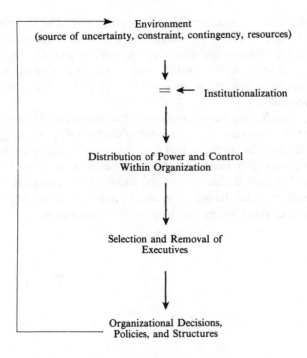

Adapted from Pfeffer and Salancik (1978: 229)

Figure 8.6
A Model of Organizational Adaptation

in the linkage between the environment and its constraints, contingencies, and resources and the distribution of power and influence within the organization. The two implications of that model are that change in organizations is largely externally induced, and that to the extent that the organization successfully buffers or insulates itself from the environment, change is forestalled. Of course, the fact of the second point is exactly what makes insulation and buffering so desirable for those in the organization's dominant coalition—they can assure their continued control for a longer period of time to the extent that they can succeed in isolating the organization from its environment.

It is important to remember that institutionalization, and the various causes of institutionalization, are variables which exist to a greater or lesser extent in organizations. To the extent that they are present, change should be more difficult to accomplish and less frequently observed. To the extent they are not present, change should be more easily affected and more frequent. Although this argument needs additional empirical testing, observation attests to the relative lack of change in institutionalized organizations and the more frequent and easier change brought about in organizations in which power and control have not been institutionalized.

Thus, those factors that are relevant in the discussion of institutionalization become important in understanding change processes in organizations more generally, to the extent that change is of such a profound nature that power also must alter for it to occur. Consequently, the factors described in this chapter become variables to be worked on by those who seek to make change easier and by those within the organization who seek to resist alterations in present arrangements.

CHAPTER 9

POWER,
POLITICS,
AND MANAGEMENT

B ased on past experience with this material, my prediction is that by this point many readers will be convinced, but uncomfortable. They will be convinced because as they have read the examples and illustrations of ideas, they will probably have been able to fill in their own stories, based on their personal experiences in organizations. Yes, most will agree, this is a pretty accurate picture of what occurs in organizations, and the analysis is basically sound. But many readers will still be uncomfortable. After all, ideology dies hard and books on organizations are supposed to tell you how to motivate people or to make the organization more efficient, not how to use the control of information and political language to obtain more influence over organizational decisions. If this is how organizations are, certainly some must be different and they shouldn't be this way. An underlying premise is that somehow power and political activity in organizations interfere with their effective or efficient operation. Power and politics in organizations, so the argument goes, exist primarily in public sector organizations or in other organizations which are protected from competitive pressure. Certainly in a competitive market, there would be no room for the kind of activity described in this book. Indeed, the assertion that the material is basically descriptive of most U.S. organizations, coupled with the assumption that power and politics are detrimental to organizational performance, has led some to conclude that this may be one of the reasons for the diminishing competitive position of U.S. industry in world markets.

Thus, the first issue to be taken up in this concluding chapter is the relationship between power and political activity and performance in organizations. There is almost no evidence on this point, but there are some materials that can help to illuminate the issue. Let's anticipate the conclusion by noting that there is no simple relationship between politics and performance, but that the presumed, inevitable negative correlation is almost certainly wrong for many organizations a great deal of the time.

The second issue is what the implications of this perspective on organizations are for managerial selection, training, and skills. Schools of administration (business, hospital, public, educational) have been very proficient in training students in technical, analytical skills as encompassed in courses such as microeconomics, cost-benefit analysis, financial analysis, and marketing and public opinion research. It is interesting to consider the skills and the role the manager assumes if one thinks of organizations in explicitly political terms.

The third issue is what some of the implications of the material are for the design of organizations. If organizations are really coalitional and political in nature, what does this imply about how they are structured and managed?

These three issues—the relationship between politics and performance, the implications for managerial selection, training, and skills, and some implications for organization design—will tie this treatment of organizations back to concerns that are covered by other theoretical perspectives. This is important because it is probable that formal organizations, at least in the U.S., are going to become more political over time. This forecast for the future and the reasons backing it will be the fourth issue considered.

Power, Politics, and Performance

The issue of whether or not organizational politics negatively impacts performance requires a specification of the dimensions that are to be used in evaluating organizational performance. There is a large and expanding controversy over the definition and usefulness of concepts such as organizational effectiveness (e.g., Goodman and Pennings, 1977), and both space and time constraints preclude taking up the issue here. For our purposes, performance refers to any of the standard indicators of organizational well-being, including profit in the case of business firms, and the ability to get projects completed and within budget with respect to non-profit organizations. The precise measure chosen is not of concern since many of those who decry political activity in organizations seem to assume that it results in decreases in almost all measures of organizational performance.

Since there is probably going to be some power in use in virtually all organizations, the statement is better rephrased in comparative terms: the greater the use of power and politics in organizational decision making, the lower the level of organizational performance. To address such a hypothesis, after first gathering some performance indicators for the sample of organizations being studied, one would need to define a measure of the extent of the use of power and politics in the organizations. Several such measures are suggested by the material in this book. In the studies of resource allocations in universities, measures of power were gathered and were then correlated with resource allocations, controlling for other, presumably more bureaucratically rational bases for such allocations. The magnitude of the coefficient of the power measure provides, then, one estimate of the extent to which power is used in decision making. One would expect, following the hypothesis, to find systems in which this coefficient was larger performing more poorly than in other systems in which power had less impact on decisions. And, decisions other than resource allocation decisions could also be investigated. Strategic decisions, promotion decisions, hiring decisions, and so forth could all presumably be studied using a similar methodology, and in each instance, the magnitude of the coefficient for the variable assessing subunit power would provide an estimate of the extent to which power was employed in the decision making process.

Alternatively, one might measure the amount of political activity that occurred in the organization, rather than assessing the extent to which decisions were made on the basis of power. In this instance one would need to delineate in advance what political activity one is looking for, such as withholding information, selectively advocating criteria that favor one's subunit's position, forming coalitions with other participants, and so forth. Allen et al. (1979) provide the start on such a list. Then, one would need to assess how frequently these various political actions occurred in the organizations under study. Again, the argument would suggest that the more political activity there was, the less effectively the system would perform.

Although no data of the type described above have been gathered, the available literature and evidence does not support the argument that power and politics leads to performance problems. Indeed, there is some evidence that the reverse may be true.

Sapolsky (1972) did a case analysis of the Polaris submarine and missile system. The Polaris has frequently been hailed as one of the most successful and effective of the military weapons development programs undertaken in the U.S. It had few, if any, critics, was a model of good management practice, and produced a weapons system that was effective and important in the development of the United States' nuclear deterrent capability. Indeed, Sapolsky undertook the study of the development of the Polaris precisely because it was so successful, and he wanted to understand how and why it had succeeded when so many other military systems development efforts had failed or at least become inordinately costly and behind schedule.

First, how did Sapolsky judge if the program were successful? As he noted:

> For the partisan, goal attainment is the only appropriate standard by which to measure the success of governmental programs and organizations. A partisan has a cause; he seeks the implementation of particular ends to the exclusion of others. . . . The neutral observer, however, needs a more inclusive standard of success in order to evaluate objectively the performance of government. He must recognize that governmental programs invariably affect the interest of several partisan groups, each of which promotes a different set of goals (Sapolsky, 1972: 230).

Sapolsky suggested as an operationalizable standard an absence of criticism of the program. He noted, "Absence of criticism, therefore, can be taken as a mark of success, for it means that no one views the operation of a particular program or organization as inimical to his own interests or goals and that some may even perceive it as beneficial" (1972: 232).

By this standard, the evidence mustered by Sapolsky suggests that the Polaris program was quite successful. In looking for reasons for the success, Sapolsky first noted the favorable environment:

> The Polaris and the other ballistic missile programs were thus clearly the beneficiaries of an unusual convergence between technological opportunities and a consensus on national needs, a convergence with parallels perhaps only in the Manhattan and Apollo projects (1972: 241).

But the favorable technological and political environment was not the only, and perhaps not even the most important, determinant of the program's success. The program still faced "problems of jurisdictional competition and interagency coordination" (Sapolsky, 1972: 242). Sapolsky maintained that:

> *Clearly the success or even the survival of the Polaris program was not assured at its establishment. The three armed services were then competing for a role in strategic offensive missiles, and it was certain that one, or perhaps two, of them would be denied (1972: 243).*

Sapolsky concluded that it was the skill in bureaucratic politics of the backers and managers of the Polaris project that largely accounted for its success. Interservice rivalry was successfully managed; congressional and administration political support was obtained; scientific expertise was garnered as needed; and the network of interagency and interorganizational contracting relationships were successfully negotiated and managed.

> *If . . . the Polaris experience has any lesson it is that programs cannot be distinguished on the basis of their need to be involved politically in order to gain support and independence. The success of the Polaris program depended upon the ability of its proponents to promote and protect the Polaris. Competitors had to be eliminated; reviewing agencies had to be outmaneuvered; congressmen, admirals, newspapermen, and academicians had to be co-opted. Politics is a system requirement. What distinguishes programs in government is not that some play politics and others do not, but rather, that some are better at it than others (Sapolsky, 1972: 244).*

Scientists were coopted repeatedly in order to ensure that the prevailing technical opinion would be that the program was feasible. Even the famed management methods such as PERT charts and critical path analysis were, it was argued, used more for window dressing and to garner support:

> *Though the program innovativeness in management methods was, as I have tried to show, as effective technically as rain dancing, it was, nevertheless, quite effective politically. The Special Projects Office quickly learned that a reputation for managerial efficiency made it difficult for anyone to challenge the . . . development plans (Sapolsky, 1972: 246).*

In the discussion of the Polaris case, many of the political strategies described in previous chapters can be seen: cooptation, the legitimation of decisions through the trappings of rational management, the formation of coalitions, and the cultivation of external allies. What Sapolsky provides in his analysis is the argument that it was these political activities which were the critical factors in the program's success.

A similar case can be made for beneficial effects of power and politics at New York University during the 1960's. Recall from Chapter 2 that NYU faced declining enrollments and the requirement for redefining an educational strategy that would make it financially viable in competition with other private universities in the East and the expanding system of city and state low cost public higher education. Such reorientation had been successfully resisted previously, as attempts to consolidate undergraduate programs to reduce duplication and expense, for example, had been unsuccessful. The combination of growing fiscal stringency and a new president made change more likely. But the reason that the changes succeeded was primarily the ability of those in the administration to play organizational politics successfully.

First, they used the strategy of cooptation. In the process of reformulating educational strategy and policy, there was at least some attempt to involve most of the major constituent groups of the university. Second, they used the strategy of coalition analysis and formation. As noted in Chapter 2, changes were instituted in such a way as to ensure that there would not be too much opposition. Policies were reformulated so that important political actors in the system would be reasonably satisfied; and those who were unhappy with the proposed changes were primarily in the less powerful departments and subunits.

But perhaps the most masterful strategy of all was the use of the Ford Foundation in the change process. The Foundation funded the institutional study of NYU's current position, and outside experts and sources were used, along with internal people, in conducting the study. Thus, the policy recommendations that emerged had the advantages of involving some cooptation of internal interests as well as having the blessing of outside experts and the imprimatur of the Ford Foundation as funding and sponsoring the entire project. This gave the project of institutional reexamination a legitimacy that it might not otherwise have. At the end of the study, NYU was able to get Ford to fund, on a challenge grant basis (they would put up so much money if NYU could raise so much on its own) the changes the report had recommended. Thus, the NYU administration had engaged an external ally with prestige, high credibility, and resources, and had made the obtaining of the resources contingent on the educational policy and strategy that needed to be undertaken in any event. Given the financial condition of the university, it would have been almost impossible not to accept the Ford money, and that acceptance meant that the changes in strategy would have to be adopted. Now, to oppose the changes would be to oppose a prestigious, externally funded report, the Ford Foundation, and the very money that the university needed for its survival. Clearly, the mustering of political support and coopting or otherwise disposing of political opposition was what made the change implementable at that time.

Both of these cases illustrate what is perhaps the greatest benefit of power and political activity in organizations—it is this organizational politicking which facilitates organizational change and adaptation to the environment. As shown in Chapter 8, the institutionalization of beliefs, practices, rules, and decisions, and the escalating commitment to present ways of doing things, makes the self-correction of errors within an administrative hierarchy a rare event. Change comes about when those presently out of power are able to articulate a new set of strategies which are more consonant with present environmental contingencies and are able to generate sufficient support for implementation within the organization. In just this way those who favored more rigorous undergraduate and professional education at New York University were finally able to wrest control of the institution away from those units that favored and benefited from an undergraduate, open-enrollment, part-time emphasis. This shift in emphasis facilitated fund raising and the attraction of students, and kept NYU alive when it otherwise would have almost certainly been forced out of existence.

The argument that power and politics leads to reduced performance derives primarily from the premise that such decision making takes too much time and resources in the negotiating and bargaining that goes on, and can lead to decisions which are not the best from the point of view of the total organization, as they reflect principally the interests of the most powerful subunits. With respect to the first issue, it is not clear that the bargaining and compromise which characterizes political decision making necessarily takes any longer than the amount of time it takes to search for facts and information to resolve uncertainty and generate alternatives that accompanies rational choice procedures. The following case illustrates the point well.

A small fairly young manufacturer of computer peripheral equipment was organized on a functional basis, with vice presidents of engineering, marketing, finance, production, and personnel. The firm was initially well funded through venture capital backers, and had hired into its management a set of very experienced and competent individuals. The company's intended market was other manufacturers of computer systems; it wanted to sell primarily to other manufacturers who would then sell a larger system directly to the end user. The strategy seemed reasonable since it would avoid the requirement of having large sales and service operations and would enable the firm to penetrate the market more rapidly than if it had to first develop strong end-user identification. It had some fairly well engineered products—primarily tape and disc drives—and had some initial customer success.

The problem continually confronted by the firm was a classic one for firms in this position in this industry: frequently a manufacturer would be interested in a tape or disc product, but only if the firm would agree to substantially re-engineer the product to change some of its performance or operating characteristics. Of course, from the point of view of the firm, it was much better to sell what it had already designed and could produce. Bidding on new products required substantial additional engineering expense, as well as increased production costs because few standard models were being made and shipped.

The problem surfaced within the firm as a conflict among the various vice presidents and their respective functions. Marketing believed that it was production and engineering's job to design and produce what the market demanded. Given that the firm had little or no market power and the industry was very competitive, the vice president of marketing argued that it was unreasonable to expect him and his department to sell whatever production and engineering had jointly decided to produce. For his part, the vice president of production argued that efficiencies in manufacturing would never be achieved until the company developed a more standardized product line. He faced problems in scheduling, training assemblers, and stocking parts, because of the continually changing product line and product characteristics. Engineering took the position that if they designed a sound product with good specifications that could be produced at a reasonable manufacturing cost, that their responsibility then ended. Finance was also concerned about manufacturing margins and profits if redesigned units were to be continually produced.

Interestingly, instead of a political struggle to resolve which point of view should prevail, the firm, which was comprised of highly professional managers, embarked on a different course. How could they decide which strategy to pursue without information? So, an outside consultant was retained to do some market research, to assess how their product stacked up against the competition, what the market looked like if they decided to do redesign, and what it would look like if they decided to sell only what they had already designed and were producing. At the same time, another consultant was hired to examine their manufacturing operations and provide financial information on the cost implications of various strategic options, as well as what it might take to implement them in terms of facilities. The finance department meanwhile worked on a corporate planning model so that it could provide financial analysis for various alternative strategies.

Unfortunately, none of this ever came to fruition. While the analysis continued, orders were lost, sales of the standard product were falling precipitously, in part because marketing did not know whether or not the firm was willing to modify the product design, and finally, the investment bankers stepped in and took over the management of the firm. In the ensuing activity, most of the previously employed vice presidents left the organization.

Although information such as that which was being gathered was undoubtedly valuable, the firm was chasing a mirage. There was the belief that somehow, if only enough data were collected, fundamental differences in opinion about strategy and values in the firm would melt away and the decision would become obvious to all. Such a scenario is unlikely to occur in many instances, regardless of how long the search process continues. But in any event, it should be clear that the search for information with which to resolve such disputes is itself a costly and time consuming process. The time and costs of political bargaining, coalition formation, and compromise need to be balanced against the reality of time pressure for decisions and the fact that the generation and evaluation of alternative courses of action takes both time and other resources.

As for the second issue of politics and power not producing decisions which are best from the point of view of the organization as a whole —that, of course, assumes that what is best from the point of view of the organization as a whole is knowable at the time the decision must be made. If everyone knew what was best and could agree on it, then there would not be any use of power in the decision making in the first place. It is because of the fundamentally irreducible nature of the uncertainty about the relationship between actions and their future consequences, and what such consequences portend for the organization, that power and its use arise. To argue that power and politics produces decisions which are suboptimal is to assume that there is knowledge about the organization and its operations which in all likelihood does not exist, for if it did, there would be much less use of power and politics.

There are seldom organizational problems with right or wrong answers except in textbooks. There may be problems that have better or worse answers, but whether or not anyone can tell which are the better decisions and which are the worse ones at the time the decision has to be made is another question. The real issue turns on whether better decisions emerge from a political decision process or from a decision process in which there is more homogeneity concerning goals, information, and understanding of technology. Clearly Sloan's institutionalizing of an advocacy system in General Motors reflects at least one person's belief that conflict and the power and politics that inevitably accompany it may produce better results.

There may be decision systems which combine some of the better features of both the rational and the political. Alexander George, a political scientist, has argued for the use of what he terms a multiple advocacy system in the making of foreign policy. The advantages of multiple advocacy over the alternatives have been described as:

> *Instead of utilizing centralized management practices to discourage or neutralize internal disagreements over policy, an executive can use a multiple advocacy model to harness diversity of views and interests in the interest of rational policy making. Diversity is also given scope in "bureaucratic politics" and "partisan mutual adjustment," but in contrast to these unregulated pluralistic systems, multiple advocacy requires management to create the basis for structured, balanced debate among policy advocates drawn from different parts of the organization (George, 1972: 751).*

A multiple advocacy system "defines the role of the chief executive as a 'magistrate' who listens in a structured setting to different, well-prepared advocates making the best case for alternative options" (George, 1972: 751). To the extent that there are disagreements and uncertainty about decisions, this more openly competitive system "is more likely to secure a critical examination and weighing of them ... than a highly centralized policy-making system" (George, 1972: 752). George has explicitly recognized the functional role of conflict and disagreement in producing higher quality decisions. What he proposes in a multiple advocacy system is a way of managing the conflict so that it produces a better decision.

If conflict is both inevitable and potentially productive within complex formal organizations, George argued that "one solution lies in ensuring that there will be multiple advocates within the ... system who, among themselves will cover a range of interesting policy options on any given issue" (George: 759). George suggested that multiple advocacy would work best and produce the best solutions when the following conditions were met:

(1) No major maldistribution among the various actors of the following resources:
 (a) Power, weight, influence.
 (b) Competence relevant to the policy issues.
 (c) Information relevant to the policy problem.
 (d) Analytical resources.
 (e) Bargaining and persuasion skills.

(2) Presidential-level participation in organizational policy making in order to monitor and regulate the workings of multiple advocacy.

(3) Time for adequate debate and give-and-take (George, 1972: 759).

It is clear the multiple advocacy is not the same as the political decision model. George has argued (1972: 760) that it is a mixed situation, in which there is centralization of the process in order to maintain and make use of internal diversity, conflict, and competition. The role of the chief executive as magistrate is an important component of the process:

> The introduction of the magistrate role into the system means that advocates are no longer competing against each other (as would be the case in a decentralized bargaining system such as "partisan mutual adjustment"); rather, the advocates are competing for the magistrate's attention (George, 1972: 761).

George's suggestion, although raised with respect to the formulation of foreign policy in the executive branch of government, would appear to be equally applicable to other situations in which the differences in points of view would improve the decision making process if they were expressed. George has clearly recognized the functional consequences of conflict for improving the quality of organizational decision making. This conclusion is consistent with a variety of evidence, including a study of experimental groups by Bower (1965) who found that conflict was an important motivator of constructive thought and analysis. Indeed, Bower found that groups were not as successful in their problem solving activities when they were instructed to be concerned about what was best for the group as a whole.

There are, however, some problems with George's multiple advocacy system. As he recognized, the conditions specified to make the system work are difficult to achieve. It is almost impossible to equalize power, much less analytical resources, bargaining skills, and information. Time pressures also often intrude to make the advocacy process too time consuming. However, even if the conditions were all met, there is still some question about the utility of the system. Clearly, George expects the chief executive to have great wisdom and insight. That person is expected to make the final decision, based on the different points of view presented by the various advocates or contesting groups. There is a presumption of the chief executive as being above the fray, of being able to get beyond parochial interests and personal concerns to make a wise and intelligent choice. Such a role requirement seems like a very tall order to fill. Executives are bound by the commitment process described in the last chapter, as well as by the limits of selective perception, socialization and training, and inculturation into organizational norms and practices that limit the ability to make strictly rational choices. It is unrealistic to expect the chief executive to be uncommitted, unbiased, and uninvolved with the various positions being presented. These two problems—the assumption of what is required to fulfill the magistrate role and the assumptions of equal power, resources, and access—make the multiple advocacy system an interesting model but probably not as effective in practice. The reliance on the all-encompassing judgment of the chief executive seems to be risky.

Of course, political decision making processes, which can and do operate in organizations, provide many of the advantages of multiple advocacy without the reliance on the impartial arbiter. If this is the case, and if, as asserted frequently throughout this book, power and politics are endemic in organizations, why isn't decision making more effective?

The problem may be that most organizations operate under the guise of rationality with some elements of power and politics thrown in, and thereby manage to obtain the worst of both worlds. Salancik and Pfeffer have argued:

> *However, institutionalized forms of power—what we prefer to call the cleaner forms of power: authority, legitimation, centralized control, regulations, and the more modern "management information systems"—tend to buffer the organization*

from reality and obscure the demands of its environment.
. . . Political processes, rather than being mechanisms for
unfair and unjust allocations and appointments, tend toward
the realistic resolution of conflicts among interests (1977b: 3).

The suggestion is that under the guise and norm of rationality, power is centralized and institutionalized in organizations, and political processes are "cleaned up." What is left is a system in which power and politics occur in a covert fashion, and in which there are elements of rational decision processes occurring simultaneously with political activity. Advocacy may not be legitimate, so different points of view are not really brought out. At the same time, the conflicts remain, so that there are problems with implementation, acquiring accurate information, and getting access to the decision process. Thus, the argument concerning the relationship between power and organizational performance might be more usefully recast to suggest that performance is negatively affected primarily when politics occurs in a system which operates largely under the guise of rationality. However, in this case, it is probably the institutionalized power and trappings of rational choice, more than the conflict and political activity, which cause organizational problems.

The relationship of organizational politics to performance is both interesting and important, and certainly the jury is still out. The constructive role of conflict and having different points of view and heterogeneous information argue for the positive consequences of power and politics on performance. At the same time, there are problems of subunit interests dominating the organization, as well as the diversion of resources into internal political squabbles. We can tentatively conclude that under those conditions specified in Chapter 3 in which power is likely to be used to resolve decisions, power and politics is probably positively related to performance. Under conditions when power and politics are not necessary to make the choice, the use of power and politics may negatively affect performance.

One final point is important in considering the relationship between power and political activity and organizational performance. The use of power in organizational decision making takes, as was shown in Chapters 5 and 6, a number of different forms, ranging from coalition formation, cooptation, and the selective presentation and use of information to the use of political language and outside expertise to legitimate decisions. It is quite plausible to presume that the different strategies of power in use may have somewhat different effects on organizational operations. It is possible that there may be "good" and "bad" political activity in organizations. Thus, a more refined analysis would need to consider how various forms of political activity impact organizational performance, rather than considering the use of power in a more global fashion.

Again, however, the reader is cautioned to recall that what is "good" or "bad" is in most instances only known long after the decision has been made and implemented. It is quite possible for a group within the organization to seize control through a variety of apparently illegitimate means but have a perspective on the organization and its functioning which turns out to make the organization more successful. Thus, though the search for the consequences of various forms of political activity is probably useful, whether or not conditions can be found which permit the specification of what is harmful or helpful political activity in organizations is very much open to question.

Managerial Skills, Selection, and Training

In addition to the question of the impact on organizational performance, another issue facing the political approach to organizational analysis is what such a view implies about the role of the manager in organizations, and what its implications are for the activities of managerial training and selection. As one colleague has suggested, even if this perspective is right, what does one do with it in terms of management education and management development?

The first important point is that this is scarcely an irrelevant issue. Several years ago business schools were graduating more than 16,000 MBA students per year and, I suspect, the number has grown since then. The management training and executive education business is huge, with whole catalogues devoted to listing the various programs, their course of study, faculty, and fees. I can think of virtually no business school which does not run some sort of executive program or management training program, and frequently more than one. These 16,000 MBA's are only the tip of the iceberg, as there are many thousands more undergraduate students majoring in business. For colleges already starved for revenues, and facing even more serious enrollment declines in the future, the education of future managers is the key to their survival.

The point that there is a large management training industry is relevant to understanding the kind of skills and roles which are currently viewed as appropriate for administrators, and to appreciating why it may be quite difficult to change these. Business education in this country was once more applied and more case oriented than it currently is. Since the late 1950's, the trend has been toward increasing analytical sophistication in the skills imparted in business schools and in other training settings. Managers and future managers learn how to do sophisticated quantitative and statistical analysis, financial analysis, and optimization methods. Training has become more disciplinary in its orientation, and business school faculties are more likely to be comprised primarily of people with doctoral degrees from basic disciplines such as economics, sociology, and psychology than they are to have faculty who have very much experience as practicing managers. Clearly, there is consensus on the importance of analytical skills, particularly quantitative analytical skills, in the training of managers. At least such a consensus is implied by curricula that have more decision or management science than any other subject matter, which is a common phenomenon.

It is reasonable to ask what the evidence is on the effectiveness of business education in producing more successful and effective managers in general, and in particular if there is any evidence relevant to the issue of the type of skills imparted. The evidence is not very hopeful with respect to business education and the kind of skills imparted by it. Livingston (1971) compared senior executives attending an advanced management course at Harvard with a sample of Harvard MBA graduates with comparable years of work experience. Because the senior managers earned about a third more, on the average, than the Harvard MBA's, Livingston argued that advanced management education had limited value. Although the methodology of this study is clearly flawed (Weinstein and Srinivasan, 1974) as it is inappropriate to compare a random sample of Harvard MBA's with a select group of senior executives, there is almost no systematic research which attempts to test or refute Livingston's contention. The numerous studies which attempt to develop predictors of career success of MBA graduates (Harrell, 1969; 1970; Williams and Harrell, 1964; Weinstein and Srinivasan, 1974) are not germane, as they do not sample a general population of managers to assess the effects of specific business training on career success. Pfeffer's (1977b) study comparing MBA graduates with those with only a bachelor's degree in business is suggestive but also not conclusive. Pfeffer found that, controlling for other factors such as socioeconomic background, years of work experience, and whether or not the person was self-employed, having an advanced degree did not have a significant effect on current compensation for a sample of graduates from a single business school. This study, of course, did not compare business school graduates with others, which is what would be required to estimate the effects of business training.

Another view of the issue is obtained by considering whether or not success in business schools is correlated with subsequent job and career success. If business schools impart valued and needed skills, one might argue that performance in mastering those skills would be correlated with subsequent managerial performance. Here, too, the evidence is not favorable. Pfeffer (1977b) reported there was no correlation between grades or admission test scores and subsequent career success, measured in terms of attained salary. Williams and Harrell (1964) reported that neither college grades nor grades in required courses predicted subsequent salary for a sample of Stanford MBA's, but that there was a positive correlation between grades in elective courses and salary. It is quite plausible to argue that elective grades measure motivation and effort as much as the mastery of cognitive skills, or alternatively that they measure the students' ability to find courses in which higher grades are easier to achieve. In either case, the relationship between skill mastery and subsequent success is not evident. Weinstein and Srinivasan (1974) did find a significant effect of grades on compensation for their subsample of line managers, but found no relationship for staff managers. The existing evidence does not support the conclusion that, to the extent grades represent mastery of concepts taught in school, there is any effect of such specific knowledge on subsequent career success.

A cursory examination of articles on executive succession in the business press indicates that executives come from a variety of backgrounds. Some are engineers, some are lawyers, some have graduated with degrees in economics, history, or political science, and some have little formal education but have worked their way up through the company. Surveys of where chief executives come from (in terms of colleges) typically list Harvard, Yale, and Princeton among the top five. Neither Princeton nor Yale had programs in business until very recently, so if specialized business training is going to be necessary in the future, it certainly was not in the recent past. Collins (1979) has argued that educational credentialing is part of the stratification system and has little to do with formal knowledge or skills required. His argument may be applicable in general, as well as in managerial positions. Degrees may be barriers to entry more than specific knowledge prerequisites.

Two questions come immediately from the literature on the determinants of managerial attainment. The first is, if business education or performance in business school does not predict subsequent career success for managers, then why not? The second question is, given the absence of any evidence arguing for the particular impact of the current

modes of training, why is such training, and the particular skills emphasized the ones that are stressed so heavily in the curricula?

There are many potential reasons to explain why performance in
schools of management, or even the acquisition of management training,
may not be related to subsequent career success. In the first place, it is
quite possible that there are class or socioeconomic effects on succession
to high management positions which operate independently of the educational system but use education, though not perhaps, specific types of
degrees, as a filter. Pfeffer's (1977b) data reveal the importance of socioeconomic background for salary attainment for both bachelor's degree
and MBA graduates. Second, career outcomes may be in part the consequence of chance factors. March and March (1978), for example, in
examining the careers of school superintendents, argued that as individuals were promoted up the career ladder, enough filtering and self-selec-
tion was accomplished that by the time the need arose to pick a superin-
tendent from among a set of candidates, the candidates were all so
similar that chance both described the process of selection and was
probably a sufficient decision rule. After all, if the candidates for a
position are all quite similar in background, skills, and experience, it
makes little sense to have an elaborate screening procedure operating on
those characteristics as such a procedure will not discriminate among the
potential job holders.

A third possibility has to do with the type of training imparted.
Business schools impart both the ideology and skills of analysis, especially economic and quantitative analysis. This is a maximizing ideology,
which emphasizes the role of numerical procedures and the belief that
there are best or optimal answers. Optimization techniques form the core
of current courses in finance (maximizing shareholder wealth, optimiz-
ing portfolio performance), decision sciences or operations research
(maximizing expected utility, inventory sizes, linear programming), marketing (optimum levels and allocation of advertising, product development, and distribution resources), economics (particularly microeconomics or the theory of the firm), and, I am sorry to report,
organizational behavior. In the latter field, the search for optimization
takes the form of a search for optimal leadership styles, compensation
systems, decision making systems, or structures, contingent on the environment and technology. Students emerge from such a program believing that there is an optimum answer or set of answers discoverable
through quantitative analysis. It is quite possible that they are thus
desensitized both to the issue of multiple goals and to the use of data to
construct arguments, explanations, and justifications. They are trained

in specialized language and techniques which make them excellent allies in political struggles, for they can assist in producing the appearance of nonsubstitutability and expertise, as well as the numbers and analyses that support one particular position. At the same time, it is clear that they may be ineffective themselves in such political contests, in large measure because they are insensitive to the game which is being played or its rules.

There is some data that indirectly bears on this third possibility. Harrell and Harrell (1979) reported data on 434 graduates of the Stanford MBA program, including 182 responses from persons who had been out fifteen years. They compared Stanford MBA's with engineering and non-engineering undergraduate majors in terms of earnings after leaving the MBA program. Presumably, the engineering majors are more likely to be quantitatively oriented and more inclined to rely on analysis and data than the non-engineering undergraduate students. McKenney and Keen (1974) have reviewed evidence which indicated that major while in undergraduate school does have effects on the individual's cognitive style and mode of approach to problems. The one problem with the Harrell data is that all the MBA's went to the same graduate business program, so that some differences which might have existed on entering the program could have been eroded over the two year course of study.

Harrell and Harrell (1979: Table 4) observed the following differences in their sample. For the MBA classes 1961–1965, the starting salary was statistically significantly higher for the engineers than for the students with non-engineering undergraduate majors. At five years after graduation, the data indicated that salaries were either comparable or slightly larger for the non-engineering majors, although the difference was not significant. At ten years after graduation, there was a statistically significant difference in salaries in favor of those with non-engineering undergraduate backgrounds, and at fifteen years, individuals who had not majored in engineering earned about ten percent more than those that had, although because of sample size and variability, this difference was not statistically significant.

Pfeffer (1977b) observed a significant effect for MBA training on starting salary, but no significant effect on current salary, when other explanatory factors were controlled. This is consistent with the Harrell data in indicating that there is evidence for a positive effect of specialized technical training at the start of one's career, but that career progress is not significantly enhanced and may come to be harmed by these specialized skills. Part of this may result from the fact that those with very advanced technical skills may get placed in staff positions which have less prospect for upward mobility than line management jobs. Part of the problem may also derive from the limited perspective on the organization that results from analytical training.

If the evidence on the effects of training is so negative, then why do the curricula look the way they do? The answer has much more to do with the politics of educational curricula than it does with the effects of such curricula on those who are exposed to it.

THE POLITICS OF CURRICULA

The increasing emphasis on quantitative analysis in business education curricula can be readily traced to a series of pressures which tended to force change in the same direction. In the 1950's the Ford Foundation sponsored a study of business school educational programs. This study, the Gordon and Howell report (1959), argued that there was too much emphasis on relating case histories of business situations and not enough attention to developing a theoretically-based knowledge of management practice. The Ford Foundation, much as in the case of New York University, was willing to spend money to help implement some of the changes recommended by the Gordon and Howell report, and began providing support for business schools to improve their research and theoretical foundations through sponsoring research projects and various types of faculty training activities.

This emphasis on increased scholarship was consistent, of course, with the generally growing research program in all aspects of universities. After 1957 when the Russians launched Sputnik, there was a tremendous expansion in federally funded research, much of which went to support research programs in universities. These grants produced, as was discussed in Chapter 4, overhead monies that provided important slack resources to the institutions involved. The expansion made possible by both the direct funding and the overhead was welcomed by universities. Faculty expansion proceeded, salaries increased, and in this climate, the importance of scholarship and research was re-emphasized throughout the university setting. This climate would have to have some impact on business schools. Even though they were professional schools and on many campuses were rather isolated from the rest of the university, the emphasis on research and scholarship affected business schools.

The expansion of graduate education programs far outstripped the expansion of the university system to employ the products of those programs—trained faculty. The one area of enrollment that has continued to expand in almost all universities is enrollment in the professional schools, particularly business. Consequently, the expansion of research-trained faculty in the disciplines, which exceeded the supply of new teaching positions in the disciplinary departments, found a ready outlet in the expanding schools of business administration. Economists, sociologists, and psychologists found a much more lucrative job market in the business schools; for their part, the business schools, which were interested in enhancing their theoretical and research bases under the stimulus of the Gordon and Howell report and the Ford Foundation, were quite willing to take in these well-qualified scholars from the basic social science departments. Indeed, the relatively slow and unsuccessful expansion of business school doctoral programs meant that there were not enough well-qualified business school graduates in many of the subject areas.

These factors—a shortage of trained business school Ph.D.'s, a surplus of doctoral graduates from the other social sciences, a generally increased emphasis on research throughout universities, the Gordon and Howell report and the Ford Foundation's support for changing business education—came together to profoundly change business school teaching methods and curricula during the period from the late 1950's through the 1960's. In many schools, the emphasis on business cases diminished. There was increased attention to computers, quantitative analysis, and the teaching of theory. The job market placed few constraints on this process. First, these changes occurred almost everywhere, so from the point of view of employers, there was little to choose. Second, employers have maintained that the function of graduate education is to train people in how to think and write. Specific skills would be better learned in the specific organization, where the particular rules, policies, and procedures that were local practice could be acquired. Thus, as long as the training was increasingly rigorous and intellectually demanding, the specific content was not of major concern. With the growing demand for admission to business education programs, the elite business schools began to play even more of a filtering or selection role, making them all the more valuable to employers.

It is clear how a set of circumstances in the environment evolved to increase the disciplinary, theoretical focus within business schools. The remaining part of the scenario is how the quantitative emphasis came to dominate other theoretical or research perspectives within business school curricula. That part of the story is also quite simple. In the first place, most business schools were the step-children of economics departments, and economics as a discipline was becoming increasingly quantitative and analytic during this period. Typical of the step-child relationship was the School of Business at the University of California at Berkeley. Although one of the oldest business schools in the country, the school did not have its own doctoral program until the late 1950's; prior to that time doctoral students interested in business went through the program in the economics department. Moreover, prior to the late 1950's all the faculty who were hired in the school, including those teaching marketing, industrial relations, and operations management had their basic training and graduate work in economics. Business schools were often seen as applied economics departments; in some universities, the economics department was actually a part of the business school. The close relationship between business education and economics, and the increasingly theoretical and quantitative emphasis in economics, helped to legitimate quantitative analysis within the business school curricula.

In the second place, economics and decision science tends to be more paradigmatically developed than many of the other business areas, especially the area of organizational behavior. As was noted in Chapter 4, a high level of paradigm development, and the consensus and certainty accompanying it, facilitates those fields in the political contests that occur within universities and within schools. The ability to demonstrate predictable results, along with the shared consensus that typically characterizes the more paradigmatically developed fields, gives them advantages in claiming academic legitimacy and rigor. In the context of universities, many of which were also dominated by the harder sciences (e.g., Pfeffer and Salancik, 1974; Lodahl and Gordon, 1973), the more quantitative subjects within the school had advantages in contests for power deriving not only from the higher level of internal consensus, but also from their ability to draw on external allies from related and powerful departments around the university, such as economics, mathematics, and statistics.

Analytic technique, precise, measurable, and quantitative came to replace less precisely understood or transmitted understanding of business situations and decision making. The internal dynamics, external allies, and the relevant labor markets and funding patterns made it almost inevitable. The critical conclusion from this discussion, as well as from the discussion of the studies of the effects of business school grades and training, is that *in no case is there evidence that the curriculum and method of instruction which evolved is any better* (or for that matter any worse) *than alternative programs of instruction, including those replaced.* Thus, it is important to remember that the now institutionalized curricula that dominate administrative education in the U.S. were in large measure the result of a set of forces which may have had little to do with the role of administrators or the skills which are needed to perform that role. Rather, the curricula tended to be produced by their own political dynamics, largely separate from consideration of training or educational needs.

AN ALTERNATIVE
PERSPECTIVE ON MANAGERIAL SKILLS

If we take seriously a political view of organizations, then the role of the manager and the skills needed to perform effectively in that role begin to look very different. The political model suggests that organizations are characterized by uncertainty and conflict. Bargaining and negotiation are the primary decision making modes, and analysis is seen as a tool in the power struggle, rather than the way through which decisions are made.

This suggests that among the critical skills which are needed by managers who are filling administrative roles in organizations in which power and politics play an important part, are a tolerance for uncertainty and ambiguity and the ability to confront and manage conflict and advocacy. Training in advocacy, case preparation and presentation, and power and politics, including the use of symbolic acts and language, may be more appropriate training for the manager in a political organization; at least such skills can be useful as supplements to the technical analytic skills that seem now to dominate business education. We have already noted the rising prominence of lawyers in executive positions and the effect of socioeconomic background on business success. In both cases, other reasons for the importance of these variables may be supplemented by the fact that both legal training and high status backgrounds may be associated with knowledge of and skill in using power and political tactics in organizational settings. Certainly, the vast majority of the legislators in the U.S. have legal backgrounds, which suggests something about what law prepares one to do. Similarly, social background may not only provide social similarity and connections but also a knowledge about power, politics, and their use which is not possessed by as many people from lower status backgrounds. Legal training may not only be increasingly critical, given governmental regulation and public scrutiny of business; such training may also be important in developing advocacy and presentation skills which are useful in political contests within organizations.

An example of the type of skills we are discussing can be found in Peters' (1978) treatment of implementation strategies, which was mentioned previously in Chapter 6. Peters argued for the importance of knowing how to use time, persistence, and settings in symbolic ways in order to accomplish organizational change and redirection a little at a time. One of the advantages of the incremental change approach which Peters advocated is that it is less likely to arouse opposition, as the change will not be perceived as being as large or as important.

The implicit recognition of the importance of at least some of these skills is evidenced by the addition of writing and speaking skills workshops at major business schools such as Stanford, Berkeley, and Carnegie-Mellon. Such courses are typically introduced on an optional or non-credit basis, however, and are generally perceived as being necessary only because of the increasingly poor job of education which is done by high schools and undergraduate colleges. While minimal competence at writing and speaking is increasingly recognized as being important for career success, the fact that presentation, advocacy, political and interpersonal skills may be critical in affecting career progress is not as widely recognized.

Whether or not the skills enumerated can be taught and, if so, how, is still open to question. Nevertheless, a review of the existing research provides little support for the institutionalized position of the strictly analytic approaches to managerial education. The point is that the political model of organizations not only has something to say about organizational analysis; it also has implications for the analysis and design of management education activities.

MATCHING PERSONAL AND ORGANIZATIONAL STYLES

It is clear that all organizations are not equally political. It is also undoubtedly true that various individuals have different skills and different styles of personal interaction. Some are comfortable with quantitative analysis; others are comfortable with presentation and argument. It is useful for both individuals and organizations to try to match their specific skills and styles to each other. This point is precisely that made by Kotter (1978) in a review of the implications of a political view of organizations for managerial careers. Kotter argued that settings within organizations, and the organizations themselves, varied in terms of the amount of interdependence and the number of relationships that needed to be managed, which he suggested were important determinants of how political the position was. Kotter suggested analyzing positions by their requirements for exercising political skills, and then deciding how much of those skills were possessed by the individual, as well as his or her taste for that kind of position.

What is being suggested is a kind of contingency theory of careers. Persons with both a taste and an aptitude for nonpolitical types of operations will probably both perform better and be somewhat happier in those kinds of settings. On the other hand, individuals with highly developed political skills and with a preference for more political types of settings will probably perform more effectively and be happier in those types of settings. In order to implement this as a career development or selection strategy, substantial additional work will need to be done in identifying political skills, analytic skills, and the characteristics of those settings that call for one kind of aptitude and interest rather than another. It is also quite possible that the two types of skills are not negatively related to each other, which opens up even more possibilities in terms of predicting success and performance.

Even at this point, however, the factors enumerated in Chapter 3 provide some guidance to diagnosing situations in which power and politics will be more or less prominent. It is important to take such factors into account in planning career moves as well as in attempting to predict a person's success and happiness in various kinds of situations.

Some Implications
for Organization Design

The analysis of power and politics in organizations, and particularly the analysis of the institutionalization of power, has implications for the design of organizations. As Pfeffer and Salancik (1977c: 15) noted, "Prescriptions for effective organization designs depend on one's view of organizations, how they operate, what their principal problems are, and how they are managed." Most approaches to organization design implicitly take the problem to be one of the effective coordination and control of the interdependent activities of the various persons performing the specialized tasks in the organization. Thus, for example, Galbraith (1973) focused on design strategies which either enhance the capacity of the structure to process information needed for coordination or control or, alternatively, which reduce the need for information processing within the structure. Mackenzie's (1978) findings on the advantages of more hierarchical structures also proceeded from the premise of the most efficient way of coordinating and controlling task processes.

However, as Weick (1969) has argued, the organizing process inherently involves a dilemma. In ecological or natural selection terms, it is the dilemma of the choice between variation and retention. Structures in which operating routines are perfectly retained and repeated will have little variation in task and decision making processes. They will do what

356

they do very well and very consistently, but they will have little novel activity from which to select adaptive responses if and when environmental circumstances change. On the other hand, structures in which there is a great amount of variation in activity and in task processes will have the raw material available from which to select adaptive responses. The problem is that in the continual variation in activity, there is very little of the economy that comes from repetition, learning, and specialization. Implementation will be problematic, though adaptation will be likely.

Pfeffer and Salancik also recognized this design dilemma:

> The principal dilemma involves the contradiction between learning what to do and executing decisions and policies. . . . From this perspective, the job of management is to be responsive. . . . The problem is that the manager as a processor and assimilator of demands is not in an action mode. An organization designed to execute decisions requires more centralization of control, more unity of direction, more orderliness in decision processes, more hierarchy, more formal structure. These very attributes of structure, which make action possible, also limit the visibility of alternatives, minimize conflicting information, and prevent the intrusion of other perspectives (1977c: 21).

The approach taken by Williamson (1975) in analyzing organizational design also recognizes the problem. Williamson's recommended solution is the adoption of the multidivisional, or M-form structure. As analyzed by Williamson, the multidivisional structure solves the problem by separating the tasks of efficient operation from the tasks of overall strategic adaptation.

The multidivisional form "involved substituting quasi-autonomous operating divisions (organized mainly along product, brand, or geographic lines) for the functional divisions of the U-form structure as the principal basis for dividing up the task and assigning responsibility" (Williamson, 1975: 136). Most large firms in the U.S. today are organized in a multidivisional structure. The evidence indicates, moreover, that the multidivisional structure tended to accompany increasing levels of diversification in the firms' activities. Chandler argued that the multidivisional form was particularly successful because:

> The basic reason for its success was simply that it clearly removed the executives responsible for the destiny of the entire

enterprise from the more routine operational activities, and so gave them the time, information, and even psychological commitment for long-term planning. . . . The new structure left the broad strategic decisions as to the allocation of existing resources and the acquisition of new ones in the hands of a top team of generalists. Relieved of operating duties and tactical decisions, a general executive was less likely to reflect the position of just one part of the whole (1966: 382–383).

Williamson summarized the characteristics and advantages of the multidivisional structure as:

1. *The responsibility for operating decisions is assigned to (essentially self-contained) operative divisions or quasifirms.*

2. *The elite staff attached to the general office performs both advisory and auditing functions. Both have the effect of securing greater control over operating division behavior.*

3. *The general office is principally concerned with strategic decisions, involving planning, appraisal, and control, including the allocation of resources among the (competing) operating divisions.*

4. *The separation of the general office from operations provides general office executives with the psychological commitment to be concerned with the overall performance of the organization rather than become absorbed in the affairs of functional parts (Williamson, 1975: 137).*

The question to be posed is whether or not the multidivisional structure really does solve the problem of commitment to unsuccessful decisions and resistance to change which hinders the innovation and adaptation process within organizations. In discussing the relative advantages and disadvantages of organizing transactions using markets or organizational arrangements, Williamson (1975) recognized the fact that there were inherent problems in organizations which limited their performance, adaptability, and efficiency. Furthermore, Williamson (1975: 117) recognized that while appropriate internal organization might shift the point at which inefficiencies and problems would occur, such problems could not be completely precluded. In a discussion that is consistent with the points concerning institutionalization and commitment which were made in the last chapter, Williamson argued that many of the problems of the firm had to do with persistence and commitment to unsuccessful operations:

> Among the more severe goal distortions of internal organiza-
> tions are the biases which it experiences that are favorable to
> the maintenance or extension of internal operations. Biases of
> three types are discussed: internal procurement, internal ex-
> pansion, and program persistence. Communication distortion
> supports all three (1975: 118–119).

Williamson argued that the existence of an internal source of supply distorted procurement decisions. Because managers were reluctant
to abolish their own jobs, and because there is some evidence that
managerial compensation is tied to organization size as well as to profits,
there was a tendency for firms to favor the maintenance and use of
internal sources of supply. Furthermore, there were biases toward internal expansion which were produced by compensation incentives as well
as power motives. And, behavior tended to persist in organizations.
Williamson noted:

> . . . existing activities embody sunk costs of both organizational
> and tangible types while new projects require initial invest-
> ments of both kinds. The sunk costs in programs and facilities
> of ongoing projects thus insulate existing projects from dis-
> placement by alternatives which, were the current program not
> already in place, might otherwise be preferred (1975: 121).

These problems of persistence and commitment have manifested
themselves in several ways in the operations of large U.S. firms. Many
firms have found it difficult to innovate and develop new products and
new markets internally. There is some evidence to indicate that the
research and development resources expended in smaller organizations
have tended to produce more results than when expended in large organizations. Evidence summarized by Pfeffer and Salancik (1978) indicated
that although the profits of larger firms were less variable than those of
smaller organizations, the overall level of profitability was not greater.
As was noted in Chapter 8, the correlation between tenure and profitability for a large, random sample of U.S. firms is so low that less than 3%
of the variation in tenure is accounted for by profitability alone. This also
provides evidence for persistence and resistance to change.

Although there is some evidence that indicates that the multidivisional form may be a more effective design and may be able to remedy
at least some of these problems (e.g., Armour and Teece, 1978), there is
also evidence to indicate that these problems are persistent features in

almost all organizational designs. For instance, in General Motors, which was one of the first of the multidivisional structures and a model of the separation of strategic decision making from operations (Chandler, 1966), De Lorean reported that there was increased intervention of the senior executives into even the most minute product design and engineering decisions (Wright, 1979). There was also evidence that General Motors, as well as the other U.S. automobile companies, was late in recognizing and acting on the shift in taste in the U.S. toward smaller, more fuel efficient automobiles. De Lorean has argued also that there have been almost no major technological breakthroughs in the automobile industry in more than twenty years.

The design problem is clear—resistance to change and persistence of activities in the face of evidence that changes in decisions are required. One design alternative, the multidivisional form, may offer some advantages but it is clearly not sufficient to overcome the various problems of commitment and institutionalization detailed in Chapter 8 and by Williamson (1975). For instance, although executives in the general management ranks may, by their separation from the operating divisions, come to take on a more global perspective toward the business, it is unlikely that they would be any less susceptible to the effects of commitment to their own strategic decisions, and persist after performance has begun to diminish.

The multidivisional form represents, to some extent, an attempt to internalize capital market allocation mechanisms—in this case, through the use of a central staff and strategic planning function. But there already exists in organizations a quasi-market, the market for power and influence. What we are suggesting is that in organizations, power may serve as an internal market substitute or as a complement for the economic market which firms attempt to replicate through structures such as the multidivisional form. Pfeffer and Salancik (1977c: 23) argued that the view of organizations as quasi-markets in which power was the transactions medium of exchange led to two implications for organization design: making information available to all participants, so that the market for power and control can work more efficiently; and keeping power and control relatively decentralized and diffuse, so that no single organizational actor or set of actors dominated the firm and could therefore institutionalize control and delimit the operation of political contests within the organization. Both of these suggestions, but particularly the latter, seem to fly in the face of at least some organization design prescriptions. For instance, the centralization of information that sometimes occurs in a multidivisional form can act to insulate those at the top of the organization from criticism and review of their decisions.

The implications of this argument for organizational design are to reinforce the use of lateral relations at lower organizational levels (e.g., Galbraith, 1973). In this context, some of the advantages of the matrix organization become apparent. A matrix organization (Davis and Lawrence, 1977) is one that is organized along two dimensions simultaneously at some point in the structure. Frequently, matrix organizations have functional managers along one axis and product or project managers along the other, as diagrammed in Figure 9.1.

Several things are evident about such organizational designs. In the first place, a certain amount of conflict has been designed into the organization. Davis and Lawrence (1977) have suggested that one of the condi-

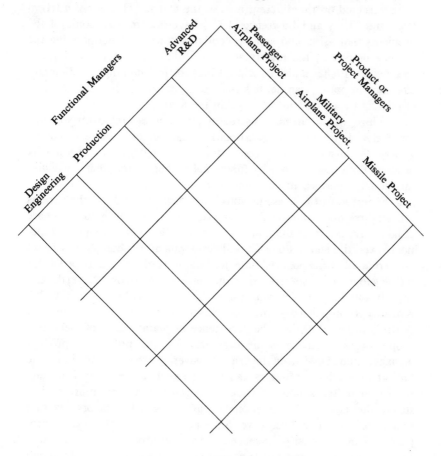

Figure 9.1
Diagram of a Typical Matrix Structure

tions in which a matrix structure should be used is a situation in which there are two or more competing perspectives and each is equally important, and thus it would be incorrect to subordinate one to another. In a product or project by function matrix, the goals of project completion and control and functional efficiency and expertise are presumed to be equally important. Of course, since persons working within the matrix have two bosses, and because the structure itself provides symbolic recognition of the importance of the different and separate goals, some degree of conflict or friction between the perspectives is to be expected.

Second, in order for the matrix organization to be successful, a balance of power must be maintained between the different perspectives, as represented on the different axes of the matrix. This is not a trivial task, and Davis and Lawrence (1977) have documented some of the problems that arise, and some potential solutions. In maintaining the balance of power, the matrix structure fulfills one of the conditions specified by Pfeffer and Salancik (1977c) for maintaining quasi-market efficiency in power transactions—namely, preventing the concentration of control by a single interest within the firm.

Third, within the matrix structure, it becomes a relatively straightforward task to build in quasi-market features of a more economic variety. For instance, many consulting firms are organized in a matrix fashion. Persons are hired by functional managers for their particular functional expertise, in economic analysis, computers, operations research, and so forth. These persons must then be "sold" to the various project directors within the firm, who staff their projects by the purchase of labor services from the functional groups. In order to maintain functional expertise and to do basic skill development, the budget may be set up so that all of the peoples' time need not be sold; some may be left for the development of specialized competence and expertise. Nevertheless, the introduction of an internal market for services within the firm, which is readily accomplished within a matrix structure, can bring in significant controls to guard against the persistence or maintenance of ineffective people or activities. In some organizations, the project or product managers must buy within the firm. However, in other organizations, the project or product managers can purchase what they need from any source, including sources outside the organization. This more radical step further ensures that functional departments within the organization remain responsive and sensitive to the needs of those running the projects. The bias against persistence and internal procurement can potentially be overcome, and in the case of permitting outside supply, it can be virtually eliminated.

362

The important point about the matrix or the variant just described, the market matrix structure, is that one of the reasons for its effectiveness is its legitimation and institutionalization of conflict, competition, and some degree of political activity within the firm. The fact that matrix structures are difficult to operate and are potentially unstable testifies to the power of the rational model to condition managers' operating styles and practices. As was noted earlier, we seem to have spent much more time worrying about how to rationalize organizations rather than exploring strategies for making them operate more effectively using a political approach.

It seems fair to state that in its basic dynamics and operation, the matrix, and particularly the matrix incorporating quasi-market mechanisms, is consistent with implications of the political model of organizations. Negotiation, competition, and a balance of power are all features emphasized in both. What this suggests is that in those organizations which are prone to power and politics in any event, a matrix design or some variant thereof may be a more effective way to structure the organization. This also suggests that conditions which predict when matrix structures will be more or less effective can be derived from the analysis of organizations as political systems. In those circumstances in which power and politics are most likely to be employed (as specified in Chapter 3), and in those instances in which the institutionalization of power is likely to occur, matrix structures may offer advantages over other designs, including the multidivisional structure. Of course, this argument requires empirical study. However, the link between matrix structures and the conditions fostering the use of power and politics in organizations is worthy of exploration.

The Politicization of Organizations

Understanding how to design organizations in which power and politics are important features, and understanding the role, skills, and training and selection of managers in such organizations is important and likely to become more important because of the increasing politicization of all organizations in the U.S., particularly large corporations. If business firms were ever not reasonably conceptualized as political coalitions, and if administrative agencies ever functioned primarily according to the classic model of bureaucracy, this is not true today and will be less true in the future. The politicization of organizations throughout society can be argued to follow from the following factors: increasing resource scarcity, and the increasing conflict and use of power engendered by such scarcity; an increasingly heterogeneous society in terms of values, beliefs, attitudes, and socialization and inculturation; the erosion of confidence in most organizations and institutions, with the concomitant erosion of the legitimacy of the power and authority exercised by and within those institutions; and more specifically, the growing movement for corporate accountability and social responsibility, which promises to challenge fundamentally the present governance arrangements of most large corporations. We consider each of these factors in turn in developing the argument that power and politics will come to play an increasing role in the decision making processes of most organizations in this society.

THE EFFECTS OF SCARCITY

In Chapter 3, we noted that scarcity was one of the fundamental conditions which predicted the use of power in organizational choice. Without scarcity there is no decision problem; to the extent that scarcity is greater, the stakes are higher for those who fail to win in organizational political activity. As scarcity increases, what was once a decision that might affect how well off a subunit might be, or how fast a person or set of organizational participants might get promoted, becomes a decision concerning the very continuation and existence of the subunit, and the retention of persons whose livelihoods depend on their employment with the organization.

Scarcity clearly promotes the use of power and political activity within those institutions that face scarcity. Thus, all that remains is to make the argument that most organizations will face increasing resource scarcity in the future in this country, and that the signs of the increased political activity within those organizations are already visible. The first point is easily made. The rate of growth of the U.S. economy has declined in virtually a secular trend since the end of World War II. There has been a corresponding decline in the rate of growth of productivity, until in recent years, productivity, or the amount of output produced per unit of labor input, has actually declined slightly or levelled off. The reasons for such declines in both economic growth and productivity are both numerous and not fully understood, and are well beyond the scope of this book. Nevertheless, both portend increasing economic scarcity in the future. Corporate profits, as a share of gross national product after allowing for inventory profits and the underdepreciation of capital assets, are at an all time low. The median income, in constant dollars, has grown much more slowly over the last ten years than it has in any period since World War II. In short, all of the symptoms and signs of scarcity are present.

The reactions to the scarcity, in terms of power and political struggles within organizations, are also apparent. Although Cohen and March

(1974) did not observe any systematic decrease in the average tenure of university presidents during periods of increased turbulence and difficulty, Pfeffer and Moore (1980a) found that the average time in office for their sample of forty academic department heads decreased strikingly as resource scarcity and the accompanying increased conflict grew during the 1970's. Though not yet empirically examined, impressionistic evidence supports the view that the tenure of executives of major U.S. corporations, as well as the tenures of many of the other major officers, has declined in recent years. Proxy fights, take-overs, and conflicts between executives, their boards, and shareholders have become increasingly frequent and bitter. Indeed, the increasing insecurity in the positions of high level corporate executives has spawned the employment contract, which provides some measure of financial protection over a period of time for corporate officers to protect and insure them against early "forced retirement." The indications are that these forms of protection are frequently used, as the risks of managing in an environment of greater scarcity become greater.

THE GROWTH OF
WORK FORCE HETEROGENEITY

In an environment of scarce resources, managers confront an even more heterogeneous work force in an environment in which many of the traditional institutions of socialization and social bonding are failing. Work force heterogeneity has increased in simple demographic terms. Whereas once the work force consisted primarily of Caucasian males, now there are significant numbers of women in all the professions and industries. In addition, there are growing numbers of various ethnic and racial minorities who have entered the work force. Some projections indicate, for instance, that by the year 2000, California will have a majority of various non-white ethnic groups comprising its population. Recent immigrants from Mexico, Vietnam, Cambodia, Cuba, and so forth will bring to the work place a greater diversity in beliefs, values, and attitudes.

At the same time various forms of demographic diversity are increasing, the various institutions which provide socialization and inculturation are having problems in their performance of that role. Ouchi and Jaeger (1978), arguing for the growing importance of the work organization as an institution of social integration, maintained that traditional U.S. institutions such as the church, the family, and neighborhood were succumbing to a growing social anomie and fragmentation. Greater geographic mobility has loosened kinship ties and the linkage to community and neighborhood, while the statistics on church attendance document the decline in this form of social integration. The schools, too, confront issues of decreased public acceptance and problems in the education and socialization of the young. One explanation of the success of the Proposition 13 property tax cut initiative in California was that people had lost confidence in the local schools; many wanted to spend their property tax savings on alternative private education. Proposals such as educational voucher systems have received attention also because of the decline of public confidence in the public education system.

To the extent that such trends continue, organizations are posed with the problem of managing ever greater diversity in attitudes, beliefs, and values. This heterogeneity in background and outlook provides both diversity and stimulus to organizations, but at the same time will clearly tend to make them more political in their governance. Indeed, one can make the case that the increasing demographic and cultural diversity found in organizations in the future will be a provocative source of positive change. The direction or consequences of the political activity is not the issue; the point is that the increasing heterogeneity promises to make organizational governance more of a political activity.

THE EROSION OF ORGANIZATIONAL AUTHORITY

Many of the recent public opinion polls document the loss of public confidence in most contemporary institutions, including corporations, unions, and government agencies. Such a decline in confidence has consequences for the decision making and governance of these institutions.

As mentioned previously, because of the power of lower level participants in organizations (Mechanic, 1962), the acceptance of authority is critical in the management of large formal organizations. It is impossible to exercise control strictly through the use of rewards and punishments; authority, legitimated power, is important in being able to make choices in a fashion that approximates the rational model. Indeed, rational choice presumes either centralized authority or shared consensus on goals and definitions of technology. To the extent that the authority of most formal organizations is eroded through the loss of public confidence and legitimacy, participants in the organizations are less likely to accept decisions and the premises for the decisions without question. What was once a potentially rational decision making process becomes transformed, through the loss of institutional authority, into a political struggle in which organizational members do not necessarily accept the values and judgments of others in the organization, and rather seek to engage in bargaining and haggling concerning the allocation and use of the resources and energy which constitute the organization.

Accompanying the loss of confidence in most contemporary organizations is a diminished willingness to be subject to their authority and a diminished concern for their survival and continued well-being. It is obviously easier to get organizational participants to make sacrifices for an organization in which they have more confidence and trust. Individuals are going to be more willing to forego their own immediate goals and objectives and to cooperate in joint efforts within a formal structure in which they have more confidence. Thus, the diminished confidence and authority in most contemporary organizations makes control over participants more difficult and reduces the willingness of organizational members to work harmoniously and in the organization's interests. With diminished confidence and respect, participants are more likely to approach the organization in terms of what they can get out of it, leading to more political contests within the organization concerning the division of resources. Gamson (1968) has argued that there are two activities which occur in every social collectivity, the coordinated effort to produce some collective product and the activity associated with determining how that product is to be allocated. What is suggested is that to the extent that the authority of the organization is eroded through a loss of confidence and respect, there is less energy expended on the production of the collective product and more time and attention given to the political activity of dividing up the resources produced by the organization.

THE POLITICIZATION
OF BUSINESS FIRMS

Many of the effects just described can be clearly seen in the growing politicization of business corporations. Examining citizen protests and political action taken directly, Vogel noted:

> Over the past fifteen years, a new way has been found to influence the decisions of corporations in the United States. No longer are public demands for change in corporate behavior addressed exclusively through government. Instead, a growing number of groups and individuals are taking their criticisms of corporate conduct directly to the firm: they are lobbying the corporation as well as the government (1978: 3).

Vogel's study examined the growing movement for corporate accountability, as that movement had emerged in shareholder resolutions and other direct forms of protest lodged against corporations. He argued that although citizen hostility against business firms has flourished in the past, it currently is taking a new form:

> What is new—and significant—is the form in which some public criticisms of business are now being made. In addition to political pressures from the state and the trade unions, the corporation today must also deal increasingly with direct pressures from organized citizen groups (1978: 3).

Vogel traced the growing use of direct protests and citizen involvement in corporate decision making to the movement for greater corporate accountability, which was accompanied by some fundamental changes in how corporations were viewed:

> The development of direct citizen protests reflects the influence of a large body of legal, academic, and popular opinion that regards the modern corporation as a private government, enjoying a substantial immunity from the constraints of both the market and the state. . . . The corporate accountability movement represents an attempt to realize in practice what scholars such as Latham, Dahl, and others have argued in theory— namely that corporations wield the power of governments and should, therefore, be treated like governments (Vogel, 1978: 5–6).

Vogel argued that the increased accountability demands and citizen protests directed against corporations reflected the diminished legitimacy of most contemporary American institutions, including the government. But whatever the reasons, the effects on corporations were evident.

> Liberalization of rules governing access to proxy machinery, politicization of shareholder suits, growth in the number and importance of outside directors, and greater willingness of both individual shareholders and institutions to vote against the recommendations of management—all these developments point to a historically important decrease in the autonomy and authority of those who manage corporations—the 1970's thus

*appear to represent a historic turning point in the distribution
of power within the corporation (Vogel, 1978: 13).*

Clearly, the increasingly diverse demands made on corporations, for investment in certain countries and not in others, for various employment and product policies, and indeed, to get in or out of certain kinds of business activity, and the fact that such demands were made by diverse groups, has made decision making within the corporation more political. If profit maximization *was* the simple rule to guide action, and there is some question if it was ever so widely used, it is no longer as applicable in a social setting in which corporations are increasingly treated as public governments and in which diverse interests claim to have some say in the corporation's decisions.

Increasing scarcity, the decline in the effectiveness of institutions of socialization and social integration, greater heterogeneity in the population and the workforce both in terms of demographics and in terms of values and attitudes, and the changing public perception of all institutions including the business corporation, have acted together to politicize decision making taken within virtually all formal organizations. To the extent that such trends continue into the future, the politicization of organizations will proceed apace, with all that this implies for the process of decision making and management of these organizations.

Conclusion

This section was originally going to be titled, "The Manager as Politician." After talking to some manager friends, however, it was learned that such an appellation was taken as an insult. Managers aren't politicians, I was told. They are rational, interested in efficiency and effectiveness, hard-working, and engaged in the serious business of resource allocation and strategy formulation in major enterprises that control vast sums of wealth and energy. They certainly are not politicians, engaged in frivolous conflict and dispute, subject to various pressures and responding to constituencies which could promise them the most votes or money. However, as they talked about their activities during their work, my informants told me about maneuvers which were relevant to their career advancement, such as showing up opponents at meetings, getting access to some critical information, making a point with the boss. I heard about maneuvers to get their subunit's point of view across more effectively, including forming alliances with other units, and about attempts to make decisions in uncertain and complex situations; in short, I heard about a lot of political activity. Fortunately, these associates were quite

369

normal in their selective perception, motivation, and responses to commitments—not at all like the calculating, disinterested, highly motivated, and completely objective paragons I seem to encounter in my books on management and organizations.

If there is one concluding message, it is that it is probably effective and it is certainly normal that these managers do behave as politicians. It is even better that some of them are quite effective at it. In situations in which technologies are uncertain, preferences are conflicting, perceptions are selective and biased, and information processing capacities are constrained, the model of the effective politician may be an appropriate one for both the individual and for the organization in the long run.

Power and politics are often part of organizations, and need to be understood as fundamental and important processes. Power and politics are basic processes which occur in many organizations much of the time, and are empirically researchable and analyzable using a set of conceptual tools which are already largely in place and which have constituted the subject matter of this book. Although ignoring these topics may be favored, given the ideology and political purposes served, it is time to begin incorporating the issues raised here in a much more systematic and comprehensive way in both the research and teaching in the field of organizations.

REFERENCES

Adams, J.S. 1965. Inequity in Social Exchange. In *Advances in Experimental Social Psychology*, Vol. 2, ed. Leonard Berkowitz, pp. 267–300. New York: Academic Press.

Allen, Michael Patrick, Panian, Sharon K., and Lotz, Roy E. 1979. Managerial Succession and Organizational Performance: A Recalcitrant Problem Revisited. *Administrative Science Quarterly* 24:167–180.

Allen, Robert W., Madison, Dan L., Porter, Lyman W., Renwick, Patricia A., and Mayes, Bronston T. 1979. Organizational Politics: Tactics and Characteristics of its Actors. *California Management Review* 22:77–83.

Allen, Thomas J. 1969. *Meeting the Technical Information Needs of Research and Development Projects. Working Paper No. 431–69.* Cambridge, MA: Massachusetts Institute of Technology, Sloan School of Management.

Allison, Graham T. 1971. *Essence of Decision.* Boston: Little, Brown and Company.

Allport, Floyd H. 1962. A Structuronomic Conception of Behavior: Individual and Collective. *Journal of Abnormal and Social Psychology* 64:3–30.

Archibald, W. Peter. 1974. Alternative Explanations for Self-Fulfilling Prophecy. *Psychological Bulletin* 81:74–84.

Armour, Henry O., and Teece, David J. 1978. Organizational Structure and Economic Performance: A Test of the Multidivisional Hypothesis. *Bell Journal of Economics* 9:106–122.

Asch, S.E. 1958. Effects of Group Pressures Upon Modification and Distortion of Judgments. In *Readings in Social Psychology*, eds. E.E. Maccoby, T.M. Newcomb, and E.L. Hartley, pp. 174–183. New York, Holt.

Bachrach, Peter, and Baratz, Morton S. 1962. Two Faces of Power. *American Political Science Review* 56:947–952.

Baldridge, J. Victor. 1971. *Power and Conflict in the University.* New York: John Wiley.

Barber, James D. 1966. *Power in Committees: An Experiment in the Governmental Process.* Chicago: Rand McNally.

Baritz, Joseph H. 1960. *The Servants of Power.* Middletown, CT: Wesleyan University Press.

Baskett, G.D. 1973. Interview Decisions as Determined by Competency and Attitude Similarity. *Journal of Applied Psychology* 57:343–345.

Bem, Daryl J. 1972. Self-Perception Theory. In *Advances in Experimental Social Psychology,* Vol. 6, Leonard Berkowitz, (ed.) pp. 1–62. New York: Academic Press.

Benson, J. Kenneth. 1973. The Analysis of Bureaucratic-Professional Conflict: Functional Versus Dialectical Approaches. *Sociological Quarterly* 14:376–394.

Beyer, Janice M., and Lodahl, Thomas M. 1976. A Comparative Study of Patterns of Influence in United States and English Universities. *Administrative Science Quarterly* 21:104–129.

Bibb, Robert, and Form, William H. 1977. The Effects of Industrial, Occupational, and Sex Stratification on Wages in Blue-Collar Markets. *Social Forces* 55:974–996.

Bierstedt, Robert. 1950. An Analysis of Social Power. *American Sociological Review* 15:730–738.

Blake, R.R., and Mouton, Jane S. 1961. Reactions to Intergroup Competition Under Win-Lose Conditions. *Management Science* 7:420–435.

Blau, Peter M. 1964. *Exchange and Power in Social Life.* New York: John Wiley.

———, and Schoenherr, Richard A. 1971. *The Structure of Organizations.* New York: Basic Books.

Bower, Joseph L. 1965. The Role of Conflict in Economic Decision-Making Groups: Some Empirical Results. *Quarterly Journal of Economics* 79:263–277.

Brehm, Jack W. 1966. *A Theory of Psychological Reactance.* New York: Academic Press.

Brown, Richard Harvey. 1978. Bureaucracy as Praxis: Toward a Political Phenomenology of Formal Organizations. *Administrative Science Quarterly* 23:365–382.

Bucher, Rue. 1970. Social Process and Power in a Medical School. In *Power in Organizations,* ed. Mayer N. Zald, pp. 3–48. Nashville, TN: Vanderbilt University Press.

Burns, Tom, and Stalker, G.M. 1961. *The Management of Innovation.* London: Tavistock.

Byrne, D. 1969. Attitudes and Attraction. In *Advances in Experimental Social Psychology,* Vol. 4, ed. Leonard Berkowitz, pp. 35–89. New York: Academic Press.

Carey, Alex. 1967. The Hawthorne Studies: A Radical Criticism. *American Sociological Review* 32:403–416.

REFERENCES

Carlson, Richard O. 1962. *Executive Succession and Organizational Change.* Danville, IL: Interstate Printers and Publishers.

————. 1972. *School Superintendents: Career and Performance.* Columbus, OH: Charles E. Merrill Publishing Co.

Cartwright, Dorwin. 1979. Contemporary Social Psychology in Historical Perspective. *Social Psychology Quarterly* 42:82–93.

Chaffee, Ellen E. 1980. *Decision Models in University Budgeting.* Unpublished Ph.D. dissertation. Palo Alto, CA: Stanford University.

Chandler, Alfred D., Jr. 1966. *Strategy and Structure.* New York: Doubleday & Co., Anchor Books Edition.

Child, John. 1972. Organizational Structure, Environment and Performance: The Role of Strategic Choice. *Sociology* 6:1–22.

————. 1973. Strategies of Control and Organizational Behavior. *Administrative Science Quarterly* 18:1–17.

Cohen, Michael D., and March, James G. 1974. *Leadership and Ambiguity: The American College President.* New York: McGraw-Hill.

————, and Olsen, Johan P. 1972. A Garbage Can Model of Organizational Choice. *Administrative Science Quarterly* 17:1–25.

————. 1976. People, Problems, Solutions, and the Ambiguity of Relevance. In *Ambiguity and Choice in Organizations,* James G. March and Johan P. Olsen, pp. 24–37. Bergen, Norway: Universitetsforlaget.

Coleman, James S. 1973. Loss of Power. *American Sociological Review* 38:1–17.

Collins, Randall. 1979. *The Credential Society.* New York: Academic Press.

Committee on Educational Policy. 1974. *Recommendations from the Committee on Educational Policy Regarding the Future of Instruction and Research in Criminology on the Berkeley Campus.* Unpublished ms. Berkeley, CA: University of California.

Crecine, J.P. 1967. A Computer Simulation Model of Municipal Budgeting. *Management Science* 13:786–815.

Crozier, Michel. 1964. *The Bureaucratic Phenomenon.* Chicago: University of Chicago Press.

Cyert, Richard M., and March, James G. 1963. *A Behavioral Theory of the Firm.* Englewood Cliffs, NJ: Prentice-Hall.

Cyert, Richard M., Simon, Herbert A., and Trow, Donald B. 1956. Observation of a Business Decision. *Journal of Business* 29:237–248.

Dahl, Robert A. 1957. The Concept of Power. *Behavioral Science* 2:201–215.

Dahrendorf, Ralf. 1959. *Class and Class Conflict in Industrial Society.* Stanford, CA: Stanford University Press.

Davis, James H. 1969. *Group Performance.* Reading, MA: Addison-Wesley.

Davis, Otto A., Dempster, M.A.H., and Wildavsky, Aaron. 1966. A Theory of the Budgeting Process. *American Political Science Review* 60:529–547.

Davis, Stanley M., and Lawrence, Paul R. 1977. *Matrix.* Reading, MA: Addison-Wesley.

Dearborn, Dewitt C., and Simon, Herbert A. 1958. Selective Perception. *Sociometry* 21:140–143.

Dornbusch, Sanford M. 1955. The Military Academy as an Assimilating Institution. *Social Forces* 33:316–321.

——, and Scott, W. Richard. 1975. *Evaluation and the Exercise of Authority: A Theory of Control Applied to Diverse Organizations.* San Francisco, CA: Jossey-Bass.

Dowling, John B. 1978. *Organizational Legitimation: The Management of Meaning.* Unpublished doctoral dissertation. Palo Alto, CA: Stanford University.

Downs, Anthony. 1957. *An Economic Theory of Democracy.* New York: Harper and Brothers.

Edelman, Murray. 1964. *The Symbolic Uses of Politics.* Urbana, IL: University of Illinois Press.

——. 1971. *Politics as Symbolic Action.* Chicago, IL: Markham.

——. 1977. *Political Language: Words That Succeed and Policies that Fail.* New York: Academic Press.

Edstrom, Anders, and Galbraith, Jay R. 1977. Transfer of Managers as a Coordination and Control Strategy in Multinational Organizations. *Administrative Science Quarterly* 22:248–263.

Edwards, Ward. 1954. The Theory of Decision Making. *Psychological Bulletin* 51:380–417.

Emerson, Richard M. 1962. Power-Dependence Relations. *American Sociological Review* 27:31–41.

Etzioni, Amitai. 1964. *Modern Organizations.* Englewood Cliffs, NJ: Prentice-Hall.

Farney, Dennis. 1979. Republicans Have What Carter Wants: The Power of Votes. *Wall Street Journal,* April 20, 1979.

Festinger, Leon. 1954. A Theory of Social Comparison Processes. *Human Relations* 7:117–140.

——, Riecken, H.W., and Schacter, S. 1956. *When Prophecy Fails.* Minneapolis, MN: University of Minnesota Press.

Following the Corporate Legend. *Business Week,* February 11, 1980, pp. 62–68.

Fornell, Claes. 1976. *Consumer Input for Marketing Decisions: A Study of Corporate Departments for Consumer Affairs.* New York: Praeger.

Fox, Frederick, and Staw, Barry M. 1979. The Trapped Administrator: Effects of Job Insecurity and Policy Resistance on Commitment to a Course of Action. *Administrative Science Quarterly* 24:449–471.

Frank, L.L., and Hackman, J.R. 1975. Effect of Interviewer-Interviewee Similarity on Interviewer Objectivity in College Admission Interviews. *Journal of Applied Psychology* 60:356–360.

Freeman, John. 1979. Going to the Well: School District Administrative Intensity and Environmental Constraint. *Administrative Science Quarterly* 24:-119–133.

Freeman, John H. 1978. The Unit of Analysis in Organizational Research. In *Environments and Organizations,* eds. Marshall W. Meyer and Associates, pp. 335–351. San Francisco: Jossey-Bass.

REFERENCES

————, and Hannan, Michael T. 1975. Growth and Decline Processes in Organizations. *American Sociological Review* 40:215–228.

French, John R.P., Jr., and Raven, Bertram. 1968. The Bases of Social Power. In *Group Dynamics,* 3rd ed., eds. Dorwin Cartwright and Alvin Zander, pp. 259–269. New York: Harper and Row.

Friedland, Edward I. 1974. *Introduction to the Concept of Rationality in Political Science.* Morristown, NJ: General Learning Press.

Friedrich, Carl J. 1937. *Constitutional Government and Democracy.* New York: Harper and Brothers.

Galbraith, Jay R. 1973. *Designing Complex Organizations.* Reading, MA: Addison-Wesley.

Gamson, William A. 1964. Experimental Studies of Coalition Formation. In *Advances in Experimental Social Psychology,* Vol. 1, ed. Leonard Berkowitz, pp. 81–110. New York: Academic Press.

————. 1968. *Power and Discontent.* Homewood, IL: Dorsey.

————, and Scotch, Norman R. 1964. Scapegoating in Baseball. *American Journal of Sociology* 70:69–76.

George, Alexander L. 1972. The Case for Multiple Advocacy in Making Foreign Policy. *American Political Science Review* 66:751–785.

Gephart, Robert P., Jr. 1978. Status Degradation and Organizational Succession: An Ethnomethodological Approach. *Administrative Science Quarterly* 23:-553–581.

Gergen, Kenneth J. 1969. *The Psychology of Behavior Exchange.* Reading, MA: Addison-Wesley.

Gerwin, Donald. 1969. A Process Model of Budgeting in a Public School System. *Management Science* 15:338–361.

Goldner, Fred H., Ritti, R. Richard, and Ference, Thomas P. 1977. The Production of Cynical Knowledge in Organizations. *American Sociological Review* 42:539–551.

Good Management is the U.S.'s Scarcest Resource, Says Dean Arjay Miller. *Campus Report,* Vol. 11, #40, July 11, 1979, pp. 2–3. Palo Alto, CA: Stanford University.

Goodman, P., and Friedman, A. 1971. An Explanation of Adams' Theory of Inequity. *Administrative Science Quarterly* 16:271–288.

Goodman, Paul S., and Pennings, Johannes M., eds. 1977. *New Perspectives on Organizational Effectiveness.* San Francisco: Jossey-Bass.

Gordon, Robert A., and Howell, James E. 1959. *Higher Education for Business.* New York: Columbia University Press.

Gouldner, Alvin. 1952. The Problem of Succession in Bureaucracy. In *Reader in Bureaucracy,* ed. Robert Merton, pp. 339–351. Glencoe, IL: Free Press.

Granovetter, Mark S. 1974. *Getting a Job: A Study of Contacts and Careers.* Cambridge, MA: Harvard University Press.

Grusky, Oscar. 1963. Managerial Succession and Organizational Effectiveness. *American Journal of Sociology* 69:21–31.

Hackman, J. Richard, and Lawler, Edward E. 1971. Employee Reactions to Job Characteristics. *Journal of Applied Psychology* 55:259–286.

Hackman, J. Richard, and Oldham, Greg R. 1975. Development of the Job Diagnostic Survey. *Journal of Applied Psychology* 60:159–170.

Hage, J., and Aiken, M. 1969. Routine Technology, Social Structure and Organizational Goals. *Administrative Science Quarterly* 14:366–376.

Hamblin, R.L. 1958. Leadership and Crisis. *Sociometry* 21:322–335.

Hamilton, Robert W. 1976. *Cases and Material on Corporations—Including Partnerships and Limited Partnerships.* St. Paul, MN: West Publishing.

Hannan, Michael T. 1978. Empirical Research. In *Environments and Organizations,* eds. Marshall W. Meyer and Associates, pp. 173–176. San Francisco: Jossey-Bass.

———, and Freeman, John H. 1977. The Population Ecology of Organizations. *American Journal of Sociology* 82:929–964.

———. 1978. Internal Politics of Growth and Decline. In *Environments and Organizations,* eds. Marshall W. Meyer and Associates, pp. 179–199. San Francisco: Jossey-Bass.

Hargens, Lowell L. 1969. Patterns of Mobility of New Ph.D.'s Among American Academic Institutions. *Sociology of Education* 42:18–37.

Harrell, Thomas W. 1969. The Personality of High Earning MBA's in Big Business. *Personnel Psychology* 22:457–463.

———. 1970. The Personality of High Earning MBA's in Small Business. *Personnel Psychology* 23:369–375.

———, and Harrell, Margaret S. 1975. *A Scale for High Earners. Technical Report No. 7, Office of Naval Research.* Palo Alto, CA: Graduate School of Business, Stanford University.

———. 1979. *Careers of Stanford MBA's with and without Engineering Undergraduate Degrees.* Unpublished ms. Palo Alto, CA: Graduate School of Business, Stanford University.

Heller, Frank, and Yukl, Gary. 1969. Participation, Managerial Decision-Making, and Situational Variables. *Organizational Behavior and Human Performance* 4:227–241.

Helmich, Donald L., and Brown, Warren B. 1972. Successor Type and Organizational Change in the Corporate Enterprise. *Administrative Science Quarterly* 17:371–381.

Hickson, D.J., Hinings, C.R., Lee, C.A., Schneck, R.H., and Pennings, J.M. 1971. A Strategic Contingencies' Theory of Intraorganizational Power. *Administrative Science Quarterly* 16:216–229.

Hills, Frederick S., and Mahoney, Thomas A. 1978. University Budgets and Organizational Decision Making. *Administrative Science Quarterly* 23:454–465.

Hinings, C.R., Hickson, D.J., Pennings, J.M., and Schneck, R.E. 1974. Structural Conditions of Intraorganizational Power. *Administrative Science Quarterly* 19:22–44.

REFERENCES

Holt, Donald D. 1979. The Unlikely Hero of McGraw-Hill. *Fortune,* May 21, 1979, pp. 97–108.

Hoos, Ida R. 1972. *Systems Analysis in Public Policy: A Critique.* Berkeley, CA: University of California Press.

Hunter, Floyd. 1953. *Community Power Structure.* Chapel Hill, NC: University of North Carolina Press.

Jacobs, R.C., and Campbell, D.T. 1961. The Perpetuation of an Arbitrary Tradition through Successive Generations of a Laboratory Microculture. *Journal of Abnormal and Social Psychology* 62:649–658.

Janis, Irving L. 1972. *Victims of Groupthink.* Boston: Houghton Mifflin.

Kahn, Robert L., Wolfe, Donald M., Quinn, Robert P., and Snoek, J. Diedrick. 1964. *Organizational Stress: Studies in Role Conflict and Ambiguity.* New York: John Wiley.

Kalleberg, Arne L., and Sorenson, Aage B. 1979. The Sociology of Labor Markets. In *Annual Review of Sociology,* Vol. 5, eds. Alex Inkeles, James Coleman and Ralph H. Turner, pp. 351–379. Palo Alto, CA: Annual Reviews.

Kanter, Rosabeth Moss. 1977. *Men and Women of the Corporation.* New York: Basic Books.

Kaplan, Abraham. 1964. *The Conduct of Inquiry.* Scranton, PA: Chandler Publishing Co.

Karpik, Lucien. 1978. Organizations, Institutions and History. In *Organization and Environment: Theory, Issues and Reality,* ed. Lucien Karpik, pp. 15–68. Beverly Hills, CA: Sage.

Katz, Daniel, and Kahn, Robert L. 1966. *The Social Psychology of Organizations.* New York: John Wiley.

Kelley, Harold H. 1971. *Attribution in Social Interaction.* Morristown, NJ: General Learning Press.

Kiesler, Charles A., and Kiesler, Sara B. 1969. *Conformity.* Reading, MA: Addison-Wesley.

King, Albert S. 1974. Expectation Effects in Organizational Change. *Administrative Science Quarterly* 19:221–230.

Korda, Michael. 1975. *Power.* New York: Ballantine Books.

Korten, David C. 1962. Situational Determinants of Leadership Structure. *Journal of Conflict Resolution* 6:222–235.

Kotin, Joel, and Sharaf, Myron. 1967. Management Succession and Administrative Style. *Psychiatry* 30:237–248.

Kotter, John P. 1978. Power, Success, and Organizational Effectiveness. *Organizational Dynamics* 6 (No. 3):27–40.

Kramer, Fred A. 1975. Policy Analysis as Ideology. *Public Administration Review* 35:509–517.

Labor Letter. *Wall Street Journal,* July 24, 1979, p. 1

Lasswell, Harold D. 1936. *Politics: Who Gets What, When, How.* New York: McGraw-Hill.

Lawrence, Paul R., and Lorsch, Jay W. 1967. *Organization and Environment.* Boston: Graduate School of Business Administration, Harvard University.

Leavitt, Harold J. 1951. Effects of Certain Communication Patterns on Group Performance. *Journal of Abnormal and Social Psychology* 46:38–50.

———. 1954. A Note on Some Experimental Findings about the Meanings of Price. *Journal of Business* 27:205–210.

Leeds, Ruth. 1964. The Absorption of Protest: A Working Paper. In *New Perspectives in Organization Research,* eds. W.W. Cooper, H.J. Leavitt, and M.W. Shelly, pp. 115–135. New York: John Wiley.

Leiserson, Michael. 1970. Coalition Government in Japan. In *The Study of Coalition Behavior,* eds. Sven Groennings, E.W. Kelley, and Michael Leiserson, pp. 80–102. New York: Holt, Rinehart and Winston.

Lieberman, Seymour. 1956. The Effects of Changes in Roles on the Attitudes of Role Occupants. *Human Relations* 9:385–402.

Lippitt, Mary E., and Mackenzie, Kenneth D. 1976. Authority-Task Problems. *Administrative Science Quarterly* 21:643–660.

Livingston, J. Sterling. 1969. Pygmalion in Management. *Harvard Business Review* 47 (July-August):81–89.

———. 1971. The Myth of the Well-Educated Manager. *Harvard Business Review* 49:79–89.

Lodahl, Janice, and Gordon, Gerald. 1972. The Structure of Scientific Fields and the Functioning of University Graduate Departments. *American Sociological Review* 37:57–72.

———. 1973. Funding the Sciences in University Departments. *Educational Record* 54:74–82.

Lowe, E.A., and Shaw, R.W. 1968. An Analysis of Managerial Biasing: Evidence from a Company's Budgeting Process. *Journal of Management Studies* 5:304–315.

Mackenzie, Kenneth D. 1978. *Organizational Structures.* Arlington Heights, IL: AHM Publishing.

Manne, Henry G. 1965. Mergers and the Market for Corporate Control. *Journal of Political Economy* 73:110–120.

March, James C., and March, James G. 1978. Performance Sampling in Social Matches. *Administrative Science Quarterly* 23:434–453.

March, James G. 1962. The Business Firm as a Political Coalition. *Journal of Politics* 24:662–678.

———. 1966. The Power of Power. In *Varieties of Political Theory,* ed. David Easton, pp. 39–70. Englewood Cliffs, NJ: Prentice-Hall.

———. 1976. The Technology of Foolishness. In *Ambiguity and Choice in Organizations,* James G. March and Johan P. Olsen, pp. 69–81. Bergen, Norway: Universitetsforlaget.

———. 1978. Bounded Rationality, Ambiguity, and the Engineering of Choice. *Bell Journal of Economics* 9:587–608.

———, and Olsen, Johan P. 1976. *Ambiguity and Choice in Organizations.* Bergen, Norway: Universitetsforlaget.

REFERENCES

March, James G., and Simon, Herbert A. 1958. *Organizations.* New York: John Wiley.

Markus, M. Lynne. 1979. *Understanding Information System Use in Organizations: A Theoretical Approach.* Unpublished Ph.D. dissertation. Cleveland, OH: Case Western Reserve.

———. 1980. *Organizational Design and Information Systems.* Unpublished ms. Cambridge, MA: MIT, Sloan School of Management.

Martin, Joanne. 1981. Relative Deprivation: A Theory of Distributive Injustice for an Era of Shrinking Resources. In *Research in Organizational Behavior,* Vol. 3 (in press), eds. Larry L. Cummings and Barry M. Staw. Greenwich, CT: JAI Press.

Mayes, Bronston T., and Allen, Robert W. 1977. Toward a Definition of Organizational Politics. *Academy of Management Review* 2:672–678.

Mayhew, L. 1969. Ascription in Modern Societies. *Sociological Inquiry* 38:-105–120.

McEachern, William A. 1975. *Managerial Control and Performance.* Lexington, MA: D.C. Heath.

McKenney, James L., and Keen, Peter G.W. 1974. How Managers' Minds Work. *Harvard Business Review* 52 (No. 3):79–90.

Mechanic, David. 1962. Sources of Power of Lower Participants in Complex Organizations. *Administrative Science Quarterly* 7:349–364.

Metz, Tim. 1979. Harold Geneen Is Seen as Driving Force Behind ITT Switch in Top Management. *Wall Street Journal,* July 13, 1979, p. 4.

Meyer, John W., and Rowan, Brian. 1977. Institutionalized Organizations: Formal Structure as Myth and Ceremony. *American Journal of Sociology* 83:-340–363.

Meyer, Marshall W. 1971. Some Constraints in Analyzing Data on Organizational Structures. *American Sociological Review* 36:294–297.

———. 1972. Size and Structure of Organizations: A Causal Analysis. *American Sociological Review* 37:434–440.

———. 1978. Leadership and Organizational Structure. In *Environments and Organizations,* eds. Marshall W. Meyer and Associates, pp. 200–232. San Francisco: Jossey-Bass.

Meyer, Pricilla S. 1979. The ITT Coup: Why Harold Geneen Got the Board to Strip Power from Hamilton. *Wall Street Journal,* July 18, 1979, pp. 1, 27.

Miller, Richard L., Brickman, Philip, and Bolen, Diana. 1975. Attribution Versus Persuasion as a Means for Modifying Behavior. *Journal of Personality and Social Psychology* 31:430–441.

Mills, C. Wright. 1956. *The Power Elite.* New York: Oxford University Press.

Mincer, Jacob. 1974. *Schooling, Experience, and Earnings.* New York: Columbia University Press.

Moore, William L. 1979. *Determinants and Outcomes of Departmental Power: A Two Campus Study.* Unpublished Ph.D. dissertation. Berkeley, CA: University of California.

———, and Pfeffer, Jeffrey. (in press) "The Relationship Between Departmental

379

Power and Faculty Careers on Two Campuses: The Case for Structural Effects on Faculty Salaries." *Research in Higher Education.*

Morris, C.W. 1949. *Signs, Language and Behavior.* New York: Prentice-Hall.

Nagel, Jack H. 1975. *The Descriptive Analysis of Power.* New Haven, CT: Yale University Press.

Nehrbass, Richard G. 1979. Ideology and the Decline of Management Theory. *Academy of Management Review* 4:427–431.

Nord, Walter R. 1974. The Failure of Current Applied Behavioral Science: A Marxian Perspective. *Journal of Applied Behavioral Science* 10:557–578.

Oldham, Greg R., and Brass, Daniel J. 1979. Employee Reactions to an Open-Plan Office: A Naturally Occurring Quasi-Experiment. *Administrative Science Quarterly* 24:267–284.

O'Reilly, Charles A., and Caldwell, David. 1979. Informational Influence as a Determinant of Perceived Task Characteristics and Job Satisfaction. *Journal of Applied Psychology* 64:157–165.

Ouchi, William G. 1980. Markets, Bureaucracies, and Clans. *Administrative Science Quarterly* 25:129–141.

———, and Jaeger, Alfred M. 1978. Type Z Organization: Stability in the Midst of Mobility. *Academy of Management Review* 3:305–314.

Ouchi, William G., and Johnson, Jerry B. 1978. Types of Organizational Control and Their Relationship to Emotional Well Being. *Administrative Science Quarterly* 23:293–317.

Ouchi, William G., and Price, Raymond L. 1978. Hierarchies, Clans and Theory Z: A New Perspective on Organization Development. *Organizational Dynamics* 7:25–44.

Parsons, Talcott, and Smelser, Neil J. 1956. *Economy and Society.* New York: Free Press.

Pellegrini, Roland, and Coates, Charles H. 1956. Absentee-Owned Corporations and Community Power Structure. *American Journal of Sociology* 61:413–419.

Pennings, Johannes M. 1975. The Relevance of the Structural-Contingency Model for Organizational Effectiveness. *Administrative Science Quarterly* 20:393–410.

Perrow, Charles. 1961. The Analysis of Goals in Complex Organizations. *American Sociological Review* 26:859–866.

———. 1970. Departmental Power and Perspectives in Industrial Firms. In *Power in Organizations,* ed. Mayer N. Zald, pp. 59–89. Nashville: Vanderbilt University Press.

———. 1972. *Complex Organizations: A Critical Essay.* Glenview, IL: Scott, Foresman.

Peters, Thomas J. 1978. Symbols, Patterns, and Settings: An Optimistic Case for Getting Things Done. *Organizational Dynamics* 7:3–23.

Pettigrew, Andrew M. 1972. Information Control as a Power Resource. *Sociology* 6:187–204.

REFERENCES

————. 1973. *The Politics of Organizational Decision-Making.* London: Travistock.

Pfeffer, Jeffrey. 1972. Size and Composition of Corporate Boards of Directors: The Organization and its Environment. *Administrative Science Quarterly* 17:218–228.

————. 1973. Size, Composition and Function of Hospital Boards of Directors: A Study of Organization-Environment Linkage. *Administrative Science Quarterly* 18:349–364.

————. 1974. Cooptation and the Composition of Electrical Utility Boards of Directors. *Pacific Sociological Review* 17:333–363.

————. 1977a. Power and Resource Allocation in Organizations. In *New Directions in Organizational Behavior,* eds., Barry M. Staw and Gerald R. Salancik, pp. 235–265. Chicago: St. Clair Press.

————. 1977b. Effects of an MBA and Socioeconomic Origins on Business School Graduates' Salaries. *Journal of Applied Psychology* 62:698–705.

————. 1977c. Toward an Examination of Stratification in Organizations. *Administrative Science Quarterly* 22:553–567.

————. 1978a. The Micropolitics of Organizations. In *Environments and Organizations,* eds. Marshall W. Meyer and Associates, pp. 29–50. San Francisco, CA: Jossey-Bass.

————. 1978b. *Organizational Design.* Arlington Heights, IL: AHM Publishing Corp.

————. 1981. Management as Symbolic Action: The Creation and Maintenance of Organizational Paradigms. In *Research in Organizational Behavior,* Vol. 3 (in press), eds. Larry L. Cummings and Barry M. Staw. Greenwich, CT: JAI Press.

————, and Lawler, John. 1980. Effects of Job Alternatives, Extrinsic Rewards, and Behavioral Commitment on Attitude Toward the Organization: A Field Test of the Insufficient Justification Paradigm. *Administrative Science Quarterly* 25:38–56.

Pfeffer, Jeffrey, and Leblebici, Huseyin. 1973a. The Effect of Competition on Some Dimensions of Organizational Structure. *Social Forces* 52:268–279.

————. 1973b. Executive Recruitment and the Development of Interfirm Organizations. *Administrative Science Quarterly* 18:449–461.

Pfeffer, Jeffrey, and Leong, Anthony. 1977. Resource Allocations in United Funds: Examination of Power and Dependence. *Social Forces* 55:775–790.

————, and Strehl, Katherine. 1977. Paradigm Development and Particularism: Journal Publication in Three Scientific Disciplines. *Social Forces* 55:938–951.

Pfeffer, Jeffrey, and Moore, William L. 1980a. Average Tenure of Academic Department Heads: The Effects of Paradigm, Size, and Departmental Demography. *Administrative Science Quarterly* 25:387–406.

————. 1980b. Power in University Budgeting: A Replication and Extension. *Administrative Science Quarterly* 25:637–653.

Pfeffer, Jeffrey, and Salancik, Gerald R. 1974. Organizational Decision Making as a Political Process: The Case of a University Budget. *Administrative Science Quarterly* 19:135–151.

———. 1977a. Administrator Effectiveness: The Effects of Advocacy and Information on Resource Allocations. *Human Relations* 30:641–656.

———. 1977b. Organizational Context and the Characteristics and Tenure of Hospital Administrators. *Academy of Management Journal* 20:74–88.

———. 1977c. Organization Design: The Case for a Coalitional Model of Organizations. *Organizational Dynamics* 6:15–29.

———. 1978. *The External Control of Organizations: A Resource Dependence Perspective.* New York: Harper and Row.

———, and Leblebici, Huseyin. 1976. The Effect of Uncertainty on the Use of Social Influence in Organizational Decision Making. *Administrative Science Quarterly* 21:227–245.

Plott, Charles R., and Levine, Michael E. 1978. A Model of Agenda Influence on Committee Decisions. *American Economic Review* 68:146–160.

Polsby, Nelson W. 1960. How to Study Community Power: The Pluralist Alternative. *Journal of Politics* 22:474–484.

Pondy, Louis R. 1969. Effects of Size, Complexity, and Ownership on Administrative Intensity. *Administrative Science Quarterly* 14:47–60.

———. 1970. Toward a Theory of Internal Resource-Allocation. In *Power in Organizations,* ed. Mayer N. Zald, pp. 270–311. Nashville: Vanderbilt University Press.

———. 1977. The Other Hand Clapping: An Information-Processing Approach to Organizational Power. In *Reward Systems and Power Distribution,* eds. Tove H. Hammer and Samuel B. Bacharach, pp. 56–91. Ithaca, NY: Cornell University, School of Industrial and Labor Relations.

———. 1978. Leadership Is a Language Game. In *Leadership: Where Else Can We Go?* eds. Morgan W. McCall Jr., and Michael M. Lombardo, pp. 87–99. Durham, NC: Duke University Press.

Provan, Keith G., Beyer, Janice M., and Kruytbosch, Carlos. 1980. Environmental Linkages and Power in Resource-Dependence Relations between Organizations. *Administrative Science Quarterly* 25:200–225.

Pugh, Derek S. 1966. Modern Organization Theory. *Psychological Bulletin* 66:235–251.

Radnor, M., and Neal, R.D. 1973. The Progress of Management Science in Large U.S. Industrial Corporations. *Operations Research* 21:427–450.

Radnor, M., Rubenstein, A.H., and Bean, A.S. 1968. Integration and Utilization of Management Science Activities in Organizations. *Operational Research Quarterly* 19:117–141.

Reibstein, David J., Youngblood, Stuart A., and Fromkin, Howard L. 1975. Number of Choices and Perceived Decision Freedom as a Determinant of Satisfaction and Consumer Behavior. *Journal of Applied Psychology* 60:434–437.

REFERENCES

Riker, William H. 1962. *The Theory of Political Coalitions.* New Haven, CT: Yale University Press.

Rosenthal, Howard. 1970. Size of Coalition and Electoral Outcomes in the Fourth French Republic. In *The Study of Coalition Behavior,* eds. Sven Groennings, E.W. Kelley, and Michael Leiserson, pp. 43–59. New York: Holt, Rinehart and Winston.

Rout, Lawrence. 1979. School History Books, Striving to Please All, Are Criticized as Bland. *Wall Street Journal,* September 5, 1979, pp. 1, 33.

Salancik, Gerald R. 1977a. Commitment and the Control of Organizational Behavior and Belief. In *New Directions in Organizational Behavior,* eds. Barry M. Staw and Gerald R. Salancik, pp. 1–54. Chicago: St. Clair Press.

———. 1977b. Commitment Is Too Easy. *Organizational Dynamics* 6:62–80.

———, and Conway, Mary. 1975. Attitude Inferences from Salient and Relevant Cognitive Content About Behavior. *Journal of Personality and Social Psychology* 32:829–840.

Salancik, Gerald R., and Lamont, V. 1975. Conflict in Societal Research: A Study of One RANN Project Suggests that Benefitting Society May Cost Universities. *Journal of Higher Education* 46:161–176.

Salancik, Gerald R., and Pfeffer, Jeffrey. 1974. The Bases and Use of Power in Organizational Decision Making: The Case of a University. *Administrative Science Quarterly* 19:453–473.

———. 1977a. An Examination of Need-Satisfaction Models of Job Attitudes. *Administrative Science Quarterly* 22:427–456.

———. 1977b. Who Gets Power—And How They Hold On to it: A Strategic-Contingency Model of Power. *Organizational Dynamics* 5:3–21.

———. 1978a. A Social Information Processing Approach to Job Attitudes and Task Design. *Administrative Science Quarterly* 23:224–253.

———. 1978b. Uncertainty, Secrecy, and the Choice of Similar Others. *Social Psychology* 41:246–255.

———. 1980. Effects of Ownership and Performance on Executive Tenure in U.S. Corporations. *Academy of Management Journal* 23: (in press).

———, and Kelly, J. Patrick. 1978. A Contingency Model of Influence in Organizational Decision-Making. *Pacific Sociological Review* 21:239–256.

Sapolsky, Harvey M. 1972. *The Polaris System Development.* Cambridge, MA: Harvard University Press.

Sargent, Lyman Tower. 1972. *Contemporary Political Ideologies.* Homewood, IL: The Dorsey Press.

Schattschneider, E.E. 1960. *The Semi-Sovereign People.* New York: Holt, Rinehart and Winston.

Schein, Edgar H. 1968. Organizational Socialization and the Profession of Management. *Industrial Management Review* 9:1–16.

Schmidt, Stuart M., and Kochan, Thomas A. 1972. Conflict: Toward Conceptual Clarity. *Administrative Science Quarterly* 17:359–370.

383

Schulze, Robert O. 1958. Economic Dominants and Community Power Structure. *American Sociological Review* 23:3–9.

Sease, Douglas R. 1980a. Steel's Priorities May Determine Winner in Race for Lewis Foy's Job at Bethlehem. *Wall Street Journal,* January 16, 1980, p. 5.

———. 1980b. Bethlehem Steel Picks Donald Trautlein, an Accountant, to be its Chief Executive. *Wall Street Journal,* February 1, 1980, p. 6.

Selznick, Philip. 1949. *TVA and the Grass Roots.* Berkeley, CA: University of California Press.

Sherif, M. 1935. A Study of Some Social Factors in Perception. *Archives of Psychology,* No. 187.

———, Harvey, O.J., White, B.J., Hood, W.R., and Sherif, C. 1961. *Intergroup Conflict and Cooperation: The Robbers Cave Experiment.* Norman, OK: University Book Exchange.

Simon, Herbert A. 1957. *Models of Man.* New York: Wiley.

———. 1964. On the Concept of Organizational Goal. *Administrative Science Quarterly,* 9:1–22.

———. 1979. Rational Decision Making in Business Organizations. *American Economic Review* 69:493–513.

Sloan, Alfred P. 1963. *My Years With General Motors.* New York: Macfadden-Bartell.

Smigel, Erwin O. 1964. *The Wall Street Lawyer.* New York: Free Press of Glencoe.

Smith, Peter B. 1973. *Groups within Organizations.* New York: Harper and Row.

Sommer, Robert. 1969. *Personal Space: The Behavioral Basis of Design.* Englewood Cliffs, NJ: Prentice-Hall.

Stagner, Ross. 1969. Corporate Decision Making: An Empirical Study. *Journal of Applied Psychology* 53:1–13.

Stava, Per. 1976. Constraints on the Politics of Public Choice. In *Ambiguity and Choice in Organizations,* James G. March and Johan P. Olsen, pp. 206–224. Bergen, Norway: Universitetsforlaget.

Staw, Barry M. 1974. Attitudinal and Behavioral Consequences of Changing a Major Organizational Reward: A Natural Field Experiment. *Journal of Personality and Social Psychology* 29:742–751.

———. 1976. Knee-Deep in the Big Muddy: A Study of Escalating Commitment to a Chosen Course of Action. *Organizational Behavior and Human Performance* 16:27–44.

———. 1979. *Commitment in an Experimenting Society.* Unpublished ms. Evanston, IL: Northwestern University, Graduate School of Management.

———, and Fox, Frederick V. 1977. Escalation: Some Determinants of Commitment to a Previously Chosen Course of Action. *Human Relations* 30:431–450.

REFERENCES

Staw, Barry M., and Ross, Jerry. 1980. Commitment in an Experimenting Society: An Experiment on the Attribution of Leadership from Administrative Scenarios. *Journal of Applied Psychology* 65:249-260.

Steele, Fred I. 1973. *Physical Settings and Organization Development.* Reading, MA: Addison-Wesley.

Stouffer, S.A., Suchman, E.A., Devinney, L.C., Star, S.A., and Williams, R.M. 1949. *The American Soldier, Vol. 1: Adjustment During Army Life.* Princeton, NJ: Princeton University Press.

Thompson, James D. 1967. *Organizations in Action.* New York: McGraw-Hill.

———, and Tuden, Arthur. 1959. Strategies, Structures and Processes of Organizational Decision. In *Comparative Studies in Administration,* eds., J.D. Thompson, P.B. Hammond, R.W. Hawkes, B.H. Junker, and A. Tuden, pp. 195–216. Pittsburgh: University of Pittsburgh Press.

Tolbert, Pamela, and Zucker, Lynne G. 1979. *Institutional Sources of Formal Structure: The Diffusion of Civil Service Reform Among Cities, 1880–1930.* Unpublished ms. Los Angeles: UCLA, Department of Sociology.

Vogel, David. 1978. *Lobbying the Corporation: Citizen Challenges to Business Authority.* New York: Basic Books.

Vroom, Victor H., and Yetton, Philip W. 1973. *Leadership and Decision-Making.* Pittsburgh, PA: University of Pittsburgh Press.

Walker, Orville C., Jr. 1970. *An Experimental Investigation of Conflict and Power in Marketing Channels.* Madison, WI: unpublished doctoral dissertation.

Warren, Roland L. 1970. Alternative Strategies of Inter-Agency Planning. *Inter-Organizational Research in Health Conference Proceedings:* 114–129. Washington, D.C.: National Center for Health Services Research and Development.

Weber, Max. 1947. *The Theory of Social and Economic Organization.* New York: Free Press.

Weick, Karl E. 1969. *The Social Psychology of Organizing.* Reading, MA: Addison-Wesley.

———. 1979. Cognitive Processes in Organization. In *Research in Organizational Behavior,* Vol. 1, ed. Barry M. Staw, pp. 41–74. Greenwich, CT: JAI Press.

Weiner, Stephen S. 1976. Participation, Deadlines, and Choice. In *Ambiguity and Choice in Organizations,* James G. March and Johan P. Olsen, pp. 225–250. Bergen, Norway: Universitetsforlaget.

Weinstein, Alan G., and Srinivasan, V. 1974. Predicting Managerial Success of Master of Business Administration (MBA) Graduates. *Journal of Applied Psychology* 59:207–212.

Wenocur, S. 1975. A Political View of the United Way. *Social Work* 20:223–239.

Whisler, Thomas. 1960. The "Assistant To" in Four Administrative Settings. *Administrative Science Quarterly* 5:181–216.

385

————. 1970. *Information Technology and Organizational Change.* Belmont, CA: Wadsworth.

————, Meyer, H., Baum, B.H., and Sorenson, P.F. Jr. 1967. Centralization of Organization Control: An Empirical Study of its Meaning and Measurement. *Journal of Business* 40:10–26.

White, Sam E., and Mitchell, Terence R. 1979. Job Enrichment Versus Social Cues: A Comparison and Competitive Test. *Journal of Applied Psychology* 64:1–9.

Wildavsky, Aaron. 1968. Budgeting as a Political Process. In *The International Encyclopedia of the Social Sciences, 2,* ed. David L. Sills, pp. 192–199. New York: Crowell, Collier and Macmillan.

————. 1979. *The Politics of the Budgeting Process,* 3rd ed. Boston: Little, Brown.

————, and Hammond, Arthur. 1965. Comprehensive Versus Incremental Budgeting in the Department of Agriculture. *Administrative Science Quarterly* 10:321–346.

Williams, F.J., and Harrell, T.W. 1964. Predicting Success in Business. *Journal of Applied Psychology* 48:164–167.

Williamson, Oliver E. 1975. *Markets and Hierarchies: Analysis and Antitrust Implications.* New York: Free Press.

Woodward, Joan. 1965. *Industrial Organization: Theory and Practice.* London: Oxford University Press.

Worchel, Stephen, Lee, Jerry, and Adewole, Akanbi. 1975. Effects of Supply and Demand on Ratings of Object Value. *Journal of Personality and Social Psychology* 32:906–914.

Wright, J. Patrick. 1979. *On a Clear Day You Can See General Motors: John Z. DeLorean's Look Inside the Automotive Giant.* Grosse Point, MI: Wright Enterprises.

Yoels, William C. 1974. The Structure of Scientific Fields and the Allocation of Editorships on Scientific Journals: Some Observations on the Politics of Knowledge. *Sociological Quarterly* 15:264–276.

Zald, Mayer N. 1965. Who Shall Rule? A Political Analysis of Succession in a Large Welfare Organization. *Pacific Sociological Review* 8:52–60.

————, and Hair, Feather Davis. 1972. The Social Control of General Hospitals. In *Organization Research on Health Institutions,* ed. Basil S. Georgopoulos, pp. 51–81. Ann Arbor: Institute for Social Research, University of Michigan.

Zalkind, Sheldon S., and Costello, Timothy W. 1962. Perception: Implications for Administration. *Administrative Science Quarterly* 7:218–235.

Zucker, Lynne G. 1977. The Role of Institutionalization in Cultural Persistence. *American Sociological Review* 42:726–743.

INDEX